DICTIONARY OF
FRENCH SLANG
AND COLLOQUIAL
EXPRESSIONS

Henry Strutz
Formerly Associate Professor of Languages
State University of New York
Alfred State College of Technology

BARRON'S

All inquiries should be addressed to:
Barron's Educational Series, Inc.
250 Wireless Boulevard
Hauppauge, NY 11788
http://www.barronseduc.com

International Standard Book Number 0-7641-0345-8

Library of Congress Catalog Card Number 98-73385

Printed in the United States of America
9 8 7 6 5 4

Contents

PREFACE

French Slang

Many researchers, including Einstein, have said that the urge to play is the source of all human creativity. Slang is playful in all languages. French slang is particularly playful, perhaps more gracefully playful than the rough play of some other languages. For instance, on the notes for "Patachou—Montmartre," an LP released by Columbia Records some decades ago, Aram Avakian balks at translating the lyrics of the traditional song "La mariée" (The Bride) "from such a supple language as French into so blunt a language as American." (Nowadays, there is less hesitation in translating the risqué, bluntly or otherwise.) The French language is famous for its lucidity, elegance, and wit. Much French slang shares in those characteristics. The ancient Babylonians, Chinese, and Greeks sometimes used terms for fruits, vegetables, and animals to designate parts of the human body. Some of those same designations are still used today in many languages, including French, but French often adds a light touch and Gallic wit.

Language at Play

Slang is lively, dynamic language, language at play. Words often get shortened by chopping off the beginning (apheresis) or the end (apocope). Words perceived as insipid, pretentious, or pompous, are livened up or taken down a peg or two by adding slang prefixes, or, more frequently, suffixes. (See the entries **-aga; -ard; -arès; -caille; -da; -muche; -ouche; -ouille; -uche; -zig.**) The French enjoy having fun with their language and have created several playful slang systems and no less than twelve series of variations on the personal pronouns. (See the entries **javanais; largonji; louchébem; mézigue, verlan.**) Verlan (backslang) is in full flower, and new words are being coined all the time. There is even **verlan** of **verlan.** The best known of these coinages are included in this dictionary.

Many words can be **"verlanized"** *(backslanged).* Just move the last syllable to the beginning and *voilà*—**verlan.** Some are easy to recognize, for instance: **deban (bande); jourbon (bonjour); fumpar (parfum); ouf (fou); tarcol (coltar).** You might want to have fun and create some yourself. Don't feel limited by the original spelling, since pronunciation (often varying pronunciations), not spelling, is the determining factor, and vowels and consonants can change. For example, the **verlan** *(backslang)* versions of **femme; flic; gauche; mec;** and **paquet** are **meuf; keuf; cheug; keum; képa.**

Javanais, not as complicated or varied as **verlan,** forms slang words by inserting **av, va,** or **ag** after a consonant. For instance, **jeudi** becomes **javeudavi** and **chatte** becomes **chagatte.**

Largonji, is another slang system. Like **javanais,** it probably originated in former French Indochina. In this system, the first letter is replaced by "l" and the original first letter starts the last syllable that ends in an often fanciful suffix such as: **-é; -ès; em; ic; iche; -oque; -uche.** As is the case with verlan, the pronunciation, not the spelling of the original word, is what counts. Examples: **lamfé (femme); latronpem (patron); laubé/laubiche (beau); lauchem (chaud); linspré (prince).**

Many have pointed out that despite a multiplicity of rich cheeses (see the entries **Franchecaille** and **fromegi**) and sauces, obesity is not as prevalent in France as elsewhere, as in North America, for instance. Some claim a connection to wine drinking. Dr. Andrew Weil, a nutritionist, ethnologist, and philosopher, speculates that this paradox may be due to something unknown—in the food, the ambiance, whatever. Might not a playfulness, a lightness of spirit be partly responsible also? Life can be made more light-hearted, more amusing, even healthier, if approached playfully. There may be a correlation between lightness of body and the enlightened mind, the mind that delights in word play. France has long been devoted to the light, in both senses—whether striving to capture the light in constructing Gothic cathedrals, in creating the technique and language of ballet, or in the lightness of a soufflé or in **nouvelle cuisine.** The light of reason shone particularly bright in the **siècle des lumières,** the eighteenth century, when the *Encylopédie* was published in the face of obscurantist opposition. Fabled French light (of the **midi,** the

Île-de-France, of Paris, the **Ville lumière,** and so on) has inspired painters. This lightness of spirit and body may, in part, account for the extent and variety of French slang. Traditionally, one function of slang, notably "thieves' cant," is to conceal. People involved in crime, drugs, nonconjugal sex, and such, want to keep outsiders in the dark about their activities. In a deeper sense, however, many slang expressions often cast light, and sometimes even a little sweetness, on what is otherwise dark and sinister.

Foreign Influences on Slang

Foreign languages are best studied in a spirit of openness, receptivity. Even more openness is desirable when studying slang. Over the centuries, French slang has been open to influences from its European neighbors and has borrowed generously from them, as well as from the gypsies, potentially everyone's neighbors. Arabic is also well represented, a reflection of France's former colonial presence in North Africa and the Middle East. Despite official attempts to discourage it, American slang is currently "in," especially in matters relating to drugs and rock music. Some of these Americanisms have been included, especially in cases where French has taken a word and modified its meaning or spelling, as in **flipper, dileur.**

Speaking French

Speakers of standard French often elide vowels, especially **e,** and leave out **ne** in negatives. As you would expect, such omissions occur more frequently in slang, as in **t'inquiète.** This is true of English as well: "wanna" for "want to," and the omission of final "g," as in "gettin." For **je ne sais pas,** you will sometimes hear **j'sais pas** or even **sais pas. Il n'y a pas** becomes **n'y a pas** or **y'a pas. Tu as** is often pronounced **t'as.** Some of the sentences illustrating the entries make these omissions but most do not, since to do so might be confusing and distract attention from the word at issue. You know enough about French and English to recognize slurred words. By no means should you get the idea that slang parlance is the sole and exclusive province of ill-spoken "lowlifes" in inner city and suburban slums, although you will certainly find it there. Books on slang sell well in France. Most who buy them are not marginal people, those on the fringes of society, but literate, articulate individuals interested in all ranges of the splendid instrument that is the French language. Some of them call themselves **argotnautes** and are involved in **argotologie.** Many who scale the heights of "high culture," **haute cuisine,** and **haute couture** also want to check out linguistic "lower depths" and incorporate slang expressions in their speech and writing. This was true even in Proust's time. He complained that the determined pursuit of slang by some writers was an affectation. You should strive to recognize slang, but use it cautiously yourself until it comes naturally to you. Slang expressions are increasingly encountered in literature and prestige publications in our day and much "street French" is also heard in the **salon** and around the table.

Creating Slang

The **passé simple** is a literary tense and therefore rarely, if at all, used in the example sentences. Yet it isn't as dead on the street as usually alleged, since, as the entry for **rappeur** points out, there are rap performers who use it extensively. Young people are traditionally users and creators of slang. Each generation wants to assert its uniqueness, its identity, in language too, but older people have taken increasingly to slang, perhaps because they are still young at heart. Some slang, still in current use, goes back to Rabelais and Villon. Balzac, Zola, Céline, and many other famous authors have used and even created slang. Many slang words have entered popular speech and are no longer felt as slang. For most speakers of French, the distinction between colloquial speech and slang is anything but rigid.

The original, basic meanings of **chier, con, cul, foutre, merde, pisse,** and so on involve sex and/or elimination. They are still "strong stuff" and some—fewer and fewer—speakers of French will not use them in polite society. Yet language is a living, evolving thing, and these words have developed different, extended meanings and also given rise to families of words that are in use at all levels of society, words in which the originally sexual or excretory connection is only minimally perceived, or no longer felt at all. See the entries **chienlit; chier; con; cul; déconner; démerdard; emmerdeur; foutre; pisseux,** among many others. The verb **baiser** has moved in the opposite direction, and is no longer used for "to kiss." Language, like all else, is involved in processes of change.

Humor in Slang

Slang expressions often deal playfully with dysfunction—excessive eating and drinking, violence, disease, mortality, and other aspects of the human condition sometimes difficult to bear. Their burden can be made lighter by shedding linguistic light on them. Humor can put things in a different light and brighten up what is dreary or ominous. French slang often consummates a particularly felicitous marriage of the visceral and cerebral, or more scientifically, a union of left and right brain, of the older parts of the brain concerned with the basics of survival (eating, drinking, sex) and the higher perceptions and functions associated with later brain development.

Freud liked to quote the Roman playwright Terence's maxim: **humani nihil a me alienum puto** (I consider nothing human foreign to me). Human experience is complex and varied. Talking about it in varied, often humorous imagery, can provide insight into problem areas. Aspects of the human condition that are distasteful to some can be made more palatable, less "foreign," if playfully expressed. This dictionary, though far from exhaustive, will give a good idea of the playful possibilities in French, and when possible, in the English translations.

Even though slang is frequently used, it isn't much taught in school, and you may have stumbled in the dark when coming across it in the written or spoken language. I hope this dictionary will help you to play a better language game—in the light.

BIBLIOGRAPHY

The following books and dictionaries may be useful to you for further study.

Boudard, Alphonse and Luc Étienne. *La Méthode à Mimile.* Paris: La Jeune Parque, 1974.

Brunet, François and Declan McCavana. *Dictionnaire bilingue de l'argot d'aujourd'hui.* Pocket, 1996.

Burke, David. *Street French Slang Dictionary and Thesaurus.* New York: Wiley, 1997.

Caradec, François. *Dictionnaire du français argotique et populaire.* Paris: Larousse, 1977.

Carrière, Jean-Claude. *Les mots et la chose.* Paris: Le Pré aux Clercs, 1991.

Colin, Jean-Paul and Jean-Pierre Mével. *Dictionnaire de l'argot.* Paris: Larousse, 1995.

Knox, Helen. *Harrap's Slang.* Edinburgh: Harrap Books, 1993.

Merle, Pierre. *Le Dico de l'argot fin de siècle.* Paris: Éditions du Seuil, 1996.

LIST OF ABBREVIATIONS

abbr. = abbreviation
adj. = adjective
Ar. = Arabic
Brit. = British
Cf. = compare
crim. = criminal
euph. = euphemism
Eng. = English
esp. = especially
f. = feminine
Fr. = French
Ger. = German
h.s. = herself/himself
hum. = humorous
It. = Italian
joc. = jocular
lit. = literally
m. = masculine
m.s. = myself
orig. = originally
o.s. = oneself
pej. = pejorative
pref. = prefix
qch. = quelque chose
qn. = quelqu'un
show biz = show business term
s.o. = someone
s.t. = something
Sp. = Spanish
t.s. = themselves
y.s. = yourself

ABATS, *m., pl.* Male genitalia, "nuts" (lit. "giblets"). *Ils devaient montrer leurs abats au toubib militaire.* "They had to show their nuts to the army doctor."

ABATTAGE, *m.* Cutting down of trees; slaughter of animals. **Avoir de l'abattage,** *idiom.* To have get-up-and-go. *Ce député a beaucoup d'abattage et se fera réélire.* "That deputy's very dynamic and will get himself reelected." **Faire de l'abattage,** *idiom.* To turn tricks constantly. *Mon maq exige que je fasse de l'abattage.* "My pimp insists that I turn lots of tricks."

ABATTIS, *n., pl.* Arms or legs (lit. "poultry giblets"). **Numéroter ses abattis,** lit. "to count one's limbs." *Après l'accident on a numéroté nos abattis.* "After the accident we checked to see that we were still in one piece." *Tu peux numéroter tes abattis!* "I'm going to knock your block off!"

ABEILLE, *f.* Bee. **Avoir les abeilles,** *idiom.* To be fidgety. *Tu bouges sans arrêt; on dirait que tu as les abeilles.* "You keep moving around; you look like you've got ants in your pants." **Mettre les abeilles,** *idiom.* To annoy. *Cesse de me mettre les abeilles!* "Quit bugging me!"

ABÎMER. To damage. **Abîmer le portrait à qn.** To bash s.o.'s face in. *Son amant lui a abîmé le portrait.* "Her boyfriend ruined her looks."

ABONNÉ, -E, *m., f.* Subscriber. **Être aux abonnés absents,** *idiom.* To be dead drunk; be out of it. **Se mettre aux abonnés absents,** *idiom.* To tune out. *Je suis aux abonnés absents toutes les fois qu'il reprend ce sujet.* "I tune out every time he takes up that subject." *Pendant ses conférences la moitié des étudiants se met aux abonnés absents.* "During his lectures, half the students turn off."

ABORDAGE, *m.* Assault. See VOL À L'ABORDAGE.

ABOULER. To hand over. *Aboule tout le fric ou je tire!* "Hand over all the dough (money) or I'll shoot!"

(S')ABOULER. To come (over). *Aboule-toi, vite!* "Come over here, quick!"

ABOYEUR, *m.* Carnival barker; hawker. *Sur les boulevards les aboyeurs hurlent les manchettes des journaux du soir.* "On the boulevards, newspaper hawkers yell the evening newspaper headlines."

ABRICOT, *m.* Female genitalia (lit. "apricot"). *Mon mari est dingue de mon abricot.* "My husband is nuts about my (apri)cunt."

ABUS, *m.* Abuse. **Il y a de l'abus!** *idiom.* That's going too far! *Le supermarché falsifie les dates limites. Il y a de l'abus!* "The supermarket fakes the 'use by' dates. Things are getting out of hand!"

ACADÉMIE, *f.* Academy. **Avoir une belle académie,** *idiom.* To be well built. *Oui, cette danseuse espagnole a une belle académie, mais tu délaisses tes études à l'Académie.* "Yes, that Spanish dancer has a gorgeous bod, but you're neglecting your studies at the Academy."

ACCORDÉON, *m.* Extensive criminal record, *police,* (lit. "accordion"). *Avec un tel accordéon tu passeras le restant de ta vie en tôle.* "With a record like yours, you'll spend the rest of your life in the slammer."

ACCOUCHER. To confess (lit. "to give birth"). *Tu as qch.à me dire. Accouche donc!* "You've got something to tell me. Come on, spit it out!"

ACCRO, *m.,* from **accroché** (hooked). **1.** Junkie. *Peu à peu il* *est devenu accro.* "Little by little, he got hooked." **2.** Ardent fan. *Les accros du jazz viendront nombreux au spectacle.* "Jazz fanatics will turn out in force for the show."

ACCROCHER. 1. To hit it off (lit. "to attach"). *Nous accrochions tout de suite.* "We hit it off right away." **2.** To arrest. *Ce n'est pas la première fois qu'on l'accroche.* "It's not the first time she's been busted."

(S')ACCROCHER. To make a great effort. *Il s'accroche pour réussir dans son métier.* "He's going all out to succeed in his profession." **Tu peux te l'accrocher.** "You can forget it. Give it up."

ACCROCHE-TOI, JEANNOT! *joc.* "Hang in there, buddy! Show your stuff!"

ACCUS, *m., pl.,* from **accumulateurs** (storage batteries). **Recharger les accus. 1.** To recharge one's batteries (by eating, drinking, resting). *On avait grand besoin de recharger les accus.* "We really needed a pick-me-up." **2.** To set 'em up again. *"Patron, rechargez les accus," dit-il, en tapant son verre sur le zinc!* "'Bartender, hit us again,' he said, banging his glass on the bar."

(D')ACHAR, *abbr.* of **acharnement** (tenacity). **Lutter; travailler d'achar.** To fight; work assiduously. *Elle travaillait d'achar, pendant que les autres ne foutaient rien.* "She worked like all get-out, while the others didn't do a damned thing."

(D')ACHAR ET D'AUTOR, (autor = autorité). Vigorously. *Elle fait tout d'achar et d'auto.* "She does everything intensely and well."

ACHILLE, *m.* **1.** Achilles (name). **2.** Knife, *crim. Il prétend posséder l'achille de Jack l'éventreur.* "He claims he owns Jack the Ripper's knife."

ACRAIS!/ACRÉ! Watch out! Cheese it! *Acré! Planque ta came—les stups sont là.* "Watch out! Hide your stash—the narcs are here."

À CROUME. On credit. *Ils ont tout acheté à croume.* "They bought everything on credit."

ACTE DE NAISSANCE. See AVALER...NAISSANCE.

ACTER, show biz. To act. *Si tu veux acter dans un des mes films, ma petite, il faut que tu sois arrangeante avec moi.* "If you want to act in one of my pictures, little girl, you'll have to be nice to me."

ACTEUSE, *f.* Lousy actress. *Cette acteuse a des fans et même un fanzine.* "That lousy actress has fans and even a fanzine."

ADJA, *m.* or *f.* To scram [from Romani **dja!**—go!]. *Si l'on ne fait pas l'adja, les poulets nous piqueront.* "If we don't disappear fast, the cops'll nab us."

ADJUDANT, *m.* **1.** Warrant officer. **Coucher avec la femme de l'adjudant,** *idiom.* To get sent to the stockade. *Après la bagarre, on les a envoyés coucher avec la femme de l'adjudant.* "After the brawl, they were sent to the guardroom." **2.** Authoritarian person. *Bien/oui, mon adjudant, tout comme mon adjudant voudra.* "OK, boss, just as you want."

ADJUPÈTE, *m., pej.* for **adjudant.**

ADO, *m., f. abbr.* of **adolescent(e).** *Il y a des cours de musique pour ados.* "There are courses in music for adolescents."

À DONF, youth, backslang* for **à fond.** Totally. *Pousse pas ta musique à donf ou tu deviendras sourdingue.* "Don't play your music at full blast or you'll go deaf."

AFANAF, *adv.* Fifty-fifty (from Eng. "half and half"). *Et si on faisait afanaf?* "How about our going Dutch?"

AFFAIRE, *f.* **1.** Affair. **La belle affaire!** Big deal!' *"Je n'ai rien à me mettre!" —"'Ah, la belle affaire!' lui répondit-il."* "'I haven't got a thing to wear.'—'So what!,' he said." **En faire une affaire d'état,** *idiom.* To make a federal case out of something. *Ce rien, il va en faire une affaire d'état.* "He's going to make a big to-do out of that little

* See explanation of **verlan,** page iv.

nothing." See LÂCHER L'AFFAIRE. **2.** Shady operation. *Le gangster a pu faire son affaire en donnant des pots-de-vin à la police.* "The gangster could do his thing after bribing the police." See FAIRE SON AFFAIRE À QN. **3.** Sexually proficient person. *Malgré sa beauté, ce n'est pas une affaire.* "Despite her beauty, she's no good in bed."

AFFAIRES, *f., pl.* Menstrual period. *Son amant aime lui faire l'amour quand elle a ses affaires.* "Her lover likes to make love to her when she has her period."

(S')AFFALER. To confess; inform, *crim.* (lit. "to collapse with fatigue"). *Si tu t'affales auprès des flics, je te casse la gueule!* "If you rat to the cops, I'll break your face."

AFFICHE, *f.* **1.** Poster. **Être à l'affiche,** *idiom.* To be playing. *Qu'est-ce qui est à l'affiche ce soir à l'Odéon?* "What's on at the Odeon tonight?" **2.** Affected homosexual. **Faire l'affiche,** *idiom.* To camp up a storm. *Faire l'affiche te défoule, mais ce soir, sois discret.* "Camping it up relaxes you, but tonight, be discreet."

AFFICHÉ, -E. Published; displayed. **C'est affiché.** "It's a sure thing."

AFFICHER. To put up posters. **Afficher un sourire.** To put on a (phony) smile. *La tueuse à gages affichait un sourire avant de le tuer.* "The hired killer put on a smile before killing him."

(S')AFFICHER. To flaunt o.s. *En dépit des gens bien-pensants, Anna Karenina s'affichait avec son amant.* "Despite the hostility of the self-righteous, Anna Karenina appeared in public with her lover."

AFFRANCHI, *m.* Shady character. *C'est une bourgeoise qui ne fréquente que les affranchis.* "She's upper middle-class, but hangs out only with lowlifes."

AFFRANCHIR. 1. To put someone wise (lit. "to liberate"). *Je l'ai affranchie sur son jules, mais macache.* "I set her wise about her boyfriend but it was no use." **2.** To initiate sexually. *Casanova voulait l'affranchir, mais elle en savait plus que lui.* "Casanova wanted to initiate her sexually but she knew more than he did."

AFFREUX, *m.* Sinister person. *C'est un affreux, ton frangin!* "Your brother's bad news."

AFFREUX JOJO, *m.* Nasty brat; trouble-making individual. *Elle n'a pas de chance. Son mari et son gamin sont deux affreux jojos.* "She has no luck. Her husband and kid are two impossible creatures."

AFFURER. To make big money. *Ce magouilleur veut nous fait croire qu'on va affurer gros.* "That slick operator is trying to make us think we're going to make a killing."

AFFÛTER. To fine-tune (lit. "to sharpen"). Affûter la forme, *idiom.* To get into shape. *Il ferait mieux d'affûter sa forme que de cultiver sa graisse.* "He should work out instead of feeding his face."

AFFÛTIAUX, *m., pl.* Trinkets. *Elle avait sorti tous ses affûtiaux pour lui plaire.* "She got out all her baubles to please him."

AFNAF = AFANAF.

AGAÇANTE, *f. adj.* Sexually provocative (lit. "annoying"). *Elle se fringue de façon très agaçante.* "She's a very sexy dresser."

AGACE-PISSETTE, *f. Quebec.* Cockteaser. *Il cherche des vierges, pas les agace-pissettes.* "He's looking for virgins, not cockteasers."

AGACER LE SOUS-PRÉFET. To masturbate (lit. "to harass the sub-prefect"). *Il s'épuise en agaçant trop le sous-préfet.* "He wears h.s. out by flogging the bishop too much."

AGATES, *f., pl.* Peepers. *Je ne pouvais voir que les agates de la fatma.* "All I could see were the Arab woman's eyes."

AGITÉ, -E, *m., f.* Agitated person. **Un(e) agité(e) du bocal,** *idiom.* A loony. *Céline a appelé Sartre un "agité du bocal".* "Celine called Sartre 'a nutcase.'"

AGITER. To shake. **Les agiter.** To clear out. *Agite-les ou je te casse la gueule.* "Beat it or I'll knock your block off."

(S')AGITER. 1. To hurry up. *Si tu t'agites, tu seras à l'heure.* "If you step on it, you'll be on time." **2. Se l'agiter.** To masturbate. *Il se l'agitait longtemps sans pouvoir bander.* "He pulled at it for a long time but couldn't get it up."

AGOBILLES, *f., pl.* **1.** Burglars' tools. *Les poulets l'ont surpris, les agobilles en main.* "The cops caught him, burglars' tools in hand." **2.** Testicles. *Je ne peux m'imaginer ce gus aboulique avec des agobilles!* "That guy's so apathetic it's hard to believe he's got balls!"

AGRAFER. 1. To arrest (lit. "to fasten"). *Le commissaire a juré que le violeur serait agrafé sous peu.* "The commissioner swore the rapist would be arrested shortly." **2.** To hold up. *Le concierge me guette pour m'agrafer avec ses ragots.* "The concierge lies in wait to buttonhole me with gossip." **3.** To steal. *Où qu'elle aille, Hedi essaye d'agrafer qch.* "Wherever she goes, Hedi tries to swipe something."

AIDÉ, -E. Pas aidé, -e. Not favored by looks or brains. *Elle n'est pas aidée mais a réussi à épouser un milliardaire.* "She's no beauty, but she managed to marry a billionaire." *Il n'est pas aidé! Que fera-t-il donc dans la vie?* "He's not bright. What's he going to do in life?"

AIGUILLER. 1. To mark cards (lit. "to point"). *Il a triché en jouant avec des cartes aiguillées.* "He cheated by playing with marked cards." **2.** To have sexually. *Don Juan aiguillait les nanas et son valet les comptait.* "Don Juan laid the ladies and his valet kept score."

AIL, *m.* Garlic. **Bouffer/vendre de l'ail** (lit. "to eat/sell garlic"). To be a lesbian. *J'adore bouffer de l'ail mais parfois un mec comme dessert, ça me plaît.* "I love being a lesbian but once in a while I enjoy a guy for dessert." **Aimer; sentir; taper l'ail** (lit. "to like; reek of garlic"), *idiom.* To be a lesbian. *Ça sent l'ail chez elles, mais c'est*

7

leur affaire. "There's a lesbian atmosphere in their house, but that's their business." See GOUSSE; MARCHANDE D'AIL.

AILE, *f.* Wing. **Avoir du plomb dans l'aile,** *idiom.* To have problems. *Ça fait longtemps qu'il a du plomb dans l'aile!* "He's been in a bad way for some time!" See BATTRE DE L'AILE; BATTRE DES AILES; COUP DANS L'AILE; ROGNER LES AILES.

AILES BRUNES/NOIRES/ROUGES, motorcyclist (Hell's Angels) slang for types of sex in which **ailes** may refer to "testicles." **Avoir ses ailes brunes,** *idiom.* To have anal sex. **Avoir ses ailes noires,** *idiom.* To have sex with a black girl. **Avoir ses ailes rouges,** *idiom.* To have intercourse with a girl during her period. *Avec sa Suédoise le motard a ses ailes tantôt brunes, tantôt rouges, mais avec son Ougandaise, il les a toujours noires.* "The motorcyclist sometimes browns his Swedish girlfriend or has her during her period, but with his Ugandan girlfriend, he always gets poontang."

AIMER. To love. **Va te faire aimer.** Get lost! Piss off! Fuck off!

AIMER L'AIL. See AIL.

AIR, *m.* **1.** Air. **Être en l'air,** *idiom.* To be without funds. *Dès les premiers tours de roulette au casino de Deauville j'étais en l'air.* "After the first few turns of the roulette wheel in the casino at Deauville, I was broke." **L'avoir en l'air,** *idiom.* To have an erection. *Il est à l'âge où il l'a toujours en l'air.* "He's at an age where he's always got it up." See BRASSER DE L'AIR; CHANGER D'AIR; CRACHER EN L'AIR; DÉPLACER DE L'AIR; (S')ENVOYER EN L'AIR; FOUTRE EN L'AIR (FOUTRE 3); (SE) FOUTRE EN L'AIR; JOUER (À) …L'AIR; (NE PAS) MANQUER D'AIR; PARTIE…AIR; PISSER EN L'AIR; POMPER **1.** PRENDRE DE L'AIR. **2.** Appearance. **Avoir l'air.** To look like. *De quoi aurais-je l'air en minijupe au milieu de ces robes longues?* "What will I look like in a miniskirt surrounded by all those evening gowns?" **Avoir l'air fin/con/couillon/cul.** To look like a real jerk/asshole. *Tu auras l'air fin si tu changes d'avis.* "You'll look like a real idiot if you change your mind." **En avoir l'air et la chanson** (a pun on meaning **3**, "tune"). To be what one looks like. *Ce con en a l'air et la chanson.* "That jerk is as dumb as he looks." **3.** Tune. See JOUER...AIR; JOUER...BAVEUSE; JOUER UN AIR...FLÛTE; (DE L')AIR! See DE L'AIR!

AIRBAGS, *m., pl.* **1.** Impressive breasts (lit. "air bags"). *J'aimerais poser ma tête entre ses airbags là!* "I'd like to rest my head between those splendid tits!" **2.** Individual endowed with large breasts. *T'as vu tous les airbags le long du bois de Boulogne?* "Have you seen all those big-busted gals all over the Bois de Boulogne?"

AIRPRO. Thoroughly professional (from **avoir l'air professionnel**). *T'inquiète! Cette infirmière est airpro.* "Relax! That nurse is thoroughly professional."

AISE, *f.* Pleasure; ease. **À l'aise/à l'aise, Blaise,** *adv.* Easily; no problem. *"On y va tout de suite?" "À l'aise."* "Can we go right away?" "No problem!"

À LA VA-COMME-JE-TE-POUSSE. See (À LA) VA-COMME ...

ALCO(O)LO, *m., f., adj.* and *n.* Lush. *Il a le pif d'un alcolo mais ne boit que du thé.* "He's got an alkie's schnozz but he's a teetotaler."

ALIGNER. Les aligner, *idiom.* To pay up (lit. "to align them" [bank notes]). *Emma Bovary, ne pouvant pas les aligner, s'est suicidée.* "Emma Bovary couldn't come up with the money and committed suicide."

(S')ALIGNER. 1. To take on s.t. difficult. *Lors de la grève des dames-pipi il a dû s'aligner le nettoyage des chiottes du musée.* "During the toilet attendants' strike he had to clean the museum's toilets." **2. Pouvoir (toujours) s'aligner,** *idiom.* To have little chance. *Tu peux toujours t'aligner —ils n'en prendront que treize sur mille.* "You can forget it—they'll only accept 13 out of 1,000."

ALLÈCHE, *f.,* youth. Poster (from **allécher,** "to tempt"). *Vise un peu l'allèche pour le concert rock.* "Take a look at that ad for the rock concert."

ALLER À LA CACASSE/AU CUL/RADADA. See CACASSE; CUL **3**; RADADA.

ALLER QUELQUE PART. See QUELQUE PART.

ALLER-RETOUR/ALLER ET RETOUR, *m.* A double slap in the face (lit. "round trip"). *Cesse d'aguicher les mecs, sinon tu auras un aller-retour.* "Stop coming on to guys or I'll box your ears."

ALLIGATOR, *m.* Barfly; lounge lizard. *Le barman a eu du mal à fermer à cause des alligators.* "The bartender had trouble closing up because of the drunks glued to the bar."

ALLONGER. 1. To align. **Les allonger.** To fork over money. *Allonge-les ou tu auras affaire à mes potes!* "Pay up or you'll have to deal with my pals." **2. Allonger qqn.** To knock s.o. down. *L'auteur menaçait d'allonger le critique.* "The author threatened to flatten the critic." **3.** To bump off. *Le gangster voulait allonger tous ses rivaux.* "The gangster wanted to rub out all his rivals."

ALLONGER UN COUP/UNE BEIGNE/CLAQUE/ TALOCHE/TARTE À QN. To give s.o. a wallop. *Si tu continues à crier, je t'allonge une taloche.* "If you keep on shouting, I'll give you a good whack."

ALLONGÉS, *pl.* The dead (lit. "stretched out"). **Être aux allongés,** *idiom.* To be among the dead. *Le pauvre, il souffrait tellement qu'il est mieux aux allongés.* "The poor guy, he suffered so much, he's better off dead." **Boulevard/jardin des allongés,** see JARDIN.

(S')ALLONGER. To own up. *Après trois heures d'interrogatoire il s'est enfin allongé.* "After three hours of questioning he finally spilled the beans."

(SE L')ALLONGER. To masturbate. *Portnoy ne pensait qu'à se l'allonger.* "All Portnoy thought about was jerking off."

ALOUETTE, *f.* Female traffic cop (lit. "swallow"). *Fais gaffe, dans une heure l'alouette te posera un papillon!* "Watch out, in an hour the meter maid'll give you a ticket."

AL(L)OUF, *f.* Match. *La gosse jouait avec la boîte d'al-loufs.* "The little girl played with the matchbox."

ALLUMÉ, -E. Lit up (lit. and figuratively). *Ils étaient tous allumés lors du viol collectif.* "They were all high at the time of the gang rape."

ALLUMÉ, E, *m., f.* Drunkard. *C'est un allumé: il n'a plus son permis (de conduire).* "He's a drunk and no longer has a driver's license."

ALLUMER. 1. To excite sexually. *Avec sa jupe ras le pétard, elle allume tous les gus.* "In her miniskirt up to her ass, she turns on all the guys." **2.** To gun down. *Les mercenaires les avait tous allumé dans le village.* "The mercenaries gunned down everyone in the village." **3.** To reprimand. *Maman va t'allumer.* "Ma's going to give you a bawling out."

ALLUMER LES BOUGIES. To elucidate (lit. "to light the candles"). *Trêve de mystification; allumons les bougies!* "That's enough of a mystery. Let's have some light on the matter."

ALLUMEUR, *m.* Con man's sidekick. *Il ne voulait plus faire l'allumeur et pensait faire de l'arnaque seul.* "He didn't want to be the decoy anymore and planned some scams of his own."

ALLUMEUSE, *f.* **1.** Bar girl. *Il n'avait bu qu'un verre avec l'allumeuse et a été sidéré en voyant la note.* "He only had one drink with the B-girl and was floored by the bill." **2.** Hooker; cockteaser. *Longtemps allumeuse, elle cherche maintenant l'illumination dans l'Himalaya.* "A longtime hooker, she's now looking for illumination in the Himalayas."

ALPAGUER. 1. To buttonhole (lit. "grabbing s.o. by the collar of the alpaga (alpaca) coat"). *Je ne me laisse plus alpaguer par ce chronophage.* "I don't allow that time waster to buttonhole me anymore." **2.** To arrest. *Il s'est fait alpaguer par la flicaille.* "He got nabbed by the cops."

ALSACO, *m., pej.* Alsatian. *Ce titi parisien a pour parents des Alsacos.* "That Parisian kid's parents are Alsatians."

AMATEUR DE ROSETTE. See ROSETTE **2.**

AMAZONE, *f., joc.* **1.** Horsewoman (orig. the legendary one-breasted female warrior). **Monter en amazone.** To ride sidesaddle. *Quand elle monte en amazone elle est très élégante.* "When she rides sidesaddle she looks very elegant." **2.** Prostitute who works out of her car. *Beaucoup d'amazones peuvent se payer des voitures de luxe.* "Many car-based prostitutes can afford luxury autos."

AMERLAUD/AMERLO(T)/AMERLOCHE/AMER- LOQUE/AMERLUCHE, *m.* American. *Elle a épousé un Amerloque.* "She married an American."

AMI-AMI. See FAIRE AMI-AMI.

AMINCHE, *m.* Friend. *Tu me le présentes, ton aminche?* "Are you going to introduce me to your pal?"

AMOCHER. To bash (from **moche** ["ugly"; "rotten"]). *Lors de l'accident sa voiture et lui furent bien amochés.* "He and his car were badly banged up the accident."

AMORTI. Over the hill (lit. "depreciated"). *Pour les jeunes, on est amorti après trente ans.* "For the young, you're over the hill once you're thirty."

AMORTISSEURS, *m., pl.* Breasts (lit. "shock absorbers"). *Tâte-les, mes amortisseurs, c'est pas du faux.* "Feel my knockers and you'll see they're not fake."

AMOUR, *m.* **1.** Love. See BALAI D'AMOUR; FILER...AMOUR; GUEULE D'AMOUR; MARCHANDE D'AMOUR; PANIER D'AMOUR; PAPILLON D'AMOUR. **2.** Charmer; darling. *Sois un amour et passe-moi la confiture.* "Be a dear and pass me the jelly."

(À L')AMOUREUSE. Lit. "lovingly." Said of a prostitute who gives extras, without charging extra. *Les michés préfèrent Julie qui travaille à l'amoureuse.* "The johns prefer Julie who labors for love."

AMOUREUX. See RAIDE DINGUE.

AMPHIBIE, *m.* Multi-moonlighter (lit. "amphibious"). *Je ne lui fais pas confiance; c'est un amphibie.* "I have no confidence in him; he's got too many jobs."

AMUSER LA GALERIE. See GALERIE.

AMYGDALES, *f., pl.* Tonsils. **Se faire lécher les amygdales,** *idiom.* To get tongue kissed. *Lèche-moi les amygdales, mais ne me mords pas la langue!* "Give me a French kiss, but don't bite my tongue!" See (SE) CALER LES AMYGDALES.

ANANAS, *m.* **1.** Hand grenade (lit. "pineapple"). *Ce groupuscule d'anars avait stocké des centaines d'ananas.* "That tiny group of anarchists had stockpiled hundreds of hand grenades." **2.** Breast. *J'aimais ses ananas fermes et tendres.* "I loved her firm and tender breasts."

ANAR/ANARCHO, *m.* or *f.,* from **anarchiste.** Anarchist. *Le fils aîné du président se veut anar.* "The president's eldest son claims to be an anarchist."

ANATOLE. See ÇA COLLE ANATOLE.

ANDEK! Watch out! (from Ar.). *"Andek!", cria le jeune beur en voyant les flics.* "Watch out," cried the young (Fr.-born) North African when he spotted the cops."

ANDOUILLE, *f.* Nerd (lit. "chitterling sausage"). *Espèce d'andouile! Tu t'es fait avoir.* "You dummy! You were had." **Faire l'andouille.** To act like a fool; horse around. *Ne fais pas l'andouille!* Quit acting like a jerk! See DÉPENDEUR.

ANDOUILLE DE CAL(E)CIF/À COL ROULÉ, *f.* Penis (lit. "sausage in the shorts; turtleneck sausage"). *Les gars ont comparé leurs andouilles de calecif.* "The young boys compared their sausages (peckers)."

ANGE, *m.* Angel. **Un ange passe, passa, a passé,** *idiom* (said when there is a lull in the conversation). *La discussion était animée; soudain un ange a passé.* "The discussion was spirited; suddenly there was an awkward silence." **Être aux anges,** *idiom.* To be in ecstasy. *Elle* *était aux anges d'avoir gagné.* "She was in seventh heaven when she won." See FAISEUR D'ANGES; VOIR LES ANGES.

ANGE GARDIEN, *m.* Pickpocket's lookout (lit. "guardian angel"). *Le tireur et son ange gardien entraient dans le métro à l'heure d'affluence.* "The pickpocket and his lookout went into the subway during rush hour."

ANGÉLINA, *f.* Passive homosexual. *C'est un bar frequenté par les angélinas.* "Passive gays hang out in that bar."

ANGLAIS, *m., pl.* Englishmen. **Avoir ses Anglais.** To have one's menstrual period (Eng. soldiers were known as "redcoats.") **Les Anglais ont débarqué; sont arrivés.** To begin to menstruate (lit. "the English have landed.") *Je me croyais enceinte, mais les Anglais ont enfin débarqué.* "I thought I was pregnant, but my period finally started."

ANGLAISER. To sodomize. *La marine anglaise était au port et les angélinas cherchaient à se faire anglaiser.* "The English fleet was in and the passive fags wanted to get fucked."

ANGLICHE/ANGLUCHE, *m., f., adj.* and *n.,* often *pej.* English/Brit./limey. *J'aime me baguenauder sur le Bvd. des Angliches à Nice.* "I like to stroll along the Boulevard des Anglais in Nice."

ANGORA, *m.* Female genitalia (from the association with the Angora cat). *Mon mari adore mon angora.* "My husband loves my pussy."

ANGUILLE DE CALEÇON/CAL(E)CIF. Penis (lit. "eel in the shorts"). *Son immense anguille de calecif n'était qu'un gode!* "His immense dick was just a dildo."

ANNEAU, *m.* **1.** Anus ring (lit. "ring"). *Pépé a de sacrées émeraudes à l'anneau.* "Grandpa has enormous hemorrhoids." **2.** Buttocks. *Il m'a donné un coup de pied dans l'anneau pour m'être moqué de lui.* "He gave me a kick in the butt for having made fun of him." See DÉFONCER…ANNEAU.

ANTENNES, *f., pl.* youth. Unisex hairstyle featuring colored "devil" horns on each side of the head (lit. "antennae").

T'as des antennes sensass! "Your horns are terrific!"

ANTIFLE, *f.* Church. *Malgré leurs familles, ils ont refusé de se marier à l'antifle.* "Despite their families, they refused to get married in church."

S'ANTIFLER. To get married. *Ni croyants ni pratiquants, ils se sont quand même antiflés à l'église.* "They neither believe nor practice their religion, but they got hitched in church anyway."

ANTIGEL, *m.* Hard liquor (lit. "antifreeze"). *Et si on prenait un petit coup d'antigel?* "How about our having a little snort?"

ANTIGRIPPE, *m.* Alcoholic drink; after-dinner drink. *Il a toujours sur lui sa petite bouteille d'antigrippe.* "He always has his little bottle of booze to keep out the cold."

ANTISÈCHE, *f.* Trot; pony. *Des étudiants essayaient de se servir de leurs antisèches à l'exam.* "Some students tried to use their ponies during the exam."

APÉRO, *m.* Aperitif. *C'est l'heure de l'apéro! Si on le prenait chez moi?* "It's aperitif time (happy hour). How about having it at my place?"

APPART(E), *m.* Apartment. *Son appart est dément!* "Her apartment is fantastic!"

APPE = APPART.

APPELER. To call. **Se faire appeler Arthur/Joseph/Jules.** See ARTHUR.

APPUYER SUR LE CHAMPIGNON. See CHAMPIGNON.

(S')APPUYER. 1. To put up with (lit. "to lean on"). *J'aime tchatcher avec elle, même si je dois m'appuyer ses gamins.* "I enjoy gabbing with her even if I have to put up with her kids." **2.** To get stuck with s.t. *Pourquoi c'est toujours moi qui m'appuie la plonge?* "Why am I the one who always gets stuck with the dishes?"

APRÈM, *m., abbr.* for **après-midi.** Afternoon. *C't'aprèm j'suis libre.* "I'm free this P.M."

À PLUSS!/À PLUTE!, *abbr.* for **à plus tard!** *À pluss, mon pote!* "See you later, my friend."

AQUARIUM, *m.* **1.** Glass-enclosed office. *Si j'étais exhibitionniste, j'aimerais travailler dans cet aquarium.* "If I were an exhibitionist, I'd like working in this fishbowl." **2.** House or place of ill repute. *Ce n'est pas un aquarium ici; partez faire votre boulot ailleurs.* "This is no sleazy dive; go elsewhere to ply your trade." **Note:** In addition to the idea of "open display," many terms for "pimp" are types of fish, such as **maquereau, merlan, poisson,** and so on. Cf. FENÊTRIÈRE.

ARABI, *m., pej.* Arab. *Ton oncle ne semble pas aimer les Arabis.* "Your uncle doesn't seem to like Arabs."

ARAIGNÉE, *f.* **Avoir une araignée au plafond**, *idiom.* To have bats in the belfry (lit. "to have a spider in the ceiling"). *Parfois je crois que tu as une araignée au plafond.* "Sometimes I think you've got bats in the belfry." See FAIRE…ARAIGNÉE.

ARBALÈTE, *f.* Penis (lit. "crossbow"). **Filer un coup d'arbalète.** To screw. *Elle aimait les préliminaires, mais il ne voulait que lui filer un coup d'arbalète.* "She liked foreplay, but all he wanted to do was stick it into her."

ARBI/ARBICOT = ARABI.

ARBRE, *m.* Tree. See GRIMPER À L'ARBRE; GRIMPER AUX ARBRES.

ARCAGNASSES/ARCAGNATS, *m., pl.* Menstrual period. *La gosse était paniquée par ses premiers arcagnasses.* "The kid was frightened by her first period."

ARCAN/ARCANDIER, *m.* Hoodlum. *Ce quartier grouille d'arcans.* "That neighborhood is full of thugs."

ARCHE, *f.* Buttocks (lit. "ark"; "strong box"; poss. influence of Eng. "arse" or Ger. **Arsch**). **Fendre l'arche,** *idiom.* To be a pain in the ass. *Tu me fends l'arche.* "You're a real pain in the ass."

ARCHER/ARCHER DU ROI, *m.* Policeman (lit. "[king's] archer"). *Monsieur le commissaire, est-ce-que vos archers sauraient me protéger si j'accepte cette mission?*

"Commissioner, will your men be able to protect me if I accept this mission?"

ARCHI-, *pref.* Extremely. **Archichiant.** Deadly dull. *Le film était archichiant.* "The movie was mind-numbing." **Archicon.** Unbelievably stupid. *Si tu crois ça, tu es archicon.* "If you believe that, you're a real idiot." **Archifaux.** Totally wrong. *Votre réponse est archifausse.* "Your answer is totally wrong." **Archifou.** Stark raving mad. *Tous les archifous ne sont pas à l'asile.* "Not all the crazies are in the asylum."

ARDILLON, *m.* Penis (lit. "prong"; "barb"). *Mon mari avait l'ardillon bien plus ardent avant!* "My husband's dick used to be much more passionate!"

-ARD. Frequently used suffix added to adjectives and nouns, usually pej., disparaging. See CORNARD; QUEUTARD; SALOPARD; TROUILLARD.

ARDOISE, *f.* **1.** Slate. See MOUILLER UNE ARDOISE; PRENDRE UNE ARDOISE À L'EAU. **2.** Debt (originally recorded on a blackboard). *Ce poivrot a des ardoises chez tous les cafetiers du coin.* "That drunk has run up a bill with all the local café owners." **3.** Toilet; "tearoom" (homosexual). *Tous les jours il drague dans les ardoises du parc.* "Every day he cruises the T rooms in the park."

-ARÈS/ARESSE. Slang suffixes that create invariable adjectives with only one form for the *m., f.,* and *pl.* See BOUCLARÈS; DÉFONCARÈS; EMBALLARÈS; PLANQUARÈS.

ARÊTES, *f., pl.* Back; ribs (lit. "fishbones"). *Elle n'a rien à se mettre sur les arêtes.* "She's got nothing to wear (put on her back)."

ARGAGNASSES = ARCAGNASSES.

ARGOMUCHE, *m.* Street talk (from **argot** [slang] and suffix **-muche**). **Jacter/jaspiner l'argomuche.** To talk slang. *Dans la zone, on ne jacte que l'argomuche.* "In the slums, all we talk is slang."

ARGOUGNER = ARPIGNER.

ARIA, *m.* Operatic aria. **Faire des arias,** *idiom.* To make a song and dance. *C'est dans son caractère de toujours faire des arias.* "It's his nature to always make a fuss."

ARISTO, *m., f., abbr.* of **aristocrate.** *Ce resto est un nid d'aristos.* "Aristocrats hang out in that restaurant."

ARLEQUINS, *m., pl.* Leftovers; bits of this and that (from Harlequin's motley costume). *Elle sait faire un gueuleton avec des arlequins.* "She knows how to make a feast out of leftovers."

ARLO, *m.* Cheap knickknack. *Tu dis que ce n'était que de l'arlo, mais ma licorne en verre avait une grande valeur sentimentale pour moi.* "You say it was worthless, but my glass unicorn had great sentimental value to me."

ARMÉNOUCHE, *m.* Armenian. *Il y a beaucoup d'armé-nouches dans notre quartier.* "There are lots of Armenians in our neighborhood."

ARMOIRE, *f.* Closet. **Armoire à glace.** Strapping hulk (lit. "clothes closet with a large mirror"). *Les gardes du corps sont souvent des armoires à glace.* "Bodyguards are often big bruisers."

ARNAQUE, *f.* Swindle. *Tu as vu les prix? C'est de l'ar-naque!* "Have you seen the prices? It's highway robbery!"

ARNAQUER 1. To arrest. *Le dealer s'est fait arnaquer par les douaniers et leurs chiens.* "The drug dealer was nabbed by the customs officials and their dogs." **2.** To swindle. *Si tu veux te faire arnaquer, va manger dans ce nouveau restaurant.* "If you want to get ripped off, go eat in that new restaurant."

ARNAQUEUR/ARNAQUEUSE, *m., f.* Swindler. *Dans le film* L'arnaque, *Newman et Redford jouaient les maîtres arnaqueurs.* "In the movie *The Sting,* Newman and Redford played master con artists."

ARPENTER (L'ASPHALTE/LE BITUME). To be a streetwalker (lit. "to walk to and fro (on the pavement)"). *J'ai commencé à arpenter très jeune.* "I started soliciting when I was very young."

ARPENTEUSE, *f.* Prostitute. *Ce prof, un de mes meilleurs michés, me dit qu'il fait des recherches sur les arpenteuses.* "That professor, one of my best customers, tells me he's doing research on working girls."

ARPÈTE/ARPETTE, *m., f.,* often *pej.* Apprentice (from Ger. **Arbeiter** [worker]). *L'arpète du sorcier avait bousillé le boulot.* "The sorcerer's apprentice botched the job."

ARPIGNER. To grab. *Ce petit voyou a arpigné mon sac (à main).* "That little hood grabbed my purse."

ARPINCHE, *m.* Miser. *Tu n'auras pas un sou de cet arpinche.* "That miser won't give you a cent."

ARPION, *m.* **1.** Foot. *Il m'a foutu un coup d'arpion.* "He gave me a kick in the pants." See TAPER DES ARPIONS. **2.** Toe. *Le danseur s'est cassé le gros arpion.* "The dancer broke his big toe."

ARQUER. To walk (lit. "to bend a bow"). *J'ai tant couru que je ne peux plus arquer.* "I ran so much, I can't take another step."

ARRACHÉ, *m.* Snatching. See VOL À L'ARRACHÉ.

ARRACHER. 1. To rip out or off; grab. **Ça arrache!** "That really grabs you." *Ce calva, ça arrache.* "This applejack brandy is strong stuff. It really gets to you!" **2. En arracher.** To work hard. *Il en a arraché aujourd'hui!* "He worked hard today!"

ARRACHER SON COPEAU. To have an orgasm (lit. "to tear off a (wood) shaving"). *Le marin rêvait d'arracher son copeau avec une fille du port.* "The sailor dreamed of getting it off with a girl in port."

(S')ARRACHER. To run away; escape. *Je ne pensais qu'à m'arracher de chez mes parents.* "All I could think of was getting away from my parents."

ARRANGER. To beat up (lit. "to arrange"). *Après cette bagarre stupide, te voilà drôlement arrangé.* "Just look at you, all beat up after that stupid fight."

ARRÊTER. To stop; arrest. **Arrête tes salades!** "Cut the crap! Stop giving me a hard time!" See FRAIS.

ARRIÈRE-TRAIN, *m.* Buttocks (lit. "animal's hindquarters." *Tu as vu l'arrière-train qu'elle se paye?* "Have you seen the ass on her?"

(S')ARRIMER. To shack up together (lit. "to link up"). *Mimi aimerait avoir un gosse, mais ne veut s'arrimer à aucun bonhomme.* "Mimi would like to have a child, but she doesn't want a committed relationship with any male."

ARRONDISSEMENT À BITUME, *m.* City district with government buildings and/or residences of prominent people. *Le Sentier n'est pas un arrondissement à bitume.* "The Paris garment district isn't a select district."

ARROSER. 1. To celebrate with a drink (lit. "to water"). See ÇA S'ARROSE; COURAGE ARROSÉ. **2.** To bribe. *Il fallait bien l'arroser pour avoir le contrat.* "His palm had to be well greased to get the contract."

ARSOUILLE, *m.* (Either from **souillon** ["slut"; "slob"] or from Eng. "arsehole.") **1.** Crook. *Cet arsouille a triché aux cartes.* "That crook cheated at cards." **2.** Tough. *Je l'ai connu arsouille, mais sa fiancée l'a civilisé et adouci.* "When I knew him he was a hooligan, but his fiancée has civilized and softened him."

(S')ARSOUILLER. 1. To get soused. *Il aimait chaque week-end s'arsouiller avec les copains.* "Every weekend he liked to booze it up with the boys." **2.** To live a life of debauchery. *Après le monastère il s'est arsouillé.* "After the monastery, he lived riotously."

ARTHUR. Se faire appeler Arthur. To get reprimanded. *Si tu sèches encore le cours, tu te feras appeler Arthur.* "If you keep cutting the course, you'll get called on the carpet."

ARTILLER. 1. To make fat profits. *Les initiés artillaient gros.* "The insiders made fat profits." **2.** To plug/bang sexually. *Les marins ne pensaient qu'à artiller les filles du port.* "All the sailors had on their mind was screwing the girls in the port."

ARTILLERIE, *f.* **1.** Loaded dice (lit. "artillery"). *Ce joueur* *porte toujours son artillerie sur lui.* "That gambler's always got his loaded dice on him." **2.** Plentiful, simple food. *J'aime la nouvelle cuisine; chez mes parents ce n'est que de l'artillerie.* "I like nouvelle cuisine; at my parents' it's just meat and potatoes." **3.** Male genitalia. *Cet exhibitionniste aime sortir son artillerie dans le métro.* "That flasher likes to take out his equipment in the subway."

ARTISTE, *m., f.* Counterfeiter. *Il est artiste de premier ordre et ses derniers billets étaient un travail d'artiste.* "He's a first-class counterfeiter and his most recent bank notes were a work of art." See TRAVAILLER EN ARTISTE.

AS *m.* Ace (cards; aviation). See AS DU VOLANT. **Être plein aux as,** *idiom.* To be loaded; filthy rich. *Son nouveau mari est plein aux as.* "Her new husband is filthy rich." **Passer à l'as,** *idiom.* To go down the drain. *Tous leurs projets sont passés à l'as.* "All their projects went down the drain." **Passer qch. chose à l'as,** *idiom.* Not to count something deliberately. *Le gangster a donné des pots-de-vin au juge qui a passé des preuves importantes à l'as.* "The gangster bribed the judge who suppressed important evidence."

AS DE PIQUE, *m.* **1.** Pope's/parson's nose (lit. "ace of spades"). *"Les derniers seront les premiers," disait-elle en mangeant l'as de pique.* "'The last shall be first', she said, eating the part that went over the fence last." **2.** Human posterior. **Être ficelé/fichu/foutu/fagoté comme l'as de pique,** *idiom.* To be dressed in an asinine manner. *Le modèle Line est souvent fagoté comme l'as de pique.* "The (artists') model, Line, often dresses grotesquely." **3.** Female genitalia. *Quand Line est à poil, les peintres admirent la splendeur de son as de pique.* "When Line is completely nude, the painters admire her big black bush."

AS DE TRÈFLE = TRÈFLE.

AS DU VOLANT, *m.* Top driver. *Il se prend pour un as du volant.* "He thinks he's a wonderful driver."

ASCENSEUR. Elevator. **Renvoyer l'ascenseur** (lit. "to

send back the elevator"). **1.** To return a favor. *J'ai été déçue qu'il ne me renvoie pas l'ascenseur.* "I was disappointed at his not returning the favor." **2.** To get back to right away. *Je suis à la bourre et ne peux te renvoyer l'ascenseur.* "I'm in a hurry and can't get back to you now."

ASPERGE, *f.* **1.** Tall, thin person (lit. "asparagus"). *Pour avoir de grands enfants, le petit roi d'Italie a choisi une asperge pour reine.* "To have tall children, the tiny king of Italy chose an asparagus as queen." **2.** Penis. **Aller/être aux asperges.** To engage in prostitution. *Je vais parfois aux asperges pour mettre du beurre dans les épinards.* "I do a little hooking occasionally to improve our financial situation." **Cultiver des asperges.** To work as a prostitute. *"Au lieu de cultiver ta flemme, va cultiver des asperges."* "Instead of loafing around, get to work (hooking)."

ASPHALTE, *m.* Pavement. **Arpenter/faire/polir/l'asphalte.** To be a hooker. *Avant le clandé j'ai longtemps poli l'asphalte.* "Before the whorehouse, I walked the streets for some time."

ASPINE, *m.* or *f.* Money. *Cet arpinche ne vit que pour son aspine.* "That miser lives only for his money."

ASPRO®, *m.* **1.** Aspirin. *Passe-moi un aspro. J'ai mal à la tête.* "Hand me an aspirin. I have a headache." **2.** Male or female prostitute (from English "ass professional"). *J'étais aspro avant de me marier.* "I used to sell my ass before I got married."

ASSAISONNER. 1. To bash (lit. "to season"). *Ses copains de classe l'ont assaisonné.* "His classmates beat him up." **2.** To kill. *Aboule le fric ou je t'assaisonne.* "Hand over the dough or I'll rub you out."

ASSEOIR. To flabbergast (lit. "to seat"; "establish"). *Sa stupidité nous assied.* "His stupidity flabbergasts us." **En rester assis,** *idiom.* To be dumbfounded. *Il a eu le premier prix; on en est resté assis.* "He got the first prize; we were knocked for a loop."

(S')ASSEOIR. To sit down. **S'asseoir dessus/sur qch.,**

idiom. To not give a damn about. *Ton choix c'est de la merde; je m'assieds dessus.* "Your choice is rotten; I don't care for it at all."

ASSIETTE AU BEURRE, *f.* Sinecure. *Il chôme car il ne cherche que l'assiette au beurre.* "He's unemployed because all he wants is a cushy job." **Avoir l'assiette au beurre,** *idiom.* To be rich and powerful; ride the gravy train. *Il rêve d'avoir l'assiette au beurre.* "He's dreaming of being on easy street."

(S')ASSIR. To sit down (for **s'asseoir**). *Je suis crevé; je vais m'assir.* "I'm bushed; I'm going to sit down."

ASSURER. 1. To know one's stuff (lit. "to assure"). *Il assure en tout, sauf en sciences.* "He's up on everything, except science." **2.** To look snazzy. *Elle a acheté une robe pour assurer dans son nouveau job.* "She bought a dress to look smart at her new job." **3.** To have well under control. *Dors tranquille, moi j'assure.* "Rest easy, I have the situation well in hand."

ASTAP(E). 1. Really funny (from **à se taper le cul par terre** ["to split one's sides laughing," lit. "to knock one's ass on the ground"]). *Elle raconte toujours des histoires astapes.* "The stories she tells are real thigh-whackers." **2.** Till this afternoon! (Contraction of **à c't'aprème,** from a contraction of **à cet après-midi.**)

ASTICOT, *m.* **1.** Maggot. See ENGRAISSER LES ASTICOTS. **2.** Wimp. *On le traitait d'asticot, mais il nous a tous surpris.* "We called him a worm but he surprised us all."

ASTICOTER. To needle. *On dirait que tu te fais un vrai plaisir de m'asticoter.* "It seems you get a real kick out of bugging me."

(S')ASTICOTER. To bicker. *Ils ne s'arrêtent pas de s'asticoter.* "They never stop squabbling."

ASTIQUER. To polish. **Bien astiqué.** Spruced up. *Depuis son service militaire il est toujours bien astiqué.* "He's always well groomed since his stint in the military."

ASTIQUER LA BAGUETTE/COLONNE/GAULE. To

jerk off. *On n'a pas de préso, mais au moins astique-moi la colonne.* "We haven't got a rubber, but give me a hand job at least."

ASTIQUER LE BOUTON. To stimulate the clitoris. *C'était le pied quand Luc, au resto, m'astiquait le bouton avec son gros orteil!* "It was mind-blowing when Luc's big toe tickled my clit in the restaurant!"

ATOUT, *m.* Clout (lit. "trump"). *Il avait reçu tant d'atouts qu'on ne le reconnaissait plus.* "He was so bashed up that he was unrecognizable."

(D')ATTAQUE. In shape. *Je me sens tout à fait d'attaque pour le faire.* "I feel entirely capable of doing it."

ATTAQUER. To give a buzz to (lit. "to attack"). *Attaque-moi vers huit plombes.* "Give me a ring around eight."

ATTIGER. 1. To beat up. *Les flics niaient l'avoir attigé.* "The cops denied having worked him over." 2. To infect with VD. *Malgré le préso il s'est fait attigé.* "Despite the condom, he got VD."

ATTIGER/ATTIGER LA CABANE. To exaggerate. *Quand elle raconte ses histoires elle attige toujours la cabane.* "When she tells her stories, she really lays it on thick."

ATTRIBUTS, *m., pl.* 1. Attributes. 2. **Attributs (virils).** Male genitalia. *Ce défroqué est écartelé entre les attributs divins, les virils, et les appas féminins.* "That defrocked priest is torn between the divine attributes (omniscience, ubiquity, and so on), male private parts, and feminine charms."

AUBERGE, *f.* Inn. **Ne pas être sorti de l'auberge,** *idiom.* Not to be out of the woods yet. *On a gagné le premier procès, mais on n'est pas encore sorti de l'auberge.* "We won the first trial, but we're not out of the woods yet."

AU BLACK/NOIR/SCHWARZ. Nondeclared (for tax purposes); under the table (Fr. **noir,** Ger. **schwarz** = "black"). *Il veut toujours être payé au black.* "He always wants to be paid under the table."

AUGE, *f.* Plate (lit. "trough"). *Mon auge est vide.* "My plate is empty."

AUSSI SEC. Quick as a flash [from **aussitôt** ("right away")]. *Aussi sec elle lui a retourné une gifle.* "She immediately slapped him back."

AUTEL, *m.* Baker's oven (lit. "altar"). *Le boulanger basané ressemble à un ange blanc quand il prépare ses pains pour l'autel.* "The dark-skinned baker looks like a white angel when he prepares his loaves for the oven."

AUTOBUS, *m.* Occasional prostitute. *Personne ne pouvait soupçonner qu'elle jouait à l'autobus.* "No one could have guessed that she hustled occasionally."

(D')AUTOR, *abbr.* of **autorité.** With determination. *Si tu t'y mets d'autor, tu finiras le projet bien avant la date limite.* "If you really apply yourself, you'll finish the project before the deadline." See also (D')ACHAR ET D'AUTOR.

AUXI/AUXIGOT, *m.* Prison trustee (from **auxiliaire**). *Les auxigots jouissaient de privilèges.* "The trustees enjoyed privileges."

AVALER LA PILULE. To grin and bear it (lit. "to swallow the pill"). *Rien à faire, il faut avaler la pilule.* "No way around it, we'll have to bite the bullet."

AVALER SON ACTE DE NAISSANCE. To die (lit. "to swallow one's birth certificate"). *Tu parles comme si demain tu allais avaler ton acte de naissance.* "You talk as if you were going to cash in your chips tomorrow."

AVALER SON DENTIER. To work overtime as a prostitute (lit. "to swallow one's dentures"). *J'ai fait peu de passes; faut que j'avale mon dentier.* "I haven't turned many tricks; I've got to get going."

AVANTAGE, *m.* Advantage. **Faire un avantage à qn.,** *idiom.* To be nice to s.o. *On m'a fait un avantage sur cette robe qui avait fait la vitrine.* "They gave me a discount on this dress that was in the window."

AVANTAGES, *m., pl.* Breasts. *Pour séduire, elle mettait ses* *avantages en valeur.* "To be seductive she showed lots of cleavage."

AVANT-POSTES, *m., pl.* Breasts (lit. "outposts"). *Elle se tenait très droite pour faire pointer ses avant-postes.* "She carried herself very erect so that her tits would stick out."

AVANT-SCÈNE, *f.* Breasts (lit. "proscenium"). *Avec une telle avant-scène elle ne peut faire que des ravages.* "With knockers like that, she can't help but break some hearts."

AVARO, *m.* Sad/bad happening (from **avarie,** "damage to goods in transit"). *Dans sa vie il n'avait que des avaros.* "His life has been a succession of kicks in the ass."

AVATAR, *m.* Mishap (orig. "manifestation of the God Vishnu [Hinduism]"). *Je vous souhaite un voyage avec moins d'avatars cette fois-ci. Que Vichnou, dans un de ses avatars nombreux, vous protège.* "I wish you a less problematic trip this time. May Vishnu, in one of his numerous manifestations, protect you."

AVEC, *m.* Bonus. *Elle travaillait dur dans l'espoir d'un avec.* "She worked hard, hoping for a bonus."

AVIATEUR, *m.* Sadomasochistic homosexual (lit. "aviator"). *Est-ce qu'il y a ici un bar pour aviateurs?* "Is there a leather S and M bar here?"

AVIRON, *m.* Spoon (lit. "oar".) *J'ai bu ma soupe à même le bol parce que tu ne m'as pas donné d'aviron.* "I drank my soup right out of the bowl, because you didn't give me a spoon."

AVOINE, *m.* Oats. **Coller/filer/refiler une avoine à qn.,** *idiom.* To beat s.o. up. *Il l'a mise dans une telle colère qu'elle lui a filé une avoine.* "He infuriated her so much that she gave him a sound thrashing."

AVOINER. 1. To beat; whip. *Le moine avoinait son cheval et s'avoinait plus tard.* "The monk beat his horse and flagellated h.s. later." **2.** To speed. *Il aime avoiner dans sa nouvelle Peugeot.* "He likes to tear up the road in his new Peugeot."

AVOIR RIEN À FOUTRE. See N'EN AVOIR RIEN À FOUTRE.

AZIMUT, *m.* Azimuth (magnetic angle used in astronomical calculations). **Dans tous les azimuts/tous azimuts,** *idiom.* Every which way; on all fronts. *On l'a cherchée dans tous les azimuts.* "We looked for her all over the place."

AZIMUTÉ, -E, *m., f., adj.* and *n.* Crazy. *C'est un azimuté; qui part toujours dans tous les azimutes.* "He's bananas, always riding off in all directions."

BA, *abbr.* of **bonne action** ("good deed"). *J'essaye chaque jour de faire ma BA.* "Every day I try to do a good deed."

BABA, *adj.* Dumbfounded. **Être baba; en rester baba,** *idiom.* To be knocked for a loop. *J'étais baba de sa forme après l'intervention.* "I was flabbergasted to see her in such good shape after the operation."

BABA, *m.* Rear end. **L'avoir dans le baba,** *idiom.* To be conned. *Je l'ai eu dans le baba, en payant cette merde beaucoup trop cher.* "I really got screwed by paying much too much for that junk."

BABA/BABA-COOL, *m.* Youth, 1970s. Hippy. *Il est baba-cool, respecte son gourou, et rejette la violence.* "He's a flower child, respects his guru, and rejects violence."

BABASSE, *f.* Pinball machine. **Secouer la babasse,** *idiom.* To play the silver ball. *Il sèche l'école pour secouer la babasse.* "He plays hooky from school to play the silver ball."

BABILLARD, *m.* **1.** Book; newspaper (**babiller,** "to babble"). *Il aime lire chaque matin son babillard.* "He likes to read his newspaper every morning." **2.** Bulletin board. *Je dois consulter mon babillard électronique.* "I have to take a look at my electronic bulletin board (computer)."

BABILLARDE/BABILLE, *f.* Letter. *Elle n'a pas le temps de lire toutes ses babillardes.* "She hasn't got time to read all his letters."

BABINES, *f., pl.* Lips. **Se (pour) lécher les babines.** To lick one's chops. *Il se léchait les babines à l'idée d'une soirée strip-tease.* "He licked his chops looking forward to an evening of striptease."

BABOULES, *f., pl.* Testicles. *Je lui ai foutu un coup dans les baboules.* "I gave him a kick in the balls."

BAB'S = BABA/BABA-COOL.

BAC, *m., abbr.* of **baccalauréat.** High school diploma. *J'ai dû passer trois fois mon bac avant de l'avoir.* "I had to take the exam three times before getting my high school diploma."

BAC À SABLE, *m.* Territory (lit. "sandbox"/ "litter box"). *Je me tiens à mon bac à sable et je me fous du reste.* "I stick to my turf and don't give a damn about the rest."

BACANTES/BACCHANTES, *f., pl.* **1.** Bacchantes (devotees of the wine god Bacchus). **2.** Mustache; whiskers (from Ger. **Backe,** "cheek"). *Il aimait lisser de sa main ses belles bacchantes.* "He loved stroking his attractive mustache."

BACCARA, *m.* Hard luck. **Être en plein baccara,** *idiom.* To be in a jam; be bankrupt. *Au Sentier, beaucoup sont en plein baccara.* "In the garment district, many are having a hard time."

BÂCHE, *f.* **1.** bed sheet; cover (lit. "canvas cover"). **Piquer une bâche,** *idiom.* To hit the sack. *J'avais besoin de piquer une bâche.* "I needed to hit the hay." **2.** Cap. *Il ne se balade jamais sans sa bâche.* "He never goes anywhere without his cap."

BACHOT, *m.* Variant of **bac.**

BACHOTER. To study hard. *Après avoir tant bachoté elle devrait réussir.* "After all that cramming she should pass."

BADA, *m.* Hat. **Faire porter le bada à qn.,** *idiom.* To frame s.o. *Mes copains m'ont fait porter le bada.* "My friends set me up and I got a bum rap."

BADABOUM, *m.* Brawl. *La flicaille a mis fin au badaboum.* "The cops stopped the free-for-all."

BADIGEON, *m.* Heavy makeup (lit. "whitewash"; "paint"). *Avec tout ton badigeon tu ressembles à une pute.* "With all that war paint you look like a whore."

BADIGOINCES, *f., pl.* Lips. *Sers-toi de tes badigoinces et affiche un sourire!* "Use your lips and put a smile on your face!" See (SE) CALER.

BAFFE, *f.* Clout. **Coller/flanquer/foutre une baffe à qqn.** To hit s.o. *Il flanque des baffes à son chien pour le faire obéir.* "He whacks his dog to get it to obey."

BAFOUILLE, *f.* Letter. *Sa bafouille était illisible.* "His letter was illegible."

(SE) BÂFRER. To stuff one's face. *Il aime se bâfrer chez les autres.* "He loves to pig out at other people's tables."

BÂFREUR, -EUSE, *m., f.* Glutton. *N'invite pas ce bâfreur.* "Don't invite that glutton."

BAGATELLE, *f.* Sexual relations. **Les bagatelles de la porte** (the idea is "little trifles before entering the gate"). Heavy petting; foreplay. *Les bagatelles de la porte l'avaient épuisé et il s'est endormi.* "Foreplay exhausted him and he fell asleep." **Être porté sur la bagatelle,** see CHOSE.

BAGNE, *m.* Sweatshop (lit. "prison"). *Ce boulot, c'est le vrai bagne.* "This place is a real salt mine/the pits."

BAGNOLE, *f.* Car. *Ma vieille bagnole a refusé de démarrer ce matin.* "My old jalopy wouldn't start this morning." **Quelle belle bagnole!** "That's some car! Quite a heap!"

BAGOUGNASSES, *f., pl.* Lips. *Essuie tes bagougnasses avant de m'embrasser.* "Wipe your lips before kissing me."

BAGOULER. To talk a blue streak. *L'entendre bagouler me fatigue.* "Listening to him rattle on wears me out."

BAGOUSE/BAGOUZE, *f.* **1.** Ring. *Elle aime couvrir ses doigts de bagouses tocardes.* "She like to cover her fingers with flashy rings." **2.** Anus. **Être/refiler de la bagouse.** To be a homosexual. *J'ai su tout de suite qu'il* *était de la bagouse.* "I knew right away he was gay." **3.** Luck. **Avoir de la bagouze,** *idiom.* To be lucky. *Il est temps qu'on ait un peu de bagouze.* "It's time we had a bit of luck."

BAGOUT, *m.* Glibness. **Avoir du bagout,** idiom. To have the gift of gab. *Ce camelot a du bagout.* "That street vendor's a smooth talker."

BAGUE = BAGOUSE.

BAGUETTES, *f., pl.* Thin legs (lit. "(chop)sticks"; "batons"). *Sa nana est une planche à pain juchée sur des baguettes.* "His chick's a bread board (flat-chested) perched on spindly legs."

BAHUT, *m.* **1.** Taxi. *Impossible d'avoir un bahut à l'heure de pointe!* "Impossible to get a taxi at rush hour." **2.** Small truck. *Son bahut est toujours en panne.* "His truck's always breaking down." **3.** School. *Chaque fin de semaine elle était heureuse de quitter le bahut.* "Every weekend she was glad to get out of school."

BAIGNER. To bathe. **Baigner dans le beurre/l'huile,** *idiom.* To go like clockwork. *Pourquoi t'inquiéter? Tout baigne dans l'huile!* "Why get upset? Everything's going great!" *Ça baigne!* "Everything's hunky-dory!"

BAIL, *m.* **1.** Lease. **Casser le bail.** To get a divorce (lit. "to break the lease"). *On a décidé de casser le bail, malgré les enfants.* "We've decided to get a divorce despite the children." **Ça fait un bail!** It's been a long time! *Ça fait un bail qu'on a dansé ensemble!* "It's been ages since we danced together!" **2.** Money (from Eng. "buy"). *As-tu besoin de bail pour le week-end?* "Do you need money for the weekend?"

BAILLE, *f.* Water (river, sea, and so on). *Ses copains l'ont mis à la baille.* "His friends threw him into the drink."

BAIN, *m.* Bath. **Être dans le bain,** *idiom.* **1.** To be in the know. *Je préfère être dans le bain avant d'attaquer un nouveau projet.* "I prefer to be well informed before tackling a new project." **2.** To be implicated. *Elle ne savait* *pas que son fils était dans le bain.* "She didn't know her son was mixed up in it."

BAIN-MARIE, *m.* Bidet (lit. "double boiler"). *Elle ferait bien d'utiliser son bain-marie après chaque passe.* "She really should use her bidet after each trick."

BAISANT, -E. Really nice. **Pas baisant.** Nasty. *Il n'est pas baisant, ce mec là.* "That guy's a mean customer."

BAISEBEIGE. Hip variant of BCBG 2.

BAISE-EN-VILLE, *m.* Overnight bag. *Il a plein de présos dans son baise-en-ville.* "He's got plenty of condoms in his overnight bag."

BAISER. 1. To have sexually; fuck (orig., but no longer, "to kiss," although the noun **le/un baiser** is still standard Fr. for "the/a kiss"). *Mon mec baise vachement bien.* "My guy's terrific in bed." See MAL-BAISÉ. **Se faire baiser.** To get screwed (in both senses). *Catherine la Grande aimait se faire baiser par une élite qu'elle sélectionnait.* "Catherine the Great enjoyed getting fucked by an elite she selected." *Nous nous sommes vraiment fait baiser.* "We really got shafted." **2.** To swipe. *Qui m'a baisé de ma montre?* "Who pinched my watch?" **3. Ne rien y baiser.** To understand nothing. *J'ai bien écouté, mais je n'y ai rien baisé.* "I listened closely but I didn't get it at all."

BAISER À LA BOURGEOISE. To copulate in the male superior position. *Elle s'est lassée de baiser à la bourgeoise.* "She got tired of the missionary position."

BAISER À LA PAPA. To copulate calmly. *Après des paroxysmes, ça fait parfois du bien baiser à la papa.* "After passionate bursts it's sometimes nice to have a good, slow screw."

BAISEUR, -EUSE, *m., f.* Sexy or horny person. *C'était un sacré baiseur, avant.* "He was a real stud, once."

BAISODROME, *m.* Brothel; place of frequent sexual encounters. *Ah, ce petit hôtel au fond du bois, c'est un vrai baisodrome.* "Ah, that little hotel deep in the woods, lots of screwing going on there."

BAISSER. To lower. See FROC.

BALADER. 1. To take for a walk. *J'aime balader mon chien.* "I like to take my dog for a walk." **Envoyer balader qn.** To send s.o. packing. *Il voulait de l'argent; je l'ai envoyé balader.* "He wanted money; I gave him his walking papers." **Envoyer balader qch.** To chuck; dump. *J'en avais marre, je voulais tout envoyer balader.* "I was fed up with it and wanted to pack it all in." **2.** To hoodwink. *Il m'a baladé avec toutes ses sornettes.* "He led me down the garden path with his tall stories." **3.** To defeat easily. *Elle a baladé toutes ses rivales au tennis.* "She had all her tennis competitors for lunch."

BALADEUR, -EUSE. Wandering. **Avoir la main baladeuse/les mains baladeuses.** To have roaming hands. *Je ne guinche plus avec lui, car il a les mains baladeuses.* "I don't dance with him any more because he paws me."

BALAI, *m.* Broom. See CON COMME UN BALAI; COUP DE BALAI; DONNER UN COUP DE BALAI; RAMASSER LES BALAIS; VOITURE.

BALAI À/DE CHIOTTES, *m.* Bristly mustache (lit. "toilet bowl brush"). *Tu te plains de mon balai à chiottes.* "You complain about my stiff mustache."

BALAI D'AMOUR, *m.* Soft mustache. *Avant tu aimais mon balai d'amour.* "You used to love my tender mustache."

BALAIS, *m., pl.* Years of age. *J'ai 95 balais, mais on me donne toujours moins.* "I'm 95, but people always take me for younger."

BALAISE. See BALÈZE.

BALANCER. 1. To swing. See BIEN BALANCÉ. **2.** To throw out. *Tous les jours je balance des quantités de magazines.* "Every day I throw out loads of magazines." **3.** To give. *Balance-moi un peu de fric pour le week-end.* "Give me some money for the weekend." **4.** To denounce. *J'ai été* *balancée par ma meilleure copine.* "I was denounced by my best friend."

BALANCER LA SEMOULE. See SEMOULE.

BALANCER UN COUP/UNE BEIGNE/UNE CLAQUE. See FILER UN COUP…À QN.

BALANCER UNE VACHERIE. See VACHERIE.

BALANCER UNE VANNE/DES VANNES. See VANNE.

(SE) BALANCER. To hurl o.s. (lit. "to rock"). *Il s'est balancé dans le vide avec son parachute.* "He bailed out over empty space."

(S'EN) BALANCER. To not give a damn. *Toutes ces histoires, je m'en balance!* "I don't give a damn about all that stuff."

BALANÇOIRE, *f.* Swing. **Envoyer qn. à la balançoire,** *idiom.* To tell s.o. to get lost. *J'avais envie de l'envoyer à la balançoire.* "I felt like telling him to get lost."

BALANÇOIRE À MICKEY/À MINOUCHE. Sanitary napkin. *Elle préfère les tampons aux balançoires à Mickey.* "She prefers tampons to rags."

BALAYETTE, *f.* Penis (lit. "whisk broom"). See DANS… BALAYETTE!

BALAYETTE INFERNALE. Very large penis. *Elle priait chaque fois qu'elle voyait sa balayette infernale!* "She prayed every time she saw his huge tool." **Une partie de balayette infernale.** A session of intense sex. *Après une partie de balayette infernale, nous étions pompés.* "After intense lovemaking we were exhausted."

BALCON, *m.* Balcony. **Il y a du monde au balcon,** *idiom, joc.* "She's amply bosomed/stacked/got big tits" (lit. "the balcony is crowded").

BALÈZE. 1. Brawny. *Il est balèze, ton jules.* "Your boy friend's a hunk." **2.** Brainy. *En manipulation de données, il est balèze.* "He's a whiz at data handling."

BALLE, *f.* Franc (lit. "ball"). *À Paris mille balles se* *dépensent en un clin d'œil.* "In Paris you can go through 1000 francs in no time flat."

BALOURD, *m.* Counterfeit (lit. "oaf"). *Tu croyais ton sac sorti de chez Vuitton mais c'est un balourd.* "You thought your handbag came from Vuitton, but it's a fake."

BALPEAU/BALLEPEAU, backslang of **peau de balle.**

BAMBOU, *m.* Bamboo. **Avoir le bambou = avoir le bâton.** See BÂTON **1;** COUP DE BAMBOU.

BAMBOULA, *m., pej.* **1.** Black person. *Lors de la fête, les Bamboulas dansaient dans la rue.* "During the holiday, the blacks danced in the street." **2.** *f.* Spree. *Mon fils ne pense qu'à faire la bamboula.* "All my son wants to do is party." (Both derive from **bambalon,** an African drum.)

BAMÉ, *m., f.* Spaced-out person. *Il y a une bande de bamés ce soir dans la boîte.* "There's a bunch of crazies in the place tonight."

BANANE, *f.* **1.** Banana. **Avoir la banane,** *idiom.* To have an erection. *J'ai la banane dès que je la vois.* "I get hard every time I see her." **Se prendre une (peau de) banane,** *idiom.* To fail. *Après ses grands tubes son dernier disque s'est pris une banane.* "Many of her songs were big hits but her last two records bombed." See PEAU DE BANANE. **2.** Military decoration. *Raconte comment tu as gagné toutes ces bananes.* "Tell us how you got all that fruit salad." **3.** Twin-rotor helicopter. *Beaucoup de bananes se sont écrasées au sol récemment.* "Many choppers have crashed recently." **4.** Fool. *Je te l'ai déjà souvent dit, banane!* "I've already told you many times, idiot."

(SE FAIRE) BANANER. To be conned. (Cf. BANANE **4.**) *Les veuves se sont fait bananer par l'escroc.* "The widows were swindled by the crook."

BANDANT, -E. 1. Sexually desirable. *Charlotte est la plus bandante de toute la classe.* "Charlotte is the sexiest girl in the whole class." **2.** Exciting. **Pas bandant.** Nothing to write home about. *Le film ce soir n'est pas bandant.* "Tonight's movie isn't very interesting."

BANDER. To get an erection (from "to bend; tighten a bow"). *Je suis en quête de dessous pour faire bander mon mari.* "I'm looking for undies that'll excite my husband." **Bander pour qn.** To turn on. *Je bande pour aucune d'elles.* "None of them turns me on." **Bander pour un mec/bander pour une fille.** To go for a guy/girl (both are now also used by women, the second one by a lesbian). *Elle savait qu'il était marié, mais elle bandait pour lui.* "She knew he was married, but she went for him."

BANDER COMME UN CERF. See CERF.

BANDER FOULARD/MOU. 1. To be scared. *Quand son mari l'a menacé, il bandait mou.* "When her husband threatened him, he got scared." **2.** To have a flabby erection. *D'habitude il bande foulard, mais hier soir il m'a surprise.* "He usually has trouble getting it up, but last night he surprised me."

BANDER GUIMAUVE. To be impotent. *Malgré son grand âge il ne bande pas guimauve.* "Despite his advanced age, he's not impotent."

BANDEUR, -EUSE, *m., f.* Sexy. *C'est une petite bandeuse!* "She's a raunchy little sexpot!"

BANNIÈRE, *f.* Banner (flag). **En bannière.** In shirttails; shirtsleeves. *Il m'a reçue en bannière, à moitié nu; j'en étais choquée!* "He received me in shirttails, half-naked; I was shocked!"

BANQUER. To pay up. *Elle peut acheter des fringues haute couture; c'est son baron qui banque!* "She can buy high-fashion clothes; it's her sugar daddy who shells out for them."

BAPTÊME, *m.* Gang rape (lit. "baptism"). *Il nie avoir participé au baptême.* "He denies having taken part in the gang bang."

BAPTISÉ AU SÉCATEUR. See SÉCATEUR.

BAPTISER AU SÉCATEUR. See SÉCATEUR.

BARAKA, *f.* Good luck (from Ar. for "blessing"). **Avoir la**

baraka, *idiom.* To be on a roll. *À Las Vegas il a eu la baraka.* "He lucked out in Las Vegas."

BARAQUE, *f.* Shack. See CASSER LA BARAQUE.

BARBAQUE, *f.* **1.** Meat. *Les végétariens nous ont invités à un barbecue sans barbaque.* "The vegetarians invited us to a meatless barbecue." **2.** Flesh. *C'est une tribu de cannibales qui sait très bien assaisonner la barbaque.* "They're a tribe of cannibals very knowledgeable in the seasoning of flesh." See MARCHAND DE BARBAQUE.

BARBE, *f.* **1.** Beard. **Se mettre une fausse barbe,** *idiom.* To practice cunnilingus (lit. "to put on a false beard"). *Mon mari n'aime pas se raser mais il adore se mettre une fausse barbe.* "My husband doesn't like to shave but he loves to eat hair pie." Cf. BARBU· **2.** S.t. annoying. **C'est la barbe! C'est la Sainte-Barbe! Quelle barbe!** What a drag! See LA BARBE!

BARBEAU, *m.* Small-time pimp (lit. "barbel" [fish]). *Son barbeau est celui qui porte des bagues tocardes.* "Her pimp's the one who wears flashy rings."

BARBER. 1. To bore; annoy. *Ce pitre me barbe.* "That clown bugs me." **2.** To trick. *T'as essayé de nous barber, couillon!* "You tried to put one over on us, dickhead!"

BARBILLON/BARBIQUET/BARBISET = BARBEAU.

BARBU, *m.* Female pubic hair (lit. "bearded man"). See DESCENTE...BARBU.

BARCA! = BARKA!

BARDER. To heat up. See ÇA VA BARDER!

BARGE/BARGEOT/BARJO/BARJOT, backslang of **jobard.** Crazy. *Il est barjot, ce motard; il roule sans casque.* "That biker's off his rocker; he rides without a helmet."

BARKA! "Enough! That will do!"

BARON, *m.* **1.** Accomplice. *Elle empochait les bijoux pendant qu'il faisait le baron.* "She pocketed the jewels while he acted as decoy." **2.** Sugar daddy. *Son baron faisait tout* *pour lui plaire.* "Her sugar daddy did everything to please her."

BARRE, *f.* Bar; rod. **Avoir barre(s) sur qn.,** *idiom.* To be one up on s.o. *Il a tout fait pour avoir barre sur moi.* "He did everything to have an edge on me." **Avoir une/la barre avec qn.,** *idiom.* To make a hit with s.o. *À son regard, j'ai vu que j'avais la barre.* "The way she looked at me told me that I'd hit it off with her." **Avoir une barre pour qn.,** *idiom.* To have the hots for s.o. *Il a une barre pour moi, mais je le déteste.* "He's got the hots for me but I despise him." See COUP DE BARRE/POMPE; COUP DE FUSIL/BARRE; (SE) PRENDRE UNE BARRE; (À) TOUTE BARRE.

BARRÉ. Être bien/mal barré. To be well/badly positioned. *Dans cette affaire on est mal barré.* "We're not in a good position in this matter."

(SE) BARRER. To scram. *Je voulais lui parler mais il s'est barré.* "I wanted to talk to him but he beat it."

BARREUR, *m.* Nightclub doorman; bouncer (lit. "helmsman"). *Le barreur de la disco a évincé les skins.* "The disco bouncer threw out the skinheads."

BARRIQUE, *f.* Barrel. See ROND...BARRIQUE.

BAS-DUC/BAS-DU-CUL, *m., adj.* and *n.* Short(y). *Elle est trop bas-du-cul pour faire un mannequin.* "Her ass is too close to the ground to make it as a model."

BASKETS, *f., pl.* Sports shoes. **Être bien/à l'aise dans ses baskets,** *idiom.* To be relaxed/together. *Dans n'importe quelle situation, il est bien dans ses baskets.* "He keeps his cool, whatever the circumstances." **Faire baskets,** *idiom.* To take French leave. *Ils ont fait baskets dans beaucoup de restos.* "They left without paying in many restaurants."

BASSINER. To grate on; harass (lit. "warm with a warming pan"; "water"). *Arrête de me bassiner avec toutes tes lamentations!* "Quit bugging me with all your moaning."

BASTA! "That's enough of that!"

BASTON = COGNE 2.

BASTRINGUE, *m.* **1.** Seedy dance hall. *Allons gigoter au bastringue du coin!* "Let's go shake our dancing legs at the local dance hall." **2.** Band. *Lui et ses copains ont créé un petit bastringue.* "He and his friends have formed a little combo." See (ET) TOUT LE BASTRINGUE. **3.** Din. *Impossible de dormir avec un tel bastringue!* "Impossible to get any sleep with that racket."

BATACLAN, *m.* Stuff. *Les enfants sont partis depuis longtemps mais leur bataclan est toujours ici.* "The kids moved out long ago, but their junk is still here." **Tout le bataclan!,** *idiom.* The whole shebang. *Je veux qu'ils prennent tout: tout le bataclan!* "I want them to take everything, the whole works!"

BAT(H). Wonderful; classy. *Elle est bath, ta bagnole!* "Your car is really gorgeous." **Bath au pieu/plumard.** Good in bed. *Je me cherche une gonzesse bath au pieu.* "I'm looking for a broad who's terrific in bed."

BÂTON, *m.* **1.** Stick. **Avoir le bâton,** *idiom.* To have an erection. *Cette vieille fille croit que les hommes ont toujours le bâton et sont prêts à la violer.* "That old maid thinks men are always erect and ready to rape her." See MENER...CHAISE. **2.** One million old francs (10,000 new francs). *Il a hérité deux cents bâtons de ses parents.* "He inherited two million new francs from his parents." **3.** Leg. *Elle a cassé son bâton gauche en patinant.* "She broke her left leg skating."

BATTANT, *m.* Heart. *Il jure qu'il l'aime du fond de son battant.* "He swears he loves her from the bottom of his heart."

BATTANT, -E, *m.*, *f.* S.o. with get-up-and-go. *C'est une battante; elle réussira.* "She's a go-getter; she'll succeed."

BATTRE DE L'AILE. To be in a bad way. *Son commerce battait de l'aile et il a dû fermer boutique.* "His business was on its last legs and he had to shut up shop."

BATTRE DES AILES. To flail one's arms about. *Il est pété et bat des ailes.* "He's high on s.t. and is flapping his arms about."

39

BAVARD, *m.* **1.** Telephone answering machine (from the adj. "talkative"). *Il n'y avait aucun message sur le bavard.* "There wasn't a single message on the answering machine." **2.** Lawyer. *Méfie-toi de ton bavard; c'est un escroc!* "Don't trust your mouthpiece; he's a crook."

BAVER. 1. To drool. **Faire baver,** *idiom.* To create difficulties. *Le maire m'en a fait baver.* "The mayor gave me a real hard time." **2.** To drool over. *Tes bijoux me font baver.* "Your jewels make me drool with envy." **3.** To speak. **Baver sur qn.** To speak ill of. *Il faut se méfier de lui; il bave sur tous.* "You've got to watch out for him; he dumps on everybody."

(EN) BAVER DES RONDS DE CHAPEAUX. To have a rough time of it. *Avant d'avoir l'autorisation j'en ai bavé des ronds de chapeaux.* "Before getting the authorization I really had to sweat it."

BAVETTE, *f.* **1.** Bib. **Tailler une bavette,** *idiom.* To chew the fat; shoot the breeze. *On se taillera une bavette demain.* "We'll have a nice chat tomorrow." **2.** Informer. *On a trouvé le cadavre de la bavette dans la cour de la taule.* "They found the informer's corpse in the prison yard."

BAVEUSE, *f.* **1.** Gossip. *Ne fréquente pas trop cette baveuse.* "Don't spend too much time with that gossip." **2.** Tongue. *Il a la baveuse bien pendue.* "He talks a blue streak."

BAVEUX, *m.* **1.** Lawyer (more "in" term for BAVARD 2). **2.** Newspaper. *Ne te cache pas derrière ton baveux; écoute-moi!* "Don't hide behind your newspaper; listen to me." **3.** Tongue kiss. *On a commencé nos ébats par un baveux.* "We began our lovemaking with a wet French kiss."

BCBG, *adj.* and *m., f., n.* **1.** Acronym for **bon chic, bon genre.** Conservatively chic; belonging to the smart set. *Pour plaire à sa mère il a épousé une BCBG.* "To please his mother he married a social register/junior league/yuppie type." **2.** Acronym for **beau cul**, **belle gueule.** A pretty face and a gorgeous bod. *Je bande pour une BCBG.* "I turn on to a nice piece of stuff."

BEAU COMME UN PAF (EN FLEUR)! Beautiful as all get out! (lit. "beautiful as a (flowering) phallus").

BEAU CUL, BELLE GUEULE. See BCBG **2**.

BEAU-DAB, *m.* Father-in-law. *Mon beau-dab était extraordinaire.* "My father-in-law was extraordinary."

BEAU GOSSE, *m.* Handsome man. *Son mec est beau gosse.* "Her guy's good-looking."

BEAUF(E), *m.* **1.** Brother-in-law (for **beau-frère**). **2.** Average **petit-bourgeois**, jingoistic Frenchman. *Sa nouvelle pièce de théâtre est raciste et devrait plaire aux beaufs.* "Her new play is racist and will probably appeal to the average prejudiced Frenchman."

BEAUJOLPIF/BEAUJOLPINCE, *m.,* the former is a composite of **Beaujolais** and the *adj.* **olpif.** Beaujolais (wine). *Le mois de novembre est enjolivé par l'arrivée du beaujolpif.* "The month of November is brightened by the arrival of the new Beaujolais wine."

BEAU LINGE, *m.* The smart set. *À l'ouverture du festival il n'y avait que du beau linge.* "Only beautiful people were at the opening of the film festival."

BÉBÉ, *m.* Baby. See BUFFET; REFILER LE BÉBÉ.

BÉBÉ ROSE, *m.* Milk with grenadine syrup. *Moi, je prendrai un bébé rose; mon mari un diabolo menthe.* "I'll have a grenadine milkshake; my husband a mint-flavored soda."

BÉBÉ SANS BRAS, *m.* One-liter wine bottle (lit. "armless baby"). *Les ouvriers du port de Brest sont très attachés à leurs bébés sans bras.* "Brest dockworkers are very attached to their bottles of wine."

BÉBÊTE, *f.* **1.** Small insect. *Ça grouille de bébêtes ici.* "This place is alive with creepy-crawlies." **2.** Foolish. *Brigitte est belle, mais bébête; sa sœur déteste ses rires bébêtes.* "Brigitte is beautiful, but childish; her sister detests her silly giggles."

BEC, *m.* Mouth (lit. "beak"). **Avoir une prise de bec avec qn.,** *idiom.* To lock horns with s.o. *J'ai eu une prise de* *bec avec la maitresse de mon mari.* "I crossed swords with my husband's mistress." See CLAQUER DU BEC; CLOUER LE BEC; RESTER LE BEC... TAPER DU BEC. **2.** Obstacle. See TOMBER...BEC.

BÉCANE, *f.* **1.** Bike; motorcycle. *Tu peux aller à pied ou prendre ta bécane.* "You can go on foot or take your bike." **2.** Tool; machine (especially computer). *Je me bats toujours avec ma bécane électronique.* "I'm still struggling with my electronic bike."

BÊCHER. 1. To put on airs. *Avec tes nouvelles fringues, tu bêches!* "You're acting stuck-up in your new clothes." **2.** To snub. *Les dames de la haute m'ont bêchée à l'opéra.* "The high-society ladies snubbed me at the opera."

(SE) BÉCOTER. To bill and coo. *Ils ont passé l'après-midi à se bécoter.* "They spent the afternoon smooching."

BEDAINE, *f.* Potbelly. *Il fait tout pour perdre sa grosse bedaine.* "He's working hard at losing his rubber tire."

BEDONNER. To get/show a paunch. *Pierre bedonne et se compare à une statue du Bouddha.* "Potbellied Pierre compares h.s. to a statue of the Buddha."

BÉGONIA, *m.* **1.** Begonia. **Être dans les bégonias,** *idiom.* To have lost consciousness. *Elle est toujours dans les bégonias.* "She's still unconscious." See CHARRIER DANS... **2.** Female genitalia. *Line réserve son bégonia à Marc.* "Line is saving her pussy for Mark."

BÉGUIN, *m.* **1.** Flirtation (lit. "bonnet"). **Avoir le béguin pour qn.,** *idiom.* To have a crush on s.o. *Elle a le béguin pour son prof de musique.* "She has a crush on her music teacher." **2.** Noncommercial love. **Y aller au béguin,** *idiom.* To grant sexual favors without charging. *Elle est sentimentale et y va souvent au béguin.* "She's very sentimental and often does it for nothing."

BÉGUINE, *f.* Rhumba-like dance from the Fr. Antilles. *Le groupe a commencé à jouer la béguine, mais j'ai n'ai pas dansé avec Luc, car je n'ai plus le béguin pour lui.* "The band began the beguine but I didn't dance with Luke because I no longer have a crush on him."

BÉGUINEUSE, *f.* Unreliable prostitute. *Mon maq ne tolère pas les béguineuses.* "My pimp doesn't tolerate those who give it away."

BEIGNE, *f.* Smack. See ALLONGER…BEIGNE; FILER…BEIGNE…; FLANQUER…BEIGNE.

BELLE. L'avoir belle. To be on easy street. *Depuis qu'il a hérité gros il l'a belle.* "Ever since he inherited a lot of money he's been on easy street." **En faire voir de belles à qn.,** *idiom.* To put s.o. through a ringer. *Son petit voyou de fils lui en faisait voir de belles.* "Her lout of a son made life rough for her." **En faire de belles,** *idiom.* To be up to no good. *Il en a fait de belles avant de se marier.* "He got into a lot of mischief before getting married."

BELLE-DABESSE/BELLE-DOCHE, *joc.,* not *pej.* Mother-in-law. *Ma belle-doche et moi, nous aimons le vin.* "My mother-in-law and I are fond of wine."

BELLE GOSSE, *f.* Beautiful girl. *Sa frangine est belle gosse.* "Her sister's a looker."

BELLE LURETTE. A considerable amount of time (from **heurette,** diminutive of **heure**). *"Il y a belle lurette que j'ai fêté mes vingt piges," dit mon grand-dab.* "'It's been some time since I celebrated my twentieth birthday,' says my grandpa."

BÉNEF, *abbr.* of **bénéfice.** Profit. *Leur commerce laissait un bon bénef.* "Their business made a good profit."

BERGE, *f.* Year (lit. "river bank"). *Elle est toujours vierge malgré ses trente berges.* "She's still a virgin despite her thirty years (of age)."

BERLUE, *m.* Illusion. **Avoir la berlue,** *idiom.* To hallucinate. *J'ai cru avoir la berlue en les revoyant ensemble.* "I thought I was seeing things when I saw them together again."

BÉSEF. A lot. *Il n'y en avait pas bésef.* "There wasn't much/many (of it/them)."

BESOGNER. To have sexually (lit. "to work away; drudge") *Le patron les avait toutes besognées.* "The boss had banged them all."

BESOINS, *m., pl.* Nature's needs. See FAIRE SES BESOINS.

BÊTE, *f.* **1.** Beast. See CHERCHER...BÊTE. **2.** Outstanding individual. **C'est la bête!** He or she is brilliant. *Il était la bête de la classe mais il a loupé son exam.* "He was the class star but he failed the exam."

BÊTE COMME CHOU. Easy as pie. *C'est bête comme chou.* "That's a cinch."

BÊTE COMME SES PIEDS. Stupid. *Il est bête comme ses pieds.* "He's as dumb as they come."

BEUR, *m., not pej.,* backslang of **arabe.** Young, French-born, second-generation North African. *Coco a épousé un jeune beur qui la rend très heureuse.* "Coco's married to a young North African who makes her very happy."

BEURRE, *m.* **1.** Butter. **Être du beurre; être un (vrai) beurre,** *idiom.* To be a cinch/snap. *C'est du beurre!* It's a piece of cake! **Compter pour du beurre,** *idiom.* To count for nothing. *Nos interêts ne comptaient que pour du beurre.* "Our interests counted for nothing." See BAIGNER...BEURRE; METTRE...ÉPINARDS; ŒIL...NOIR. **2.** Money. **Faire son beurre,** *idiom.* To make a bundle, pile. *Ce financier a profité de la crise économique pour faire son beurre.* "That financier took advantage of the economic crisis to make a bundle." See ASSIETTE AU BEURRE.

(SE) BEURRER. 1. To make a bundle. *Il s'est beurré pendant la guerre en faisant du marché noir.* "During the war my brother made a bundle dealing in the black market." **2.** To get soused. *Ils se sont tous bien beurrés.* "They all got dead drunk."

BÉZEF = BÉSEF.

BIBELOT, *m.* Burglar's tool (lit. "ornament"). *Le cambrioleur maugréait contre son bibelot en panne.* "The burglar grumbled about his skeleton key that didn't work."

BIBELOTS, *m., pl.* Male genitalia. *Je préfère les bibelots* *de mon mari à tous les bijoux du monde.* "I prefer my husband's family jewels to all the jewels in the world."

BIBERONNER. To booze (from **biberon,** "baby's bottle"). *Il ne fout rien depuis qu'il biberonne.* "He hasn't worked at anything ever since he hit the bottle."

BIDOCHE, *f.* **1.** Meat. *Ils boudent la bidoche britannique.* "They're leery of British meat." **2.** Flesh. *Le marchand de Venise ne voulait pas se séparer d'une livre de sa bidoche.* "The merchant of Venice didn't want to part with a pound of his flesh." See MARCHAND DE BIDOCHE.

BIDON, *m.* **1.** Belly (lit. "can"; "flask"). *J'en ai plein le bidon.* "My tummy is stuffed." **2.** Bullshit. *C'est du bidon!* "That's a load of crap!"

BIDON, *adj.* Phony. *Il a mis en scène un attentat bidon.* "He staged a phony assassination attempt."

BIDONNER. To cheat. **Bidonner un travail,** *idiom.* To do a half-assed job. *Si on ne le surveille pas, il bidonne son boulot.* "If you don't keep an eye on him, he'll botch the job."

(SE) BIDONNER. To laugh one's head off. *On s'est bidonné en regardant ce comique.* "We laughed our heads off watching that comic."

BIDOUILLEUR, -EUSE, *m., f.* **1.** S.o. who tinkers with gadgets. *Mon mari se croit un parfait bidouilleur.* "My husband thinks he has a way with machines." **2.** Computer hacker/expert. *C'est une bidouilleuse, spécialiste en programmation.* "She's a computer programming specialist."

BIDULE, *m.* What-do-you-call-it. *J'ai un tiroir plein de bidules que je devrais balancer.* "I've got a draw full of thingamajigs I ought to throw out."

BIEN BALANCÉ, -E. Attractive; well built. *Quelle nana! Pas seulement intello, mais bien balancée.* "What a chick! Not only a brain but a looker too!"

BIÈRE, *f.* Beer. **Ce n'est pas de la petite bière,** *idiom.* "That's no small potatoes/not to be sneezed at." **Ne pas se prendre pour de la petite bière.** To be conceited; swell-headed. *Il ne se prend pas pour de la petite bière, et à juste titre, peut-être.* "He has a high opinion of h.s., and maybe he's right." (A stronger equivalent is **ne pas se prendre pour de la petite merde.** See MERDE.)

BIGLER. To take a look at (lit. "to squint"; "have poor eyesight"). *Viens bigler ce que j'ai trouvé pour toi.* "Take a gander at what I've found for you."

BIGO/BIGOPHONE, *m.* Telephone. **Donner/filer/passer un coup de bigo(phone).** To phone. *N'oublie pas de me passer un coup de bigo demain.* "Don't forget to give me a ring tomorrow."

BIN'S/BINZ, *m.* **1.** Disorder. *Quel bin's dans son bureau!* "His office is a real mess." **2.** Complicated procedure. *C'est tout un binz pour arriver chez eux.* "It's a real hassle getting to their place."

BIQUE, *f.* Female goat. **Bique et bouc** (lit. "nanny and billy goat"). Active and passive homosexual. *En tôle il a appris à être bique et bouc.* "In jail he learned how to be a flip-flopper."

BIROUTE, *m.* Penis. *"Cette biroute, où avait-elle été avant?", se demandait-elle.* "'Where's this dick been before?' she wondered."

BISCOTOS, *m., pl.* Biceps. See ROULER LES BISCOTOS.

BITE, *m.* = **BITUME.** See RASE-BITE.

BIT(T)E, *f.* Penis. *Raspoutine était archifier de sa maxi bite.* "Rasputin was very proud of his huge cock." See CON À...BITE; PEAU DE BITE; RENTRER... BRAS; SAC À BITES.

BITE À JEAN-PIERRE, *f.* Policeman's billy club (lit. "Jean-Pierre's dick"). *Dans la manif il a reçu un coup de bite à Jean-Pierre.* "He got hit by a policeman's billy club during the demonstration."

BITER. 1. To understand. *Je n'ai rien bité à ton histoire.* "I don't know what you're talking about." **2.** To have carnal knowledge of. *Le philosophe m'a bien bitée et je me sens pleine de sagesse.* "The philosopher gave me a good screwing and I feel full of wisdom."

BITONIAU/BITONIO, *m.* Thingamajig. *Il manque un bitonio à cette lampe.* "There's a whatsit missing in this lamp."

BITUME, *m.* Pavement. **Arpenter/faire/polir le bitume.** To be a streetwalker. *Elle a l'habitude d'arpenter le bitume de la rue d'Aboukir.* "She usually works Aboukir Street." See ARRONDISSEMENT À BITUME; RASE-BITE/BITUME.

BITURE, *f.* Bender. **Prendre une biture,** *idiom.* To tie one on. *Il a pris une telle biture qu'il ne pouvait pas conduire.* "He got so loaded he couldn't drive." See (À) TOUTE BARRE/BITURE.

BIZET = BARBEAU.

BIZUT(H), *m.* Freshman. *C'est un bizut et ne connaît pas les règles du bahut.* "He's a frosh and doesn't know the school's rules."

BIZUTAGE, *m.* Hazing. *Le censeur a essayé de supprimer le bizutage.* "The vice principal tried to stop hazing."

BIZUTER. To haze. *Quelques sadiques éprouvaient un plaisir à les bizuter.* "A few sadists took pleasure in hazing them."

BLABLATER. To babble on. *Personne n'écoutait mais il continuait de blablater.* "No one was listening but he kept rattling on."

BLAGUE, *f.* Joke; hoax. *C'est de la (haute) blague!* "That's a bunch of baloney!" See SANS BLAGUE!

BLAGUER. To joke. *Elle ne le prenait pas au sérieux car il aimait blaguer.* "She didn't take him seriously because he liked to kid around."

BLAIRER. To stand. *Elle ne peut pas me blairer, mais moi, je l'adore.* "She can't stand me, but I adore her."

BLANC LIME/BLANC LIMÉ = LIME/LIMÉ.

BLÉ, *m.* Money; "bread" (lit. "wheat"). See FAUCHÉ (COMME LES BLÉS).

BLED, *m.* from Arabic. **1.** Remote place. *Il habite un bled perdu en Bretagne.* "He lives in the boonies in Brittany."

2. Hometown. *Mon bled c'est Bordeaux.* "My hometown is Bordeaux."

BLINDÉ, -E. 1. Thick-skinned (lit. "armor-plated"). *Assez de baratin; je suis blindé.* "Enough soft talk. I'm impervious to it." **2.** Drunk. *Je chante quand je suis blindée.* "I sing when I'm drunk."

BLOBLOS, *f., pl.* Ample, pendulous breasts. *Il est obnubilé par les nanas à bloblos.* "He's hung up on broads with big boobs."

BLOC, *m.* Station house jail. *Après la bagarre de cette nuit, il a passé la nuit au bloc.* "After the brawl, he spent the night in the jug." **Gonflé à bloc.** To be full of beans. *Elles étaient parties gonflées à bloc au rallye mais n'ont pas gagné.* "They were raring to go when they left for the car rally, but they didn't win."

BLOUSER. To swindle. *Les promoteurs les ont blousés.* "The property developers took them for a ride."

BOBARD, *m.* Lie; tall story. *Tu ne racontes que des bobards!* "You're talking a load of bull."

BOBINE, *m.* Face (lit. "reel"; "bobbin"). *Tu en fais une drôle de bobine.* "You've got an odd/sour look about you."

BOBONNE, *f., pej.* Wife. *Ma bobonne ne me comprend pas.* "My wife doesn't understand me."

BOCAL, *m.* Head (lit. "jar"). *Tu n'as rien dans le bocal.* "You've got nothing between the ears." See AGITÉ DU BOCAL.

BOCHE, *m., pej.* German. *Pépé nie avoir été collabo et râle contre les Boches, et les Italboches aussi.* "Grandpa denies having been a collaborator and complains about the krauts, and the wops too."

BOF! Big deal! So what? Who cares?

BOGE, *m., f.* Bourgeois. *Il était plein de mépris pour les boges.* "He was full of contempt for the bourgeois."

BOIRE COMME UN TROU. See TROU.

BOIRE DU PETIT LAIT. See LAIT.

BOIRE SEC. See SEC.

BOIRE UN BOUILLON. See BOUILLON.

BOL, *m.* **1.** Bowl. **Prendre un bol d'air,** *idiom.* To get some fresh air. *Il me fallait prendre un bon bol d'air après la réunion politique.* "I needed some good fresh air after the political meeting." **2.** Luck. See COUP DE BOL. **3.** Posterior. **En avoir ras le bol,** *idiom.* To be fed up. *J'en ai ras le bol de toutes tes minauderies.* "I've had it up to here with your affected mannerisms." **4.** Motorcyclist's helmet. *Pour l'épate, il se balade avec son bol sur la tête.* "To impress people he walks around with his helmet on his head."

BONBON, *m.* **1.** Candy. **Coûter bonbon.** To be expensive. *Ta petite fantaisie, ça m'a coûté bonbon!* "Your little whim cost me a pretty penny!" **2.** Hard drugs. *Tu mourras d'une overdose si tu bouffes tant de bonbons.* "You'll OD if you keep consuming all those drugs." **3.** Clitoris. *J'avais le bonbon très excité.* "My clitoris was very excited." See RAS LE BONBON. **4.** Testicles. **Casser les bonbons.** To annoy. *Ils nous cassent les bonbons avec leurs drames familiaux.* "They bug us with their domestic dramas." See CASSE-BONBONS. BON CHIC, BON GENRE. See BCBG **1.**

BONDIEUSERIE, *f.* **1.** Ostentatious piety. *Ma grand-tante exagère un peu avec sa bondieuserie.* "My great-aunt overdoes it a bit with her show of religiosity." **2.** Kitchy ecclesiastical knicknack. *On a acheté de l'eau bénite du robinet, des assiettes où les yeux s'ouvrent et se ferment, et d'autres bondieuseries.* "We bought holy water from the tap, plates with eyes that open and close, and other religious trinkets."

BONHOMME, *m.* **1.** Husband. *Mon bonhomme va bien.* "My husband is well." **2.** Guy. *Qu'est-ce qu'il nous veut, ce bonhomme?* "What does that guy want from us?" **3.** Erect penis. *Il lui courait après, en tenant son bonhomme.* "He ran after her holding his stiff dick." See CHEMIN.

BONI = BÉNEF.

BONICHE, *f., pej.* Servant. *Tu me prends pour ta boniche?* "Do you think I'm your slave?"

BONIMENT, *m.* Sales talk. *Arrête tes boniments!* "Cut the crap!" **Faire du boniment,** *idiom.* To feed someone a line. *Je ne te fais pas de boniment; t'es la femme de ma vie!* "I'm not handing you a line; you're the love of my life."

BONJOUR LES DÉGÂTS! That means trouble!

BONNE BOURRE! See BOURRE.

BONNE FEMME, *f.* **1.** Wife. *J'arriverai avec ma bonne femme.* "The missus and I will be coming." **2.** Woman, *pej.*, unless accompanied by an *adj.* expressing admiration, such as **une grande bonne femme; une bonne femme charmante.** *Je ne peux pas la blairer, cette bonne femme.* "I can't stand that broad."

BONNE POIRE = POIRE 3.

BONNES FEMMES, *f., pl.* Females. *Les bonnes femmes sont parties faire les boutiques aujourd'hui.* "The ladies went out shopping today."

BONNICHE, *f.* = **BONICHE.**

BONSHOMMES, *m., pl.* Men. *Les bonshommes sont partis à la pêche.* "The men have gone fishing."

BORDEL, *m.* **1.** Brothel. *Lautrec était comme chez lui dans les bordels.* "Toulouse-Lautrec felt right at home in whorehouses." **2.** Disorder. *Sa piaule, c'est un véritable bordel.* "His pad is a real shambles."

BORDÉLIQUE. Messy. *Fais un effort pour être moins bordélique.* "Try to be less messy."

BORDS, *m., pl.* Edges. **Sur les bords.** Somewhat. *Il est un peu cinglé sur les bords.* "He's a bit cracked (but not over the line)."

BORGNE, *m.* Penis (lit. "one-eyed person"). **Étrangler le borgne,** *idiom.* To masturbate (lit. "to choke the one-eyed man," a reference to the meatus (urinary opening). *J'étrangle souvent le borgne, mais il est increvable.* "I keep strangling (whacking off) the one eyed monster, but he's indestructible."

BOSSE, *f.* **1.** Hump; bump. **Rouler sa bosse,** *idiom.* To knock about; globe-trot. *Nous avons pas mal roulé notre bosse.* "We've done a lot of traveling." **2.** Flair. **Avoir la bosse de qch,** *idiom.* To have a knack for s.t. *Elle a la bosse des maths.* "She has a flair for math."

BOSSER. To work hard. *Il faut que tu bosses si tu veux finir à l'heure.* "You'll have to hustle if you want to finish on time."

BOSSEUR, -EUSE, *m., f.* Hard worker. *C'est une bosseuse: elle a réussi dans la vie.* "She's a hard worker: she's been successful."

BOTTE, *f.* Boot. See CIRER LES BOTTES; LÈCHE-BOTTES; TOMBER EN BOTTE(S).

BOUC. See BIQUE.

BOUCHÉ, -E. Stupid (lit. "blocked"). **Bouché à l'émeri.** Really stupid. *Il reste bouché à l'émeri malgré toutes les explications.* "He's still as thick as ever despite all the explanations."

BOUCHÉE, *f.* Mouthful. **Mettre les bouchées doubles,** *idiom.* To double one's efforts. *Il va falloir mettre les bouchées doubles.* "We're going to have to go all out."

BOUCHER. To cork; stop up. **En boucher un coin à qn.,** *idiom.* To astound s.o. *Elle m'en a bouché un coin par sa rapidité d'agir.* "She floored me by acting so rapidly."

BOUCHON, *m.* **1.** Cork. **Mettre un bouchon à qn.,** *idiom.* To shut s.o. up. *Mets-toi un bouchon!* "Put a lid on it!" **Pousser le bouchon (un peu/trop loin).** To exaggerate. *Il pousse toujours le bouchon trop loin en parlant de ses amours.* "He always lays it on thick when talking of his love life." See PRENDRE...DU BOUCHON. **2.** Youngest child. *Papa dorlote son petit bouchon.* "Pop pampers the baby of the family."

BOUCLARÈS. Closed; off limits. *Ce bar est bouclarès.* "This bar is off limits."

BOUCLARÈS! "Shut up!" "Put a lid on it!"

BOUCLER. 1. To buckle. **La boucler.** To keep one's mouth shut. *Tu vas la boucler!* "Will you keep your trap shut!" **Boucler la boucle.** To come full circle; loop the loop. *On voulait revenir par Paris pour boucler la boucle.* "We returned via Paris to make it a round trip." *C'est une affaire bouclée.* "It's a done deal." **2.** To imprison. *J'avais trop d'alcool dans le sang; ils m'ont bouclé et retiré mon permis.* "I had too high a blood alcohol level; they locked me up and took away my driving license." **Être bouclé chez soi/à la maison.** To be cooped up at home. *Mes parents m'ont bouclé toute la semaine.* "My parents grounded me all week."

BOUDIN, *m.* **1.** Blood sausage. **S'en aller/finir/partir/ tourner en eau de boudin,** *idiom.* To flop. *Tous mes efforts sont partis en eau de boudin.* "All my efforts went down the drain." **2.** Sulking (pun on **bouder** [to sulk]). **Faire du/son boudin,** *idiom.* To pout; sulk. *Oui, fais ton boudin, tu n'auras rien de moi.* "Go ahead and sulk—you'll get nothing from me." **3.** Fat girl. *Il préfère un boudin à une maigrichonne.* "He prefers a plump girl to a thin one." **4.** An easy piece/lay. *Yvette n'est pas le boudin que tu crois.* "Yvette isn't the pushover you take her for."

BOUFFE, *f.* Food. *Tu me fatigues; tu ne penses qu'à la bouffe.* "You wear me out; all you think about is eating."

BOUFFER. To eat. **Bouffer du...** To be anti, very hostile to, as in **bouffer du curé/juif.** To be anticlerical/anti-semitic. *Après avoir quitté la prêtrise, il bouffait du curé.* "After leaving the priesthood, he became anticlerical."

BOUFFER DE LA BITE. See CON À...BITE.

BOUFFER DE L'AIL. See AIL.

BOUFFER DES BRIQUES. See BRIQUES.

(SE) BOUFFER LE NEZ. To quarrel. *On ne peut les laisser ensemble sans qu'il se bouffent le nez.* "You can't leave them alone without their getting into each other's hair/at each other's throats."

BOUFFETANCE, *f.* = **BOUFFE.**

BOUFFI. Puffy. *Tu l'as dit, bouffi!* "You said it, Eddy!" "You can say that again, Henry!" (**Bouffi** serves merely as a rhyming intensifier.)

BOUGNOUL(E), *pej.* Dark-skinned foreigner. *Il est raciste et plein de mépris pour ceux qu'il appelle "bougnoules".* "He's a racist and full of contempt for those he calls 'niggers.'"

BOUGRE, *m.* Individual. *C'est un bon/mauvais/pauvre/ bougre.* "He's a good/rotten/miserable guy/sort/fellow."

BOUGRE! Damn (it)!

BOUGRE D'ÂNE/IMBÉCILE. "You jackass!/idiot!"

BOUGRE DE TEMPS! Rotten weather!

BOUGREMENT. Extremely. *Elle est bougrement sexy.* "She's extremely sexy."

BOUGRESSE, *f.* **1.** Female. *Sa bougresse est hommasse.* "His broad's butchy." **2.** Bitch. *Je ne peux la blairer, la bougresse.* "I can't stand that bitch."

BOUI-BOUI/BOUIBOUIS, *m.* **1.** Low dive. *Pour se changer les idées le millionaire aimait se soûler dans les bouibouis.* "For a change of scenery, the millionaire liked getting drunk in low dives." **2.** Brothel. *Les filles de ce boui-boui ne sont pas très alléchantes.* "The girls in this whorehouse aren't very enticing."

BOUIF, *m.* Shoemaker. *Je cherchais un bouif pour mon talon cassé.* "I looked for a shoemaker for my broken heel."

BOUILLE, *f.* **1.** Face. **Avoir une bonne bouille.** To have a pleasing face. *Il ne peut pas être dangereux, ce mec; il a une bonne bouille.* "That guy can't be dangerous; he's got a friendly face." **2.** Naïve individual; potential mark for a swindler. *L'arnaqueur savait où trouver les bonnes bouilles.* "The con man knew where to find likely marks."

BOUILLON, *m.* **1.** Water (lit. "broth"). **Boire/prendre un**

bouillon. To go under. *Il ne savait pas gérer son commerce et a pris un sacré bouillon.* "He didn't know how to manage his business and went flat broke." **2.** Poor restaurant. *Il y a toujours du monde dans ce bouillon.* "This greasy spoon's crowded." **3.** Criminal's hideout. *La police les a enfin pris dans leur bouillon.* "The police finally captured them in their hideout."

BOUILLONNER. To have many unsold copies (lit. "to bubble"; "boil"). *Ce magazine bouillonne un max.* "That magazine has huge quantities of unsold copies."

BOUL', ** *m.* from **boulevard. *On se retrouvait toujours aux restos du Boul' Mich'.* "We always met in restaurants on the Boulevard Saint-Michel."

BOULE, *f.* Head (lit. "bowling ball; billiard ball"). **Avoir les boules,** *idiom.* **1.** To be ill at ease/angry. *Ça se voyait qu'il avait les boules.* "It was obvious he was upset." **2.** To be very frightened. *J'avais les boules quand les flics m'ont demandé mes papiers.* "I was scared shitless/witless when the cops asked for my ID." **Avoir la boule à zéro,** *idiom.* To be totally bald. *Il a la boule à zéro et porte une perruque.* "He's completely bald and wears a rug." **Coup de boule.** Blow delivered by the head. *Dans le film,* Les compères, *Depardieu montre à Richard comment donner un coup de boule.* "In the movie *Les compères,* Depardieu shows Richard how to give a blow with the head."

BOULER. To roll. **Envoyer bouler qn.,** *idiom.* To tell s.o. to get lost. *Je ne pouvais plus le voir, je l'ai envoyé bouler.* "I couldn't stand the sight of him anymore and sent him packing."

BOULETTE, *f.* Blunder (lit. "pellet"). *J'ai fait une boulette en disant avoir vu son mari avec une fille.* "I made a blunder when I said I'd seen her husband with a girl."

BOULEVARD DES ALLONGÉS = JARDIN DES ALLONGÉS.

BOULONNER. To slave away at a job (lit. "to bolt"). *Je boulonne toute la journée.* "I slave away all day."

BOULOT, *m.* Job. **Au boulot!** "Let's get to work!" **Être boulot-boulot.** To be hard-working. *Il n'est pas baisant le mec; trop boulot-boulot.* "That guy's no fun; too much of a workaholic."

BOULOTTER. 1. To eat. *On n'avait rien à boulotter à la maison.* "We had nothing to eat in the house." **2.** To squander. *Le marin a boulotté sa paye avec les filles du port.* "The sailor blew his wages on the girls in the port."

BOUM, *f.* Young people's party. *On a passé des disques de Trenet à la boum.* "We played Charles Trenet records at the bash." See SURBOUM.

BOUMER. To be in full swing; go well. **Ça boume?** "Everything going OK?"

BOUQUET. Bouquet. **C'est le bouquet!** That's the limit/last straw; that takes the cake!

BOUQUIN, *m.* Book. *Elle traîne ses bouquins partout.* "She carries her books around with her everywhere."

BOUQUINER. To read. *Elle bouquine dans le métro.* "She reads in the subway."

BOUQUINEUR, -EUSE, *m., f.* Bookworm. *Elle a toujours le nez dans les bouquins; c'est une vraie bouquineuse.* "She's always got her nose in a book; she's a real bookworm."

BOURDE, *f.* Blunder. **Faire une bourde,** *idiom.* To put one's foot in it. *Tu as fait une bourde en parlant de son ancien amant.* "You put your foot in it when you talked about her former lover."

BOURDON, *m.* Bumblebee. **Avoir le bourdon,** *idiom.* To feel depressed. *Toutes les fois qu'il part elle a le bourdon.* "Every time he leaves, she has the blues."

BOURGEOISE, *f.* Wife (lit. "middle-class woman"). *Ma bourgoise ne veut pas aller.* "The missus doesn't want to go." See BAISER À LA BOURGEOISE.

BOURLINGUER. To be a globetrotter. *Il ne s'est jamais marié car il aimait trop bourlinguer.* "He never got married because he was too fond of traveling around."

BOURRATIF, -IVE. Filling. *Je cale; ce pain est trop bourratif.* "I'm not eating any more; this bread is too filling."

BOURRE, *f.* Stuffing (upholstery); wad of hair. **De première bourre.** First rate. *Tout ce qu'il nous a montré était de première bourre.* "Everything he showed us was of excellent quality." **Être à la bourre,** *idiom.* To be pressed for time. *Je ne peux plus attendre; je suis à la bourre.* "I can't wait any longer; I'm in a hurry." **Bonne bourre!** "Give her a good plugging; have fun!" **Être en pleine bourre,** *idiom.* To be in top shape. *Ce grand tombeur se dit être en pleine bourre mais il me laisse insatisfaite.* "That great ladykiller claims he's in top form but he leaves me unsatisfied." See (SE) TIRER LA BOURRE.

BOURRE, *m.* Policeman. *Ce con de bourre insistait pour me faire souffler dans le ballon.* "That idiot cop insisted on my taking a breath test."

BOURRÉ, -E. Soused. *Il est revenu de la discothèque complètement bourré.* "He came back dead drunk from the discotheque."

BOURRÉ, E COMME UNE CANTINE = BOURRÉ.

BOURRE-MOU, *m.* Hogwash. *Tu ne racontes que du bourre-mou.* "Everything you're saying is a lot of hogwash."

BOURRER. 1. To have sexually (lit. "to stuff"). *Les routiers avaient envie de bourrer la nouvelle serveuse du resto routier.* "The truck drivers wanted to plug the new waitress at the truck stop restaurant." **2.** To beat up. *Les voyous l'avaient bourré de coups.* "The thugs really worked him over." **3.** To accelerate; drive recklessly. *Luc est un chauffard et n'aime que bourrer.* "Luke's a bad driver and just likes to tear up the road."

BOURRER LA GUEULE À QN. To bash s.o.'s face in. *Ferme-la ou je te bourre la gueule.* "Shut your trap or I'll knock your block off."

BOURRER LE CRÂNE/MOU/LA CAISSE À QN. To feed s.o. a bunch of baloney. *Tu veux me faire accroire* *ça? Va bourrer le mou de qn. d'autre.* "You want me to swallow that? Go try your line on s.o. else."

(SE) BOURRER. 1. To make fat profits. *Il a profité de notre misère pour se bourrer.* "He took advantage of our poverty to make a bundle." **2.** To get plastered. *Si tu me montrais un peu plus de tendresse, je me bourrerais moins.* "If you showed me a little more tenderness, I'd get soused less."

BOURRIQUE, *f.* Pig-headed individual (lit. "donkey"). *Il est têtu comme une bourrique.* "He's as stubborn as a mule."

BOUSEUX, -EUSE, *m., f., pej.* Yokel (from **bouse,** "cow dung"). *Je ne peux plus blairer ce bled, ni ses bouseux.* "I can't stand this hick town or its rubes any more."

BOUSILLAGE, *m.* Tattooing (lit. "screw up"). *Admire mon dernier bousillage!* "Admire my new tattoo!"

BOUSILLE, *f.* = **BOUSILLAGE.**

BOUSILLER. 1. To botch. *En bricolant ma radio, tu l'as bousillée.* "You screwed up my radio when you tinkered with it." **2.** To kill. *Il a bousillé ses complices.* "He rubbed out his accomplices."

BOUSILLEUR, -EUSE, *m., f.* Tattooer (lit. "bungler"). *Le bousilleur attendait les marins pétés.* "The tattoo artist waited for the drunken sailors."

BOUSOUX = BOUSEUX.

BOUSSOLE, *f.* Compass. **Perdre la boussole,** *idiom.* To go off one's rocker. *Je crois que tu perds la boussole.* "I think you're going nuts."

BOUSTIFAILLE, *f.* Food. *Quand est-ce-qu'elle arrive, la boustifaille?* "When's the grub coming?"

BOUSTIFAILLER. To chow down; guzzle. *Arrête de boustifailler et tu seras moins gros.* "Stop eating and drinking so much and you won't be so fat."

BOUSTIFFE, *f.* = **BOUSTIFAILLE.**

BOUT, *m.* End. **Tenir le bon bout,** *idiom.* To be close to succeeding. *Nous tenons le bon bout.* "We're on the right track." **En connaître un bout.** To be well informed. *Sur le jazz elle en connaît un bout.* "She's knows a thing or two about jazz."

BOUTANCHE, *f.* Bottle. *La boutanche, on va se la faire à nous deux.* "The two of us will split this bottle."

BOUTEILLE, *f.* Bottle. **Avoir/prendre de la bouteille,** *idiom.* To be getting on in years. *Nous prenons tous de la bouteille!* "We're all getting older."

BOUTEROLE, *f.* Church. *La basilique de Montmartre est une sacrée bouterole!* "The basilica of Montmartre is some church!"

BOUTIQUE, *m.* **1.** Shop. **Faire boutique son cul,** *Fr. Caribbean sl.* To prostitute o.s. *Si tu ne me donnes pas le fric je ferai boutique mon cul.* "If you don't give me the money, I'll sell my ass." **2.** Male/female genitalia. **Montrer sa boutique.** To expose one's genitals; flash. *Quand ce satyr lui a montré sa boutique, ma grand-tante est tombée dans les pommes.* "When that flasher exposed himself to my great-aunt, she almost passed out."

BOUTON, *m.* **1.** Button. See CIRER. **2.** Pimple. *Elle le trouve beau, malgré ses boutons.* She finds him handsome despite his pimples. **3.** Clitoris. *Il n'a qu'à appuyer sur mon bouton, et je mouille.* "All he has to do is press my button (stimulate my clit) and I get hot." See ASTIQUER LE BOUTON.

BOUTON DE ROSE = BOUTON 3.

BOYAU, *m.* Guts. **Avoir le boyau de la rigolade,** *idiom.* To have the giggles/a laughing fit. *Nous avions tous le boyau de la rigolade.* "We all couldn't stop laughing." See TORD-BOYAUX; (SE) TORDRE LES BOYAUX.

BOYAUTANT. Sidesplitting. *C'est boyautant de le voir en trav.* "It's a howl to see him in drag."

(SE) BOYAUTER. To laugh uproariously. *On s'est boyauté pendant son sketch.* "We busted a gut laughing during her sketch."

BRAGUETTE, *f.* **1.** Fly (pants). See ESCALADEUSE DE BRAGUETTE; PÉTER…BRAGUETTE. **2.** Prostitute who works in doorways. *Quand je suis pressé, je m'envoie une braguette, d'ailleurs je ne peux pas me payer une grande horizontale.* "When I'm pressed for time, I get it off with an upright whore; besides, I can't afford a horizontal one."

BRAISE, *f.* Money (lit. "embers"). *Peux-tu me filer de la braise?* "Can you let me have some dough."

BRAISEUX, -EUSE. Wealthy. *Elle n'avait d'yeux que pour les braiseux.* "She was only interested in rich guys."

BRANCHÉ, -E. 1. Up to date; trendy. *Les piercés se croient branchés.* "People who've had piercing (forehead, and so on) think they're very cool." **2.** To be in the know. *Elle est branchée opéra.* "She's a knowledgeable opera buff."

BRANCHER. 1. To connect; plug in. *Le hockey sur glace, ça le branche.* "Ice hockey really turns him on." **2.** To acquaint s.o. with s.t. *Il faut que tu me branches sur ce sujet.* "You'll have to familiarize me with that subject." **3.** To pick up. *Il l'a branchée dans la rue.* "He picked her up on the street."

(SE) BRANCHER. To take up; get interested in. *Mamie s'est branchée sur l'informatique.* "Grandma's gotten interested in computer science."

BRANDON, *m.* Penis (lit. "firebrand"). *Il avait le brandon en l'air.* "His dick was up."

BRANLAGE, *m.* Masturbation. *Il ne pensait qu'au branlage.* "All he thought about was beating the meat."

BRANLÉE, *f.* Severe beating/defeat. *Il a reçu une de ces branlées!* "He got one hell of a beating!"

BRANLER. 1. To do. **Qu'est que tu branles?** "Just what are you doing?" **N'en avoir rien à branler,** *abbr.* **R.A.B.,** *idiom.* Not to give a damn. *Tes ébats amoureux, je n'en ai rien à branler.* "I couldn't care less about your love life." **2.** Masturbate. *Je l'ai branlé pour avoir la paix.* "I jerked him off so he'd leave me in peace."

(SE) BRANLER. 1. To masturbate. *Il se branlait en reluquant du porno.* "He whacked off while ogling porn." **2. Se les branler/se branler les couilles.** Not to do a goddamned thing (lit. "to jerk off one's balls"). *Pendant que je bosse, toi, tu te les branles!* "While I slave away, you don't do a fuckin' thing."

(S'EN) BRANLER. Not to care. *De tes sornettes, je m'en branle!* "I don't give a damn about your stupid stories!"

BRANLERIE, *f.* Empty dreams. *Tu t'adonnes trop à la branlerie.* "You indulge in too many idle fancies."

BRANLETTE, *f.* Masturbation. *Plutôt la branlette que le SIDA!* "Better to consult Dr. Jerkoff than to get AIDS!"

BRANLEUR, *m.* **1.** Masturbator. *Les deux branleurs aimaient se masturber de concert.* "The two meat beaters liked to whack off together." **2.** Good-for-nothing boy. *Je refuse que tu sortes avec ce petit branleur.* "I refuse to let you go out with that bum."

BRANLEUSE, *f.* **1.** Very young girl. *Je ne m'intéresse pas aux branleuses.* "I'm not interested in very young girls." **2.** Masturbatrix. *C'est une branleuse extra.* "She gives a great hand job."

BRANLOCHER = BRANLER.

BRANQUE, *m.* = **BRANQUIGNOL.**

BRANQUIGNOL/BRANQUIGNOLLE, *m., f.* Crazy person. *Tu me prends pour un branquignol?* "Do you take me for a nut?"

BRAQUE. Crazy. *Ta frangine est un peu braque.* "Your sister's a little cracked."

BRAQUEMARD, *m.* Penis. *Je connais des braquemards de toute taille.* "I'm familiar with cocks of every size."

BRAQUER. To commit armed robbery. **1.** *Le supermarché a été braqué.* "The supermarket was held up." **2.** Barge in on; annoy. *Tu aurais pu me bigophoner au lieu de me braquer.* "You could've given me a call instead of dropping in unannounced."

BRAQUOS, *m.* Penis. **Avoir le braquos,** *idiom.* To have an erection. *Il avait le braquos en pensant à elle.* "He had a hard-on thinking of her."

BRAS, *m.* Arm. **Faire le bras d'honneur.** To give someone the finger. *La bagarre a commencé quand il a fait le bras d'honneur à son rival.* "The brawl began when he gave the finger to his rival."

BRASSER DE L'AIR = DÉPLACER DE L'AIR.

BREDOUILLE. Empty-handed. *Il voulait faire fortune mais il est revenu bredouille.* "He wanted to make a fortune but came back with nothing."

BRÉSILIENNE-RASOIR, *f.* Transsexual prostitute. *La brésilienne-rasoir a un prix d'attaque trop fort.* "The TS/transi whore's basic price is too steep."

BRIC, *m.* Brothel. *C'est un bric classe!* "That's a first-class whorehouse!"

BRICHETON, *m.* Bread. *N'oublie pas le bricheton ce soir.* "Don't forget the bread tonight."

BRICOLEUR, -EUSE, *m., f.* **1.** Handyman; do-it-your-selfer. *Ce bricoleur ne veut pas être déclaré.* "That handyman doesn't want his work to be declared (for taxes)." **2.** Incompetent worker. *Ce n'est qu'une équipe de bricoleurs.* "They're just a bunch of amateurs."

BRICOLO, *m., abbr.* of **bricoleur.**

BRIEFER. To brief. *Tu peux me briefer là-dessus?* "Can you put me in the picture about that?"

BRIFFER. To eat. *J'ai très faim; allons briffer!* "I'm very hungry; let's go eat."

BRILLER. To have an orgasm (lit. "to shine"). *Il est le seul à me faire briller.* "He's the only one who makes me come."

BRINDEZINGUE. Crazy. *Il nous a raconté des histoires brindezingues.* "He told us nutty stories."

BRINGUE, *f.* Binge. *Aux vacances de Pâques on fera la bringue en Floride.* "During Easter vacation we'll have a ball in Florida."

BRIOCHE, *f.* Belly. *La bière me donne de la brioche.* "Beer is making me paunchy."

BRIQUE, *f.* **1.** Brick. **Bouffer des briques,** *idiom.* To have nothing to eat. *Si tu ne trouves pas de boulot on bouffera des briques.* "If you don't get a job we'll starve." See (NE PAS) CASSER DES BRIQUES. **2.** Ten thousand francs. *Peux-tu me prêter une brique?* "Can you lend me ten grand?"

BRONZE, *m.* Turd. **Couler/mouler un bronze** (lit. "to cast a bronze [statue]"). To defecate. *Il lisait le canard en coulant son bronze.* "He read the newspaper while taking a crap."

BROUTER LA FRISÉE/LE CRESSON. To practice cunnilingus (lit. "to graze the curly endive/watercress") *Il bande peu mais broute à merveille le cresson.* "He rarely gets it up but he's great at muff diving."

BROUTER LA TIGE. To fellate (lit. "to nibble on the stalk"). *Elle rêvait de brouter tige après tige.* "She dreamed of sucking one cock after another."

BROUTEUSE, *f.* Lesbian. *Les brouteuses aiment se brouter le cresson.* "Dykes like to eat hair pie."

BÛCHE, *f.* Log. See PRENDRE/RAMASSER...BÛCHE.

BÛCHER. To fell trees. **Bûcher un examen,** *idiom.* To cram for an exam. *Elle a réussi son bac sans bûcher.* "She passed her high school exam without having to cram for it."

BUFFET, *m.* Belly (lit. "sideboard"; "buffet"). **Avoir un bébé dans le buffet,** *idiom.* To be pregnant. *J'avais un bébé dans le buffet quand il m'a planquée.* "I had s.t. in the oven when he ditched me." **En avoir dans le buffet.** To have guts/balls. *Il est super, ce mec; il en a dans le buffet.* "That guy's terrific; he's got guts."

BULLE, *f.* Bubble. See COINCER LA BULLE.

BULLER. To loaf. *Il n'aime que buller.* "All he wants to do is hang out."

BURETTE, *f.* **1.** Face (lit. "cruet"). *Quel plaisir revoir ta* *burette souriante!* "I'm really glad to see your smiling face." **2.** Penis. *Le cureton inspectait la burette de l'enfant de chœur.* "The priest checked out the altar boy's dick."

BURETTES, *f., pl.* Testicles. **Vider les burettes.** To ejaculate (lit. "to empty the cruets"). *Il avait besoin de se vider les burettes.* "He needed to gets his rocks off."

BURNÉ. Large-testicled. *Il était burné et ça se voyait.* "It was obvious that he had big balls."

BURNES, *f., pl.* Testicles. **Casser les burnes à qn.** To be a ball buster. *Tu me casses les burnes!* "You're a real pain in the neck/ass." See CASSE-BURNES.

BUVABLE. Tolerable (lit. "drinkable"). *Il n'est pas buvable, ce mec.* "That guy's unbearable."

BYZANCE, Byzantium. **Être Byzance!,** youth. To be terrific/the berries (poss. associated with **aisance, plaisance,** and so on, rather than anything Byzantine, such as icons, iconoclasts, corruption, conspiracies, scholars, violence—quite the opposite of "être Byzance!") *Le soleil brillait, les filles m'aimaient. Ah, c'était Byzance!* "The sun was shining, the girls loved me. Ah, that was really living!"

ÇA ARRACHE! See ARRACHER.

ÇA BAIGNE! See BAIGNER.

ÇA CHIE! "What a mess!" See ÇA VA CHIER.

ÇA COINCE! What a stink!

ÇA COLLE, ANATOLE? "How's tricks, Dick?" "Everything OK, Kay?"

ÇA M'INTERPELLE!, See INTERPELLER.

ÇA S'ARROSE! "That calls for a drink!"

ÇA TE LA COUPE! "Top that if you can! That leaves you speechless, doesn't it?"

ÇA VA BARDER = ÇA VA CHAUFFER!

ÇA VA CHAUFFER! Sparks will fly. *Les étudiants sont descendus dans la rue. Ça va chauffer!* "The students are demonstrating in the streets. Things are going to heat up!"

ÇA VA CHERCHER DANS… To add up to approximately…. *Ça va chercher dans les combien, tous ces meubles?* "About how much money is all that furniture going to cost?"

ÇA VA CHIER! "The shit's going to hit the fan!"

ÇA Y EST! "That's it! That's settled! That's done!"

CABANE, *f.* **1.** Ramshackle house; small outbuilding (such as a doghouse). **Faire de la cabane,** *idiom.* To be a burglar. **Faire une cabane,** *idiom.* To do a burglary job. *Mon frangin il a fait de la cabane toujours seul, mais fera une prochaine cabane à l'aide de complices.* "He's always done his breaking and entering alone, but he'll do his next job with accomplices." See ATTIGER LA CABANE. **2.** Jail. *Son frangin est toujours en cabane.* "Her brother's still in stir."

CABANE À LAPINS, *f.* Shack. *Je n'aimerais pas habiter leur cabane à lapins.* "I wouldn't like to live in that dump of theirs."

CABANON, *m.* **1.** Provençal cottage. *Le week-end on quitte Marseille pour le cabanon—c'est toute notre vie.* "Weekends we leave Marseilles for our country cottage—that's our whole life." **2.** Loony bin. *Ton oncle est bon pour le cabanon.* "Your uncle's ready for the nuthouse."

CÂBLÉ, -E. Être câblé. To be hip; trendy (lit. "to have cable TV"). *Nous ne sommes ni branchés, ni câblés: ce ne sont que les valeurs éternelles qui nous intéressent.* "We're neither with it nor up-to-date; we're interested only in eternal values."

CABOCHE, *m.* Head. **Avoir une sacrée/sale caboche,** *idiom.* To be really pigheaded. *Ton dab a une sale caboche.* "Your dad's really pigheaded."

CABOT, *m.* **1.** Corporal. *Ce petit cabot se prend déjà pour Napoléon ou Hitler.* "That little corporal already thinks he's Napoleon or Hitler." **2.** Dog. *Elle a laissé toute sa fortune aux cabots sans foyer.* "She left her fortune to homeless dogs."

CABOTIN, -E, *m., f.* **1.** Ham actor. *Ne traite pas de cabotin ce grand artiste.* "Don't call that great artist a ham." **2.** Show-off. *Arrête de faire le cabotin!* "Quit showing off!"

CABOTINAGE, *m.* Bad acting. *Des critiques trouvaient que la divine Sarah faisait du cabotinage.* "Some critics thought the divine Sarah's (Bernhardt) acting was hammy."

CABOULOT, *m.* Low dive or dump. *"Quel caboulot!" disait Bette.* "'What a dump,' said Bette."

CABOULOTE, *f.* Waitress in a cheap tavern. *La caboulote rêvait de devenir une star de cinéma.* "The waitress in the dive dreamed of becoming a movie star."

CABOULOTIÈRE = CABOULOTE.

CACA, *m.,* children. Poop. *As-tu fait caca?* "Have you done number two?" *C'est du caca.* "That's worthless trash."

CACADE, *f.* Diarrhea (from **caca** and **cascade**). *Il a la cacade et reste à la maison.* "He's got the runs and is staying home."

CACASSE, *f., obs.* for "ass," used only in: **Aller à la cacasse.** To have sex (not necessarily anal). *Mon mec n'a jamais le temps pour la tendresse; il va tout de suite à la cacasse.* "My guy's never got time for tenderness; he just wants nooky right away."

CACHE-FRIFRI, *m.* G-string; skimpy panties. *La stripteaseuse a pété son cache-frifri.* "The stripper snapped her G-string."

CACHEMIRE, *m.* Cashmere. **Donner un coup de cachemire sur le piano,** *ironic.* To give the counter a quick wipe. *Ici on ne donne pas souvent un coup de cachemire sur le piano.* "They don't wipe the counter very often here."

CACTUS, *m.* Problem (lit. "cactus"). *Tout s'est passé sans cactus.* "Everything went off without a hitch." **Avoir un cactus dans la poche/le portefeuille,** *idiom.* To be a miser. *Son oncle a un cactus dans la poche.* "His uncle's a skinflint."

CADAVRE, *m.* Empty bottle/"dead soldier" (lit. "corpse"). *Au nombre de cadavres, on mesurait leur cuite.* "You could tell how drunk they were by the number of empty bottles."

CADEAU, *m.* Gift. **Ne pas être un cadeau.** To be very troublesome. *Son nouvel jules n'est pas un cadeau.* "Her new boyfriend's no bargain." **Ne pas faire de cadeau,** *idiom.* To pull no punches. *La vie ne lui a pas fait de cadeau.* "Life hasn't treated him gently." See PETIT CADEAU.

CAFÉ, *m.* Coffee. **Fort de café.** Strong stuff; exaggerated. *Ton histoire est un peu fort de café.* "Your story is a bit much." See PRENDRE…PAUVRE.

CAFÉ-COUETTE, *m.* Bed and breakfast (lit. "coffee quilt"). *Une bretonne en coiffe tient un chouette de café-couette.* "A Breton woman wearing a traditional headdress runs a very nice B & B."

CAFEMAR/CAFEMON = CAFETON.

CAFETER, *school.* To inform; tell tales out of school. *C'est toi qui as cafeté.* "You're the one who squealed."

CAFETEUR, -EUSE, *m., f.* School. *Ils ont passé le cafeteur à tabac.* "They beat up the snitch."

CAFETIÈRE, *f.* Head (lit "coffeepot; coffeemaker"). *Il n'a rien dans la cafetière.* "He's got nothing upstairs."

CAFETON, *m.* **1.** Coffee. *Son cafeton n'est pas dégueu.* "Her coffee's pretty good." **2.** Café. *Rendève demain au cafeton d'en face.* "It's a date tomorrow at the café across the street."

CAFOUILLADE = CAFOUILLAGE.

CAFOUILLAGE, *m.* Something wrong; a mess. *Il y a eu des cafouillages lors des dernières elections.* "There were irregularities in the last elections."

CAFOUILLER. **1.** To blunder. *J'ai cafouillé pour venir ici.* "I made one mistake after another in getting here." **2.** To not work right. *Le téléphone portatif cafouille encore.* "The cordless telephone is acting up again."

CAFOUILLIS, *m.* Mess. *Quel cafouillis chez eux!* "Their place is a shambles!"

CAFTER = CAFETER.

CAFTEUR = CAFETEUR.

CAGE À LAPINS, *f.* = CABANE À LAPINS.

CAGEOT, *m.* Unattractive female (lit. "crate"). *As-tu vu ce cageot?* "Have you seen that dog?"

CAGES À LAPINS. Cheap public housing. *On va démolir les cages à lapins de la banlieue.* "They're going to tear down the public housing in the suburbs."

CAGNA, *f.* Room. *Leur cagna était cracra mais ils étaient heureux.* "Their pad was filthy but they were happy." See CASSER LA CAGNA.

CAGNARD, *m.* Sun. *Je rêve de partir au cagnard.* "I'm dreaming of going off to someplace sunny."

CAÏD, *m.* Top dog (from Ar.). *Il a essayé de se faire passer pour un caïd de l'industrie.* "He tried to pass himself off as a big tycoon."

-CAILLE. Slang suffix, sometimes *pej.* Examples: **mouscaille** (excrement; dire poverty); **Franchecaille** (France).

CAILLER. To be cold (lit. "to curdle"). *Ça caille aujourd'hui.* "It's freezing today."

(SE LES) CAILLER = Se les geler. See (SE) GELER.

SE CAILLER LE RAISIN/SANG. To be extremely disturbed. *Mon fils et sa vie de débauche me caillent le raisin.* "My son's debauched life is worrying me sick."

(SE) CAILLER LES MICHES. To be extremely cold. *On se caillait les miches dans cet hôtel non chauffé.* "We froze our asses off in that hotel with no heat."

CAILLOU, *m.* Head (lit. "pebble"). *Tu es tombé sur le caillou?* "Have you gone off your rocker?"

CAISSE, *m.* = QUÈS, *m.*

CAISSE, *f.* **1.** Head. See BOURRER...CAISSE; RAS. **2.** Chest. *Tu vas souffrir de la caisse si tu ne t'arrêtes pas de fumer.* "You're going to have lung problems if you don't stop smoking." See ROULER LA CAISSE. **3.** Vehicle. See (À) FOND LA CAISSE. **4.** Fart. See LÂCHER...CAISSE. **5.** Drunkenness. See PRENDRE...CAISSE.

CAISSE À SAVON, *f.* Rattletrap vehicle. *Je ne veux plus* *voyager dans ta caisse à savon.* "I don't want to travel in your beat-up old crate anymore."

CAISSON, *m.* Head. **(Se) faire sauter le caisson,** *idiom.* To kill (o.s.). *Très déprimé, il s'est fait sauter le caisson.* "He was very depressed and blew his brains out."

CAL(E)CIF, *m.,* slang for **caleçon.** Boxer shorts. See ANDOUILLE...CALCIF; ANGUILLE; FILER...CALCIF.

CALE, *f.* Ship's hold. See (À) FOND DE CALE; RAS...CALE.

CALECIF = CALCIF.

CALEÇON, *m.* Shorts. See ANGUILLE.

CALENDOS/CALENDOT, *m.* Camembert cheese. *Le calendos de Camembert était le plus dégueu de tous.* "The camembert from Camembert was the yuckiest of all."

(SE) CALER LES AMYGDALES/BADIGOINCES/ JOUES/MOUSTACHES. To eat heartily (lit. "to fill one's tonsils/lips/cheeks/mustache." Cf. Eng. "to stuff one's face.") *On pétait la faim et on s'est calé les amygdales.* "We were starving and really put it away."

CALETER = CALTER.

CALMOS. Quietly. *On va y arriver calmos.* "We'll get it done without sweating it."

CALMOS! Cool it!

CALTER/SE CALTER. To scram. *Je me suis calté directo.* "I hit the road right away."

CAMBRONNE (Pierre). Napoleonic general who, in one version, replied "Merde!" when asked to surrender at Waterloo. Cf. General McAuliffe's answer "Nuts! Shit!" to a later surrender demand, also in Belgium. See MOT DE CAMBRONNE; CHAMBRE DE CAMBRONNE.

CAMBROUS(S)ARD, -E, *m., f.* Hick. *Je suis heureuse de vivre comme une cambrousarde.* "I'm happy living like a country bumpkin."

CAMBROUS(S)E, *f.* Country. *J'ai quitté la ville pour la cambrousse.* "I left the city for the sticks."

CAMBUSE, *f.* Hovel. *Et si l'on allait à ma cambuse?* "How about going to my pad?"

CAME, *f.* **1.** Merchandise. *Je n'achète que de la bonne came.* "I only buy good stuff." **2.** Drugs. *Elle fait un mémoire sur le rôle de la came dans la religion.* "She's doing a thesis on the role of drugs in religion."

CAMÉ, -E. Stoned; addicted. *Il est camé depuis longtemps mais il s'en sortira.* "He's been a drug addict for a long time but he'll kick the habit."

CAMÉLIA, *f.* High-class kept woman (from Dumas' *La dame aux camélias.* Note that the flower **camélia** is *m.*). *Je suis lasse d'être ta camélia; je pense faire des études et changer de métier.* "I'm tired of being your houseplant (mistress); I'm planning to go to school and change professions."

CAMELOTE, *f.* **1.** Trash. *Ce bidule, c'est de la camelote.* "That thing's a piece of junk." **2.** Goods. *Il a vendu toute sa camelote sur le marché.* "He sold all his stuff at the marketplace." **3.** Sperm. *Il lance trop vite sa camelote.* "He shoots his load too fast."

(SE) CAMER. To take drugs. *Il ne se came plus.* "He's no longer a junkie."

CAMP, *m.* Camp. See FOUTRE LE CAMP.

CAMTAR, *m.* Truck. *Les camtars sur la route, c'est l'enfer.* "Trucks on the road mean sheer hell!"

CANARD, *m.* **1.** Lump of sugar in coffee (lit. "duck"). *C'est le canard qui boit mon cafeton.* "It's the sugar that drinks my coffee." See FROID DE CANARD. **2.** Newspaper. See 3 for use in a sentence. **3.** False report; hoax. Le canard enchaîné *est un canard de qualité sans canards.* "*Le canard enchaîné* (The Tied Up Duck) is a quality newspaper without canards." **4.** False note. *Malgré les canards, elle reste une grande diva.* "Despite the wrong notes, she's still a great diva." **5.** Wet kiss, youth. *Ils se sont quittés sur un canard.* "They kissed passionately when they parted."

CANON, *m.* Glass of wine. *On a bu un canon sur le zinc du caboulot.* "We had a glass of wine at the bar."

CANTALOU(P), *m.* Native of the Auvergne. *J'ai goûté aux chansons et au cantal de ce Cantaloup.* "I sampled that Auvergnat's songs and Cantal (cow-sheep-goat cheese)."

CANTINE, *f.* Belly (lit. "cafeteria"; "canteen"). *J'ai la cantine bien remplie.* "I'm stuffed." See BOURRÉ…CANTINE.

CANTINER, *crim.* To buy goods in the prison store. *Si j'avais de l'oseille, je cantinerais des clopes sans avoir à me vendre.* "If I had any bread, I'd buy cigarettes at the store without having to sell m.s."

CANTOCHE, *f.* Canteen. *Et si l'on allait au resto? J'en ai marre de la cantoche.* "How about going to the restaurant? I'm sick of the canteen." See BOURRÉ…CANTOCHE.

CAOUA, *m.* Coffee. *Et un petit caoua pour se mettre en route.* "And a cuppa java to help us get started."

CAP, from **capable.** *T'es cap?* "Can you cut the mustard?"

CAPOTE/CAPOTE ANGLAISE, *f.* Condom (lit. "Eng. hooded coat"). (Note: in Brit. slang, "French letter" means "condom.") *Je refuse les michés qui veulent marcher sans capote.* "I reject johns who want to get it on without a rubber."

CARABINÉ, -E. Very powerful. *J'ai une migraine carabinée.* "I've got one hell of a headache."

CARAFE, *f.* Head (lit. "carafe"). *Tu n'as rien dans la carafe.* "You're birdbrained." See TOMBER EN CARAFE; RESTER EN CARAFE.

CARAMBOLAGE, *m.* Multiple highway accident. *Quel carambolage sur la route verglacée!* "That was some pileup on the icy road."

CARAMBOLER. To have sexually. *Ils m'ont carambolée sur la plage.* "They banged me on the beach."

(SE) CARAMBOLER. To crash into. *Les deux motos se sont carambolées superbement.* "The two bikes really smashed into each other."

(SE) CARAPATER. To scram. *L'orage arrive; je me carapate.* "The storm's coming; I'm making tracks."

CARAT, *m.* Year (lit. "carat"). *Il a vingt carats.* "He's twenty." See DERNIER CARAT; PRENDRE DU CARAT.

CARAVELLE. Expensive prostitute, often in a car. (Caravel(le) has been used at various times for types of ships, planes, and cars. Cf. **amazone, autobus, montgolfière, wagonnière.**) *Il s'ennuie chez lui et rêve de s'envoyer en l'air avec une caravelle.* "He's bored at home and dreams of getting it off with a high-class hooker."

CARBURANT, *m.* Liquor (lit. "fuel"). *Son carburant c'est le calva.* "Applejack's the drink that keeps him going."

CARBURER À L'ALCOOL = MARCHER À L'ALCOOL.

CARNE, *f.* Inferior meat. *Ils t'ont refilé de la carne, mais je rejetterais même du tournedos Rossini, car je prépare ma réincarnation.* "They sold you tough meat, but I'd reject even tournedos Rossini because I'm preparing my reincarnation."

CAROLINE, *f.* Passive homosexual. *Il s'est lassé d'être toujours la Caroline.* "He got tired of always being the receiver."

CAROSSÉE = BALANCÉE.

CAROTTE, *f.* Carrot. **Les carottes sont cuites!** *idiom.* "It's all over (for him, for us); our goose is cooked."

CARPETTE, *f.* Spineless person (lit. "rug"). *Ne joue pas la carpette, défends-toi!* "Don't be a wimp; defend y.s."

CARREAU, *m.* Diamonds (cards). See (SE) TENIR À CARREAU.

CARREAUX, *m., pl.* Eyeglasses (lit. "windowpanes"). *J'ai paumé mes carreaux.* "I've lost my glasses."

CARTE DE FRANCE/DE GÉOGRAPHIE. Semen stains on sheets after sex/nocturnal emission. *Enfant il pissait au lit; maintenant il trace la carte de France chaque nuit.* "As a child he used to wet the bed; now he starches his sheets every night."

CASE, *f.* Cabin; cell; box. See MANQUER UNE CASE.

CASQUE, *m.* Helmet. See RAYER LE CASQUE.

CASQUER. To pay. *À toi de casquer aujourd'hui.* "It's your turn to shell out today."

CASSE, *f.* **1.** Damage. *L'ouragan n'a pas fait trop de casse.* "The hurricane didn't do too much damage." **2.** Violent confrontation. *Il risque d'y avoir de la casse pour la manif.* "There'll probably be some rough stuff during the demonstration." **3.** Scrapyard. *Ta bagnole est bonne à foutre à la casse.* "Your jalopy is ready for the scrapyard."

CASSE, *m.* Burglary. *On a fait un casse dans l'imeuble.* "There was a break-in in the building."

CASSE-BONBONS, *m., f., adj.* and *n.* Annoying; annoying person. *Qu'est-ce qu'il peut être casse-bonbons.* "He can be a real ball buster." See BONBON **4.**

CASSE-BURNES = CASSE-BONBONS.

CASSE-COU, *m., f., adj.* and *n.* Daredevil(ish). *C'est une skieuse casse-cou qui descend à une vitesse folle.* "She's a daredevil skier who descends at breakneck speed."

CASSE-COUILLES = CASSE-BONBONS.

CASSE-CUL, *m.* Annoying person. *T'es on ne peut plus casse-cul.* "You couldn't be more of a pain in the ass if you tried."

CASSE-GUEULE, *m., adj.* and *n.* Risky/dangerous place. *Un vrai casse-gueule la route pour monter chez toi.* "The uphill road to your house is full of accidents waiting to happen."

CASSEMENT = CASSE 1.

CASSE-NOISETTES, *m., pl.* Voluntary vaginal contractions during intercourse (lit. "nutcracker"). *Ma moule sait faire casse-noisettes et traire un max les mecs.* "My pussy knows how to flex its muscles and milk guys dry."

CASSE-PIEDS, *m., f., adj.* and *n.* Annoying or boring person or situation. *Ce film est d'un casse-pieds fini.* "This film is totally boring."

CASSE-PIPE, *m*. Bloody war. *Il refusait de partir au casse-pipe.* "He refused to go to war (and be cannon fodder)." See CASSER SA PIPE.

CASSER. To break. **À tout casser. 1.** Stupendous. *Ils ont fait un banquet à tout casser.* "They prepared a fantastic banquet." **2.** At the very most. *Ça vaut 20.000 à tout casser.* "That's worth 20,000, tops."

CASSER DU SUCRE SUR LE DOS DE QN. See SUCRE.

CASSER LA BARAQUE. 1. To have a great theatrical success (lit. "to break the cabin"). *La diva a cassé la baraque.* "The diva brought down the house." **2.** To ruin s.o.'s chances/plans. *Méfie-toi de ton associé: il risque de nous casser la baraque.* "Be careful of your partner; he's likely to pull the rug out from under us."

CASSER LA CAGNA. To bust up the joint. *Sacrés gosses! Vous finirez par casser la cagna.* "Damned brats! You'll wind up wrecking the place."

CASSER LA/UNE CROÛTE/GRAINE. To eat. *Et si on cassait la croûte.* "How about a break for a bite to eat?"

CASSER/SE CASSER LA MARGOULETTE/ GUEULE. See MARGOULETTE.

CASSER LA RONDELLE/LE POT/L'ANNEAU/ OIGNON = DÉFONCER....

CASSER LA TÊTE/LES PIEDS. To bore; annoy. *Ça me casse les pieds d'aller à cette réunion.* "Going to that meeting is a real drag."

CASSER LE BAIL. See BAIL.

CASSER LES BONBONS/BURNES/COUILLES/ GLAOUÏS/LES CASSER. See BONBONS; BURNES.

CASSER SA PIPE. To die. *Avant de casser ma pipe, je voudrais me défouler un peu.* "Before kicking the bucket, I'd like to kick up my heels a bit."

CASSER SON ŒUF. To have a miscarriage. *Elle a cassé son œuf la première fois mais s'est rattrapée en faisant un doublé.* "She had a miscarriage the first time but made up for it by giving birth to twins."

(NE PAS) CASSER DES BRIQUES/NE RIEN CASSER.
To be of little or no interest (lit. "to not break any bricks; to break nothing"). *Ça ne casse pas des briques.* "That's nothing to write home about." *Ton bouquin ne casse rien.* "Your book's hardly earthshaking."

(SE) CASSER LA FIGURE/GUEULE. To fail (lit. "to break one's face"). *Son entreprise est sur le point de se casser la gueule.* "His business is about to go bust."

(SE) CASSER LA TÊTE/NÉNETTE. To rack one's brains. *Je me suis cassé la nénette pour trouver la réponse.* "I racked my brains to find the answer."

(SE) CASSER LE CUL/FION/LES COUILLES. To work one's ass off; bust one's buns/balls. *Il s'est cassé le cul pour élever ses gosses.* "He busted his buns to raise his kids."

CASSEUR, *m.* Burglar. *La bande de casseurs a été enfin agrafée.* "The gang of second-story men was finally nabbed."

(SE) CASSER LE NEZ. To get no answer at the door or on the phone (lit. "to break one's nose"). *On s'est cassé le nez au Musée d'Orsay le jour de fermeture.* "We got no answer at the Orsay Museum on the day it was closed."

CASSE-TÊTE, *m.* Difficult. *Ce problème, c'est un vrai casse-tête.* "That problem's a real headache."

CASTAPIANE, *f.* Gonorrhea. *(Il) y a des castapianes qui résistent aux antibios.* "Antibiotics don't cure all kinds of clap."

CATHO = CATHOLIQUE.

CATHOLE, *m., f., pej.* Very devout Catholic. *Notre grand-tante était une cathole folle.* "Our grand-aunt was a religious nut."

CATHOLIQUE. Catholic. **Pas très catholique,** *idiom.* Not on the up-and-up; not "kosher." *Qch. de pas très catholique se passe là.* "S.t. fishy's going on there."

CATIN, *f.* Prostitute. *Il était mordu de cette catin.* "He was nuts about that slut."

CAVALE, *f.* Escape (lit. "mare"). **Être en cavale,** *idiom.* To be a fugitive. *Son fils est en cavale; on ne sait où.* "Her son is on the run; no one knows where he is."

CAVE, *f.* Cellar. See DESCENTE À LA CAVE.

CEINTURE, *f.* Belt. **Faire ceinture; se serrer la ceinture,** *idioms.* To do without. *On a fait longtemps ceinture et maintenant on en profite.* "We tightened our belt for some time and now we're reaping the benefits."

(À) CENT SOUS DE L'HEURE. See (S')EMMERDER; (SE) RASER.

CERF, *m.* Stag. **Bander comme un cerf.** To have a very firm erection. *Ce con croit que la corne de rhinocéros le fera bander comme un cerf.* "That idiot thinks that rhino horn is going to make him get it up bone hard."

CERVELLE, *f.* Brain. See (SE) CREUSER.

CÉZIG(UE) = **SÉZIG(UE).**

CHACUN, -E SON TRUC. Whatever turns you on.

CHAGATTE, *f., javanais** of **chatte.** Pussy. *Sa petite chagatte est bien étroite.* "She's got a nice tight pussy."

CHAILLE, *f.* Tooth. *À vingt piges il n'avait déjà plus de chailles.* "At twenty he was already toothless."

CHAISE, *f.* Chair. **Avoir le cul entre deux chaises,** *idiom.* See CUL…CHAISES.

CHALEUR, *f.* Heat. **Être en chaleur,** *idiom.* To be sexually aroused. *Vas-y; elle est en chaleur.* "Go to it; she's hot!"

CHAMBARD, *m.* Commotion. *Quel chambard chez les voisins.* "What a racket at the neighbors'!"

CHAMBARDEMENT, *m.* Upheaval. *On s'attend à un sacré chambardement après les elections.* "A major shake-up is expected after the elections."

CHAMBRE DE CAMBRONNE, *f., euph.* Toilet. *Au château hôtel on appelait les chiottes "la chambre de Cambronne".* "In the chateau hotel they called the can 'Cambronne's room.'" See CAMBRONNE.

* See explanation of **javanais,** page 189.

CHAMP/CHAMPE, *m.* Champagne. *J'ai mis le champe au frais.* "I've put the bubbly on ice."

CHAMPIGNON, *m.* Accelerator (lit. "mushroom"). **Appuyer sur le champignon.** To keep one's foot on the accelerator. *Tu nous tueras tous si tu continues d'appuyer sur le champignon.* "If you keep speeding like this, you'll kill us all."

CHANGER D'AIR. To hit the road. *Je n'avais qu'une hâte, changer d'air.* "All I wanted was to get out of there."

CHAPEAU, *m.* Head (lit. "hat"). See (EN) BAVER DES RONDS DE CHAPEAU; PETIT CHAPEAU; TRAVAILLER DU CHAPEAU.

CHAPEAU DE ROUE, *m.* Hubcap. **Démarrer/partir sur les chapeaux de roues,** *idiom.* To leave at top speed. *L'alarme a sonné et les casseurs sont partis sur les chapeaux de roues.* "The alarm sounded and the burglars made tracks."

CHARCLO, *m.,* backslang of **clochard** ("vagrant"; "bum"). *Ce quartier grouille de charclos.* "This district is full of homeless people."

CHARCUTIER, *m.* Bad surgeon (lit. "pork butcher"; "delicatessen dealer"). *Quel charcutier as-tu vu pour cette jambe cassée?* "Who was the sawbones you went to for that broken leg?"

CHARIVARI, *m.* Uproar; noise. *J'ai toujours du charivari dans la boudine.* "My tummy's still upset/acting up."

CHAROGNE, *f.* Bitch; SOB (lit. "carrion"). *Tu fréquentes toujours cette charogne?* "You're still seeing that swine/sow?"

CHARRIDA, *m.* Crook; con man. *C'était un charrida charmeur et elle lui a fait confiance, hélas.* "He was a winsome con artist and she trusted him, unfortunately."

CHARRIER. To make fun of. *Cesse de me charrier.* "Quit putting me on."

CHARRIER (DANS LES BÉGONIAS). To exaggerate. *Assez de gasconnades—faut pas charrier!* "Enough of your tall stories—you don't have to overdo it."

CHARRIEUR = CHARRIDA.

CHASSE. Slightly drunk. *Un verre suffit pour que je sois chasse.* "One glass is enough to make me tipsy."

CHASSELAS, *m.* Type of grape used for making white wine. **Avoir un coup de chasselas; être de chasselas,** *idioms.* To be drunk. *Il a une sacrée descente pour le Fendant mais prétend qu'il n'a jamais un coup de chasselas.* "He really tanks up on Fendant (Swiss white wine) but says he's never drunk."

CHÂSSIS, *m.* Attractive female body (lit. "chassis"). *Avec ce beau châssis elle ira loin.* "With her classy chassis she'll go far."

CHAT, *m.* = **CHATTE.**

CHÂTAIGNE, *m.* Punch; electric shock (lit. "chestnut"). *J'ai pris une châtaigne avec ce foutu fer à repasser.* "That damned iron gave me a jolt."

CHÂTEAU-LA-POMPE/CHÂTEAU LAPOMPE, *m.* Drinking water (not necessarily pumped from a well). *Après sa crise de foie il ne boit que du Château Lapompe.* "After problems with his liver he just drinks nature's champagne."

CHATTE, *f.* Pussy (lit. "female cat"). *Ma chatte n'a jamais besoin de lubrifiant.* "My pussy never needs a lubricant."

CHAUD, -E. Enthusiastic (lit. "hot"). *Je ne suis pas chaud pour ton project.* "I'm not really sold on your project." See NI CHAUD NI FROID; QUARTIER CHAUD.

CHAUD-CHAUD/CHAUDE-CHAUDE = CHAUD, -E.

CHAUD!/CHAUD DEVANT! "Watch out! Coming through!" (as announced by waiters carrying dishes).

CHAUD LAPIN, *m.* Hot number. *Elles étaient trois à se partager ce chaud lapin.* "The three of them shared that hot stud."

CHAUDE-LANCE = CHAUDE PISSE.

CHAUDE LAPINE, *f.* Hot number. *J'ai goûté à sa lamdé;*

quelle chaude lapine! "I got a taste of his woman; what a horny broad!"

CHAUDE-PISSE/CHAUDE-PINCE, *f.* Gonorrhea. *Il a couché à droite et à gauche sans capote et a attrapé la chaude-pisse.* "He slept around without rubbers and got the clap."

CHAUFFER. To heat. See ÇA VA CHAUFFER.

CHAUSSETTE, *m.* Sock. See JUS…CHAUSSETTE; LAISSER…CHAUSSETTE; RETOURNER…CHAUSSETTE.

CHAUVE À COL ROULÉ = PETIT CHAUVE À COL ROULÉ.

CHÉBRAN, *m.* backslang of **branché.** Hip individual. *Les chébrans ont largué cette boîte.* "The trendy people have deserted that spot."

CHEMIN, *m.* Path. **Aller/(pour)suivre son petit bonhomme de chemin.** To advance slowly but surely, in one's own way. *Il faut que je poursuive mon petit bonhomme de chemin sans que tu me perturbes.* "I've got to keep on going without you upsetting me."

CHÈQUE EN BOIS, *m.* Rubber (lit. "wooden") check. *Après une foultitude de chèques en bois il a été interdit de chéquier.* "After bouncing many checks he wasn't allowed to write any more."

CHERCHER. To look for. See ÇA VA CHERCHER.

CHERCHER BASTON. To look for; pick a fight. *Calme-toi; cherche pas toujours baston.* "Calm down; don't be so pugnacious."

CHERCHER DES CROSSES À QN./CHERCHER QN. To pick a fight. *Si tu me cherches des crosses, fais gaffe!* "If you're looking for a fight with me, watch out!"

CHERCHER L'HÉMATOME. To look for a fight (lit. "bruise"). *Tu cherches l'hématome?* "You lookin' for a fat lip?"

CHERCHER LA PETITE BÊTE. To split hairs. *Ne cherche pas la petite bête.* "Quit nitpicking."

CHÉROT. Expensive. *Tout est chérot chez cet antiquaire.* "Everything's pricey at that antique dealer's."

CHETRON, *m.,* backslang of **tronche.**

CHEVALIER DE LA ROSETTE. See ROSETTE **2.**

CHEVEU, *m.* **1.** Hair. See COMME...SOUPE. **2.** Problem. *Il y a un cheveu.* "There's a hitch/snag!"

CHEVILLE, *f.* Ankle. **Avoir les chevilles qui enflent,** *idiom.* To be swell-headed. *Depuis qu'il a hérité il a les chevilles qui enflent.* "After coming into that inheritance he's become too big for his britches."

(EN) CHEVILLE. In cahoots with. *Le maire s'est mis en cheville avec la pègre.* "The mayor's in bed with the mob."

CHÈVRE, *m., pej.* Bitch; slut (lit. "nanny goat"). See DEVENIR CHÈVRE.

CHEVREUIL, *m., pej.* Informer (lit. "male deer"). *Le gangster cherche la planque du chevreuil.* "The gangster is looking for the informer's hideout."

CHIADER. 1. To study hard. *J'ai chiadé mon exam.* "I went all out studying for my exam." **2.** To do s.t. painstakingly. *Ça c'est chiadé!* "That's a thorough job!"

CHIALER. To bawl. *Son gosse n'arrête pas de chialer.* "Her kid never stops crying."

CHIANT, -E. Extremely dull; annoying; shitty. *Ne sois pas chiant!* "Don't be a pain in the ass!"

CHIARD, *m., pej.* Brat (orig. one still in diapers). *J'ai fait semblant d'aimer leurs chiards.* "I pretended to like their dirty little brats."

CHIASSE, *f.* **1.** Diarrhea. *La bouffe d'hier m'a foutu la chiasse.* "Yesterday's dinner gave me the runs." See COUPE-CHIASSE. **2.** Unpleasantness. See QUELLE CHIASSE!

CHICHA, *m.* backslang of **haschisch.** See H.

CHICON = CHICHA.

CHICOS. Chic. *Que t'es chicos aujourd'hui!* "My, how elegant you are today!"

CHICOS! Fantastic!

CHIÉ, -E. 1. Remarkable; wonderful. *Quel chié prof tu as!* "What an awesome professor you've got." **2.** Rotten. *C'est chié, leur musique.* "Their music's awful." **3.** Brazen. *Elle est chiée de réclamer sans cesse du fric.* "She's got some nerve, constantly asking for money."

CHIÉ!/CHIÉ DE MERDE! Holy shit!

CHIÉE, *m.* Large amount. *Une chiée de courrier arrive chaque jour.* "Everyday a shit pile of mail arrives."

CHIEN, -NE. Mean, rotten. *Qu'est-ce qu'il a été chien avec elle!* "He treated her like a dog!"

CHIEN, *m.* Dog. **Avoir du chien,** *idiom.* To have charm; allure. *Cette fille n'est pas laide; elle a du chien.* "That girl's no dog; she has a certain fascinating s.t." See (SE) DONNER…; GARDER…CHIEN; MAL DE CHIEN; PEAU DE CHIEN.

CHIENLIT, *f.* Disorder (lit. "shit in the bed"). *"La réforme, oui; la chienlit, non" a dit de Gaulle. "La chienlit, c'est lui" scandaient les étudiants.* "'Reform yes, chaos no,' said de Gaulle." "'He's the stinking mess,' chanted the students."

CHIENNE, *f.* Female dog; bitch. **Quelle chienne de vie!** Life's a bitch; a kick in the ass!

CHIER. 1. To defecate. *Son foutu animal a chié partout!* "Her damned animal shit all over the place!" See ÇA VA CHIER; ENVOYER CHIER; FAUT…CHIE; GUEULE À CHIER…; NUL À CHIER; TRONCHE À CHIER…. **2. Se faire chier,** *idiom.* To be bored to death. *On s'est fait chier ici depuis trop longtemps. Foutons le camp!* "We've been bored to death here for too long. Let's get the hell out!" To take a great deal of trouble. *On s'est fait chier pour installer la nouvelle maison.* "We busted our buns settling into the new house." **3. Ne pas se faire chier,** *idiom.* To not give a damn; be inconsiderate. *Il ne s'est pas fait chier, celui-là en passant devant tout le monde.* "That guy didn't think twice about pushing in ahead of everybody else."

CHIER DANS LES BOTTES DE QN./FAIRE CHIER QN. To bug s.o. (lit. "to shit in s.o.'s boots"; "make s.o. shit"). *Quand aura-t-il fini de nous faire chier?* "When is he gonna stop pissing us off?"

CHIER DANS SA CULOTTE/SON FROC = FAIRE DANS...CULOTTE.

(EN) CHIER. To go through hell. *Ils en ont chié lors de l'inondation.* "They went through hell during the flood."

CHIERIE, *f.* Unpleasant situation. *Cette grève est une sacrée chierie.* "This strike's a real pain in the ass." See QUELLE CHIERIE!

CHIEUR, -EUSE, *m., f., adj.* and *n.* Lousy person (lit. "shitter"). *Ta gonzesse est une vraie chieuse.* "Your broad's a real stinker."

CHIEUR D'ENCRE. Hack journalist (lit. "ink shitter"). *Ce chieur d'encre a descendu en flammes la diva.* "That ink pisser did a hack job on the diva."

CHIFFE MOLLE, *f.* Wimp (lit. "limp rag"). *Quelle chiffe molle tu fais!* "You really come on like a dishrag."

CHINE, *f.* Flea market. *Il a vendu tout son Saint-Frusquin à la Chine.* "He sold all his stuff at the flea market."

CHINER. 1. To deal in secondhand bric-à-brac. *Chiner, c'était son premier métier.* "Antique dealing was his first occupation." **2.** To kid s.o. *Tu ne sais que chiner les autres.* "All you can do is make fun of others."

CHINER AUX PUCES. To go antiquing. *Si on allait chiner aus Puces de Clignancourt?* "How about going antique hunting at the Clignancourt flea market?"

CHINETOC/CHINETOQUE, *pej., adj.* and *n.* Chinese/Asian. *Nous sommes partis manger chez les Chinetocs.* "We went out to eat Chinese food."

CHINEUR, -EUSE, *m., f.* **1.** Antique dealer. *Il est chineur de profession.* "He's in the antiques trade." **2.** Practical joker; leg puller. *N'essaie pas de chiner un chineur.* "Don't try to kid a kidder."

CHINOIS, *m.* **1.** Chinese man. See JAMBE DU CHINOIS. **2.** Penis. See PATINER LE CHINOIS; POLIR LE CHINOIS.

CHIOTTES, *f., pl.* Toilet. *Où sont les chiottes?* "Where's the head?" See BALAI À CHIOTTES.

CHIPER. To swipe. *Qui m'a chipé mes lunettes de soleil?* "Who pinched my sunglasses."

CHIPOLATA, *m.* Penis (lit. "sausage"). *La tantouse avait très faim de chipolata.* "The queen was hungry for meat."

CHIQUE, *f.* Chewing tobacco. See COUPER LA CHIQUE.

CHIQUÉ, *m.* Pretentiousness. *Ne fais pas de chiqué avec moi.* "Don't try to put on airs with me."

(AU) CHIQUÉ. As a bluff. *Il y va toujours au chiqué.* "He always bluffs it out."

(DU) CHIQUÉ. S.t. phony. *Son arrêt de travail pour maladie, c'était du chiqué.* "His work-related disability was a put-up job."

CHLAFFE = SCHLAFFE.

CHLOF = SCHLOF.

CHNOQUE = SCHNOQUE.

CHNOUFFE = SCHNOUFFE.

CHNOUFFER = SCHNOUFFER.

CHOCHOTTE, *f.* Affected; fussy person. *Ne fais pas ta chochotte.* "Quit your silly fussing."

CHOCOLAT, *m.* Chocolate. **Faire chocolat,** *idiom.* To deceive. *Il a réussi à me faire chocolat.* "He succeeded in putting one over on me." **Être chocolat,** *idiom.* To feel frustrated. *J'ai été chocolat quand il est parti au concert avec une autre.* "I felt let down when he went to the concert with s.o. else."

CHOCOTTES, *f., pl.* Teeth. *Cesse de grincer des chocottes.* "Stop gnashing your teeth." **Avoir les chocottes,** *idiom.* To be afraid. *J'ai les chocottes quand il roule à donf.* "My teeth chatter with fear when he drives at top speed."

CHOILLE = CHOUÏA.

CHÔMDU = CHÔMEDU.

CHÔME, *f.,* from **chômage.** *J'en ai ralbol d'être à la chôme.* "I'm sick and tired of being unemployed."

CHÔMEDU, *m.* **1.** Unemployed person. *Les chômedus font une manif.* "The unemployed are demonstrating." **2.** Unemployment. *Il n'est plus au chômedu.* "He's no longer on unemployment."

CHOPER. To catch. *J'ai chopé la grippe cet hiver.* "I got the flu this winter."

CHOPINE, *f.* **1.** Bottle or glass of wine. *Il téte trop la chopine.* "He's too fond of the bottle." **2.** Large penis. *Cuit qu'il était, sa chopine m'a fait une belle jambe.* "Drunk as he was, his big dick was of no use to me."

CHOPOTTE = CHOPINE.

CHOQUOTTES = CHOCOTTES.

CHOSE, *f.* Thing. **Être porté sur la chose.** To be much interested in sex. *Mon grand-dab était très porté sur la chose.* "My granddad was a horny old devil."

CHOU, *m.* **1.** Cabbage. **Dans les choux.** Too late; failed. *C'est dans les choux, hélas, mon petit chou.* "I'm afraid it's gone down the drain, my sweet." See BÊTE…CHOU; FEUILLE DE CHOU; MON…CHOU. **2.** Head. **En avoir dans le chou,** *idiom.* To be smart. *Son mec en a dans le chou; il ira loin.* "Her guy's got a lot upstairs; he'll go far." See RENTRER…CHOU; FEUILLE…CHOU; TRAVAILLER DU CHOU.

CHOUAYE = CHOUÏA.

CHOUAGA = CHOUCARD, -E.

CHOUARD, -E = CHOUCARD, -E.

CHOUCARD, -E. Wonderful (from Romany for "beautiful"). *Ils ont fait un petit mariage choucard.* "They threw a terrific wedding feast."

CHOUCROUTE, *f.* **1.** Sauerkraut. See PÉDALER. **2.** Curly hair. *Tu as vu la choucroute qu'elle se paye, la nana?* "Have you seen that chick's beehive hairdo?" **3.** Hard drug. *C'est un accro de la choucroute.* "He's hooked on the hard stuff."

CHOUETTE, *adj.* Nice. *Elle a dégoté un chouette de boulot.* "She's found a pleasant job."

CHOUETTE, *f.* Nasty woman (lit. "owl"). *Quelle vieille chouette, ta mère.* "Your mother's a nasty old shrew."

CHOUETTE, *m.* Anus. See FILER...CHOUETTE; PRENDRE...CHOUETTE.

CHOUETTE!/CHOUETTE ALORS! That's terrific!

CHOUETTES, *m., pl.* Genuine ID. *Ce jeune sans chouettes vient d'être pincé.* "That minor with a fake ID just got pinched."

CHOUÏA, *m.* from Ar. Tiny bit. *Je reprendrais bien un chouïa du gâteau.* "I'd love just another smidgin of the cake."

CHOUQUETTE, *f.* Effeminate homosexual (lit. "sugared cream puff"). *Ne fais pas la chouquette.* "Don't be such a queen."

CHOURAVER. To steal. *C'est pas la première bagnole qu'il a chouravé.* "That's not the first car he's stolen."

CHOURAVEUR, *m.* Thief. *Elle sait qu'il est chouraveur, mais elle l'aime quand même.* "She knows he's a thief but loves him anyway."

CHPROUM = SCHPROUM.

CHTIBE = SCHTIBE.

CHTILIBEN = SCHTILIBEN.

CHTOUILLE, *f.* Gonorrhea. *Il avait la trouille que les antibios ne guérissent pas sa chtouille.* "He was afraid the antibiotics wouldn't cure his clap."

CHTUC = SCHTUC.

CIAO = TCHAO.

CIBICHE, *f.* Cigarette. *Ses cibiches puent moins que ses cigares.* "His cigarettes don't stink as much as his stogies."

CIBOULOT, *m.* Head. *Tu n'as rien dans le ciboulot pour* *dire une telle connerie.* "You haven't got a brain in your head if you can say a stupid thing like that." See (SE) CREUSER.

CIFELLE, *f.* Thread. *Ça tient avec des bouts de cifelle.* "That's hanging together by a thread."

CIFLARD = SAUCIFLARD.

CIGARE, *m.* **1.** Head. *Il n'a rien dans le cigare.* "He's empty-headed." See COUPE-CIGARE **1. 2.** Penis. **Couper le cigare.** To circumcise (lit. "to cut the cigar"). *Le Zoroastrien Zubin avait peur de se faire couper le cigare.* "Zoroastrian Zubin was afraid to be circumcised." **3.** Turd. *Il a pris le bidet pour un ouatère et a posé un cigare dedans.* "He took the bidet for a toilet and crapped in it." See COUPE-CIGARE **2.**

CIGARE À MOUSTACHES, *m.* Penis. *Freud disait: "Nous savons tous que le cigare est symbole du cigare à moustaches, mais il restera toujours un cigare."* Freud said: "We all know the cigar's a phallic symbol, but it'll always be a cigar too."

CINÉ, *abbr.* of **cinéma.** Movies; movie theater. *Samedi soir on va au ciné.* "Saturday night we go to the flicks."

CINOCHE = CINÉ.

CINOCHIER, -ÈRE, *m., f.* Movie enthusiast. *C'est une cinochière de première.* "She's an all-out movie buff."

CINOQUE = SINOQUE.

CINTRÉ, -E. Crazy (lit. "curved"). *Ne crois pas que je sois cintrée; je ne déconne pas.* "Don't think I'm bananas; I'm not kidding."

CIRAGE, *m.* Polishing. **Être dans le cirage; être en plein cirage,** *idioms.* To be in a fog (due to fatigue, alcohol, and so on). *Il ne peut pas te répondre; il est dans le cirage.* "He can't answer you; he's groggy."

CIRER. To polish. **N'en avoir rien à cirer,** *idiom.* To not care. *Ton voyou de fils, je n'en ai rien à cirer.* "Your hoodlum son is no concern of mine."

CIRER LES BOTTES/POMPES À QN. To be sycophantic (lit. "to shine s.o.'s boots or shoes"). *Pour avoir le poste, il cire les bottes du patron.* "He's sucking up to the boss to get the job."

CIRER TOUJOURS LE MÊME BOUTON. To put on the same broken record. *Il ne se lasse pas de cirer toujours le même bouton.* "He never tires of harping on the same string."

CIRQUE, *m.* **1.** Hubub; confusion (lit. "circus"). *Avec la grève, la circulation, quel cirque!* "What with the strike, the traffic's some hassle." See EMMENER…CIRQUE; MENER…CIRQUE. **2.** Carrying on. *Arrête ton cirque.* "Cool it! Stop your song and dance!"

CISAILLER. 1. To fleece (lit. "to shear") *Il s'est fait cisailler.* "He got taken to the cleaners." **2.** To be astounded. *La nouvelle de leur mort m'a cisaillé.* "The news of their death hit me where I live."

CITRON, *m.* Head (lit. "lemon"). See (SE) CREUSER.

CLAMECER = CLAMSER.

CLAMSER. To die. *Avant de clamser, le milliardaire veut se faire cloner.* "Before kicking the bucket, the billionaire wants to have h.s. cloned."

CLANDÉ, *abbr.* of **clandestin. 1.** Illegal brothel; gambling den. *Il allait régulièrement dans un clandé.* "He was a regular patron of an illegal cathouse." **2.** Prostitute in an illegal brothel. *L'été j'arpente; l'hiver je suis clandé.* "I walk the streets in the summer; in the winter I work indoors."

CLAOUIS = GLAOUIS.

CLAPET, *m.* Mouth (lit. "valve"). See FERMER SON CLAPET.

CLAPSER = CLAMSER.

CLAQUE, *f.* **1.** Whack. **En avoir sa claque,** *idiom.* To be fed up. *J'en ai ma claque de travailler la nuit.* "I've had it up to here with working nights." See ALLONGER; TÊTE À CLAQUES. **2.** Severe loss. See PRENDRE UNE CLAQUE.

CLAQUE, *m.* Whorehouse. See TÊTE À CLAQUE (*m.*).

CLAQUE-MERDE, *m.* Mouth. See FERMER SON CLAQUE-MERDE.

CLAQUER. 1. To throw money around (lit. "to slam"). *Il claque tout son fric en misant sur les chevaux.* "He blows all his money on the horses." **2.** To exhaust. *Son boulot l'a claquée totalement.* "Her job's really taken it out of her." **3.** To expire. *Il va en claquer de boire comme un trou.* "It'll be the death of him if he keeps on drinking like that."

CLAQUER DANS LES DOIGTS/MAINS/PATTES. To fail; die; go bust. *Ma bagnole m'a claqué dans les mains.* "My car conked out on me."

CLAQUER DU BEC. To be hungry. *Ils ont claqué du bec pendant leur enfance.* "They often went hungry during their childhood."

CLARINETTE, *f.* Penis. See JOUER...CLARINETTE BAVEUSE.

CLASS, *adj.* and *adv.* Finished. *C'est class!* "That's enough, it's all over." **En avoir class de,** *idiom.* To be sick and tired of. *Il en a class de sa nana.* "He's sick and tired of his woman."

CLASSE, *f.* Class. **Avoir (de) la classe; être la classe,** *idioms.* To be classy/wonderful. *C'est la classe!* "That's top-notch."

CLASSE, *adj.* Classy; great. *C'est classe ton bouquin.* "Your book's terrific."

CLEB/CLEBS = CLÉBARD.

CLÉBARD, *m.,* sometimes *pej.* Hound. *On ne le voit jamais sans son clébard.* "You never see him without his mutt."

CLÉOPATRE, *proper n.* Cleopatra. *Elle croit avoir le nez de Cléopâtre.* "She thinks she's hot stuff." **Faire Cléopâtre.** To fellate. *Il crache vite son venin quand je lui fais Cléopâtre.* "He comes fast when I suck him off."

CLEPO/CLEUPO, backslang forms of **clope.**

CLICLI, *m.* Clitoris. *Viens me faire guili-guili au clicli.* "Come tickle my clit."

CLITO, *m., abbr.* of clitoris. **Clitoris.** *Mon clito manifestait, mais il s'en foutait.* "My clit was very excited, but he didn't care."

CLOCHE, *adj.* Stupid; ridiculous. *Ce que tu peux être cloche!* "Sometimes you're really thick."

CLOCHE, *f.* **1.** Bell. See SONNER. **2.** Stupid person. *Son père, quelle cloche!* "Her father's some dingbat!" **3.** Stomach. See (SE) TAPER LA CLOCHE; (SE) TASSER LA CLOCHE.

CLOCHE, *f.,* from **clochard** (vagrant; bum). Vagrancy. *Il vit à la cloche.* "He's a hobo."

CLODO, from **clochard.** Bum. *La nuit le métro est plein de clodos.* "The subway's full of bums at night."

CLOPE, *f., m.* Cigarette. *File-moi une clope.* "Give me a cigarette."

CLOPE, *m.* Cigarette butt. *Ses mouflets suçaient les clopes perdus dans le sable.* "Her brats sucked on the cigarette butts left in the sand." See DES CLOPES.

CLOPINETTES. See DES CLOPINETTES/DES CLOPINETTES!

CLOPORTE, *f., m.,* play on **clôt porte** (one who locks up). Concierge. *Le cloporte m'apporte chaque jour mon courrier.* "The super brings me my mail every day."

CLOPORTE, *m.* Creep (lit. "woodlouse"). *Je ne peux pas le voir, ce cloporte.* "I can't stand the sight of that creep."

CLOQUE, *f.* Blister. See EN CLOQUE.

CLOU, *m.* Small amount (lit. "nail"). **Ne pas valoir un clou,** *idiom.* To be worthless. *Ta bagnole ne vaut pas un clou.* "Your car's worthless." See DES CLOUX.

CLOUER LE BEC À QN. To shut s.o. up. *Je lui ai cloué le bec en lui disant la vérité.* "I shut him up by telling him the truth."

COALTAR = COLTAR.

COCHE, *m.* Stagecoach. See LOUPER LE COCHE.

COCHON, *m.* Pig. **Copains comme cochons,** *idiom.* Fast friends. *Ils étaient copains comme cochons avant de ren-*

contrer Mimi. "They were great buddies before meeting Mimi." See TÊTE DE COCHON.

COCO, *m., f.* Communist. *C'est un ancien coco.* "He's a former Commie."

COCOTIER, *m.* Coconut palm tree. See DÉCROCHER LE COCOTIER/GRIMPER AU COCOTIER.

COCOTTE, *f.* **1.** Prostitute, *dated* (lit. "hen"). *Elle écrit un mémoire sur cocottes et courtisanes de la Belle Époque.* "She's writing a thesis on tarts and high-class whores of the Belle Époque." **2.** Pressure cooker. See COCOTTE-MINUTE®.

COCOTTE-MINUTE®, *f.* Prostitute who turns many tricks quickly (lit. "pressure cooker"). *Les cocottes-minute encaissaient un fric fou.* "The fast-working hookers made big bucks."

COGNOTER. To stink. *Les chiottes cognotent un max.* "The toilet stinks to high heaven."

COIN, *m.* Corner. See BOUCHER; PETIT COIN.

COINCER. To stink (lit. "to wedge"). See ÇA COINCE.

COINCER LA BULLE. To nap. *Il roule la nuit sans coincer la bulle.* "He drives at night without getting any sleep."

COING, *m.* Quince. **Beurré/bourré comme un coing.** Dead drunk. *Il est rentré beurré comme un coing.* "He came home soused to the gills." See GELÉE DE COING.

COLBAC/COLBAK/COLBAQUE = COLBACK.

COLBACK, *m.* **1.** Collar. *Il a pris son fils par le colback.* "He grabbed his son by the collar." **2.** Throat. *Je me prendrais bien un petit coup de rouge dans le colbac.* "A bit of red wine would sure hit the spot." **3.** Back. *J'en ai trop sur le colback.* "I've got too much on my plate."

COLIBRI, *m.* Disloyal friend (lit. "hummingbird"). *Ne lui fais pas confiance; c'est un colibri.* "Don't trust him; he's a double-crosser."

COLIS, *m.* **1.** Good-looking girl (lit. "package"). *Vise un* *peu ce beau colis.* "Take a look at that nice chick." **2.** Fart. See LÂCHER UN COLIS.

COLLABO, *m., pej., abbr.* of **collaborateur.** *Ce collabo prétend avoir été résistant.* "That collaborator claims to have been a member of the Resistance in World War II."

COLLE, *f.* Glue. **Être à la colle** = VIVRE À LA COLLE.

COLLER. 1. To glue. See ÇA COLLE, ANATOLE? **2.** To give or put forcefully. See AVOINE; BAFFE; COLLER UN GOSSE.

COLLER AU CUL/TRAIN DE QN. To harass by tagging onto s.o. *J'en ai marre de ce mec qui ne cesse de me coller au cul.* "I'm tired of that guy who follows me around everywhere."

COLLER AUX FESSES = COLLER AU CUL.

COLLER UN GOSSE À UNE FEMME. To get a woman pregnant. *Il lui a collé un gosse mais il dit n'en avoir rien à cirer.* "He got her pregnant but he says it's none of his business."

(SE) COLLER. To shack up with. *Elle l'aime mais ne veut pas encore se coller.* "She loves him but doesn't want to move in with him yet."

(S'EN) COLLER. To not give a damn. *Tes problèmes, je m'en colle!* "What do I care about your problems?"

COLLETAR = COLTAR.

COLLINE, *f.* Hill. See RATIBOISER.

COLO, *f.* from **colonie de vacances.** *Elle a envoyé ses gosses en colo.* "She sent her kids off to summer camp."

COLONNE, *f.* Penis (lit. "column"). See ASTIQUER LA COLONNE.

COL ROULÉ. See ANDOUILLE...ROULÉ; CHAUVE...ROULÉ; PETIT...ROULÉ.

COLTAR, *m.* Coal tar. **Être dans le coltar; être en plein coltar,** *idioms.* To be in a daze. *Après leur accident de voiture ils étaient en plein coltar.* "After their car accident they were in a stupor."

(SE) COLTINER. 1. To endure. *Non seulement je dois me*

coltiner un boulot chiant mais aussi le patron et sa sale caboche. "Not only do I have to put up with that rotten job, I've also got to endure the boss and his lousy temper." **2.** To fight. *Les deux frères se sont coltinés à cause d'une nana.* "The two brothers came to blows over a broad."

COMAC/COMAQUE = COMACO.

COMACO. Enormous. *Elle était comaco en attendant ses triplets.* "She was really humongous when expecting her triplets."

COMACOS = COMACO.

COMINGUE = COMMIS.

COMME = COMMISS.

COMMENCER À RENDRE LA MONNAIE. To show signs of age (said of prostitutes who, in better days, didn't have to make change for large bills). *Je suis bien loin de commencer à rendre la monnaie.* "I'm still a long way from having to cut my rates."

COMME PAS DEUX. Like nobody else. *Il a joué aujourd'hui aux échecs comme pas deux.* "Nobody could have played chess today the way he did."

COMME SES PIEDS. See CON…PIEDS.

COMME UN CHEVEU SUR LA SOUPE. At an inopportune time (lit. "like a hair on the soup"). *Cette nouvelle arrive comme un cheveu sur la soupe.* "That news has come at an awkward moment."

COMME UN PIED. Very poorly. *Il chante, danse, et joue comme un pied, mais ça lui fait plaisir.* "His singing, dancing, and playing are lousy, but he enjoys h.s."

COMME UNE FLEUR. 1. Easily. *J'ai fini le boulot comme une fleur.* "I finished the job with no sweat." **2.** Unexpectedly. *Comme une fleur elle m'a annoncé qu'elle me quittait.* "Just like that, she announced she was leaving me."

COMMISS, *f.,* short for **commission.** Accomplice's share of the loot; percentage. *Il travaille à la commiss.* "He works on a commission basis."

COMMISSIONS, *f., pl.* Errands. See FAIRE SES COMMISSIONS.

COMPAS, *m., pl.* Legs (from the "legs" of a compass). See JOUER DES COMPAS.

COMPÈTE, from **compétition.** Sports competition. *Elle s'entraîne pour la compète.* "She's in training for the meet."

COMPRENETTE, *f.* Intelligence. *T'as pas la comprenette facile.* "You're slow on the uptake."

COMPRENOIRE = COMPRENETTE.

COMPTER POUR DU BEURRE. See BEURRE 1.

CON, *m.* **1.** External female genitalia. *Elle ferait bien de foutre plus souvent son con sur le bidet.* "She should wash her snatch more often." **2.** Jerk. *Ne fais pas le con!* "Don't be such an asshole." See CONNE; DUCON; (SE) RETROUVER...CON.

CON, -NE. Idiotic. *Qu'est-ce qu'il (elle) est con (conne)!* "He's (she's) really foolish." (Note: The *m.* **con** is often used for women also, as in *Qu'est qu'elle est con!*) **Avoir l'air con,** *idiom,* see AIR. See also CON À...; CON COMME....

CON À BOUFFER DE LA BITE/COMME UNE BITE, stronger equivalents of **con comme un balai/panier; con comme ses pieds/la lune.** Absolutely stupid. *Ton pote est con comme une bite.* "Your chum is a dumb dickhead. He doesn't know his ass from his elbow."

CONARD, -E = CONNARD, -E.

CON COMME UN BALAI/PANIER; CON COMME SES PIEDS/LA LUNE. Very stupid (lit. "dumb as a broom or basket; dumb as his feet or the moon"). *Pas la peine de lui parler; il est con comme un balai.* "No point in talking to him; he's a dumb jerk."

(À LA) CON. Worthless; ridiculous. *C'était un film à la con.* "The movie was trash."

CONASSE = CONNASSE.

CONCEPIGE, *m., f.* Building superintendent. *Mon mari était le concepige; c'est moi maintenant la concepige.* "My husband was the concierge; now I'm the concierge."

CONCETÉ, *f.* Idiocies. *Ne dis pas de concetés!* "Don't talk rot."

CONDÉ, *m.* **1.** Policeman. *Ce petit voyou est maintenant condé.* "That little hood's a cop now." **Avoir le condé,** *idiom.* To enjoy police protection for s.t. illicit in return for providing information. *La pègre se méfie de lui, car il a le condé.* "The mob doesn't trust him because he's in cahoots with the cops."

CONDUITE, *f.* Behavior. **S'acheter une conduite,** *idiom.* To turn over a new leaf. *Après la tôle il s'est acheté une conduite.* "After doing time he went straight."

CONDUITE DE GRENOBLE, *f.* Walking papers. *Peu s'en faudrait que je lui fasse la conduite de Grenoble.* "It won't take much more for me to give him the boot."

(EN) CONNAÎTRE UN BOUT. See BOUT.

CONNARD. *m.* Jackass; SOB. *Ce connard a embouti ma voiture.* "That dumb bastard smashed into my car."

CONNARDE = CONNASSE.

CONNASSE, *f.* **1.** Contemptible female. *Laisse tomber; c'est une connasse!* "Drop her; she's a dumb bitch." **2.** Cunt. See CON **1.**

CONNE, *f.* Foolish woman. *Quelle conne! Son mec la mène par le bout du nez.* "What a dumb broad; her guy walks all over her."

CONNEAU = CONNARD.

CONNEMENT. Stupidly. *Il a agi connement avec elle.* "He behaved like a real fool with her."

CONNERIE, *f.* Stupid action or speech. *Tout ce que tu dis ou fais, ce ne sont que des conneries.* "Everything you do and say is idiotic."

CONOMÈTRE, *m.* Stupidity gauge (hum. coinage, cf.

pifomètre; trouillomètre). Faire péter le conomètre, *idiom.* To break all records for idiocy. *Une histoire pareille, c'est à faire péter le conomètre.* "S.t. like that is the idiocy to end all idiocy."

CONSPIGE = CONCEPIGE.

CONSTIPÉ, -E. Constipated; strained. **Constipé du mor-lingue,** see MORLINGUE.

CONTREDANSE, *f.* Parking fine (lit. "quadrille"). *Partons d'ici pour éviter une contredanse.* "Let's get out of here before we get a ticket."

(SE) CONTREFICHE DE QCH. = SE CONTRE-FOUTRE DE QCH.

(SE) CONTREFOUTRE DE QCH., intensifies **se foutre de qch.** To not care at all. *Je me contrefous de ce que tu penses.* "I don't give a good goddamn what you think."

(S'EN) CONTREFOUTRE = (SE) CONTREFOUTRE DE QCH. *Tu vas où tu veux, je m'en contrefous.* "Go wherever you want, I couldn't care less."

COPAIN-COPAIN, *adj.* Buddy-buddy. *Luc a toujours été copain-copain avec Marc.* "Luke and Mark have always been great buddies."

COPAINS COMME COCHONS. Thick as thieves. See COCHON.

COQUELICOTS, *m., pl.* Menstrual period (lit. "poppies" [a red flower]). *Après son doublé, elle attend le retour de ses coquelicots.* "After giving birth to twins, she's waiting for her period to return."

CORMORAN, *m.* Undertaker (lit. "cormorant," a black bird). *Pas baisant, le type avec la gueule d'un cormoran.* "Not very appealing, that guy with his gravedigger face."

CORNARD, *m.* Cuckolded husband (see next entry). *Ce con de cornard ignore qu'elle le trompe avec tous.* "Her chump of a husband doesn't know she's putting horns on him."

CORNOUAILLES. Cornwall (in Brittany). **Aller en**

Cornouailles (play on **cornes** [horns], associated with husbands whose wives cheat on them). To be a cuckold. *Ça fait un moment que son mari va en Cornouailles.* "Her husband's been wearing horns for some time."

COSTARD, *m.* Man's suit. *Tu portes un chié de costard.* "That's a real snappy suit you're wearing."

COT(H)URNE/CO-T(H)URNE, *m.* Roommate. *Quel casse couilles, mon coturne!* "My roommate's a real ball buster." See THURNE.

COU, *m.* Neck. See CASSE-COU.

COUCHE, *f.* Layer. See TENIR.

COUCHER AVEC LA FEMME DE L'ADJUDANT. See ADJUDANT.

COUDE, *m.* Elbow. See HUILE DE COUDE; LÂCHER…COUDE; LEVER LE COUDE.

COUIC. See (N'Y) PIGER QUE COUIC.

COUILLE, *f.* **1.** Testicle. See COUILLES. **2.** Mistake. *J'ai fait une belle couille.* "I made a beaut of a mistake." **C'est de la couille (en barres, en bâtons).** Worthless. *Tout ce que tu as pris, c'est de la couille en barres.* "Everything you bought is a load of crap."

COUILLE MOLLE, *f.* Gutless person (lit. "flabby testicle"). *Je refuse de faire quoi que ce soit avec cette couille molle.* "I don't want to do anything at all with that wimp."

COUILLES, *f., pl.* Testicles. **Avoir des couilles (au cul); en avoir,** *idiom.* To be ballsy or gutsy. *Cette gonzesse a des couilles au cul.* "She's a real gutsy lady" (lit. "That broad's got balls on her ass"). **Se faire des couilles en or,** *idiom.* To make a lot of money. *Ils pensaient se faire des couilles en or.* "They thought they were going to make a bundle." See (SE) BRANLER 2; CASSE-COUILLES; CASSER LES COUILLES; (SE) CASSER LES COUILLES; DE MES DEUX; LÂCHER…COUILLES; MES COUILLES!; PARTIR EN COUILLE(S); RAS; TOMBER EN COUILLE(S).

COUILLER = COUILLONNER.

COUILLON, -NE, Really stupid. *Que tu es couillon!* "You're a real idiot." **Avoir l'air couillon,** see AIR.

COUILLON, *m.* Jerk. *Ne fais pas le couillon.* "Don't act like such an idiot."

COUILLONNADE, *f.* Nonsense. *Ça c'est une sacrée couillonnade!* "That's a whole bunch of baloney."

COUILLONNER. To deceive. *On s'est fait tous couillonné par le patron.* "All of us were conned by the boss."

COUILLONNERIE = COUILLONNADE.

COUINER. To whine. *Ne couine pas pour rien.* "Quit bawling for nothing."

COULER. To bring down (lit. "to sink"). *Il a coulé les économies de sa famille en jouant sur les chevaux.* "He went through his family's savings by betting on the ponies."

COULER UN BRONZE. To defecate (lit. "to cast a bronze statue"). See BRONZE.

(SE LA) COULER DOUCE. To take it easy; live a cushy life. *Lennie rêvait de se la couler douce.* "Lenny dreamed of living off the fat of the land."

COULEUVRE, *f.* Snake. **Avaler des couleuvres.** To face up to hostility (lit. "to swallow snakes"). *Dans mon métier il faut savoir avaler des couleuvres.* "In my profession, you've got to be able to take the heat."

COUP, *m.* **1.** Blow. See ALLONGER; BOURRER 2; ÉCRASER LE COUP; MARQUER LE COUP; TENIR LE COUP; TIRER UN COUP. **2.** Scheme; scam. **Faire un coup,** *idiom. Ils ont fait le coup ensemble.* "They pulled off the operation together." **3.** Drink. **Boire or prendre un coup,** *idiom.* To have a drink. *Allons boire un coup.* "Let's have a drink." **4.** Skill. **Avoir le coup,** *idiom.* To be competent. *Pour diriger son monde, il a le coup.* "He's got what it takes to get people to do what he wants." See TIRER UN COUP.

COUP À BOIRE, *m.* Drink. *Donne-lui un coup à boire.* "Give him a drink."

COUP DANS L'AILE. Tipsy condition. *Il a déjà un coup dans l'aile mais il réclame toujours à boire.* "He's already half-loaded but still wants more."

COUP DANS LE NEZ. Drunkenness. *Il a pris un coup dans le nez.* "He got loaded!"

COUP DE BALAI, *m.* Police raid. *Dans ce coup de balai, tous les toxicos des Halles ont été agrafés.* "All the Les Halles area junkies got nabbed during that raid."

COUP DE BARRE/POMPE. See POMPE 2.

COUP DE BOL/VEINE, *m.* Stroke of luck. *C'était un coup de bol de sortir vivant de cet accident.* "Surviving that accident was real luck."

COUP DE BOULE. See BOULE.

COUP DE FEU, *m.* Period of peak activity. *Impossible de se faire servir au resto; c'était le coup de feu.* "Impossible to get any service; the restaurant was packed."

COUP DE FIL/BIGO/BIGOPHONE, *m.* See BIGO.

COUP DE FILET = COUP DE BALAI.

COUP DE FOUDRE, *m.* Love at first sight (lit. "flash of lightning"). *Ce bracelet, c'était le coup de foudre.* "I saw that bracelet and just had to have it."

COUP DE FOURCHETTE, *m.* Big appetite. *Quel sacré coup de fourchette!* "What a gargantuan appetite!"

COUP DE FUSIL/BAMBOU/BARRE, *m.* Steep bill. *Je ne m'attendais pas à un tel coup de fusil dans ce resto.* "I didn't expect to get fleeced like that in that restaurant."

COUP DE GUEULE, *m.* See POUSSER...GUEULE.

COUP DE JARNAC, *m.* **1.** Unexpected, decisive blow (from a duel fought by Guy de Jarnac). *Ils m'ont filé le coup de Jarnac et c'était la fin des haricots.* "They caught me off guard, thrust home, and it was curtains." **2.** Stab in the back; low blow. *Bourré de cognac, il m'a fait un coup de Jarnac.* "Tanked up on cognac, he pulled a dirty trick on me."

COUP DE PIED DE VÉNUS, *m.* See VÉNUS.

COUP (DE PIED) EN VACHE = COUP DE JARNAC 2.

COUP DE QUEUE/SABRE/GUISOT, *m.* See FILER LE COUP DE GUISOT; SABRE.

COUP DE TÊTE, *m.* Impulse. *Je l'a acheté sur un coup de tête.* "I bought it on impulse."

COUP DE TRAFALGAR, *m.* Violent situation or behavior (from the site of a Fr. naval defeat in 1805). *Mai 1968, c'était le coup de Trafalgar.* "May 1968 was a powder keg."

COUP DE TROP, *m.* Drunkenness. *Il a bu un coup de trop.* "He's had one too many."

COUP DE VIEUX. See PRENDRE…VIEUX.

COUP DU LAPIN, *m.* **1.** Rabbit punch (brutal blow to the neck). *Le truand lui avait fait le coup du lapin.* "The hood rabbit-punched him." **2.** Whiplash. *Il est sorti de l'accident de voiture avec le coup du lapin.* "He suffered a whiplash injury in the car accident."

COUP DUR, *m.* Unpleasant happening. *Elle vient de perdre son boulot; c'est un coup dur.* "She's just lost her job; that's real hard luck."

COUPE-CHIASSE, *m.* Pharmacist (lit. "diarrhea stopper"). *Je pars chez le coupe-chiasse chercher des médicaments.* "I'm going to the drugstore for medicine."

COUPE-CIGARE, *m.* **1.** Guillotine (Lit. "cigar cutter"). *Beaucoup d'aristos ont échappé au coupe-cigare.* "Many aristocrats escaped the guillotine." See CIGARE **1. 2.** Anus. *Il a des émeraudes au coupe-cigare.* "He's got piles." See CIGARE **3.**

COUPE-LA-SOIF, *m.* Drink (usually alcoholic). *N'oublie pas le coupe-la-soif pour le pique-nique.* "Don't forget the booze for the picnic."

COUPER. To cut. **Couper à qch.** To avoid s.t. *J'ai coupé à l'attente du bus en faisant du stop.* "I avoided having to wait for the bus by hitching a ride." **Ne pas y couper.** To be unavoidable. *Si je rentre tard, l'engueulade, je n'y* *couperai pas.* "If I get home late, there's no way I'll avoid getting bawled out."

COUPER COMME LES GENOUX D'UNE BONNE SŒUR. To have a dull blade (lit. "to cut like a nun's knees" [blunted by frequent kneeling]). *Je ne peux rien faire avec ce couteau qui coupe comme les genoux d'une bonne sœur.* "I can't do anything with this dull knife."

COUPER LA CHIQUE/LE SIFFLET À QN/LA COUPER À QN. To interrupt. *J'ai perdu le fil; tu m'as coupé la chique.* "I've lost the thread; you cut me off." See ÇA TE LA COUPE!

COUPER LE CIGARE. See CIGARE **2.**

COUPE-TIFS, *m.* Hairdresser. *Mon coupe-tifs est dans le coup.* "My hairdresser's up on the latest styles."

COUP FOURRÉ, *m.* **1.** Sticky situation. *Il a réussi à se sortir de ce coup fourré.* "He managed to get out of a hairy situation." **2.** Dirty trick. *Il avait monté un coup fourré pour divorcer.* "He resorted to underhanded means to get a divorce."

COUPER LE JUS. See JUS **2.**

COUPS DE PIED (AU CUL) QUI SE PERDENT, *m., pl.* Useless disciplining. *Il y a des coups de pied qui se perdent.* "Some people are hopeless cases."

COURAGE ARROSÉ, *m.* Alcohol-inspired courage. *Sans son petit courage arrosé il n'aurait jamais dit ça au chef.* "He never would have said that to the boss without Dutch courage."

COUREUR DE JUPONS, *m.* Skirt chaser. *Elle a eu la malchance d'épouser un coureur de jupons.* "She had the misfortune to marry a womanizer."

COUREUSE, *f.* Promiscuous woman. *Ce coureur de jupons préfère les vierges aux coureuses.* "That philanderer prefers virgins to easy lays."

COURIR. To run. See LAISSE COURIR.

COURIR LE GUILLEDOU. To look for love (more gal-

lant than **draguer**). *Son dab court toujours le guilledou.*
"Her father's still game for a little amorous adventure."

COURIR SUR LE HARICOT/SYSTÈME. To exasperate.
Ce dragueur commence à me courir sur le haricot. "That
guy's coming on to me is getting on my nerves."

COURT, -E. Short. **La faire courte.** To make a long story
short. *Tu peux me la faire courte?* "Can you cut to the
bottom line?"

COURT-JUS, *m.* Short circuit. *Il y a un court-jus dans cette
prise.* "There's a short circuit in this outlet."

COURT-JUS DANS LA PENSEUSE, *m.* Headache. *Je me
suis levé avec un court-jus dans la penseuse.* "I woke up
with a headache."

COÛTER BONBON. See BONBON 1.

**COÛTER LES YEUX DE LA TÊTE = COÛTER LA
PEAU DES FESSES.** See PEAU DES FESSES.

**COUVERT TROIS PIÈCES = SERVICE TROIS
PIÈCES.**

CRABE, *m.* Crab. See FACE DE CRABE; PANIER DE CRABES.

CRAC, *m.* Female genitalia. See SAUTE-AU-CRAC.

CRACHER EN L'AIR. To make a wasted effort. *Lui donner des conseils, c'est cracher en l'air.* "Giving him
advice is like spitting in the wind."

CRACHER LE MORCEAU. See MORCEAU.

CRACHER SON VENIN. See VENIN.

CRACRA. Filthy. *Sa baraque est cracra.* "His place is
filthy."

CRADE/CRADINGUE/CRADO = CRACRA.

CRAMOUILLE, *f.* Female genitalia. *Sa cramouille mouille
bien.* "Her pussy gets excited easily."

CRAMPE, *f.* Cramp. See TIRER SA CRAMPE.

CRAMPETTE = CRAMPE.

CRAMSER/CRAMPSER = CLAMSER.

CRÂNE, *m.* **1.** Head. See BOURRER LE CRÂNE. **2.** Arrest. *Il y a eu un crâne dans le village.* "There was an arrest made in the village."

CRAPAUD, *m.* Toad. See REGARDER…CRAPAUD MORT.

CRAPOTEUX, -EUSE. Filthy. *Après avoir crapahuté toute la journée, on était crapoteux.* "After hiking over rough terrain all day, we were filthy."

CRAPSER = CLAMSER.

CRASPEC. Filthy. *Je n'ai jamais vu qch. d'aussi craspec.* "I've never seen anything so grungy."

CRASSOUILLE, *f.* Dirt. *Il est d'une crassouille repoussante.* "He's revoltingly dirty."

CRAVATE, *f.* Necktie. See (S'EN) JETER UN.

CRAYONS, *m., pl.* Legs (lit. "pencils"). See (S') EMMÊLER LES CRAYONS.

CRÊME, *f.* **1.** High society. *La créme de la crème sera là.* "The highest of high society will be there." **2.** Sperm. See LÂCHER…CRÈME.

CRÊPE. See RETOURNER…CRÊPE.

CRESSON, *m.* Female pubic hair (lit. "watercress"). See BROUTER LE CRESSON; IDEM…; RAS…CRESSON.

(SE) CREUSER LA TÊTE/CERVELLE/LE CIBOULOT/ CITRON = (SE) CASSER LA TÊTE.

CRÈVE, *f.* Rotten cold. *Quelle crève je tiens!* "What a rotten cold I've got."

CREVER LA FAIM/DALLE. To be extremely hungry. See DALLE.

CREVER LA GUEULE OUVERTE. To be utterly abandoned (lit. "to croak open-mouthed [with one's tongue hanging out]"). *Elle s'est taillée avec son jules en laissant son mari crever la gueule ouverte.* "She took off with her lover and left her husband to go to hell."

(SE) CREVER LE CUL = (S')ESQUINTER LES TRIPES.

CRIME, *f.,* for **la brigade criminelle,** Fr. equivalent of the FBI. Criminal investigation squad. *La crime a mis la main sur le gangster.* "The Feds caught the gangster."

CROCS, *m., pl.* Teeth. **Avoir les crocs,** *idiom.* To be ravenously hungry. *On avait les crocs après cette grande balade.* "We wanted to get our teeth into food after that long walk."

CROSSE, *f.* Quarrel (lit. "stick"; "crozier"). See CHERCHER DES CROSSES.

CROTTE! *euph.* for **merde!** "Damn it! Shoot! Sugar!"

CROTTE VINEUSE, *f.* Excrement that reeks of wine. *Cet engrais sent la crotte vineuse.* "That fertilizer smells of winey shit."

CROUME, *m.* Credit. See À CROUME.

CROÛTE, *f.* Food. See CASSER LA CROÛTE; GAGNER SA CROÛTE.

CUCU(L)/CUCUL LA PRALINE. Silly; nuts. *Qu'est-qu'il est cucul la praline, ton frangin.* "Your brother's really zany."

CUILLER/CUILLÈRE, *f.* **1.** Spoon. **Ne pas y aller avec le dos de la cuiller,** *idiom.* To be unstinting. *Quand tu offres des cadeaux, tu n'y vas pas avec le dos de la cuiller.* "When you give presents, you really go all out." **2.** Hand. See SERRER...CUILLER.

CUISSE, *f.* Thigh. **Avoir la cuisse légère** *idiom.* To be an easy lay. *Ne croyez pas que j'ai la cuisse légère.* "Don't think it's easy to get into my pants."

CUIT, -E. Drunk (lit. "cooked"). *Il est rentré complètement cuit.* "He came home totally soused."

CUITE, *f.* Drunkenness. See PRENDRE UNE CUITE.

CUL, *adj.* Stupid. **Avoir l'air cul,** *idiom.* See AIR.

CUL, *m.* **1.** Posterior; bottom. **L'avoir dans le cul = l'avoir dans le baba,** *idiom.* See BABA. See ASTAP(E); BOUTIQUE 1; (SE) CASSER LE CUL; COLLER AU CUL; COUILLES AU CUL; COUPS DE PIED AU CUL; FEU AU CUL; GROS CUL; LÈCHE-CUL;

(SE) MAGNER LE CUL; MON CUL!; PÉTER...CUL; PAPIER-CUL; PISSER AU CUL; RAS; (EN) RESTER...CUL; TAPE-CUL; TIRE-AU-CUL; TORCHE-CUL. **2.** Jackass. *Épouser un cul pareil, quelle conne!* "Marrying an asshole like that, what a dumb broad!" See CASSE-CUL; TROU DU CUL. **3.** Sexual activity. **Aller au cul,** *idiom.* To have sex, a "piece of ass." *Il a la trouille du SIDA et ne va plus du tout au cul.* "He's afraid of AIDS and has stopped having sex." **4.** Pornography. *Le cul, il n'y a que ça qui le branche.* "The only thing that turns him on is porn." See DE CUL. **5.** Luck. *On a eu un sacré cul de trouver cette maison.* "We were incredibly lucky to find this house."

CUL BÉNI, *m.* Holy Joe: prayer sister (lit. "blessed asshole"). *Quel casse-cul, ce cul béni et sa tartuferie; c'est un cul béni sur un cul-de-sac spirituel.* "What a pain in the ass, Mr. Holier-than-thou and his sanctimonious moralizing; he's a Holy Joe on a spiritual dead-end road."

CULBUTER. To have sexually (lit. "to tumble"). *Mussolini, souvent pressé, culbutaient les nanas dans son bureau.* "Mussolini, often in a hurry, used to ball chicks in his office."

CUL ENTRE DEUX CHAISES. In an uncertain state (lit. "ass between two stools"). *T'as encloqué cette loute. Ne reste pas le cul entre deux chaises; épouse-la.* "You knocked up that broad. Don't wait around with a finger up your ass; marry her."

CUL ET CHEMISE. On close terms (lit. "ass and shirt"). *Ma femme est cul et chemise avec les curetons.* "My wife and the priests piss in one pot."

CULOT, *m.* Impudence. *Quel culot il a!* "He's got some nerve!"

CULOTTE, *f.* Underpants. **Baisser sa culotte = baisser son froc.** See FROC. See also CHIER...CULOTTE.

CULOTTÉ, -E. Impudent. *Il fait souvent des remarques culottées.* "He often makes impudent remarks."

CUL SEC! Bottoms up!

CUL-TERREUX, *m., pej.* Rube. *Je suis cul-terreux et fier de l'être.* "I'm a country bumpkin and proud of it."

CULTIVER DES ASPERGES. See ASPERGES.

CURETON, *m., pej. Le cureton défroqué a épousé une ancienne réligieuse.* "The defrocked priest married an ex-nun."

CURETOT/CURETOSSE = CURETON.

CUVER SON VIN. To sleep it off (lit. "to ferment one's wine"). *Va couver ton vin et fous-moi la paix.* "Go sleep it off and leave me alone."

CYNOQUE = CINOQUE.

D, *m*. D. See SYSTÈME D.

-DA. Slang suffix. See CHARRIDA; FLAGADA; FLAGDA; MARIDA.

DAB/DABE, *m*. **1.** Father. *Son dab faisait tout pour bien l'élever.* "His dad did all he could to bring him up right." **2.** Boss. **Le Grand Dab.** God. *Elle rejette les parrains mafieux et l'idée patriarcale du Grand Dab au ciel.* "She rejects Mafia godfathers and the patriarchal idea of the Big Boss in the sky."

DABE, *f*. Mother. *Elle s'intéresse plutôt à la Déesse-Dabe.* "She's more interested in the Mother-Goddess."

DABES, *m., pl*. Parents. *Mes dabes pètent la forme.* "My parents are in excellent health."

DABESSE = DABE, *f*.

DABUCHE = DABE, *f*.

D'ACHAR/D'ACHAR ET D'AUTOR. See (D')ACHAR.

(À) DACHE. Very far away. *Ils ont envie d'habiter à dache.* "They want to move to the boonies."

DALLE, *f*. Throat (lit. "flagstone"). **Avoir la dalle en pente,** *idiom*. To be forever thirsty. *Nous avons la dalle en pente.* "We need a drink." **Avoir la dalle/crever/péter la dalle,** *idiom*. To be very hungry. *Le boulot fini, je crève la dalle.* "I'm starved after work." See QUE DALLE; (SE) RINCER…DALLE.

DALLEPÉ, backslang of **pédale.**

DAME-PIPI, *f.* Female toilet attendant. *La dame-pipi criait: "N'oubliez pas le service!"* "The toilet attendant cried out: 'Don't forget the service charge!'"

DANS LE CUL LA BALAYETTE!/DANS LE DOS LA BALAYETTE! "It's all over! Curtains! We've been shafted! We've had it up the ass!"

DANS TOUS LES AZIMUTS. See AZIMUT.

DARD, *m.* Penis (lit. "sting"). See POMPER LE DARD.

DARDILLON, *m., dim.* of **dard.** Penis. **Avoir le dardillon,** *idiom.* To have an erection. *Il avait le dardillon.* "His prick was up."

DARGEOT/DARGIF, *m.* Buttocks. *Elle avait un dargeot prometteur.* "She had an inviting derriere."

DATTE, *f.* Date. **Ne pas en ficher; foutre une datte,** *idioms.* See DES DATTES.

DEALER = DILEUR.

DEB = DÈBE.

DÉBALLER. To confess (lit. "to unpack"). *Il m'a enfin déballé toute son histoire.* "He finally revealed the whole story to me."

DÉBALLER LE JAR(S). To talk (thieves') slang. *Ils déballaient le jars pour ne pas être compris.* "They talked slang so as not to be understood."

DÉBANDER. 1. To lose one's erection. *Il débande pour un rien.* "He goes limp at the slightest little thing." **2.** To be afraid. *Ne débande pas devant les flics.* "Don't turn chicken when the cops question you." See SANS DÉBANDER.

DÈBE, from **débile** (mental). Lamebrained. *Cesse de me traiter de dèbe.* "Quit calling me a retard."

DÉBECTANT, -E. Repulsive. *Cette carne pleine de mouches est débectante.* "That meat covered with flies is yucky."

DÉBECTER. To disgust. *Ça me débecte!* "That makes me want to throw up."

DÉBILOS = DÈBE.

DEBS = DÈBE.

DÉBINE, *f.* Extreme poverty. *Elle l'a épousé quand il était en pleine débine.* "She married him when he was at rock bottom."

DÉBINER. To inform on. *Son meilleur copain l'a débiné.* "His best friend ratted on him."

(SE) DÉBINER. To scram. *Ils se sont débinés avant la fin du spectacle.* "They ran off before the end of the show."

DÉBLOQUER. 1. To work inefficiently (lit. "to release"). *Ma voiture débloque.* "My car is acting up." **2.** To talk nonsense. *Mes vioques débloquent complètement.* "My parents feed me a load of crap."

DÉBOISÉ, -E. Bald (lit. "deforested"). *Gershwin avait la trouille de se trouver totalement déboisé.* "Gershwin was terrified of winding up totally bald."

(SE) DÉBOISER. To be losing one's hair. *Mon dab ne s'est jamais déboisé.* "My father never lost his hair."

DÉBROUILLE, *f.* Resourcefulness. *Elle s'y connaît dans la débrouille.* "She knows her way around." See SYSTÈME D.

DÈC, backslang of **condé.**

DÉCA, *m.,* from **décaféiné.** Decaffeinated coffee. *Il lui faut son petit déca avant de dormir.* "He needs his little cup of decaf before going to bed."

(SE) DÉCALCIFIER. To take one's underpants off (from **calcif** (shorts); lit. "to lose calcium"). *Il dort sans se décalcifier.* "He sleeps in his briefs."

DÉCANILLER. To beat it. *Et si on décanillait?* "How about us blowing this hole?"

DÉCAPANT, *m.* Lousy wine (from the *adj.* **décapant** [abrasive]). *Dans la cave de mon dab il n'y a pas de place pour le décapant.* "In my father's wine cellar, there's no room for any poor-quality wine."

DÈCHE, *f.* Extreme poverty; misfortune. **Être dans la dèche,** *idiom.* To be flat broke. *Tu seras dans la dèche si* *tu continues à jeter l'argent par les fenêtres.* "You'll be a pauper if you keep wasting money."

DECK = DÈC.

DÉCONNAGE, *m.* Stupid talk or behavior. *Quel splendide déconnage, le discours du sénateur!* "What a bunch of bull the senator's speech was!"

DÉCONNER. 1. To withdraw from the vagina. *Ma chienne n'a pas été couverte; le grand champion a déconné.* "My bitch wasn't served; the great champion (dog) pulled out." **2.** To malfunction (said of anything, not just a faltering phallus, as in **1**). *L'allumage de ta bagnole déconne.* "Your car's ignition is on the blink." **3.** To do or say foolish things. *Qu'est-ce qu'il peut déconner ce soir!* "God, he's really full of crap tonight!" See FAUT PAS DÉCONNER! **4.** To enjoy saying or doing foolish things. *On a passé le dimanche à déconner.* "We had fun fooling around on Sunday." See SANS DEC'.

DÉCONNER À PLEINS TUBES. To do or say totally foolish things. *La gniole le fait déconner à pleins tubes.* "Booze makes him a total jerk."

DÉCONTRACT'. Relaxed; casual. *Elle est très décontract'.* "She's very laid back."

DÉCROCHER. To go off drugs (lit. "to unhook"). *Sa mère s'est battue pour qu'il décroche.* "His mother did all she could to get him to kick the habit."

DÉCROCHER LE COCOTIER/GROS LOT/JACKPOT. To hit the jackpot; make it big. *Il a décroché le cocotier en étant reçu premier au concours.* "He scored a triumph by coming in first in the competition."

DE CUL = DE FESSE.

DEDANS. Inside. See FOUTRE **2**; (SE) FOUTRE DEDANS; RENTRE-DEDANS; RENTRER DEDANS.

DE DERRIÈRE LES FAGOTS. From a special reserve. *Mon grand-dab nous en a sorti une de derrière les fagots.* "My grandpa got out one of his special reserve bottles for us."

DE FESSE. Pornographic. *Pour lui, la vie n'est qu'une histoire de fesse.* "For him, life is only about tits, ass, and pussy."

DEF. See RAIDE DEF.

DEFFE, *f.* Cap; beret. *J'ai paumé ma deffe.* "I've lost my cap."

DÉFONÇARÈS = DÉFONCÉ.

DÉFONCE, *f.* To be in a drug-induced state (high or down). *Ils étaient tous en état de défonce.* "They were all spaced out."

DÉFONCÉ, -E. *m., f., adj.* and *n.* Drugged; drunk. *Il est souvent défoncé à mort.* "He's often totally smashed."

DÉFONCER L'ANNEAU/OIGNON/LE POT/LA RONDELLE. To sodomize (lit. "to break into the anus"). See OIGNON **2.**

(SE) DÉFONCER. 1. To take drugs; get high. *Ils se défoncent en groupe.* "They shoot up together." **2.** To go all out. *Elle s'est défoncée pour élever son môme.* "She did her utmost to bring up her child."

DÉFONCEUSE, *f.* Penis. *Il était heureux que sa défonceuse ne déconnait plus.* "He was glad his tool was in good working order again."

DÉFRINGUER = DÉFRUSQUER.

DÉFROMAGER. To remove smegma by having sex (lit. "to de-cheese"). *Le bled manquait d'eau mais la putain défromagait les mecs.* "The village's water supply was short, but the whore kept all the guys' dicks clean."

DÉFROMAGER LE MINARET, dated. To have one's smegmatic penis serviced (said by former Fr. colonials in areas with mosques and minarets). *Le légionnaire cherchait une fatma pour se défromager le minaret.* "The legionnaire looked for a female to clean his pipe." Cf. DÉGRAISSER/DÉROUILLER SON PANAIS.

DÉFRUSQUER. To undress. *Défrusque-toi rapidos.* "Take your clothes off, right away!"

DÉG = DÉGUEULASSE.

DÉGAGE! Buzz off!

DÉGAT, *m.* Damage. See BONJOUR LES DÉGATS.

DÉGLINGUER. To break down. *La télé est de nouveau déglinguée.* "The TV's on the fritz again."

(SE) DÉGLINGUER. To deteriorate. *Il se déglingue à force de défonce.* "He's going downhill because of his drug habit."

DÉGOBILLER. To vomit. *Il a dégobillé dans les toilettes de l'avion.* "He barfed in the plane's toilets."

DÉGONFLARD, -E = DÉGONFLÉ.

DÉGONFLÉ, -E. *m., f., adj.* and *n.* Coward; cowardly (lit. "deflated"). *Vous n'êtes qu'une bande de dégonflés.* "You're all chicken."

(SE) DÉGONFLER. To lose one's courage. *Tu ne vas pas te dégonfler au dernier moment?* "You're not going to get cold feet at the last minute, are you?"

DÉGONFLEUR, -EUSE = DÉGONFLÉ.

DÉGOT(T)ER. To find. *J'ai dégoté qch. de super.* "I turned up s.t. marvelous."

DÉGRAISSER SON PANAIS. To have sexually (lit. "to trim the fat off one's parsnip"). See PANAIS.

DÉGROUILLER/SE DÉGROUILLER. To hurry up. *Dégrouille-toi!* "Get a move on."

DÉGUEU = DÉGUEULASSE.

DÉGUEULASSE, *m., f., adj.* and *n.* **1.** Very dirty. *Ce resto est dégueulasse.* "This restaurant is filthy." **2.** Repulsive. *C'est un dégueulasse de lui avoir fait un coup pareil.* "He's a sleaze bag for having done s.t. like that to her." See PAS DÉGUEULASSE.

DÉGUEULASSER. To make a mess. *Ils avaient tout dégueulassé.* "They mucked up everything."

DÉGUEULASSERIE, *f.* Reprehensible act. *Quelle dégueulasserie!* "What a dirty trick!"

DÉGUEULBIF = DÉGUEULASSE.

DÉGUEULER. 1. To vomit. *Il a dégueulé sur la moquette.* "He puked on the carpet." **2.** To bad-mouth. *Cesse de dégueuler sur tout le monde.* "Stop running everybody down."

DÉGUEULIS, *m.* Vomit. *Il a fallu nettoyer tout le dégueulis de la nuit.* "Last night's puke had to be cleaned up."

DÉGUEULOIR, *m.* Mouth. *Tu ferais mieux de la fermer, ton dégueuloir.* "You really ought to keep your trap shut."

DÉGUSTER. 1. To get scolded (ironic use of the lit. "to enjoy"; "taste"). *Qu'est-ce qu'il va déguster quand il rentrera.* "He'll get a real chewing out when he comes back." **2.** To get beat up. *Qu'est-ce qu'ils lui ont fait déguster.* "They gave him a hell of a beating." **3.** To endure. *Avec leur voyou de fils, qu'est-ce qu'ils n'ont pas dégusté!* "They've been through the tortures of the damned with their son."

DÉJ, *abbr.* of **déjeuner.** See PETIT DÉJ.

DE L'AIR! Back off! *De l'air, les mômes; vous faites trop de bruit.* "Beat it, you brats; you're making too much noise."

DÉLOURDER. To open a door. *Elle refuse de délourder quand il arrive bourré.* "She won't open up when he comes home loaded." Cf. LOURDE **1.**

(SE) DÉMAQUER. To separate; divorce. *Ils ne parviennent pas à se démaquer malgré leurs querelles.* "They can't bring t.s. to split up in spite of their quarrels."

DÉMARRER SUR LES CHAPEAUX DE ROUES. See CHAPEAU DE ROUE.

DÉMENT, -E. Marvelous (lit. "demented"). *La fête était démente.* "The party was mind-blowing."

DÉMERDARD, -E = DÉMERDEUR, -EUSE.

DE MERDE. See PUTAIN DE MERDE.

DÉMERDE = DÉBROUILLE. See SYSTÈME D.

(SE) DÉMERDER. 1. To operate successfully. *Je peux me démerder toute seule.* "I can manage it myself." **2.** To hurry up. *Démerde-toi; l'heure passe.* "Step on it; time's a-wasting."

DÉMERDEUR, -EUSE, *m., f., adj.* and *n.* Resourceful person; shrewd customer. *C'est un sacré démerdeur!* "That guy knows his way around."

DE MES DEUX (COUILLES/FESSES)! Nuts to you! Kiss my ass!

DE MES FESSES. Rotten. *Où as-tu déniché ce bahut de mes fesses?* "Where'd you find this broken-down old heap?"

DEMI-PORTION, *f.* Small person. *Lui est maousse; son frangin est demi-portion.* "He's huge; his brother's a half-pint."

DEMI-SEL, *m., pej.* Small-time punk or pimp (lit. "lightly salted"). *Ce demi-sel est surveillé par les flics.* "That little shit of a lowlife is being watched by the police."

DE MON CUL = DE MES FESSES.

(SE) DÉMOUSCAILLER = (SE) DÉMERDER.

DENTIER, *m.* Dentures. See AVALER SON DENTIER.

DEP, backslang of **pédé.**

(SE) DÉPATOUILLER. To get out of trouble. *Tu es assez grand pour te dépatouiller tout seul.* "You're old enough to pick your own chestnuts out of the fire."

DÉPENDEUR D'ANDOUILLES, *m.* Tall, thin man. *Ce dépendeur d'andouille a épousé une naine.* "That beanpole married a dwarf."

(SE) DÉPIEUTER. To get out of bed. *Il s'est dépieuté ce matin du pied gauche.* "He got up on the wrong side of the bed today."

DÉPLACER DE L'AIR. To talk a lot of hot air; waste time. *Son travail n'avance pas car il déplace de l'air.* "His work's getting nowhere because he's chasing his tail."

DÉPOSER LE/SON BILAN. To die. (lit. "to file for bankruptcy; liquidation"). *T'en fais pas; tu es loin de déposer ton bilan.* "Don't get upset; you're hardly at death's door."

DÉPUCELER. To use or open up s.t. (usually a bottle) for the first time; (lit. "to take s.o.'s virginity"). *On a dépucelé une bouteille de derrière les fagots.* "We cracked out a bottle from the special reserve."

DER, *m., f.,* from **dernier. Der des ders,** *m.* **1.** Lowest of the low; last straggler. *Tu ne vas pas épouser ce der des ders?* "You're not going to marry that scum of the earth, are you?" **2.** *f.* The war to end all wars. *Le prof parlait d'une guerre nucléaire et se moquait de Wilson et de sa der des ders.* "The professor talked about a nuclear war and made fun of Wilson and his war to end all wars." **3.** *m.* Last drink before leaving. *On se boit le der des ders et on y va.* "We'll have one for the road and get underway."

DERCHE, *m.* Posterior. *La pauvre bête a reçu un coup de pied dans le derche.* "The poor animal got a kick in the ass."

DERGE = DERCHE.

DERNIER CARAT. The final limit. *Je t'attends jusqu'à midi, dernier carat.* "I'll wait for you till noon, no longer."

DÉROUILLADE/DÉROUILLE = DÉROUILLÉE.

DÉROUILLÉE, *f.* Beating. *L'équipe de hockey a pris une dérouillée magistrale.* "Our hockey team was soundly beaten."

DÉROUILLER = DÉGUSTER.

DÉROUILLER SON PANAIS. See PANAIS.

(SE) DÉROUILLER. To limber up (lit. "to get the rust off"). *Je vais me dérouiller les gambettes un peu avant le petit déj.* "I'm going to stretch my legs a bit before breakfast."

DESCENDRE. To kill. *Les truands l'ont descendu.* "The crooks bumped him off."

DESCENDRE EN FLAMMES. To be attacked verbally. *Faut pas me descendre en flammes tout de suite.* "You don't have to chop my head off right away."

DESCENTE, *f.* Going down; descent. **Avoir une bonne descente,** *idiom.* To be fond of the bottle. *Qu'est-ce qu'il a une bonne descente!* "He can really knock 'em back!"

DESCENTE À LA CAVE/AU BARBU/LAC, *m.* Cunnilingus. *Il commence toujours ses ébats par une descente à la cave.* "He always begins his lovemaking with a muff dive (lit. "going to the cellar." A "cellar" in France is usually a "wine cellar" too)."

DESCENTE DE LIT, *f.* Spineless person (lit. "bedside rug"). *Je ne veux pas sortir avec cette descente de lit.* "I don't want to go out with that doormat."

DES CLOPES/CLOPINETTES. Nothing; practically nothing. *À la mort de son mari elle a hérité des clopinettes.* "At her husband's death she got next to nothing."

DES CLOPINETTES!/CLOUX! = DES DATTES!

DES DATTES! Nothing doing! No way! Not on your life!

DESSOUS. Under. See TRENTE-SIXIÈME.

DESSALÉ, -E. *adj.* and *m., f., n.* Sexually aware (person). *Elle n'est pas assez dessalée.* "She hasn't been around enough."

DESSALER. To put s.o. wise (sexually); lit. "to desalinate." *Cette nana a besoin d'être dessalée.* "That chick needs to learn a few things."

DEUIL, *m.* Mourning. **Avoir les ongles en deuil,** *idiom.* To have dirty fingernails. *Je ne couche pas avec les mecs qui ont les ongles en deuil.* "I don't sleep with guys who've got dirty fingernails."

DEUSIO = DEUXIO.

DEUX. Two. **Ça fait deux.** To be poles apart. *Le patron et moi, ça fait deux.* "The boss and I don't see eye to eye." See COMME PAS DEUX; DE MES DEUX; EN MOINS DE DEUX.

DEUXIO/DEUZIO. Secondly. *On nous a servi primo l'apéro, deuxio le champagne.* "First they served us the aperitif, then the champagne."

DÉVEINE, *f.* Bad luck. *Les pauvres, ils ont eu la déveine.*

"The poor guys, they had bad luck." **Être dans la déveine,** *idiom.* To be down on one's luck. *On est toujours dans la déveine.* "We're still going through a bad patch."

DEVENIR CHÈVRE. To go mad with rage (lit. "to become a nanny goat"). *Cette gamine me fera devenir chèvre.* "That kid's going to drive me out of my bird."

DÉVISSER. 1. To wound; kill (lit. "to unscrew"). *Ils lui ont dévissé la tête.* "They inflicted head wounds on him." **2.** To leave. *Et si on dévissait?* "How about our hitting the road?" **3.** To die. *Il était dévissé depuis huit jours.* "He'd been dead for eight days."

DÉZINGUER. To destroy s.t. or s.o. *Ses complices enragés l'ont dézingué.* "His enraged accomplices bumped him off."

DIAM, *m.,* from **diamant.** *Le meilleur ami d'une fille, ce sont les diams, dit la chanson.* "Diamonds are a girl's best friend, says the song."

DICO, *m.,* from **dictionnaire.** Dictionary. *Elle a toujours le nez dans les dicos.* "She's always got her nose buried in a dictionary."

DILEUR, *m.,* transcription of Eng. "dealer." Drug dealer. *C'est un dileur de petite envergure.* "He's a small-time dealer."

DINGO, *adj.* and *n.* Crazy. *Complètement dingo, ce mec.* "That guy's completely bonkers."

DINGUE, *adj.* and *n.* **1.** Crazy. *Ce dingue va la faire crever en la frappant ainsi.* "That nutcase'll do her in, beating her like that." **2. Être dingue de qn,** *idiom.* To be nuts about s.o. *Ils sont dingues l'un de l'autre.* "They're crazy about each other." **3.** Incredible. **C'est dingue!** "That's mind-blowing!" See RAIDE DINGUE.

DINGUER. To tumble. See ENVOYER DINGUER.

DIRECTO, from **directement.** Right away. *Dis-le directo.* "Come straight out and say it."

DIRLINGUE = DIRLO.

DIRLO/DIRLOTE, *m., f.,* from **directeur. 1.** Principal. *Le dirlo a mis à la porte deux élèves défoncés.* "The principal expelled two junkie students." **2.** Boss. *Le dirlo a dit non.* "The boss said no."

DISJONCTER. To crack up (lit. "to disconnect"). *Il a complètement disjoncté.* "He totally flipped out."

DOCHE, *f.* Mother. *La doche et son gone sont partis en vacances.* "The mother and her kid have gone on vacation."

DODO, *m., children, hum.* Sleep. **Aller au dodo; faire dodo,** *idioms.* To go to bed. *Je veux faire dodo.* "I want to go beddy-bye."

DODOCHES = DOUDOUNES.

DOIGT, *m.* Finger. See CLAQUER...DOIGTS; OBÉIR AU DOIGT....

DOIGT DANS L'ŒIL. See (SE) FOURRER.

(LES) DOIGTS DANS LE NEZ. Very easily (lit. "with one's fingers in one's nose"). *Je pourrais faire ça les doigts dans le nez.* "I could do that with one hand tied behind my back."

DOIGTS DE PIEDS, *m., pl.* Toes. **Avoir les doigts de pieds en éventail; bouquet de violettes.** To experience orgasm; great pleasure (lit. "have one's toes spread out like a fan; in a bouquet of violets"). *À Toulouse on avait souvent les doigts de pieds en bouquet de violettes.* "In Toulouse we often had great orgasms."

DOLLUCHE, *m.* Dollar. *Cet un Amerluche plein de dolluches.* "He's a yank with big bucks."

DOMB = DOMBI.

DOMBI, backslang of **bidon.** *C'est pas du dombi!* "That's no load of bull!"

DOMINO, *m.* Tooth. *Un domino de perdu, réaction en chaîne—les autres ont suivi!* "First I lost one tooth, then the others—the domino effect!"

DONDON, *f.* Hefty lady. See GROSSE DONDON.

DONNER. To inform on. *On ne sait pas qui l'a donné.* "Nobody knows who ratted on him."

DONNER DU CHOUETTE = FILER DU CHOUETTE.

(LE) DONNER EN MILLE. To ask s.o. to guess and guess again. *Qu'est-ce qu'il a bien pu m'offrir? Je te le donne en mille.* "What do you suppose he gave me? You'll never guess!"

DONNER LA GOMME = METTRE LA GOMME.

DONNER SA LANGUE AU CHAT. See LANGUE.

DONNER UN COUP DE BALAI. To eliminate unproductive staff (lit. "to sweep up"). *Le nouveau PDG a donné un coup de balai dans l'entreprise.* "The new CEO got rid of some deadwood; made a clean sweep in the company."

DONNER UN COUP DE CACHEMIRE SUR LE PIANO. See CACHEMIRE.

(SE) DONNER UN MAL DE CHIEN. To take great pains. *Je me suis donné un mal de chien pour préparer la fête.* "I worked like a dog to prepare for the party."

(S'EN) DONNER. To give unstintingly of o.s. *Elle s'en donne pour que ses parents ne manquent de rien.* "She doesn't spare h.s. to see to it that her parents don't want for anything."

(S'EN) DONNER À CŒUR JOIE. To enjoy o.s. to the hilt. *Qu'est-ce qu'on s'en est donné à cœur joie hier soir!* "Man, did we have a super time last night!"

DONNEUR, -EUSE, *m., f.* Informant (lit. "donor"). *Les flics ont trouvé en lui un bon donneur.* "The cops found a fine fink in him."

DOPE, *f.* Drugs (from Eng.). *Il est toujours en manque de dope.* "He always needs a fix."

DORER. To gild. **Se faire dorer,** *idiom.* To get sodomized (lit. "to get suntanned"). *Le Duc de Choiseul-Praslin aimait se faire dorer.* "The Duke of Choiseul-Praslin loved being buggered."

DORER LA PILULE. To sweeten the (bitter) pill. *Je le lui dirai, mais je voudrais lui dorer la pilule.* "I'll tell him, but I'd like to cushion the blow."

DORME, *f.* Sleep. *Elle a la dorme légère.* "She's a light sleeper."

DOS, *m.* Back. **En avoir plein le dos,** *idiom.* To be fed up with s.t. *J'en ai plein le dos de bosser comme une damnée.* "I'm sick and tired of slaving away." **L'avoir dans le dos,** *idiom.* To lose out. *Pas de chance pour lui, il l'a eu dans le dos.* "He was unlucky and got shafted."

DOUBLÉ, *m.* **1.** Double. **Faire un doublé,** *idiom.* To give birth to twins. *Elle vient d'apprendre qu'elle fera un doublé.* "She's just learned that she's going to have twins." **2.** Second lay (shortly after the first one). (lit. "double"). *Elle se réjouissait toujours du doublé.* "She always enjoyed the second coming."

DOUBLER. To betray. *Il a doublé et son associé et sa femme.* "He double-crossed his partner and two-timed his wife."

DOUCE. *f.* Soft drugs; marijuana. *Il est dingue de la douce.* "He's nuts about grass."

DOUCE, See EN DOUCE; (SE LA) COULER DOUCE.

DOUDOUNES, *f.* Breasts. *Vas y doucement quand tu me tâtes les doudounes.* "Be gentle when you touch my breasts."

DOUILLER. 1. To pay out or up. *Il s'arrange toujours pour ne pas avoir à douiller.* "He always sees to it that he's not the one who shells out." **2. Ça douille.** That's a gold mine! *Son commerce, ça douille!* "His business is a big money-maker." or: "That costs a fortune." *Élever un môme, ça douille.* "Raising a child means no end of expenses."

DOUL/DOULE, *m.* **1.** Hat. *N'oublie pas ton doul.* "Don't forget your chapeau." **2.** Police informant. *Il avait la gueule d'un doule.* "He looked like a stool pigeon."

DOULOS = DOUL.

DOULOUREUSE, *f.* Hotel bill; restaurant check (lit. "the painful one"). *Aujourd'hui la douloureuse c'est pour moi.* "Today I'll take care of the bad news."

DRAGUE, *f.* Search for sex; cruising (homosexual) (lit. "dredging"). *On est parti à trois pour la drague.* "The three of us went out hunting/wolfing/cruising together."

DRAGUER. 1. To look for sex (lit. "to dredge"). *Où qu'il aille, il drague.* "Wherever he goes, he's on the make." To cruise (homosexual). *Rorem raconte que lui et Poulenc draguaient souvent ensemble.* "Rorem relates that he and Poulenc often went cruising together." **2.** To pick up (transitive). *Je l'ai draguée au Bois de Boulogne.* "I picked her up in the Bois de Boulogne." Note: **1** is intransitive, used for the sexual impulse in search of an object.

DRAGUEUR, *m.* Skirt chaser; chronic cruiser (homosexual). *Ce café est toujours plein de dragueurs.* "This café is always full of guys on the make."

DRAGUEUSE, *f.* Flirt. *C'est une dragueuse de première.* "She's a first-class flirt."

DUCHNOQUE, *m.* Fool. *Ce duchnoque nous a cassé les pieds.* "That jackass bugged us."

DUCON/DUCONNO/DUCONNOSO(F) = **DUCH-NOQUE.**

DUCON-LA-JOIE, *m.* Blissful simpleton; grinning idiot. *Laisse ce ducon-la-joie tranquille.* "Let him live in his fool's paradise."

DUR. Hard. See COUP DUR.

DUR À CUIRE = **DUR DE DUR.**

DUR!/AH, DUR! Tough luck!

DUR DE DUR, *m.* Masterful tough guy. *Jean Gabin et John Wayne jouaient souvent les durs des durs.* "Jean Gabin and John Wayne often played tough guys."

DUR, -E DE LA FEUILLE. A bit deaf. *Parle plus fort; grand-dab est dur de la feuille.* "Talk louder; gramps is a little hard of hearing."

DUR-DUR! = DUR!

(À LA) DURE. In a rough way. *Tous ses enfants ont été élevés à la dure.* "All his children were brought up without sparing the rod."

DUSCHNOQUE = DUCHNOQUE.

DYNAMITE, *f.* Cocaine (lit. "dynamite"). *La dynamite a détruit la carrière de la présentatrice.* "Coke destroyed the TV newscaster's career."

EAU, *f.* Water. See TOMBER À L'EAU.

EAU DE BOUDIN, see BOUDIN **1.**

(S') ÉCLATER. 1. To have a rip-roaring time. *On s'est éclaté au concert rock.* "We let it all hang it out at the rock concert." **2.** To get high on drugs. *Lui et sa copine s'éclatent chaque soir.* "He and his girlfriend trip every night."

ÉCLUSER. 1. To drink (lit. "to operate sluice gates"). *Le groupe au bar écluse un max.* "That bunch at the bar is really belting them down." **2.** To urinate. *La bière les fait beaucoup écluser.* "Beer makes them piss a lot." See LÂCHER…L'ÉCLUSE.

ÉCOLO, from **écologique.** Ecological. *Un plan écolo a été dressé pour combattre les marées noires.* "An environmental plan has been drawn up to deal with black tides."

ÉCOLO, *m., f.,* from **écologiste.** *Les écolos sont très engagés.* "The greens are very committed."

ÉCRASE-MERDE, *m., f., pl.* Oversize shoes (lit. "shit mincers"). *Essuie tes écrase-merde avant d'entrer.* "Wipe your clodhoppers before coming in."

ÉCRASE! Put a lid on it! Shut up!

ÉCRASER LE COUP. To make peace. *Après deux ans de mésentente, les deux frères ont écrasé le coup.* "After two years of misunderstanding, the two brothers buried the hatchet."

(EN) ÉCRASER. To sleep long or well. *J'attends le dimanche pour en écraser.* "I wait for Sunday to get a good sleep."

ÉCRASER L'AFFAIRE/LE COUP. To keep s.t. quiet. *Enceinte à douze ans, on a essayé d'écraser l'affaire.* "She was pregnant at twelve and they tried to hush it up."

(S')ÉCRASER. To become less acute. *Le scandale s'est enfin écrasé.* "The dust has finally settled on the scandal."

EFFEUILLAGE, *m.* Striptease. *L'effeuilleuse pense faire un effeuillage spirituel pour découvrir l'essentiel.* "The stripper plans to strip down spiritually to discover the essential."

EFFEUILLER LA MARGUERITE. 1. To play "she loves me, loves me not" (lit. "to thin the daisy"). *Elle effeuillait la marguerite en répétant, "(il m'aime) un peu, beaucoup, passionément, à la folie, du tout".* "She plucked the daisy's petals and repeated, "He loves me, loves me not." **2.** To make sexual advances. *Il était trop bourré pour effeuiller la marguerite.* "He was too drunk to come on to anybody." **3.** To strip. *Elle effeuille la marguerite pour son amant.* "She does a striptease for her lover."

EFFEUILLEUSE, *f.* Stripper. *Mencken savait apprécier les effeuilleuses.* "Mencken knew how to appreciate ecdysiasts."

ÉGOÏNER. To copulate (lit. "to saw"). *Othello l'égoïnait chaque nuit.* "Othello gave it to her nightly."

ÉGOUTTER LA/SA SARDINE. To urinate (lit. "to drain the sardine"). *En conduisant il égoutte sa sardine dans une bouteille.* "When driving he takes a leak into a bottle."

EMBALLAGE, *m.* Arrest (lit. "packaging; wrapping up"). *Dans le quartier il y a eu plusieurs emballages.* "Lots of people got busted in the neighborhood."

EMBALLARÈS. Arrested; rounded up. *Je me suis sauvé, mais tous les potes sont emballarès.* "I got away, but all my buddies got busted."

EMBALLER. 1. To arrest (lit. "to wrap up"). *Les flics les ont emballés.* "The cops carted them off." **2.** To please. *Ton projet ne m'emballe pas.* "Your project doesn't do anything for me." **3.** To seduce; have sexually. *Il avait une forte envie de l'emballer.* "He really wanted to make it with her."

(S')EMBALLER. 1. To fly into a rage. *Ce n'est pas grave; ne t'emballe pas.* "It isn't serious; don't fly off the handle." **2.** To be enthusiastic. *La foule s'emballait au match de foot.* "The crowd got carried away at the football game."

EMBARQUER. 1. To arrest. *Cesse la bagarre ou tu seras embarqué par les keufs.* "Stop fighting or the cops will arrest you." **2.** To involve. *Je me suis laissé embarquer dans ses combines.* "I got mixed up in his shady deals." **3.** To take away; swipe. *Mon gamin m'a embarqué tous mes crayons.* "My kid has made off with all my pencils."

EMBISTROUILLER. To pester. *Va embistrouiller qn. d'autre.* "Go bug s.o. else."

EMBRINGUER. To drag into. *J'ai été embringué dans une affaire qui m'a coûté cher.* "I got mixed up in s.t. that cost me dearly."

(S')EMBRINGUER. To get involved. *Pourquoi t'embringuer là-dedans?* "What are you getting mixed up in that for?"

(S')EMBRINGUER MAL. To get off to a bad start. *Leur mariage s'embringue mal.* "Their marriage is getting off to a bad start."

EMBROUILLE, *f.* **1.** Snag; confusion. *Tout s'est passé sans embrouille.* "Everything went off without a hitch." **2.** Shady deal. *Je me tiens à l'écart de ses embrouilles.* "I steer clear of his fishy schemes." **3.** Paris stock exchange. *Les initiés ont fait fortune à l'Embrouille.* "Inside traders made a fortune on the exchange."

ÉMERAUDES, *f., pl.* Hemorrhoids (lit. "emeralds"). *Faire du vélo, c'est rude pour les émeraudes.* "Bicycling is rough on piles."

ÉMERI, *m.* Emery. See BOUCHÉ À L'ÉMERI.

EMMANCHÉ, *m.* Idiot. *Quel emmanché, celui-là!* "That guy's a real jerk!"

EMMANCHER. To sodomize (lit. "to screw in a handle"). *Il ne pense qu'à se faire emmancher.* "All he thinks about is getting fucked."

(S')EMMANCHER. To have sex. *Les enfants ont surpris leurs parents en train de s'emmancher.* "The children surprised their parents while they were doing it."

(S')EMMÊLER LES CRAYONS/PÉDALES/PIEDS/PINCEAUX. To get mixed up (lit. "to tangle one's feet"). *Grand-mère, tu t'emmêles les pinceaux.* "Grandmother, you're getting your wires crossed."

EMMENER LE PETIT/POPAUL AU CIRQUE = MENER...CIRQUE.

EMMERDANT, -E. Very annoying. *Avoir un problème avec le fisc, c'est emmerdant.* "Having a problem with the tax collector is a real bummer."

EMMERDANT COMME LA PLUIE. Extremely displeasing. *Tu es emmerdant comme la pluie.* "You're a real pain in the ass."

EMMERDE, *m., f.* = **EMMERDEMENT.**

EMMERDÉ, -E. In difficulty. *Ils sont emmerdés jusqu'au cou.* "They're really in deep shit."

EMMERDEMENT, *m.* Trouble. *Ils ont des emmerdements avec leurs gosses.* "They've got big problems with their kids."

EMMERDER. 1. To bore; annoy. *Cesse de pleurnicher; tu m'emmerdes.* "Quit bawling; you bug me." **2.** To tell to go to hell. *Je t'emmerde! Je vous emmerde!* "Up yours! Fuck off!"

(S')EMMERDER. 1. To be bored to death. *On s'est emmerdé en campant sous la pluie.* "We were bored out of our minds camping in the rain." **2.** To fret. *Pourquoi t'emmerder pour une chose pareille?* "Why worry your head for s.t. like that?"

(S')EMMERDER À CENT SOUS DE L'HEURE = **(S')EMMERDER 1.**

(S')EMMERDER COMME UN RAT MORT. See RAT.

(NE PAS) S'EMMERDER. 1. To not trouble o.s. about anyone else. *Celle-là, elle ne s'emmerde pas, en se garant sur ma pelouse!* "That broad doesn't give a shit; she parks her car on my lawn." **2.** To have a trouble-free life. *Ils boivent des grands crus à chaque repas; ils ne s'emmerdent pas!* "They drink great vintage wines with every meal. They're not doing badly for t.s.!"

EMMERDEUR, -EUSE. Troublemaker; nuisance. *Quel emmerdeur!* "What a pain in the ass!"

EMMIELLER, *euph.* for **emmerder.** *Qu'est-ce que je m'emmielle!* "God, what a bore; hassle!"

EMMOUSCAILLER, *euph.* for **emmerder 1.** To annoy. *J'étais emmouscaillé par une foultitude de papiers à remplir.* "I was hassled by heaps of papers that had to be filled out."

EMPAFFÉ, *m.* Dumb bugger. *Espèce d'empaffé!* "You asshole, you!"

EMPAFFER. To sodomize. *Va te faire empaffer!* "Go fuck y.s.! Go get fucked up the ass!"

EMPÊCHEUR DE TOURNER EN ROND. Spoilsport. *N'amène pas à la teuf cet empêcheur de tourner en rond.* "Don't bring that party pooper to the bash."

EMPLÂTRE, *m.* Clod; wimp (lit. "medicated plaster"). *Ne fais pas l'emplâtre.* "Don't be such a jelly doughnut."

EN AVOIR. To be ballsy; tough. See COUILLES.

EN-BOURGEOIS = **HAMBOURGEOIS.**

ENCADRER. 1. To beat up severely (lit. "to frame [picture]"). *Il l'ont sacrément encadré.* "They really beat him up." **2.** To collide. *Sa voiture a encadré le réverbère.* "Her car wrapped itself around the streetlight." **3.** To endure. *Je ne peux plus l'encadrer.* "I can't put up with him anymore."

ENCAISSER 1. To get hit. *Il a dû encaisser pas mal pour être esquinté à ce point.* "He probably got severely pummeled, judging by the extent of his injuries." **2.** To stand. *Elle ne pouvait plus encaisser sa tyrannie.* "She could no longer bear his tyranny."

ENCEINTER/ENCEINTRER. To impregnate. *Elle refusait de dire qui l'avait enceintée.* "She wouldn't say who'd knocked her up."

EN CLOQUE. Pregnant (from **cloque**). **Être en cloque,** *idiom.* To be pregnant. *La lapine est de nouveau en cloque.* "The constant babymaker's pregnant again." **Mettre en cloque,** *idiom.* To impregnate. *Mais on ne sait pas qui l'a mise en cloque.* "But no one knows who got her pregnant."

ENCLOQUER. To impregnate. *C'est pas moi qui l'ai encloquée.* "I didn't knock her up."

ENCROUMÉ, -E. In debt. *Je ne supporte pas être encroumée.* "I can't stand being in debt."

(S')ENCROUMER. To go into debt. *Ils se sont encroumés pour construire leur maison.* "They went into hock to build their house."

ENCULADE = ENCULAGE.

ENCULAGE, *m.* Sodomizing. *Il se lubrifie avant l'enculage.* "He lubricates himself before taking it up the ass."

ENCULÉ, *m.* **1.** Sodomite. *Ils sont tous les deux des enculés.* "They're both asshole buddies." **2.** Rotten person. *Espèce d'enculé, fous-moi la paix!* "You bastard, bugger off!"

ENCULER. To sodomize. *Il se met toujours une capote avant de l'enculer.* "He always puts on a rubber before sodomizing her."

ENCULER LES MOUCHES. To quibble (lit. "to sodomize flies"). *Les curetons enculaient les mouches à propos du sexe des anges.* "The priests split hairs concerning the gender of angels."

EN DOUCE. On the quiet; sly. *Elle s'arrange toujours pour* *sortir en douce.* "She always manages to sneak out discreetly."

EN ÊTRE/EN ÊTRE COMME UN PHOQUE. To be one of them (esp. homosexuals). *Ça crève les yeux qu'il en est.* "It's obvious he's one of them."

EN FAIRE DE BELLES. See BELLE.

EN FAIRE VOIR DE BELLES. See BELLE.

ENFANT, *m., f.* Child. **Faire un enfant dans le dos à qn.,** *idiom.* To betray s.o. *Ce n'est pas la première fois que tu me fais un enfant dans le dos.* "It's not the first time you've stabbed me in the back."

ENFANT DE CHŒUR, *m.* Choirboy. *Le petit copain de ta fille n'est pas un enfant de chœur.* "Your daughter's little friend is no angel."

ENFANT DE SALOPE! "You bastard! SOB" (lit. "trollop's son").

ENFER, *m.* Hell. *J'ai vécu un enfer avec lui.* "Living with him was hell." **D'enfer.** Fantastic; impressive. *Ce joueur de tennis a un service d'enfer.* "That tennis player has a wicked serve."

ENFILER. To have sexually. *Il avait juste le temps de l'enfiler.* "He had just enough time to throw her one."

(S')ENFILER. 1. To copulate. *Ils cherchaient un coin tranquille pour s'enfiler.* "They looked for a quiet nook to make love in." **2.** To guzzle; devour. *J'ai pris le temps de m'enfiler un sandwich.* "I took the time to gobble down a sandwich." **3.** To take on s.t. difficult. *C'est toujours moi qui m'enfile les corvées.* "It's always me who gets stuck with the tough jobs."

ENFOIRÉ, -E. *m., f., adj.* and *n.* Stupid bastard. *Bande d'enfoirés—foutez le camp!* "You bunch of shitheads—get the hell out."

ENFOIRÉ, *m.* Homosexual. *Il croyait à tort qu'il était le seul enfoiré du bled.* "He believed, mistakenly, that he was the only queer in town."

ENFOIRER. To sodomize. *La tantouse rêvait de se faire enfoirer par toute l'équipe.* "The queen dreamed of being had by the whole team."

EN GAMIN. Female superior position. *Tous les deux aimaient mieux biter en gamin.* "Both of them preferred screwing with her on top."

ENGIN, *m.* Large penis (lit. "device"). *J'ai pris peur quand il a sorti son engin.* "I got frightened when he took out his weapon."

ENGRAISSER LES ASTICOTS. To be dead and buried (lit. "to fatten the maggots"). *Ça fait belle lurette qu'elle engraisse les asticots.* "She's been pushing up daisies for some time now."

ENGUEULADE, *f.* **1.** Severe reprimand. *Il aura une engueulade maison pour avoir découché.* "He'll get one hell of a bawling out for not having come home last night." **2.** Big argument. *Ils se sont quittés sur une engueulade.* "They parted after a stinking row."

ENGUEULER. To scold. *Ils ont engueulé leur gosse pour rien.* "They bawled out their kid for nothing."

ENGUEULER COMME DU POISSON POURRI. See POISSON.

(S')ENGUEULER. To quarrel. *Ils ne peuvent pas se parler sans s'engueuler.* "They can't talk to each other without getting into an argument."

ENGUIRLANDER. To reprimand (ironic use of "to garland"). *Je suis en retard; qu'est-ce que je vais me faire enguirlander par mes vioques.* "I'm late; my parents are going to read me the riot act."

ÉNIÈME. Umpteenth. *Je te demande pour la énième fois d'être polie avec mon nouveau mari.* "I'm asking you for the umpteenth time to be polite to my new husband."

EN LOUCÉDÉ/LOUCÉDOC/LOUSDÉ/LOUSDOC, largonji* forms of **en douce.**

* See explanation of **largonji,** page 205.

EN MOINS DE DEUX. On the double. *En moins de deux j'ai fait mes valises.* "I packed my bags in two shakes of a lamb's tail."

(S')ENNUYER COMME UN RAT MORT, see RAT.

ENSUQUER. To exhaust. *La balade à ski et la Williamine nous avaient ensuqués.* "We were really knocked out by the ski outing and the pear brandy."

ENTIFLE = ANTIFLE.

ENTORTILLER. To cajole (lit. "to wind"). *Je l'ai entortillée un max pour qu'elle sorte avec moi.* "I sweet-talked her a lot so she'd go out with me."

ENTOURLOUPE/ENTOURLOUPETTE, *f.* Swindle. *N'essaie plus de me faire des entourloupettes.* "Don't try to pull any more dirty tricks on me."

(D')ENTRÉE. From the outset. *D'entrée j'ai refusé de marcher dans leur combine.* "From the beginning I refused to have anything to do with their scam."

ENTRÉE DES ARTISTES/DE SERVICE, *f.* Anus (lit. "stage/service entrance"). *Pour ne pas l'engrosser, je la baise par l'entrée de service.* "So as not to knock her up, I bugger her."

ENTREFESSON = ENTREMICHON.

ENTREJOUFFLU = ENTREMICHON.

ENTREMICHON, *m.* Cleft separating the buttocks. *Elle portait un string pour qu'on admire son entremichon.* "She wore a G-string so people could admire her anal cleavage."

ENTUBER. 1. To sodomize. *Elle n'était pas d'accord pour se faire entuber.* "She didn't agree to take it up the ass." **2.** To swindle. *Je ne me laisserai plus entuber par ce vendeur.* "I won't get taken in again by that salesman."

ENVAPÉ, -E. Drunk; stoned. *Ils étaient tous envapés par cette gniole.* "They were all soused on that hooch." Cf. VAPÉ.

ENVOYÉ, -E. Sent. **(Bien) envoyé!** Well said! Well done! *Ça c'est bien envoyé!* "Right on! You said it!"

ENVOYER BALADER QN/QCH. See BALADER.

ENVOYER BOULER QN. See BOULER.

ENVOYER CHIER QN. To tell s.o. to go to hell. *Il me baratinait mais je l'ai envoyé chier.* "He fed me a line but I told him to piss off."

ENVOYER DINGUER/VALDINGUER QN. See VALDINGUER.

ENVOYER LA SAUCE. See SAUCE 1.

ENVOYER LA SEMOULE. See SEMOULE.

ENVOYER PAÎTRE QN. = ENVOYER BALADER QN.

ENVOYER PROMENER QN. = ENVOYER BALADER QN.

ENVOYER QN. SE FAIRE FOUTRE. To tell s.o. to fuck off. *Je les ai envoyés se faire foutre.* "I told them to fuck off."

ENVOYER SUR LES FRAISES = ENVOYER SUR LES ROSES.

ENVOYER SUR LES ROSES. See ROSE.

ENVOYER UNE VANNE/DES VANNES. See VANNE.

(S')ENVOYER. 1. To consume rapidly. *Il s'est envoyé un whisky et un sandwich.* "He belted down a whisky and gobbled a sandwich." **2.** To take on a difficult job. *Qui s'envoie la corvée du nettoyage?* "Who's going to tackle the cleaning up?" **3.** To have sexually. *Cette gonzesse, je me l'enverrais bien.* "I'd sure like to get into that broad's pants."

(S')ENVOYER DES FLEURS. 1. To trade compliments (lit. "to send one another flowers"). *Ils s'envoient des fleurs.* "They're a mutual admiration society." **2.** To trade insults, ironic. *Vous n'avez pas fini de vous envoyer des fleurs?* "Are you through throwing brickbats at each other?"

(S')ENVOYER EN L'AIR. To have sex. *Ils se sont retirés pour s'envoyer en l'air.* "They went off to make love."

ÉPATE, *f.* Ostentation. **Y aller à l'épate,** *idiom.* To show off. *Il y va toujours à l'épate.* "He's always trying to put on the dog."

ÉPATER LA GALERIE. To impress people. *C'est pour épater la galerie que tu t'es fringuée de la sorte?* "Have you gotten y.s. up like that to get people to notice you?"

ÉPINARDS, *m., pl.* Spinach. See METTRE…ÉPINARDS.

ÉPINGLER. To arrest (lit. "to pin"). *On a rapidement épinglé les casseurs.* "The burglars got nabbed fast."

ÉPONGE, *f.* Drunk (lit. "sponge"). *C'est une éponge finie.* "He's a confirmed alcoholic."

ÉPONGES, *f., pl.* Lungs. *Je suis partie au bord de la mer pour mes éponges.* "I went to the seashore for my lungs."

ESCALADEUSE DE BRAGUETTE, *f.* **1.** Prostitute (lit. "zipper climber"). *Le Sentier grouille d'escaladeuses de braguette.* "The Paris garment district is crawling with hookers." **2.** Nymphomaniac. *Il y avait plusieurs escaladeuses de braguette dans notre classe.* "There were several girls with hot pants in our class."

ESCALOPE, *f.* Tongue (lit. "cutlet [meat]"). See ROULER…ESCALOPE.

ESCALOPES, *f., pl.* **1.** Ears. *Ouvre bien tes escalopes.* "Open your ears now." **2.** The labia majora. *J'avais les escalopes en flammes.* "My lips were hot."

ESCOFFIER. 1. To steal. *Il a escoffié la formule de mon élixir d'amour.* "He stole the formula for my love potion." **2.** To kill. *Qui voulait escoffier les grands cuisiniers?* "Who wanted to kill the great chefs?"

ESGOURDER. To listen; hear. *Esgourdez, Edith va goualer.* "Listen up! Edith's going to sing."

ESGOURDES, *f., pl.* Ears. *Ouvre tes esgourdes; j'ai qch. d'important à te dire.* "Open your ears; I've got s.t. important to tell you."

ESPADOCHES/ESPAGAS, *f., pl.* Sandals. *Porter des espagas dans la neige? T'es barjo!* "Wearing sandals in the snow? You're nuts!"

ESPINGO, *m. adj.* and *n., pej.* Spaniard. *Goya et d'autres espingos vivaient en exil à Bordeaux.* "Goya and other Spaniards lived in exile in Bordeaux."

ESPINGOUIN = ESPINGO.

(S')ESQUINTER LA SANTÉ. To make a great effort (ironic for the lit. "to ruin one's health"). *Feignant que tu es, tu ne risques pas de t'esquinter la santé.* "Lazy lout that you are, you're in no danger of wearing y.s. out."

(S')ESQUINTER LES TRIPES. To knock o.s. out to do s.t. (lit. "to ruin one's guts"). *Je me suis esquinté les tripes pour toi, et tu t'en fous!* "I busted my buns for you and you don't give a damn!"

ESSOREUSE, *f.* Noisy motorbike (lit. "spindryer"). *Les essoreuses m'agressent les esgourdes.* "Noisy bikes bother my ears."

ESTAMPER. To fleece. *Si on va dans ce resto, on se fera estamper.* "If we go to that restaurant, we'll get taken."

ESTANCO, *m.* Small café (from Sp. "tobacco shop"). *On va s'arrêter au petit estanco du bled pour boire un pot.* "We'll stop at the town's little café to have a drink."

ESTOGOME = ESTOME.

ESTOME, *m.* Stomach. *J'ai l'estome fragile.* "I've got a sensitive tummy."

ET DES POUSSIÈRES. A bit more. *Elle a dix ans et des poussières.* "She's just a little over ten."

ET TA SŒUR! Mind your own business!

ÉTENDRE. 1. To floor (lit. "to spread out"). *Il a été étendu d'un crochet de gauche.* "He was knocked out by a left hook." **2.** To fail an exam. *Je bosse dure pour ne pas me faire étendre en maths.* "I work hard so as not to get shot down in math."

ÉTOILE FILANTE, *f.* Occasional prostitute (lit. "shooting star"). *Je défends mon coin et chasse les étoiles filantes.* "I defend my turf and chase away the amateurs."

ÉTOUFFER LE COUP = ÉCRASER LE COUP.

ÉTOUFFER L'ORPHELIN. To pinch money or chips from the pot in a card game (lit. "to smother the orphan"). *Je n'aime pas jouer avec qn. qui étouffe l'orphelin.* "I don't like playing with s.o. who sneaks from the kitty."

ÉTOUFFER UN PERROQUET. To have a pastis with mint (lit. "to choke a parrot"). *Et si on s'arrêtait pour étouffer un perroquet?* "How about stopping for a mint pastis?"

ÉTRANGLER LE BORGNE/POPAUL. See BORGNE.

ÊTRE. To be. See EN ÊTRE; Y ÊTRE; Y ÊTRE POUR QCH.

EUZIG(UE)S = LEUR(S)ZIGUE(S).

ÉVENTAIL, *m.* Fan. **Avoir les doigts de pieds; avoir les orteils en éventail** (lit. "to have one's toes spread out like a fan"). 1. To laze around. *Ce week-end j'aimerais bien avoir les orteils en éventail.* "I'd like to put my feet up this weekend." 2. To have an orgasm. See DOIGTS DE PIED.

(S')EXPLIQUER. 1. To quarrel. *"Allez vous expliquer ailleurs," a dit le barman.* "'Go fight/have it out someplace else,' said the bartender." **2.** To practice prostitution. *Celles qui s'expliquent dans le 8ème sont bien fringuées et vous offrent le champagne.* "Those who work the 8th arrondissement are well dressed and offer you champagne."

EXTRA, from **extraordinaire.** Marvelous. *La soirée était extra.* "It was a wonderful evening."

EXTRA, *m.* Special treat. **Se faire/s'offrir un extra.** To splurge. *Si l'on se faisait un extra chez Bocuse?* "How about splurging and going to Bocuse?"

FABRIQUER. To do (lit. "to manufacture"). *Qu'est-ce que tu fabriques là-bas?* "What are you up to over there?"

FAC, *f., abbr.* of **faculté.** *Ce prof enseigne à la fac.* "That professor teaches at the university."

FACE DE CRABE/RAT/D'ŒUF! Dog/pig/rat face!

FACHO, *adj.* and *m. n., pej.* Fascist. *Les fachos et les cocos se sont bagarrés.* "The Fascists and the Commies slugged it out."

FADA, *adj.* and *m. n.* Crazy. *Ça ne peut être qu'un fada qui a fait ça.* "Only a nut could have done that."

FAF = FACHO.

FAFFES, *m., pl.* Identity paper. *On m'a piqué mes faffes.* "S.o. swiped my ID."

FAGOT, *m.* **1.** Firewood. **Sentir le fagot** (lit. "to smell of kindling wood"). To be a burning offense. *"Les opinions de ce cureton sentent le fagot," pensait le cardinal.* "'That little priest's opinions smell of heresy,' thought the cardinal." See DE DERRIÈRE LES FAGOTS. **2.** Ex-convict. *On ignorait qu'il était un fagot.* "We didn't know he was an ex-con."

FAGOTÉ, -E. Dressed. *Elle était ahurie de se trouver sur la liste des plus mal fagotées de l'année.* "She was shocked to find h.s. on the list of the year's worst-dressed women." See AS DE PIQUE.

FAIBLE. Weak. See TOMBER FAIBLE.

FAIM, *f.* Hunger. See CREVER LA FAIM; PÉTER LA FAIM.

FAIRE. To do. **La faire à qn.,** *idiom.* To fool s.o. *On ne me la fera pas!* "They won't pull the wool over my eyes!" **Être fait (comme un rat).** To get arrested. *Après des mois de planque il a été fait.* "After hiding out for months they finally busted/cornered him." See FAUT LE FAIRE; SAVOIR Y FAIRE; (ÇA) COMMENCE À BIEN FAIRE.

FAIRE AMI-AMI. To make friends; be reconciled. *Cessons de nous disputer; faisons ami-ami.* "Let's stop quarreling and make up."

FAIRE DANS SON FROC/SA CULOTTE. To be very afraid. *Il fait dans son froc pour rien.* "He shits/pisses in his pants for the slightest little thing."

FAIRE DES MAGNES. To puff o.s. up (be pretentious); inflate a situation. *Ne fais plus de magnes.* "Stop putting on airs; stop complicating things."

FAIRE DES PATTES D'ARAIGNÉE. To gently caress erogenous zones (lit. "to make spider legs"). *Il aimait lui faire des pattes d'araignée tout autour de son angora.* "He enjoyed making love taps around her pussy."

FAIRE DU RAB. See RAB.

FAIRE LES POCHES À QN. To go through s.o.'s pockets; to pick a pocket. *Son gosse lui fait les poches.* "His kid pilfers from his pockets."

FAIRE NI UNE NI DEUX. To do s.t. unhesitatingly. *Il est parti sans faire ni une ni deux.* "He left just like that."

FAIRE SES BESOINS/COMMISSIONS, *euph.*, children. To eliminate waste. *Je sors le chien pour qu'il fasse ses besoins.* "I take the dog out so he can do his business." *As-tu fait toutes tes commissions, la petite et la grande.* "Did you do number 1 and number 2?"

FAIRE SON AFFAIRE À QN. To rub out. *Malgré ses gardes du corps, la flingueuse lui a fait son affaire.* "Despite his bodyguards, the contract killer bumped him off."

FAIRE UN FROMAGE DE QCH. To dramatize (lit. "to make a cheese of s.t."). *C'est pas la peine d'en faire un fromage.* "It's not worth making a big thing out of it."

FAIRE UN MONDE/SAC/UNE HISTOIRE DE QCH. = **FAIRE UN FROMAGE.**

FAIRE UN TABAC. See TABAC **2.**

FAIRE UNE TOUCHE. See TOUCHE.

FAIRE VINAIGRE. See VINAIGRE.

(SE) FAIRE. To earn. *Je me fais un bon mois dans ce boulot.* "I take home a good salary every month."

(SE) FAIRE DU FRIC/POGNON = **(SE) FAIRE.**

(SE) FAIRE QN. 1. To put up with s.o. *Je ne peux plus me les faire, ses mômes.* "I can't stand her brats anymore." **2.** To have sex with s.o. *Nous nous la sommes faite!* "We banged her."

(SE) FAIRE ROULER. To get swindled. *Je me suis vraiment fait rouler par ce garagiste.* "That mechanic really took me for a ride."

(S'EN) FAIRE. To worry. *"Dans la vie faut pas s'en faire; moi, j'ne m'en fais pas,"* chantait Maurice Chevalier. "'Life's not for fretting; I don't sweat it,' sang Maurice Chevalier."

FAISAN, *m.* Crook (lit. "pheasant"). *Tu crois à ce faisan de promoteur?* "You believe that con artist real estate developer?"

FAISANDÉ, -E, *adj.* and *m. n.* (S.t.) fishy (lit. "gamey"). *L'officier trouvait qu'il y avait qch. de faisandé au Danemark.* "The officer thought there was s.t. rotten in Denmark."

FAISEUR, -EUSE D'ANGES, *m., f.* Illegal abortionist. *Les faiseurs d'anges râlaient quand on a légalisé l'avortement.* "The back alley abortionists complained when abortion was legalized."

FAISANDIER = **FAISAN.**

FAIT, -E. Drunk. *Cette fois-ci il est bien fait.* "This time he's really soused."

FALZAR, *m.* Pants. *Il voulait des falzars rouges, comme ceux des pêcheurs.* "He wanted red pants, like the fishermen's."

(DES) FAMILLES. Homestyle; simple. *C'était une petite fête des familles.* "It was an unpretentious get-together."

FANA, *abbr.* of **fanatique.** Enthusiastic about. *Il est fana de vélo.* "He's nuts about biking."

FANA, *m., f.* Devoted fan. *C'est une fana d'opéra.* "She's an opera buff."

FANTAISIE, *f.* Fellatio (lit. "imagination"; "whim"). *Elle aimait commencer par une fantaisie.* "She liked to start things off with a little blow job."

FARCIR. 1. To riddle with bullets (lit. "to stuff"). *Après le braquage, la devanture de la banque était farcie de balles.* "After the holdup, the front of the bank was all shot up."

(SE) FARCIR. 1. To have sexually. *Je me la farcirais bien.* "I'd sure like to plug her." **2.** To endure. *Je me suis farci une longue attente chez le dentiste.* "I had to put up with a long wait at the dentist's."

FARD, *m.* Makeup. See PIQUER UN FARD.

FASTOCHE. Easy. *Ton problème est fastoche.* "Your problem's easy."

FATMA/FATMUCHE, *f., pej.* Ar. woman; woman (from Fatima, Mohammed's daughter, a popular Ar. first name). *Dans ta cape tu ressembles à une fatma.* "Your cape makes you look like an Arab woman."

FAUCHE, *f.* Petty theft. *Cet accro vit de la fauche.* "That junky lives by shoplifting."

FAUCHÉ, -E (COMME LES BLÉS). Penniless (lit. "cut down like stalks of wheat"). *Pas de vacs cette année; nous sommes fauchés comme les blés.* "No vacation this year; we're flat broke."

FAUCHER. To steal (lit. "to mow"; "reap"). *On a fauché mon pépin.* "Somebody swiped my umbrella."

FAUCHMAN = FAUCHÉ.

FAUT LE FAIRE! That's really s.t.! *Débarquer avec sa smala sans prévenir—faut le faire!* "Descending unannounced on us with her tribe—what do you think of that!"

FAUT PAS DÉCONNER! Cut the crap!

FAUT QUE ÇA CHIE!, (lit. "it's got to shit!"). "No more dawdling. Let's get this show on the road!"

FAUX COMME UN JETON = FAUX JETON.

FAUX CUL/DERCHE, *m.* Hypocrite (lit. "fake ass"). *Je ne veux plus voir ce faux cul.* "I don't want to see that two-faced bastard again."

FAUX JETON, *m.,* Phony. *C'est un faux jeton.* "He's as phony as a three-dollar bill."

FAVEUR, *f.* Fellatio (lit. "favor"). *Par courtoisie elle lui fait souvent une faveur.* "As a courtesy, she often gives him head."

FAVOUILLE, javanais of **fouille.**

FAYOT, *m.* Toady (lit. "bean"). *Je l'insupporte, ce fayot.* "I can't stand that ass-kisser."

FÉBOU, *f.,* backslang of **bouffe.** Food. *Qui fait la fébou ce soir.* "Who's cooking dinner tonight?"

FÉCA, *m.,* backslang of **café.** *Ton féca, c'est de la pisse d'âne.* "Your coffee's dishwater."

FÉE BLANCHE, *f.* Cocaine (lit. "white fairy"). *La fée blanche le faisait dialoguer avec Freud et Sherlock Holmes.* "Under the spell of cocaine, he talked with Freud and Sherlock Holmes."

FÉE BRUNE, *f.* Opium (lit. "dark fairy"). *Elle n'achetait que des ivoires jaunis dans les fumeries de la fée brune.* "She bought only ivory carvings yellowed in opium dens."

FÉE DU LOGIS, *f.* Perfect housewife (lit. "the home's fairy"). *Sa femme est une occase et la fée du logis.* "His wife's an occasional prostitute and a perfect homemaker."

FÉE VERTE, *f.* Hashish. *Il ne pouvait pas vivre sans la magie de la fée verte, magie qui s'est transformée en fée Carabosse.* "He couldn't live without the magic of hash, magic that turned bad."

FEIGNANT, -E/FEIGNARD, -E/FEIGNASSE. Lazy. *Si tu pouvais être moins feignant!* "If only you could be less of a couch potato!"

FEINTER. To deceive. *N'essaie pas de me feinter; je sais tout.* "Don't try to put one over on me; I know all about it."

FÊLÉ, -E. Cracked. *Il ne serait pas un peu fêlé, par hasard?* "Isn't he a little off his rocker?"

FEMME, *f.* See BONNE FEMME; BONNES FEMMES.

FEMMELETTE, *f.* **1.** Weak woman. *Elle aimait jouer à la femmelette.* "She liked playing the clinging vine." **2.** Wimp. *Le critique traitait Hamlet de femmelette.* "The critic called Hamlet a wimp."

FENDANT, -E. Hilarious (lit. "splitting"). *Quelle histoire fendante!* "What a side-splitting story!"

FENDANT, *m.* Pants. *Il vient d'acheter un nouveau fendant.* "He just bought a new pair of pants."

FENDARD = FENDANT.

FENDASSE, *f.* Female genitalia; female, *pej. Cette fendasse se gratte toujours la fendasse.* "That cunt's always scratching her cunt."

FENDRE L'ARCHE. See ARCHE.

(SE) FENDRE DE. To shell out money grudgingly. *Il ne voulait pas se fendre d'une brique pour me payer une bagnole.* "He wouldn't spring for 10,000 francs to buy me a car."

(SE) FENDRE LA GUEULE/PÊCHE/PIPE. To laugh one's head off. *Il n'y a pas de quoi se fendre la gueule.* "That's anything but a laughing matter."

FENDUE = FENDASSE.

FENÊTRIÈRE, *f.* Prostitute who solicits from her window; prostitute on display in a brothel window. *Elle a été fenêtrière et à Amsterdam et à Hambourg.* "She was showcased in both Amsterdam and Hamburg."

FERME-LA!/LA FERME!/FERME TA GUEULE!. "Shut your face/trap! Put a lid on it!"

FERMER SON CLAPET/SA GUEULE. To shut up. *Il pourrait bien fermer son clapet!* "I wish that guy would keep his trap shut!"

FERMER SON CLAQUE-MERDE, stronger version of previous entry. *Ferme ton claque-merde.* "Shut your fucking mouth!"

FERRAILLE, *f.* Small change (lit. "scrap metal"). *Je n'avais que de la ferraille.* "All I had were a few measly coins." See TAS DE FERRAILLE.

FESSE, *f.* **1.** Buttock. *Les cannibales ont coupé une fesse à la servante de Cunégonde.* "The cannibals cut one buttock off Cunegonde's servant's butt." **2.** Woman as sex object. *Si tu cherches de la fesse, va dans ce troquet.* "If you're looking for a piece of ass, go to that bar." See DE FESSE; (N')Y ALLER QUE D'UNE FESSE.

FESSES, *f., pl.* Buttocks. **Mes fesses!** "My ass!" See COLLER AUX FESSES; DE MES DEUX; DE MES FESSES; (SE) MAGNER LES FESSES; OCCUPE...FESSES; PEAU DES FESSES; SERRER LES FESSES; TIRE-FESSES.

FESTOUILLE, *f.* Party. *Une petite festouille de temps en temps ça fait du bien.* "A nice little bash or shindig now and then is just the thing."

FÊTE, *f.* Party. **Faire sa fête à qn.,** ironic. To beat s.o. up. *On lui a fait sa fête à la sortie du bar.* "They beat him up when he left the bar." **Ça va être ta fête!** ironic. "You're going to get what's coming to you!"

FEU, *m.* Fire. **(Il n') y a pas le feu!** "Where's the fire? What's the rush?" See COUP DE FEU; PÉTER LE FEU.

(AVOIR LE) FEU AU CUL/AUX FESSES/QQ. PART. **1.** To be in a great hurry. *Tu pars déjà? Tu as le feu qq.*

part? "You're leaving already? Do you have to catch a train/put out a fire somewhere?" **2.** To be horny. *Déjà à quatorze ans elle avait le feu aux fesses.* "Already at fourteen, she was a sexpot."

FEUILLE, *f.* **1.** Leaf. **Regarder/voir la feuille à l'envers.** To have sex in the country or under a tree (lit. "to see the underside of the leaf"). *Après le déj sur l'herbe ils ont regardé la feuille à l'envers.* "After eating on the grass they had a roll in the hay." **2.** Ear. See DUR…FEUILLE.

FEUILLE DE CHOU, *f.* Newspaper. *Ne te cache pas derrière ta feuille de chou.* "Don't hide behind your newspaper." **Avoir les oreilles en feuilles de chou.** To have cauliflower ears. *Le boxeur a les oreilles en feuilles de chou.* "The boxer has cauliflower ears."

FEUILLE DE ROSE, *f.* Anilinctus. *Même quand c'est lavé, elle refuse de faire feuille de rose.* "She won't ream/do a rim job even on a washed rosebud."

FEUJ, *adj.* and *m. n.,* backslang of **juif.** Jew; Jewish. *Nous aimons la cuisine feuj.* "We like Jewish cooking."

FIASC/FIASQUE, *m.* from **fiasco.** Failure. *C'était le fiasc total.* "It was a total flop."

FICELLE, *f.* String. See TIRER SUR LA FICELLE; TIRER LES FICELLES; CONNAÎTRE…FICELLES.

FICELLÉ, -E. Dressed up. *Regarde comme tu es mal ficelée.* "Look at how badly you've gotten y.s. up." See AS DE PIQUE.

FICHAISE = FOUTAISE.

FICHER, dated, less vigorous synonym of FOUTRE.

(SE) FICHER = (SE) FOUTRE.

(S'EN) FICHER = (S'EN) FOUTRE.

FICHTREMENT = FOUTREMENT.

FICHU, -E = FOUTU, -E. See AS DE PIQUE.

FICHUMENT = FOUTUMENT.

FIEF, *m.* Stronghold (lit. "fief"). *Ce village était un fief des cocos.* "That village used to be a communist stronghold."

FIEFFÉ, -E. Out-and-out. *"Je ne suis ni phallo ni facho." "Tu es un menteur fieffé."* "I'm neither a sexist nor a fascist." "You're a damned liar."

FIÉROT, *adj.* and *m. noun.* Swell-headed. *Il n'y pas de quoi faire le fiérot.* "You've got little reason to be so stuck-up."

FIEU, *m.* **1.** Son. *Elle est fier de son fieu.* "She's proud of her son." **2.** Lad. *C'était un bon fieu mais la drogue l'a tué.* "He was a good guy but drugs ruined him."

FIFILLE, *f.* Sweet little girl. *C'est bien la fifille à sa maman.* "She's her mother's little darling."

FIFINE, *f.* Sanitary napkin. *Ne jette pas ta fifine dans le pot.* "Don't throw your rag down the toilet bowl."

FIGNARD/FIGNARÈS = FIGNE.

FIGNE, *m.* Anus. **Donner/lâcher du figne.** To practice passive homosexuality. *Jean Genet a commencé très jeune à lâcher du figne.* "Jean Genet began putting out when he was very young."

FIGNEDÉ/FIGNOLET/FIGNON = FIGNE.

FIGUE, *f.* Female genitalia (lit. "fig"). *Sa figue ne se détendait pas.* "Her snatch didn't relax."

FIGUES, *f., pl.* Testicles. **Avoir les figues molles.** To have low sexual desire. *Je sais faire bander même ceux qui ont les figues molles.* "I know how to get even the limpest dicks up."

FIL, *m.* Thread. See COUP DE FIL; LÂCHER UN FIL.

FILER. 1. To spin. See FILER…AMOUR. **2.** To give. *File-moi des ronds.* "Give me some money." **3.** To follow. *Il ne savait pas que les flics le filaient.* "He didn't know the cops were tailing him."

FILER À L'ANGLAISE. To take French leave; slip off. *Nous avons filé avant la fin du concert.* "We left discreetly before the end of the concert."

FILER DE LA JAQUETTE. See JAQUETTE.

FILER DU CHOUETTE/EN FILER. To be homosexually passive. *Des fois il aime filer du chouette, mais pas tou-*

jours. "Sometimes he likes playing the female role, but not always."

FILER LE COUP DE GUIZOT. To have sex. *Cet historien godant a toujours envie de filer le coup de guizot.* "That horny historian always wants to get his end in."

FILER LE PARFAIT AMOUR. To live together blissfully with the love of one's life (lit. "to spin out [weave a web of] perfect love"). *Malgré ses cinq divorces, il rêve toujours de filer le parfait amour.* "Despite his five divorces, he's still dreaming of romantic love."

FILER UN COUP/UNE BEIGNE/JAVA/PÊCHE/ RACLÉE/TREMPE À QN. To smack s.o. *Si tu continues ton cirque, je vais te filer une raclée.* "If you keep acting up like that, I'll give you a whack."

FILER UN COUP DANS LE CALCIF = FILER... GUIZOT.

FILER UN COUP D'ARBALÈTE. See ARBALÈTE.

FILER UN COUP DE SABRE. See SABRE.

FILER SON VENIN. See VENIN.

FILER UNE AVOINE. See AVOINE.

FILET, *m.* Net. See COUP DE FILET.

FILLE, *f.* Prostitute (lit. "girl"). *Il aime se payer une fille de temps en temps.* "He likes an occasional encounter with a working girl."

FILLE D'AMOUR, *f.* Full-time prostitute working for a pimp or madam. *Malheureuse enfant, elle était heureuse de devenir une fille d'amour.* "After a troubled childhood, she was happy to become a full-fledged, totally pledged whore."

FILLE DE JOIE, *f.,* dated for **fille.**

FILLE DE L'AIR. See JOUER...AIR.

FILOCHE, *f.* Shadowing. **Prendre qn. en filoche,** *idiom.* To have s.o. followed. *Ce dileur a été pris en filoche.* "They put a tail on that dealer."

FILS À PAPA, *f.* Son whose father makes things easy for him. *Ne fais pas de ton fils un fils à papa.* "Don't turn your boy into a daddy's boy without initiative."

FILS DE PUTE/PUTAIN. SOB (lit. "whore's son"). *Fous le camp, fils de pute.* "Fuck off, dickhead."

FIN. Entirely. *Je suis fin prêt; on peut partir.* "I'm completely ready; we can leave."

FIN DES HARICOTS, *f.* Curtains; all done for. *Ce sera la fin des haricots si la star tombe malade.* "It'll be all over if the star gets sick."

FINE GUEULE, *f.* Gourmet. *On invitera cette fine gueule chez maman.* "We'll invite that connoisseur of fine food to Mom's house."

FINI, -E. 1. Done for. *Je ne suis pas encore finie, malgré mon grand âge.* "It's not over and done with for me, despite my advanced age." **2.** Complete. *Ce gosse est un paresseux fini.* "That kid's as lazy as they come."

FION, *m.* **1.** Anus. See (SE) MAGNER LE FION; (SE) CASS-ER...FION. **2.** Luck. **Avoir du fion,** *idiom.* To be lucky. *Il a eu du fion, tomber sur une femme pareille.* "He was lucky, finding a woman like that."

FISSURE, *f.* Fissure. **Avoir une fissure,** *idiom.* To be a bit cracked. *Son mac a une fissure.* "Her guy's got a screw loose."

FISTON, *m.* Son; boy. *Tu sais que je veux ton bien, mon fiston.* "You know I want what's best for you, my boy."

FISTULE, *f.* Fistula. **Avoir de la fistule,** *idiom.* To be lucky. *Malgré tout, il a eu de la fistule.* "Despite everything, he was lucky."

FIX/FIXE, *m.* Injected drug. *Il a besoin d'un fixe.* "He needs a fix."

SE FIXER. To shoot up drugs. *Il se fixe toujours avec une seringue à jeter.* "He always shoots up with a disposable needle."

FLAG, from *in flagrante delicto.* **Être pris en flag,** *idiom.* To be caught red-handed. *Sa femme l'a pris en flag avec sa* *maîtresse.* "His wife caught him and his mistress in the act."

FLAGADA. Exhausted. *Surexcité hier, flagada aujourd'hui.* "Frenetic yesterday, pooped out today."

FLAGDA, *m.,* argot for **flageolet.** Bean. *J'aime bien le gigot, mais sans flagdas.* "I like leg of lamb, but without beans." Note: In America, mint often accompanies leg of lamb; in France, leg of lamb is usually served with little lima beans.

FLAMBER. To be a big gambler or spender; to squander. *Il a flambé toute ses économies avec sa nana.* "He blew all his savings on his girlfriend."

FLAMBEUR, -EUSE. Professional/chronic gambler. *Dostoyevski était un grand flambeur.* "Dostoyevski was a chronic gambler."

FLAN, *m.* Nonsense (lit. "custard"). **C'est du flan.** "That's horse manure." See (EN) RESTER…FLAN.

FLANC, *m.* Side. **Être sur le flanc,** *idiom.* To be exhausted. *Après ce travail j'étais sur le flanc.* "I was all done in after that job." See TIRER AU FLANC.

FLANCHER. To weaken; abandon. *Tu ne vas pas flancher si près du but?* "You're not going to give up so close to the goal?"

FLANQUER UNE BAFFE/BEIGNE/RACLÉE À QN. To slap s.o. *Le prof avait envie de lui flanquer une beigne.* "The teacher felt like whacking him."

FLAPI, -E. Exhausted. *Dieu merci, c'est vendredi; je suis flapie.* "Thank God it's Friday; I'm bushed."

FLASHER SUR QN./QCH. To feel a sudden rush for s.o./s.t. *J'ai flashé sur les deux, la nana et sa bagnole.* "I really went for both of them, the chick and her car."

FLÉMINGITE, *f.* Lazy. *Pour ce qui est de faire le ménage, j'ai la flémingite aiguë.* "When it comes to doing the housework, I'm the laziest guy in the world."

FLEMME, *f.* Laziness. *J'ai la flemme d'y aller.* "I'm too lazy to go there." See TIRER SA FLEMME.

FLEUR, *f.* Favor (lit. "flower"). *Il m'a fait une fleur en me remplaçant au boulot.* "He did me a favor by taking my place at work." See COMME UNE FLEUR; (S')ENVOYER DES FLEURS; MARCHAND DE FLEURS; PERDRE SA FLEUR.

FLEUR BLEUE, *f.* Incurably romantic. *J'aime son côté fleur bleue.* "I like his sentimental side."

FLIBUSTIER, *m.* Swindler. *Cet antiquaire est un flibustier.* "That antique dealer's a crook."

FLIC, *m.* Policeman. *Il est devenu flic comme son dab.* "He became a cop like his dad."

FLICAILLE, *f.* The police. *La flicaille est partout à cause de la manif.* "The fuzz are everywhere because of the demonstration."

FLINGUE, *m.* Pistol. *Son flingue est toujours à portée de main.* "His piece is always within reach."

FLINGUER. To shoot. *Les truands l'ont flingué pour se sauver.* "The crooks blew him away so they could escape."

(SE) FLINGUER. To be very depressed (lit. "to commit suicide"). *Ne te flingue pas pour une amourette perdue.* "Don't worry y.s. sick over a broken love affair."

FLINGUEUR, -EUSE, *m., f.* Trigger-happy killer; contract killer. *La flicaille se méfiait de ce flingueur de première.* "The cops were on their guard around the notorious killer."

FLIP, *m.* Drug-induced depression; depression. *Ce livre est le flip fini.* "That book's a total downer."

FLIPPANT, -E. Depressing; creepy. *C'est flippant de voir tant de sans abris.* "It's depressing to see so many home-less people."

FLIPPER. 1. To be or get depressed (orig. as a result of tak-ing drugs). *Tous ces mendigots dans le métro, ça me fait flipper.* "All those beggars in the subway get me down." **2.** To be stressed. *Je flippais avant de passer à l'exam.* "I was keyed up before the exam." (Note that neither mean-ing is "to flip out," although meaning **2** moves in that direction.)

FLOP(P)ÉE, *m.* A large amount. *On a acheté une flopée de réserves.* "We stocked up on a whole bunch of stuff."

FLOTTE, *f.* Water; rain; drink. *J'ai reçu toute la flotte.* "I got soaked to the skin."

FLOTTER. To rain. *Il a flotté toute la journée.* "It poured all day."

FLOTTEURS, *m., pl.* Big breasts. *Avec des flotteurs pareils elle ne risque pas de se noyer!* "With bazooms like that, she's in no danger of drowning!"

FLOUSE/FLOUZE, *m.* Money. *Il se balade toujours avec du flouse plein les poches.* "He always walks around with plenty of dough on him."

FLOUSER. To fart. *Les fayots nous ont fait flouser toute la nuit.* "The beans made us fart all night."

FLÛTE, *f.* **1.** Flute. See JOUER...FLÛTE; **2.** Leg. See JOUER DES FLÛTES.

FLÛTE!, *euph.* for **foutre!** Gosh darn! Gosh damn!

FOFOLLE, *f. adj.* and *n.* Scatterbrained. *Ne fais pas attention; elle fait sa fofolle.* "Don't bother about her; she's acting crazy."

FOIN, *m.* **1.** Hay. **Faire du foin,** *idiom.* To make noise; create scandal. *Quand les flics ont fouillé leur appart, ça a fait du foin.* "There was quite a rumpus when the fuzz searched their apartment." **2.** Poor-grade tobacco; marijuana. *Il plantait du foin dans le jardin de sa grand-mère.* "He planted 'grass' in his grandmother's garden."

FOIRADE, *f.* **1.** Diarrhea. *Nous avons terminé notre gueuleton avec une bonne foirade.* "Our fine feast ended up with everyone having the runs." **2.** Fear. *Il avait la foirade en voyant les gangsters.* "He was scared shitless when he saw the gangsters." **3.** Failure. *Je ne m'attendais pas à une telle foirade.* "I wasn't expecting everything to go down the toilet/to be a total washout like that."

FOIRARD, -E = FOIREUX, -EUSE.

FOIRE, *f.* Fair. **C'est la foire ici!** "This place is a madhouse!" **Faire la foire,** *idiom.* To celebrate. *Les bonshommes sont partis faire la foire.* "The guys have gone out on a binge."

FOIRE D'EMPOIGNE. Free-for-all; rat race. *Lors des soldes, c'est la foire d'empoigne dans les grands magasins.* "When it's sale time in the department stores, it's everyone for h.s."

FOIRER. 1. To defecate. *Le chien a foiré sur la moquette.* "The dog crapped on the carpet." **2.** To go wrong; fail. *J'ai foiré complètement à l'exam.* "I really screwed up on the exam."

FOIREUX, -EUSE. Unlikely to succeed. *La plupart de ses projets sont foireux.* "Most of his projects are of doubtful value."

FOIRIDON/FOIRIDONDAINE = FOIRE.

FOLDINGUE. Crazy. *Il conduit à une vitesse foldingue.* "He speeds like a madman."

FOLICHON, -ONNE. Pleasant. See PAS FOLICHON.

FOL(L)INGUE = FOLDINGUE.

FOLKEUX, -EUSE, *m., f.* Folk music player or enthusiast. *On ira au festival des folkeux.* "We'll go to the folk musicians' festival."

FOLKLO *m.,* from **folklorique.** Old-fashioned; weird. *Toute la famille est folklo.* "The whole family are eccentrics."

FOLLE, *f.* Effeminate homosexual (lit. "madwoman"). *Les grandes folles éclataient de rire.* "The mad queens burst out laughing."

FOLLE PERDUE/FOLLE TORDUE, more emphatic for FOLLE.

(À) FOND DE CALE. Flat broke (lit. "at the bottom of the ship's hold"). *Le chômage l'a mis à fond de cale.* "He's unemployed and at rock bottom."

(À) FOND LA CAISSE. 1. At top speed (car or motorcycle). *Il roule toujours à fond la caisse.* "He always drives at top speed." **2.** All out. *Il marche toujours à fond la caisse.* "He always gives it everything he's got."

FORMIDABLE, *m.* Large glass of beer (one liter in northeast Fr.; a half-liter (pint) elsewhere). *Il buvait formidable sur formidable.* "He drank one mug of beer after another."

FORMIDE, from *adj.* **formidable.** Wonderful. *Elle est formide sa nana.* "His broad's terrific."

FORT. Strongly. **Y aller fort,** *idiom.* To exaggerate. *Tu y vas un peu fort.* "You're overdoing it a bit." **Faire fort,** *idiom.* To have great success. *Bravo! Tu as fait fort!* "Bravo! You made it big!"

FORTICHE, *m., f.* Brainy. *Tu es fortiche.* "You've got smarts."

FOUDRE, *m.* Lightning. See COUP DE FOUDRE.

FOUFOU. Crazy. *Il est un peu foufou ce jeunot.* "That kid's a bit cracked."

FOUFOUNE/FOUFOUNETTE, *f.* Female genitalia. *Elle portait une jolie robe à froufrous mais je ne pensais qu'à dévoiler sa foufoune.* "She was wearing a nice frilly dress, but all I could think about was getting at her snatch."

FOUILLE, *f.* Pocket (lit. "search"; "archaeological dig"). **C'est dans la fouille!** "It's in the bag." **En avoir plein les fouilles,** *idiom.* To be very rich. *Tes vioques en ont plein les fouilles.* "Your parents are loaded."

FOUILLE-MERDE, *m., f.* Muckraking journalist; scandal-monger. *La vie sans histoires du prince faisait le désespoir des fouille-merde.* "The prince's uneventful life made the muckrakers very unhappy."

FOUILLE PERCÉE, *f.* Person with holes in his or her pocket. *Pas possible d'économiser avec ma fouille percée de mari.* "Impossible to save anything with a spendthrift husband like mine."

FOUILLER. To have sexually (lit. "to rummage"). *Il avait une envie folle de la fouiller.* "He really wanted to plug her."

(SE) FOUILLER. To go through one's pockets. **Tu peux te fouiller.** "No way! Go to hell!"

FOUILLETTE = FOUILLE.

FOUILLOUSE = FOUILLE.

FOUINARD, -E, *m., f.* Busybody. *Je ne suis pas fouinarde, mais je fais les poches de mon mari.* "I'm not a snoop but I go through my husband's pockets."

FOULARD, *m.* Scarf. See BANDER FOULARD.

(SE) FOULER. To work hard. See RATE.

FOULTITUDE, *f.* Crowd; large amount. *La prêtresse énonce une foultitude de béatitudes pour nous aider à vaincre nos mauvaises attitudes.* "The priestess expounds heaps of beatitudes to help us overcome our bad attitudes."

FOUNETTE = FOUFOUNE.

FOUR, *m.* Flop (lit. "oven"). *Les dernières pièces de Tennessee Williams, descendues en flammes par la critique, ont été des fours.* "Tennessee Williams' last plays, roasted by the critics, were flops."

FOURBI, *m.* Stuff. *Il avait tout un fourbi dans le grenier des vioques.* "He had a pile of junk in his parents' attic."

FOURCHETTE, *f.* Fork. See COUP DE FOURCHETTE.

FOURCHETTES, *f., pl.* Legs. See JOUER...FOURCHETTES.

FOURMI, *f.* Small-time drug dealer (lit. "ant"). *Cette fourmi a été écrasée par les grands dileurs.* "That pissant dealer got crushed by the big guys."

FOURRÉ. See COUP FOURRÉ.

FOURRER. To have sexually (lit. "to stuff"). *Ma grandtante, vieille fille, n'a jamais voulu être fourrée.* "My oldmaid great-aunt never wanted to get laid."

(SE) FOURRER. To make a mistake. **Se fourrer le doigt dans l'œil (jusqu'au coude),** *idiom.* To make a whale of a mistake (lit. "to stuff one's finger into one's eye [as far as one's elbow]"). *Je me suis fourré le doigt dans l'œil en imaginant qu'il avait une maîtresse.* "I was very much mistaken when I thought he had a mistress."

151

FOUTAISE, *m.* Nonsense. *Tes arguments, c'est de la foutaise.* "Your arguments are a bunch of baloney."

FOUTEUR, -EUSE DE MERDE, *m., f.* Troublemaker. *Méfie-toi de cette fouteuse de merde.* "Watch out for that shitmixer."

FOUTOIR, *m.* Messy place; dump. *Je ne retrouve rien dans ce foutoir.* "I can't find anything in this mess."

FOUTRE, *m.* Sperm. *Ce gosse se branle sans arrêt et sent toujours le foutre.* "That kid never stops jerking off and always smells of sperm."

FOUTRE. 1. To have sex. *Il aimait la foutre sous le cerisier.* "He liked to lay her under the cherry tree." **2.** To put. *Le prof nous a dit de ne pas foutre le verbe "foutre" partout.* "The teacher told us not to put (use) the verb *foutre* everywhere." **3.** To do. *Il n'a jamais rien foutu à l'école.* "He never did any work at school." See RAME.

FOUTRE! Fuck it! Damn it to hell!

(SE) FOUTRE À. To begin. *Quand vas-tu te foutre au boulot?* "When are you going to get to work?"

FOUTRE À LA PORTE, FOUTRE DEHORS, *idiom.* To throw out. *Je l'ai foutu à la porte.* "I threw him out."

(S'EN) FOUTRE COMME DE L'AN QUARANTE/ S'EN FOUTRE PAS MAL/COMME DE SA DERNIÈRE CHEMISE/COMPLÈTEMENT. To not give a damn. *De tes conseils, je m'en fous pas mal.* "I couldn't care less about your advice."

FOUTRE DEDANS, *idiom.* To mislead. *Il m'a foutu dedans avec ses explications à la gomme.* "He really put me up shit's creek with his lousy explanations." See MERDE; MERDIER.

(SE) FOUTRE DEDANS, *idiom.* To make a mistake. *Je me suis foutu dedans, pour mes calculs.* "I crewed up in my calculations."

(SE) FOUTRE DE QCH. = S'EN FOUTRE...

(SE) FOUTRE DE QN./DE LA GUEULE DE QN. To pull s.o.'s leg. *Ne te fous pas de ma gueule.* "Don't put me on."

(SE) FOUTRE DU MONDE. To not care about anyone or anything and behave outrageously. *Tu nous redemandes du fric? Tu te fous du monde?* "You're asking us for money again? Who the hell do you think you think you are?"

FOUTRE EN L'AIR, *idiom.* To ruin. *L'ordinateur a foiré et tout son travail a ête foutu en l'air.* "The computer screwed up and all his work is in the electricity."

(SE) FOUTRE EN L'AIR, *idiom.* To commit suicide. *Hedda voulait qu'il se foute en l'air de façon élégante.* "Hedda wanted him to do h.s. in elegantly."

FOUTRE EN POUBELLE, *idiom.* To junk. *Toutes ses peintures sont à foutre en poubelle.* "All his paintings should be trashed."

(SE) FOUTRE EN ROGNE. See ROGNE.

FOUTRE LA PAIX. See PAIX.

FOUTRE L'ARGENT PAR LES FENÊTRES, *idiom.* To waste money. *Je n'ai pas d'argent à foutre par les fenêtres.* "I haven't got money to throw down the drain."

FOUTRE LE CAMP. To clear out. *Fous-moi le camp!* "Get the hell out! Fuck off! Piss off!"

FOUTRE LE TRAC/LA TROUILLE, *idiom.* To frighten. *Le film d'épouvante nous a foutu la trouille.* "The horror film gave us the willies."

FOUTREMENT. Extremely. *C'était foutrement bon ton frichti!* "Your meal was damned good!"

FOUTRE PAR TERRE, *idiom.* To chuck it all. *Parfois j'ai envie de tout foutre par terre.* "Sometimes I feel like saying to hell with it all."

FOUTRE RIEN. Not a goddamned thing. *Je n'en sais foutre rien.* "I don't know a fucking thing about it."

FOUTU, -E. 1. Done for. *C'est foutu d'avance!* "It's doomed before starting!" **2.** No good; useless; lousy. *Quelle foutue maison!* "What a dump!" **3.** Broken; *Ton magnétoscope est foutu.* "Your VCR's busted." **4.** Built. *C'est appareil est mal foutu.* "This appliance is poorly constructed." *Cette nana est bien foutue.* "That broad's stacked."

FOUTU, -E COMME L'AS DE PIQUE/COMME QUATRE SOUS. Badly dressed. See AS DE PIQUE.

FOUTU DE. Capable of; likely to. *Il n'est pas foutu d'arriver à l'heure.* "He's incapable of arriving on time."

FOUTUMENT = FOUTREMENT.

FRAÎCHE, *f.* Cash. *Au marché ils exigent de la fraîche.* "At the market, they want to be paid in cash."

FRAIS, *m., pl.* Expenses. **Arrêter les frais,** *idiom.* To call it quits. *C'est fini! J'arrête les frais.* "That's it. I've had enough." See PRINCESSE.

FRAISE, *f.* **1.** Strawberry. See ENVOYER…FRAISES; SUCRER LES FRAISES. **2.** Face; individual. **Ma/ta/sa/fraise/nos fraises,** and so on. *Vos fraises, qu'est-ce que vous en pensez?* "You guys, what do you think of that?" See RAMENER SA FRAISE.

FRAMBOISE, *f.* Clitoris (lit. "raspberry"). *J'avais la framboise très excitée.* "My clit was very excited."

FRANCFORTS, *m., pl.* Fingers. *Mimi avait les francforts gelés.* "Mimi's fingers were cold."

FRANCHECAILLE, *f.* France. *Churchill trouvait la Franchecaille archifromagère ingouvernable.* "Churchill thought cheese-producing France impossible to govern."

FRANCHOUILLARD, -E. French; chauvinistically Fr. *Mon beau-dab n'achète que franchouillard.* "My father-in-law only buys French."

FRANCHOUILLARD, *m.* French. *L'Académie franchouillarde défend le franchouillard.* "The French Academy defends the French language."

FRANCO. Right away. *Vas-y franco. Épouse-la!* "Get cracking! Marry her!"

FRANCOUILLARD, *m.* France. *La Franchecaille pleure déjà son francouillard.* "France is already unhappy about giving up the franc."

FRANGIN, *m.* Brother; buddy. *Son frangin l'accompagne partout.* "Her brother accompanies her everywhere."

FRANGINE, *f.* Sister. *Il fait passer sa petite amie pour sa frangine.* "He passes off his girlfriend as his sister."

FRANGINS, *m., pl.* Freemasons. *Tolstoy décrit les rites secrets des frangins.* "Tolstoy describes the secret rites of the Masons."

FRAPPADINGUE. Completely crazy. *Il est frappadingue, mais heureux.* "He's totally bananas, but happy."

(SE) FRAPPER. To hit or tap o.s. **Ne pas se frapper.** Not to worry. *Ne te frappe pas!* "Don't sweat it!"

FRÉROT, *m.* Younger brother. *Son frérot l'a surpris avec sa nana.* "His kid brother caught him and his girlfriend by surprise."

FRIC, *m.* Money. *Il est plein de fric.* "He's got lots of bread." See SAINT-FRIC.

FRIC-FRAC, *m.* Burglary. *Ils ont subi plusieurs fric-frac.* "They've been burgled frequently."

FRICHTI, *m.* Meal. *Ça sent le bon frichti.* "That smells like good cooking."

FRICOT = FRICHTI.

FRICOTER. 1. To cook. *Tout ce qu'il fricote est drôlement bon.* "Everything he cooks is super." **2.** To plot. *Qu'est-ce qu'ils peuvent bien fricoter ensemble?* "I wonder what they're cooking up together." **3.** To have sex. *Ils ont longtemps fricoté avant de se marier.* "They were shacking up long before they got married."

FRI-FRI. Female genitalia. See CACHE-FRI-FRI.

FRIGO. Cold. *Il fait frigo aujourd'hui.* "It's cold today."

FRIGO, *m.,* from **frigorifique.** Refrigerator. *Les nouveaux frigos respectent l'environnement.* "New fridges are environmentally friendly."

FRIME, *f.* Face; sham. *C'est de la frime, tout ce qu'il dit.* "That's all phony, everything he says."

FRIMER. To pretend. *Elle se plaît à frimer.* "She enjoys showing off."

FRIMEUR, -EUSE, *m., f.* Show-off. *Quel frimeur!* "What a show-off."

(SE) FRINGUER. To get dressed; buy clothes. *Il se fringue aux puces.* "He gets his clothes at the flea market."

FRINGUES, *f., pl.* Clothes. *Les fringues, c'est son dada.* "Clothes are her hobby."

FRIPES, *f., pl.* Clothes. *Ils vendent des fripes sur le marché.* "They sell clothes in the market."

FRISÉE, *f.* Female pubic hair (lit. "curly endive"). See BROUTER LA FRISÉE.

FRISQUET. Chilly. *Couvre-toi; le vent est frisquet.* "Bundle up; the wind's nippy."

FRITE, *f.* French fry. **Avoir la frite,** *idiom.* To be in great shape. *Je n'ai pas la frite aujourd'hui.* "I'm not feeling so hot today."

FROC, *m.* Pants. **Baisser son froc,** *idiom.* To eat humble pie. *Il avait tort mais refusait de baisser son froc.* "He was wrong but wouldn't get off his high horse." See FAIRE...FROC; CHIER...FROC.

FROID DE CANARD, *m.* Very cold weather. *Quel froid de canard!* "Boy it's cold!"

FROM = FROMEGI.

FROMAGE, *m.* Cheese. See FAIRE UN FROMAGE.

FROMAGES, *m., pl.* Feet. *Ses fromages tapent un max.* "His feet really stink."

FROMEGI, from **fromage.** *De Gaulle était fier des fromegis de la Franchecaille.* "De Gaulle was proud of France's cheeses."

FROMETEGOM/FROMETON/FROMGOM = FROMEGI.

FRUSQUES, *f., pl.* Clothes. *D'où viennent ces frusques?* "Where do those clothes come from?"

FRUSQUIN = SAINT FRUSQUIN.

FUMACE/FUMASSE. Furious. *Je suis fumace d'avoir loupé mon rendève.* "I am really ticked off at having missed my appointment."

FUMANT, -E. Marvelous. *Quelle histoire fumante!* "What a wonderful story!"

FUMER. To be angry (lit. "to smoke"). *J'ai attendu deux heures. Je fumais.* "I waited two hours. I was furious."

FUMIER, *m.* SOB (lit. "fertilizer"). *Je ne parle plus à ce fumier.* "I don't talk to that bastard anymore."

FURAX, -E. Furious. *J'étais furaxe d'avoir crevé.* "I was boiling mad at having had a flat tire."

FURIBARD, -E. Angry. *Les dabs était furibards qu'elle parte avec ce flambeur.* "Her parents were enraged at her going off with that professional gambler."

FUSEAUX, *m., pl.* Legs. See JOUER DES FUSEAUX.

FUSIL, *m.* Stomach (lit. "rifle"). *Depuis ce matin je ne me suis rien mis dans le fusil.* "I haven't had anything to eat since this morning." See COUP DE FUSIL.

FUSIL À TROIS COUPS/TROUS, *m.* Prostitute practicing oral, vaginal, and anal sex (lit. "triple-barreled shotgun"). *Line, vrai fusil à trois coups, est très recherchée.* "Line, a versatile working girl, is much in demand."

FUSILLER. To fleece (lit. "to shoot"). *Il s'est fait fusiller par son avocat.* "His lawyer took him to the cleaners."

GÂCHE, *f.* Job (lit. "trowel"). *J'ai une gâche qui me permet d'élever mes mômes.* "I've got a job that allows me to bring up my kids."

GÂCHER. 1. To work. *Gâcher ne m'a jamais fait peur.* "I was never afraid of work." **2.** To spoil. **Gâcher le métier.** To work or sell for less than the standard rate. *Les travailleurs au noir nous gâchent le métier.* "The undeclared workers are spoiling it for us."

GADIN, *m.* **1.** Head. *J'ai mal au gadin.* "I have a headache." **2.** Fall. See PRENDRE UN GADIN; RAMASSER UN GADIN.

GADOUE, *f.* **1.** Mud; muck; slush. *La neige fond; il y a de la gadoue partout.* "The snow's melting and there's slush everywhere." **2.** Mess. *Ils ne savent que foutre de la gadoue partout.* "All they can do is mess up everything."

GADOUILLE = GADOUE.

GAFFE, *m.* Prison guard. *Les gaffes participaient aux partouses.* "The prison guards took part in the orgies/daisy chains."

GAFFE, *f.* **1.** Blunder. *J'ai fait une gaffe en lui parlant de la visite de son mari.* "I made a mistake telling her about her husband's visit." **2.** Guard duty; sentinel. **Faire gaffe,** *idiom.* To be on one's guard. *Fais gaffe ou la flicaille t'agrafera.* "Watch out or the cops will get you."

GAGA. Gaga. *À 82 ans elle est loin d'être gaga.* "She's far from senile at 82." **Être gaga de qn.,** *idiom.* To be gone

158

on s.o. *Il est complètement gaga de son chien.* "He dotes on his dog."

GAGNE-PAIN, *m.* Posterior (lit. "livelihood"). *Rien que par sa démarche, son gagne-pain vous fait une invite.* "Her wiggling fanny alone is an invitation."

GAGNER SA CROÛTE. To earn one's living (lit. "to earn one's crust [of bread]"). *Il bossait dur pour gagner sa croûte.* "He worked hard to make a living."

GAGNEUSE, *f.* Prostitute who makes big money. *Cette gagneuse travaille pour sa famille.* "That expensive prostitute works for her family."

GALE, *f.* Repulsive person (lit. "mange; scabies"). *Je ne peux voir cette gale.* "I can't stand the sight of that scuzzball."

GALÈRE, *f.* Hard work. *Mon travail de nuit, c'est la galère!* "My night job's a real grind!"

GALÉRER. To work hard; have a rough time. *J'ai galéré pour réussir mes exams et galéré deux ans au chômage.* "I worked like a dog to pass my exams and I spent two rough years on unemployment."

GALERIE, *f.* Crowd (lit. "gallery"). **Amuser la galerie.** To be the life of the party. *Il n'est bon que pour amuser la galerie.* "All he's good for is clowning around."

GALÉRIEN, *m.* Galley slave. **Mener une vie de galérien,** *idiom.* To lead a dog's life. *J'ai mené une vie de galérien pour construire ma maison.* "I worked like a slave to build my house."

GALÉRIENNE, *f.* Shopping center prostitute. *La galérienne racolait en regardant les vitrines.* "The prostitute solicited as she looked at the shop windows."

GALETTE, *f.* Money (lit. "crêpe"). *Les voisins ont de la galette.* "The neighbors are rolling in dough."

GALIPETTE, *f.* Somersault. **Faire des galipettes,** *idiom.* To fool around; fool around sexually. *Ce n'est ni l'endroit ni le moment pour faire des galipettes.* "This is neither the time nor the place for a roll in the hay."

GALOCHE, *f.* Clog. See ROULER...GALOCHE.

GALOCHER = ROULER UNE GALOCHE.

GALON, *m.* Stripe (military). See PRENDRE DU GALLON.

GALOPIN, *m.* Small glass of beer. *Juste le temps pour un galopin.* "Just enough time for a short one."

GALUCHE, *f.* Gauloise® cigarette. *Mon dab ne fumait que des galuches bleues.* "My pop smoked only Gauloises in the blue pack."

GALURE/GALURIN, *m.* Hat. *Il oubliait toujours son galurin.* "He always forgot his hat."

GAMAHUCHE, *f.* Oral sex (fellatio and cunnilingus). *Ils prenaient un grand plaisir à la gamahuche.* "They really enjoyed 69."

GAMAHUCHER. To have oral sex. *Gamahucher, c'est pas son genre.* "Oral sex isn't her thing."

GAMBERGE, *f.* Deep thought. *Après mûre gamberge, j'ai fini par dire oui.* "After careful consideration, I finally said yes."

GAMBERGER. To think hard; worry. *Tu gamberges trop à ce problème.* "You worry your head/give too much thought to that issue."

GAMBETTE, *f.* Leg. *Mistinguette et Marlene Dietrich étaient très fières de leurs gambettes.* "Mistinguette and Marlene Dietrich were very proud of their legs."

GAMELLE, *f.* Dish. See PRENDRE…GAMELLE; RAMASSER…GAMELLE.

GAMIN, *m.* Lad; Young boy. *J'aime fredonner* Un gamin de Paris, *de M. Micheyl.* "I like to hum *A Paris Lad*, by M. Micheyl." See EN GAMIN.

GAMINE, *f.* Little girl. *Ma grand-tante s'habille comme une gamine.* "My great-aunt dresses like a little girl."

GAMME, *f.* Musical scale. *Chez Greuze on a voulu goûter à toute la gamme des desserts.* "In the restaurant Greuze we wanted to try the whole range of their desserts."

GANACHE, *f.* Imbecile (lit. "lower jaw [horse]"). *Cette* *vieille ganache ne t'apportera rien de bon.* "That old fool won't do you any good."

GARDER UN CHIEN DE SA CHIENNE À QN. To bear a grudge against s.o. *Elle lui garde toujours un chien de sa chienne pour avoir été trompée.* "She still has it in for him because he cheated on her."

(SE) GARGARISER DE QCH. To revel in (lit "to gargle in"). *La skieuse se gargarisait de sa médaille d'or.* "The skier delighted in her gold medal."

GARGUE, *f.* Throat. *Le tenor a toujours mal à la gargue.* "The tenor's still got a sore throat."

GÂTEAU, *m.* **C'est du gâteau!** "That's a piece of cake, a cinch."

GÂTERIE, *f.* Oral sex (lit. "little treat"). *J'adore lui faire une gâterie.* "I love giving him a present down there."

GAUCHO, *adj.* and *n.* Left wing; left-winger. *Le prof est gaucho mais pas bolcho.* "The professor's a leftist but not a Commie."

GAUFRE, *f.* See MOULE À GAUFRES; PRENDRE...GAUFRE; RAMASSER...GAUFRE.

GAULDO/GOLDO = GALUCHE.

GAULE, *f.* Penis (lit. "long pole/rod"). See ASTIQUER LA GAULE.

GAULUCHE = GALUCHE.

GAVOUSSE, javanais of **gousse.**

GAY, *adj.* and *n.* Male homosexual. *Ce sont des gays et des gousses qui fréquentent cette disco.* "Gay guys and lesbos go to that disco."

GAZER. To go (fast/well/bad, and so on) [lit. "to gas"]). *"Ça gaze avec ton mec?" "Pour l'instant ça ne gaze pas fort."* "Everything going OK with you and your guy?" "Right now things aren't too hot."

G.D.B. = GUEULE DE BOIS.

GÉANT, -E. Terrific (lit. "gigantic"). *La teuf était géante!* "The party was fantastic!"

(SE) GELER. To freeze. **Se geler les couilles; glaouis; Se les geler,** *idioms.* To be very cold; to freeze one's balls off. *On se les gèle. Rentrons vite!* "It's cold enough to freeze the balls off a brass monkey. Let's go back fast."

GERBE, *f.* Vomit (lit. "bouquet"). *Pendant la tempête il y avait de la gerbe partout sur le bateau.* "During the storm there was puke all over the boat."

GERBER. To vomit. *Ta lèche, c'est à gerber.* "Your ass-kissing makes me want to throw up."

GERBOISE, *f.* = GITON.

GI! = GY!

GICLÉE, *f.* Spurt; squirt. See LÂCHER…GICLÉE.

GICLER. To scram. *Ralbol de tes magouilles; tu vas gicler, vite fait.* "I've had it with your conniving; get out of here fast."

GIFLE, *f.* Slap. See TÊTE À GIFLES.

GIGI = GIGOLETTE.

GIGO! = GY!

GIGOLETTE, *f.* Young girl; floozy (lit. "turkey leg"). *Une gigolette m'a dragué au bar.* "A tart tried to pick me up at the bar."

GIGOLO, *m.* **1.** Gigolo. *Elle est généreuse avec ses gigolos.* "She's generous with her gigolos." **2.** Jack (cards). *Sa dame a pris son gigolo.* "Her queen took his jack."

GIGOLPINCE, *m.* Gigolo. *Son gigolpince guinche bien.* "Her gigolo's a good dancer."

GIGOT, *m.,* Leg; thigh; buttock (lit. "leg of lamb"). *Ses gigots étaient serrés un max dans son jean.* "Her ample legs were squeezed into her tight jeans."

GIGOT! = GY!

GIGOTER. To dance (lit. "to fidget; wriggle"). *Allons gigoter ce soir!* "Let's shake our dancing legs tonight."

GIGOTEUR, *m.* Dancer. *C'est un beau couple de gigoteurs.* "They're an attractive dancing couple."

GINGIN = JINJIN 2.

GIRAFE, *m.* Giraffe. See PEIGNER LA GIRAFE.

GITON, *m.* Young passive homosexual. *Le richard choyait son giton.* "The old moneybags pampered his darling boy."

GIROFLÉE (À CINQ FEUILLES), *f.* Slap (lit. "five-leaved gillyflower"). *Il avait mérité cette belle giroflée à cinq feuilles.* "He deserved the good whack he got."

GIVRÉ, -E. Crazy; drunk (lit. "frosted over"). *Lui il est né givré et elle est givrée dès le matin.* "He was born crazy, and she's drunk all day."

GLAND, -E. Stupid. *Je ne te croyais pas aussi glande.* "I didn't think you were that much of a dope."

GLAND, *m.* Penis (lit. "acorn"; "glans penis"). See POMPER LE GLAND.

GLANDER. To waste time. *J'aime glander le week-end.* "I like to loaf on weekends." **N'avoir rien à glander,** *idiom.* To not give a damn. *Nous n'avons rien à glander de toutes tes histoires.* "We couldn't care less about your actions."

GLANDES, *f., pl.* Glands. **1. Avoir les glandes,** *idiom.* To be angry. *J'ai les glandes dès que je la vois.* "Just the sight of her infuriates me." **2. Foutre les glandes à qn.,** *idiom.* To irritate s.o. *Fous le camp, tu me fous les glandes!* "Fuck off. You piss me off!"

GLANDEUR, -EUSE, *m., f.* Loafer. *Je ne veux pas embaucher ce glandeur.* "I don't want to hire that lazy bum."

GLANDILLEUX, -EUSE. Difficult; tricky. *Il s'est lancé dans des investissements glandilleux.* "He took a chance on risky investments."

GLANDOUILLER = GLANDER.

GLANDOUILLEUR, -EUSE = GLANDEUR, -EUSE.

GLANDOUILLEUX, -EUSE = GLANDILLEUX, -EUSE.

GLANDU, *m.* Fool. *Quel glandu!* "What a jerk!"

GLAOUIS, *m., pl.* Testicles. See CASSER; (SE) GELER.

GLAVIOT, *m.* Gob of spit. *Quelle infection, ces glaviots sur le trottoir!* "How revolting, all those gobs of spit on the sidewalk."

GLAVIOT(T)ER. To spit. **Glavioter sur qn.,** *idiom.* To treat s.o. like dirt. *Il glaviote sur tous à la mairie.* "He's full of contempt for everybody at city hall."

GLINGLIN, *m.,* children. Ringing. *Ça fait glinglin.* "It's going ding-dong." See SAINT-GLINGLIN.

GLISSER UN FIL = LÂCHER UN FIL.

GNAF, *m.* Shoemaker (from "Gnafron," character in traditional Lyon puppet theater). *J'ai porté mes godasses chez le gnaf.* "I took my shoes to the shoemaker."

GNANGNAN. Silly; trashy; spineless. *L'actrice est gnangnan est le film aussi.* "The actress is silly and the film too."

GNARD, -E = GNIARD, -E.

GNAULE = GNÔLE.

GNIARD, -E, *m.* **1.** Child. *Ce week-end, pas de gniards avec nous.* "Let's spend the weekend without the kids." **2.** Individual. *Comment s'appelle-t-il (elle) ce gniard (cette gniarde)?* "What's that guy's/broad's name?"

GNIAULE/GNIÔLE = GNÔLE.

GNIOUF = GNOUF.

GNOGNO(T)TE, *f.* Trifle. *Le travail qu'il te reste, c'est de la gnognotte.* "The work you've still got to do doesn't amount to a hill of beans."

GNÔLE, *f.* Hard liquor. *Son dab fabrique une sacrée gnôle.* "Her dad makes terrific hooch."

GNON, *m.* Punch; dent. *Ma voiture a pris deux gnons dans le parking.* "My car got dented in two places in the parking lot."

GNOUF, *m.* Prison. *Il vient de sortir du gnouf.* "He just got out of the slammer."

GO. See TOUT DE GO.

GOBER. 1. To swallow. *Son mec l'embobine et elle gobe tout.* "Her guy's feeding her a line and she falls for it all." **2.** To stand. *Je ne peux plus le gober, ce type.* "I can't stomach that guy anymore."

GOBER LES MOUCHES. To stand by idly (lit. "to gulp down flies"). *Au lieu de gober les mouches, agis donc!* "Instead of just twiddling your thumbs, do s.t!"

GODANT = GODEUR.

GODASSE, *f.* Shoe. *La mer a emmené mes godasses que j'avais laissées sur le sable.* "The sea claimed the shoes I left on the sand."

GODE = GODEMICHÉ; GODET.

GODEMICHÉ, *m.* Codpiece. *Elle a toute une collection de godemichés.* "She has quite a collection of codpieces."

GODER. To be sexually excited; to have an erection (lit. "to bulge"). *Par sa démarche ondulante elle fait goder tous les mecs.* "Her sexy walk gets all the guys horny."

GODET, *m.* Glass. **Avoir le godet,** *idiom.* To be lucky. *Dans sa vie il a eu le godet.* "He's been lucky in life."

GODEUR, -EUSE. Horny. *Elle n'est pas du tout guindée, plutôt godeuse.* "She's not at all stuffy; she's randy."

GODILLER = GODER.

GODILLEUR, -EUSE, *m., f.* Highly sexed person. *Les partouzards cherchaient des godilleurs.* "Those into group sex looked for strongly sexed people."

GODILLOT, *m.* Boot. *Je me suis payé une paire de godillots pour la montagne.* "I bought a pair of boots for mountain climbing."

GODILLOT, *adj.* and *m. n.* Party hack; party regular. *Ils ont triomphé grâce aux godillots.* "Thanks to the regulars, they won."

(À) GOGO. Galore. *On servait du champagne à gogo.* "They served champagne in abundance."

GOGO, *m.* Sucker. *C'est qch. pour les gogos.* "That's s.t. for chumps."

GOGOL = GOL.

GOGUENOTS, *m., pl.* Toilet. *Vise la propreté des goguenots.* "See whether the john's clean."

GOGUES = GOGUENOTS.

(EN) GOGUETTE. Tipsy. *Les marins en goguette faisaient les guinguettes.* "The drunken sailors toured the waterfront bars."

(SE) GOINFRER. To make a bundle (lit. "to stuff o.s."). *Ce maq se goinfre sur le dos de ses filles.* "That pimp is making a pile by exploiting his girls."

GOL, *adj.* and *m. n.* Fool; foolish. *Je serais vraiment gol de marcher dans les combines de ce gol.* "I'd have to be a real moron to fall for that jerk's schemes."

GOLDO = GAULDO.

GOMME, *f.* Gum. See METTRE LA GOMME.

(À LA) GOMME. Useless. *Qu'est-ce, ce truc à la gomme?* "What is this piece of junk?"

GONCE = GONZE.

GONCESSE = GONZESSE.

GONDOLANT, -E. Hilarious. *Ce film est vraiment gondolant.* "That film's a real scream."

(SE) GONDOLER. To laugh uproariously (lit. "to buckle"). *On s'est gondolé toute la soirée.* "We laughed our heads off all night."

GONE, *m.* Child (popular in Lyon, but used elsewhere too). *Les gones lui ont foutu une raclée.* "The kids beat him up."

GONESSE, *f.* Child. *La gonesse a déjà trop de poupées.* "That brat's already got too many dolls."

GONFLAGA = GONFLÉ.

GONFLANT, -E. Irritating. *Qu'est qu'elle est gonflante!* "God, is she a pain!"

GONFLE, *f.* Lie (lit. "swelling"). *La gonfle c'est son fort.* "He's good at making up tall stories."

GONFLÉ, -E. 1. Brave (lit. "swollen"). *Elle est gonflée de partir seule.* "She's got guts, leaving on her own." **2.** Impudent. *Il est vraiment gonflé de me demander une chose pareille.* "He's got some nerve asking me for s.t. like that."

GONFLÉ, -E À BLOC. See BLOC.

GONFLER. To exasperate (lit. "to inflate"). **Gonfler qn.; les gonfler à qn.** *Qu'est-ce qu'il me les gonfle!* "My God, does he get on my nerves!"

GONFLETTE, *f.* Bodybuilding. *Ce titi s'est mis à la gonflette.* "That little kid has taken to pumping iron."

GONSE = GONZE.

GONSESSE = GONZESSE.

GONZE, *m.* Fellow. *C'est un brave gonze.* "He's a swell guy."

GONZESSE, *f.* Female; wife; girlfriend. *Sa gonzesse est bien balancée.* "His babe's really stacked."

GONZIER = GONZE.

GORGEON, *m.* Glass; drink. *Et si l'on se tapait un gorgeon?* "How about our having a drink?"

(SE) GORGEONNER. To get drunk. *Il aime se gorgeonner au pastis.* "He likes to get soused on pastis."

GORILLE, *m.* Bodyguard. *Le ministre ne sort jamais sans ses gorilles.* "The minister never goes out without his bodyguards."

GOSSE, *m., f.* Child. *Elle est venue avec sa flopée de gosses.* "She came with her pack of kids." See BEAU GOSSE; TIRE-GOSSE.

GOTHA, *m.* Elite (from the registry of royals formerly published in *Gotha*, Ger.). *Son dab appartient au gotha de la pub.* "Her father's an advertising bigwig."

GOUALANTE, *m.* Popular song. *Vas y de ta petite goualante.* "Go ahead and sing your little song now."

GOUALER. To sing (loud). *Edith Piaf et Ethel Merman savaient les goualer.* "Edith Piaf and Ethel Merman knew how to belt them out."

GOUDOU, *f.* Lesbian. *J'ai horreur des mecs; je n'aime que les goudous.* "I can't stand men; I only like lesbos."

GOUGNE = GOUGNOT(T)E.

GOUGNOTTAGE, *m.* Lesbianism. *Elle est mariée, mais très tentée par le gougnottage.* "She's married, but very tempted by Sapphic love."

GOUGNOT(T)E = GOUINE.

GOUGNOT(T)ER. To be a lesbian. *Elle gougnotte depuis de nombreuses années.* "She's been a dyke for many years."

(SE) GOUGNOTTER = SE GOUINER.

GOUINE, *f.* Lesbian. *Les gouines au bar sont superbes.* "The dykes at the bar are beauties."

(SE) GOUINER. To practice lesbianism. *Sa patronne et elle se gouinent.* "She and her female boss are getting it on together."

(SE) GOUPILLER. To turn out. *Tout s'est bien goupillé.* "Everything went off without a hitch."

GOUPILLON, *m.* Penis (lit. "holy water sprinkler"). See MOUILLER LE GOUPILLON.

GOUPILLONER = MOUILLER LE GOUPILLON.

GOURBI, *m.* Hovel. *Ils devraient nettoyer leur gourbi.* "They ought to clean up their pad."

GOURDE. Stupid. *Pour prendre une initiative, qu'est-ce qu'elle est gourde!* "When it comes to showing some initiative she's really dim-witted!"

(SE) GOURER. To make a mistake. *Je me suis gouré de date.* "I got the dates mixed up."

GOURMANDISE, *f.* Fellatio (lit. "gluttony"). *La gourmandise, est un des sept péchés capitaux, mais lui faire une gourmandise, c'est mon péché mignon.* "Gluttony is one of the seven deadly sins, but eating him is my delicious little indulgence."

GOUSSE/GOUSSE D'AIL, *f. Elle est gousse et il est gay et c'est un couple heureux.* "She's a dyke and he's gay and they're a happy couple."

(SE) GOUSSER = (SE) GOUINER.

GOUZI-GOUZI, *m.* Tickle-tickle. **Faire des gouzi-gouzis; faire gouzi-gouzi.** To tickle. *Je ne ris pas quand tu me fais gouzi-gouzi car je sais me concentrer.* "I don't laugh when you tickle me because I know how to concentrate."

GRAF, *m., abbr.* of **graffito, -i.** *Ce gone se balade avec sa bombe à graf.* "That guy walks around with his can of graffiti spray."

GRAILLE, *f.* Food. *À la graille!* "Come and get it! Soup's on!"

GRAILLER. To eat. *Filons au resto; (il n')y a rien à grailler à la maison.* "Let's go to the restaurant; there's nothing to eat in the house."

GRAIN, *m.* **Avoir un (petit) grain,** *idiom.* To be crazy. *Il n'aurait pas un grain, par hasard?* "Isn't he a bit touched?"

GRAIN DE CAFÉ, *m.* Clitoris (lit. "coffeebean"). *Mâchouiller mon grain de café l'excite.* "Munching on my clit excites him."

GRAINE, *f.* Seed. **Bonne/mauvaise graine.** The right/wrong stuff. *Lui c'est de la mauvaise graine, sa frangine de la bonne (graine).* "He's a bad egg/bad news, but his sister's got the right stuff." **Graine de…** Potential. *C'est une graine d'artiste.* "She's a budding artist." See CASSER LA GRAINE; (EN) PRENDRE…GRAINE.

GRAINER = GRAILLER.

GRAISSE D'OIE/GRAISSE DE CHEVAUX DE BOIS. Snake oil. *Tout le laïus de ce camelot est à la graisse d'oie.* "That peddler's line is phony."

GRAISSER LA PATTE. To bribe. *On obtient tout de lui en lui graissant la patte.* "If you cross his palm with silver you can get anything you want."

GRAND-DAB(E), *m.* Grandfather. *Grand-dab aime guincher.* "Gramps likes to dance."

GRAND-DABE, *f. Il ne sort pas toujours avec grand-dabe.* "He doesn't always go out with Grandma."

GRANDS-DAB(E)S, *m. pl.* Grandparents. *Mes grands-dabs sont très chouettes.* "My grandparents are super."

GRAND-DUC, *m.* Grand Duke. See TOURNÉE…

GRAND-MÈRE, *f.* Double bass (musical instrument). *Il prenait grand soin de sa grand-mère en la transportant.* "He was very careful of his double bass when traveling." See PELOTEUR DE GRAND-MÈRE.

GRANDE FOLLE = FOLLE.

GRANDE GUEULE, *f.* Bigmouth. *Cette grande gueule aura toujours le dernier mot.* "That bigmouth will always have the last word."

GRAPPE, *f.* Male genitalia (lit. "bunch/cluster [grapes, for example"]). See LÂCHER LA GRAPPE.

GRAPPIN, *m.* Hand (lit. "grapnel"). See METTRE LE GRAPPIN.

GRATIN, *m.* The elite. *Elle fréquente le gratin.* "She hangs out with the upper crust."

GRATINÉ, -E. Excessive. *Sa gaffe était bien gratinée.* "He made a whale of a blooper."

GRATTE, *f.* **1.** Guitar (**gratter** = "to scratch"). See JOUER…GRATTE. **2.** Money on the side. *Cet avocat s'est enrichi en faisant des grattes.* "That lawyer got rich by a taking his cut (of transactions)."

GRATTICHE, *f.* Scabies. *Son môme avait la grattiche.* "Her kid had scabies."

GRAT(T)OS, from **gratis.** Free of charge. *Le vin était gratos au resto.* "The wine was free at the restaurant."

(SE) GRATTER LA HURE. To shave (lit. "to scratch one's hairy face." **Hure de sanglier** means "boar's head"). *Je me suis coupé en me grattant la hure.* "I cut m.s. shaving."

GRAT(T)OUILLER. To scratch; itch. *Ses papillons d'amour le gratouillent.* "His crabs make him itchy."

GRATTOUSE = GRATTICHE.

GRAVOS/GRAVOSSE, *adj.* and *m., f. nouns; javanais* of **gros/grosse.** *Tu es trop gravos pour entrer dans ce blouson.* "You're too fat to get into that jacket."

GRELOTS, *m., pl.* Testicles (lit. "little bells"). *Elle sait bien me jouer de la flute et faire sonner mes grelots.* "She sure knows how to blow me and ring my chimes."

GRELUCHE, *f.* Woman. *La greluche d'à côté passe la tondeuse.* "The broad next door's mowing the lawn."

GRENOBLE. See CONDUITE DE GRENOBLE.

GRENOUILLAGE, *m.* Wheeling and dealing (business). *C'est un spécialiste du grenouillage.* "He's good at wheeling and dealing."

GRENOUILLE DE BÉNITIER, *f.* Holy Joe (lit. "frog in the holy water font"). *La grenouille de bénitier, devenue panthéiste, est partie vivre près d'un étang aux grenouilles.* "The church lady, turned pantheist, has gone to live by a frog pond."

GRENOUILLES DE BIDET, police. Semen stains. *Après le viol, les flics recherchaient des grenouilles de bidet.* "After the rape, the cops looked for traces of semen."

GRENOUILLEUR, -EUSE. Wheeler and dealer. *Quel fameux grenouilleur!* "What a sleazy operator!"

GREUMAI, backslang of **maigre.** Thin. *Tu es trop greumai.* "You're too thin."

(SE) GRIFFER (LA TRONCHE). To put on one's makeup (lit. "to scratch [one's face]"). *J'attendais qu'elle ait fini de se griffer.* "I waited for her to finish putting on her war paint."

(SE) GRIFFER LE MACARONI. To masturbate. *Il s'est griffé le macaroni en buvant du chianti.* "He jerked off while drinking chianti."

GRILLER. To grill. **C'est grillé!** "That's all over." **Être grillé.** To be found out. *Le double agent a été grillé.* "The double agent's cover was exposed."

GRILLER UNE CIBICHE/CLOPE/TIGE. To light up a cigarette. *Je grille une clope vite fait avant le boulot.* "I have a quick smoke before work."

GRILLER UN FEU (ROUGE). To go through a (red) traffic light. *Il a une suspension de permis pour avoir grillé un feu.* "His driver's license has been suspended because he went through a red light."

(EN) GRILLER UNE = GRILLER UNE CIBICHE.

GRIMACE, *f.* Grimace. See SOUPE À LA GRIMACE.

GRIMPER. To have sexually (lit. "to climb"). *Il m'a grimpée dans la grange.* "He had me in the barn."

GRIMPER À L'ARBRE/AU COCOTIER. To hit the ceiling. *Ne grimpe pas au cocotier quand j'aborde ce sujet.* "Don't fly off the handle every time I bring up that subject."

GRIMPER AUX ARBRES, legal. To exaggerate. *Le témoin a grimpé aux arbres.* "The witness laid it on thick."

GRINGUE, *m.* **Faire du gringue à qn.,** *idiom.* To make advances to s.o. *Il me fait du gringue pour me grimper.* "He comes on to me because he wants to get into my pants."

GRINGUER. To flirt with. *Il m'a gringuée au bal.* "He made a pass at me at the dance."

GRISBI, *m.* Money. *Gary, lourd de grisbi, engageait un orchestre gitan.* "Gary, rolling in dough, hired a gypsy orchestra."

GRISETTE, historical. Shop girl of easy virtue. *Elle chante le rôle d'une des grisettes de* La veuve joyeuse. "She's singing the role of one of the grisettes in *The Merry Widow.*"

GROGNASSE, *f. pej.* Unattractive, elderly female; floozy. *Quelle grognasse, la concierge!* "What an old bag/hag, the concierge!"

GROLLE, *f.* Shoe. See TRAÎNER SES GROLLES.

GROLLES, *f., pl.* Fear. **Avoir les grolles,** *idiom.* To be afraid. *On avait les grolles dans la maison hantée.* "We had the willies in the haunted house."

GROS, *m.* Fat cat. *Tu vas avoir à faire à un gros; sois prudent.* "You'll be dealing with a big shot; be careful."

GROS, GROSSE. Excessive (lit. "fat"). *Ta gonfle est un peu grosse.* "Your tall story's a bit much."

GROS BONNET, *m.* Bigwig; **GROS,** *m.*

GROS COMME UNE MAISON. As plain as the nose on your face. *C'était gros comme une maison mais tu n'as rien vu.* "It was plain as day but you didn't see anything."

GROS-CUL, *m.* Big truck (lit. "fat ass"). *Impossible de doubler ce gros-cul.* "Impossible to pass that juggernaut."

GROS LARD/GROS PLEIN DE SOUPE, *m.* Fat guy. *Ce gros lard se la coule douce.* "That fatso takes things easy."

GROS ROUGE (QUI TACHE). Cheap, hearty red wine (that makes stains). *Un pique-nique sans gros rouge n'est pas un pique-nique.* "A picnic without good old red wine isn't a picnic."

GROS SOUS, *m., pl.* Big money. *Ils s'engueulent pour une affaire de gros sous.* "They're at each other's throats over a matter involving big bucks."

GROSSE DONDON, *f.* Very fat woman. *Il n'aime que les grosses dondons.* "He likes only fat broads."

GROSSE LÉGUME, *f.* Prominent person. *Des grosses légumes assistaient au marriage.* "VIPs attended the wedding."

GROSSIUM = GROS, *m.*

(SE) GROUILLER. To hurry up. *Il faut se grouiller avant l'orage.* "We better get cracking before the storm."

GRUE, *f.* Prostitute (lit. "crane"). *Les grues veulent se syndicaliser.* "The whores want to form a union." See PIED DE GRUE.

GUÉDRO, backslang of **drogué.** Drug addict. *C'est un guédro de longue date.* "He's been a junkie for some time."

GUENON, *f.* Ugly woman (lit. "female monkey"). *C'est une guenon, mais il l'adore.* "She's ugly, but he adores her." **Avoir la guenon,** *idiom,* Drugs. To have a monkey on one's back. *Quand il a la guenon, il est hystéro un max.* "When he needs a fix, he's wired."

GUÊPE, *f.* Wasp. **Avoir la guêpe = avoir la guenon.** See PAS…GUÊPE.

GUETTE-AU-TROU, *m., f.* Midwife (lit. "watcher at the hole"). *La guette-au-trou a beaucoup de boulot les nuits de pleine lune.* "The midwife is very busy on nights when the moon is full."

GUEULANTE, *f.* Yell. See POUSSER…GUEULANTE.

GUELARD, -E. Flashy. *Quelle couleur gueularde!* "What a loud color!"

GUEULE, *f.* 1. Face. **Faire la gueule; faire/tirer une de ces gueules; faire une gueule longue comme ça,** *idioms.* To sulk; pull a long face. *Il me fait la gueule; je ne sais pas pourquoi.* "He gives me dirty looks; I don't know why." **Avoir de la gueule,** *idiom.* To look great. *Qu'est-ce que tu as de la gueule avec ce chapeau.* "You look terrific in that hat." **2. Ma/ta/sa gueule.** Individual. See POMME 2. See also: BOURRER LA GUEULE; CASSE GUEULE; (SE) CASSER LA GUEULE; COUP DE GUEULE; CREVER LA GUEULE OUVERTE; (S'EN) METTRE…GUEULE; (EN) PRENDRE… GUEULE; (SE) FENDRE LA GUEULE; FERME…; FERMER…; FINE GUEULE; (SE) PAYER LA GUEULE; (SE) PÉTER LA GUEULE; POUSSER…GUEULE; SALE GUEULE.

(TA) GUEULE! VOS GUEULES! Shut your trap!

GUEULE À CHIER DESSUS. Disgusting face (lit. "face you want to shit on," vulgar equivalent of SALE GUEULE).

GUEULE À COUCHER DEHORS (AVEC UN BILLET DE LOGEMENT DANS SA POCHE) = SÂLE GUEULE.

GUEULE D'AMOUR, *f.* Don Juan; Lothario. *Quelle gueule d'amour cet acteur!* "What a Casanova, that actor!"

GUEULE DE BOIS, *f.* Hangover. *Trop de champagne et*

c'est la gueule de bois. "Drink too much champagne and you'll have a hangover."

GUEULE DE CON = SÂLE GUEULE.

GUEULE D'ENTERREMENT, *f.* To look like one is at a funeral. *Il est arrivé avec une gueule d'enterrement car elle avait bousillé sa voiture.* "He arrived looking depressed because she had banged up his car."

GUEULE DE L'EMPLOI, *f.* To look the part. *Ce croquemort a vraiment la gueule de l'emploi.* "That undertaker really looks the part."

GUEULE D'EMPEIGNE = SÂLE GUEULE.

GUEULE DE RAIE = SÂLE GUEULE.

GUEULE DE TRAVERS = SÂLE GUEULE.

GUEULER. 1. To yell. *Il ne peut s'empêcher de gueuler sur tous et sur tout.* "He can't help sounding off at everything and everybody." **2.** To have a loud, garish color. *Ils ont choisi un mobilier qui gueule.* "They selected gaudy furnishings." Cf. GUEULARD.

GUEULER COMME UN SOURD. To yell one's head off. *J'ai beau gueuler comme un sourd; ce môme n'en fait qu'à sa tête.* "Fat lot of good it does for me to yell my head off; that kid just does what he wants."

GUEULER COMME UN VEAU. To weep profusely. *Le gosse gueulait comme un veau après une raclée bien méritée.* "The brat bawled his eyes out after a well-deserved beating."

GUEULETON, *m.* Feast. *Leur gueuleton était super.* "Their big feed was terrific."

GUEULETONNER. To feast. *Ils gueuletonnent chaque samedi soir.* "They like to have a hearty meal every Saturday night."

GUGUS = GUS(SE).

GUIBOLLES, *f., pl.* Legs. *J'en ai plein les guibolles après une journée de boulot.* "My legs really feel it after a day at work."

175

GUICHET. See PETIT GUICHET.

GUIGNE, *f.* Bad luck. **Avoir la guigne,** *idiom.* To have hard luck. *J'ai vraiment la guigne depuis quelque temps.* "I've really been down on my luck for some time."

GUIGNOL, *m.* Eccentric. *C'est un guignol; il ne passera pas aux élections!* "He's a crackpot; he won't be reelected."

GUIGNON = GUIGNE.

GUILI-GUILI = GOUZI-GOUZI.

GUILLEDOU. See COURIR LE GUILLEDOU.

GUIMAUVE, *f.* **1.** Slushy sentiment (lit. "marshmallow"). *Tes poèmes, c'ést de la guimauve.* "Your poems are treacly/shmaltzy." See BANDER GUIMAUVE. **2.** Guitar. *Je me suis payé une nouvelle guimauve.* "I bought a new guitar."

GUIMBARDE, *f.* Old car. *Comment peux-tu rouler avec cette guimbarde?* "How can you drive that old heap?"

GUINCHE, *f.* **1.** Dance. *On y va pour cette guinche?* "Shall we dance?" **2.** Dance hall. *La guinche est pleine à craquer ce soir.* "The dance hall's bursting at the seams tonight."

GUINCHER. To dance. *Tous veulent guincher avec moi.* "Everybody wants to dance with me."

GUINCHEUR, -EUSE, *m., f.* Dancer. *C'est un bon guincheur de tango.* "He's a good tango dancer."

GUINDE = GUIMBARDE.

GUISE = GUISOT.

GUISOT/GUIZOT. 1. Leg. *Mes guizots lâchent.* "My legs are giving out." **2.** Penis. See FILER LE COUP DE GUIZOT.

GUS(SE), *m.* Guy. *Tu connais ce gus?* "Do you know that dude?"

GY! OK! Affirmative! Roger!

H, *m.,* from **hachisch.** Hashish; heroin; narcotics. *Il dit qu'il fume du H pour sa santé.* "He says he smokes hash for his health."

HABILLÉ, *m.* Uniformed policeman. *Les habillés défilaient pour la Saint Patrick.* "The boys in blue paraded on St. Patrick's Day."

HACHÈS/HACHESSE, *pron.* of *abbr.* HS **(hors service).** Exhausted (lit. "out of order"). *J'arrête pour aujourd'hui; je suis hachès.* "I'm calling it a day; I'm knocked out."

HAFNAF = AFANAF.

HALLUCINÉ, -E, *m., f.* Crazy person. *C'est un halluciné, mais fascinant dans ses intervalles lucides.* "He's a crackpot, but fascinating in his lucid intervals."

HAMBOURGEOIS, *m.,* from **en-bourgeois.** Plainclothes policeman (lit. "hamburger"). *Des hambourgeois se sont mêlés à la foule.* "Plainclothes policemen took positions in the crowd."

HANNETON, *m.* Cockchafer; May/June bug. See (PAS) PIQUÉ...

HARD, *m.* Hard-core porn; hard rock. *Il n'aime que le hard mais il bande de moins en moins.* "All he likes is hard-core porn and hard rock but he doesn't get hard much any more."

HARICOT, *m.* **1.** Clitoris (lit. "bean"). *J'ai mis son doigt*

177

sur mon haricot. "I put his finger on my clit." **2.** Foot; toe. See COURIR SUR…; (LA) FIN…

(DES) HARICOTS! Practically nothing! *Je refuse de turbiner pour des haricots.* "I won't work my ass off for peanuts."

(SE) HARNACHER. To dress (lit. "to harness up"). *Juste le temps de m'harnacher et j'arrive.* "I'll get into my gear and be right over."

HARNAIS, *m., pl.* Clothes; fashion accessories (lit. "harnesses"). *Pour le concert je me ferai belle en mettant tous mes harnais.* "I'll get all dolled up for the concert."

HARPION = ARPION.

HARPONNER. To buttonhole (lit. "to harpoon"). *J'évite de me faire harponner par des chronophages.* "I avoid getting buttonholed by time-wasters."

HASCH = H.

HAUTE, *f.,* short for **haute societé.** High society. *Notre boniche est obnubilée par les gens de la haute.* "Our maid's obsessed with the upper crust."

HEBDO, *m., abbr.* of **hebdomadaire.** Weekly periodical. *Je suis rédactrice-en-chef d'un hebdo pour clodos.* "I'm editor-in-chief of a weekly news magazine for hobos."

HÉLICO, *m., abbr.* of **hélicoptère.** Helicopter. *Qui a perfectioné l'hélico, Sikorsky ou Seversky?* "Was it Sikorsky or Seversky who perfected the chopper?"

HÉMATOME, *m.* Bruise. See CHERCHER.

HÉNAURME. Enormous. *Elle fait d'hénaurmes fautes d'orthographe.* "She makes humongous spelling errors."

HÉRISSON, *m.,* police. Problem suspect (lit. "porcupine"). *Le psychiatre a indiqué aux flics comment s'y prendre avec ce hérisson.* "The psychiatrist told the cops how they should handle that hard nut to crack."

HEURE, *f.* Hour. **Ne pas demander l'heure (qu'il est) à qn.** Not to ask for s.o.'s advice. *Je préfère agir seule, je ne* *t'ai pas demandé l'heure.* "I'd rather go it alone; I didn't ask for your advice."

HIBISCUS, *m.* Female genitalia. *Elle se caressait l'hibiscus sous le bananier.* "She fondled herself under the banana tree."

HIC, *m.* Snag. *C'est là le hic!* "That's where the trouble is."

HIRONDELLE, *f.* Uninvited guest (lit. "swallow"). *À la teuf il y avait plus d'hirondelles que d'invités.* "There were more gate-crashers than invited guests at the bash."

HISTOIRE, *f.* Story; history. *Qu'est-ce que c'est que cette histoire?* "Just what's going on here?" *Quelle histoire!* "What a fuss!" See FAIRE UNE HISTOIRE DE QCH.

HISTOIRE DE. In order to. *On va à la foire histoire de s'amuser.* "We're going to the fair to have a good time."

HISTOIRES, *f., pl.* Menstruation. *Quand la dame aux camélias avait ses histoires elle portait un camélia rouge.* "When the lady of the camellias had her period she wore a red camellia."

HIVIAU/HIVIO, *m.* Winter. *On se les caille en hivio chez toi.* "Your house is freezing in winter."

HOLKIF/HOLPÈTE = OLPICHE/OLPIF.

HOMMELETTE, *f.,* (play on **homme** *and* **omelette**). Wimp. *Quelle hommelette tu fais!* "You're a real Caspar Milquetoast."

HOMME-ORCHESTRE, *m.* **1.** One-man band. *Il fait l'homme-orchestre au bal du samedi soir.* "He's the one-man band at the Saturday night dance." **2.** Man of many talents. *Mon mari, c'est un vrai homme-orchestre.* "My husband's multitalented."

HORLOGE, *f.* Clock. L'horloge; la petite horloge. Heart. *Son horloge battait normalement durant la montée du Mont Blanc.* "His heart beat normally when climbing Mont Blanc."

HOSTO, *m.,* from **hôpital.** Hospital. *Elle est pique-fesse à l'hosto.* "She's a nurse at the hospital."

HÔTEL DE PASSE = MAISON DE PASSE.

HOURI(E), *f.* Girl; broad (orig. "paradise maiden" in the Koran). *Le mollah n'aimait pas qu'on appelle une fille non-céleste "houri".* "The mullah didn't like noncelestial girls being called 'houris'."

HOUST(E)! = OUST(E)!

HS = HACHÈS.

HUBLOTS, *m., pl.* Eyes; eyeglasses (lit. "portholes"). *Sans ses hublots il ne voit que dalle.* "He's as blind as a bat without his glasses."

HUILE, *f.* **1.** Oil. See BAIGNER DANS L'HUILE. **2.** Big shot. *Toutes les huiles assistaient à la première.* "All the VIPs were present at the premiere."

HUILE DE BRAS/COUDE, *f.* (lit. "elbow grease"). *Ce boulot, je l'ai fait à l'huile de coude.* "I used elbow grease to do that job."

HUÎTRE, *f.* Idiot (lit. "oyster"). *Ne reste pas planté là, comme une huître.* "Don't just sit there like an idiot."

(S')HUMECTER LE GOSIER/LES AMYGDALES. To have a drink (lit. "to moisten one's gullet/tonsils"). *Pendant le prèche il avait envie de s'humecter le gosier.* "During the sermon he felt like wetting his whistle."

HUPPÉ, -E. Upper crust (lit. "crested [bird]"). *Il respirait mal dans ce milieu huppé.* "He felt ill at ease in those upper-class surroundings."

HURE, *f.* Head; hairy face. See (SE) GRATTER.

HURLUBERLU, -E, *adj.* and *m., f. n.* Oddball; kook. *Il est un peu hurluberlu et je n'écoute que la moitié de ce qu'il raconte.* "He's a bit scatterbrained and I only listen to half of what he says."

HYPER/HYPRA. Very. *Elle est hypra calée en maths.* "She's super-smart in math."

HYSTÉRIQUE. Promiscuous (said of women). *Son frangin refusait de croire qu'elle était hystérique.* "Her brother wouldn't believe she slept around."

HYSTÉRIQUE, *f.* Nymphomaniac. *Son fiancé ne savait pas qu'elle était une hystérique.* "Her fiancé didn't know she was a nympho."

HYSTÉRO, *abbr.* of **hystérique.** Hysterical. *Tous ça l'a rendu hystéro.* "All that made him hysterical."

HYSTÉRO, *m., f.* Bundle of nerves. *C'est un hystéro de premiére.* "He's a nervous wreck."

ICICAILLE/ICIDÉ/ICIGO/ICITE. Here. *Ça ne se fait pas icigo.* "That isn't done here."

IDEM. Ditto. *Il sera baisé et toi idem.* "He'll be screwed and so will you."

IDEM AU CRESSON. All the same. *Avec ou sans, c'est idem au cresson.* "With or without, it doesn't matter."

IÈCHE, backslang of **chier.** To be extremely bored. *Qu'est-ce qu'on s'est fait ièche ce week-end!* "God what a shitty, boring weekend!"

ILLICO (PRESTO). Right away. *L'hélico va décoller illico.* "The chopper's taking off right away."

ILLUSE, *f.,* from **illusion. Se faire des illusions,** *idiom.* To imagine things. *Ne te fais pas d'illuses!* "Don't fool yourself!"

IMBÉCILE HEUREUX!/HEUREUSE! Ignorance is bliss! (lit. "(you) happy idiot").

IMBITABLE. Incomprehensible. *Son laïus m'était imbitable.* "His spiel was all Greek to me."

IMBLAIRABLE. Unbearable. *Il est imblairable quand il est soûl.* "He's impossible when he's drunk."

IMBUVABLE. Insufferable (lit. "undrinkable"). *Ne l'invite plus; il est imbuvable.* "Don't invite him again; he's too much to take."

IMPAIR, *m.,* criminal. Sell-out (lit. "uneven number"; "social indiscretion"). *"Tu sais ce qui t'attend après ton impair," lui dit le parrain.* " 'You know what's in store for you after your little song to the cops,' said the godfather."

IMPASSE, *f.* Dead end. **Faire l'impasse/une impasse sur qch.,** school. To skip over part of the syllabus when studying for an exam. *J'ai fait une impasse sur Victor Hugo; hélas, je l'ai payée!* "I didn't bother to review Victor Hugo, and boy did I regret it!"

IMPAYABLE. Hilarious (lit. "unpayable"). *Tonton est impayable quand il mime Charlot.* "Uncle's a scream when he imitates Charlie Chaplin."

IMPEC, *abbr.* of **impeccable.** Marvelous. *On descend au Ritz! C'est impec!* "We'll stay at the Ritz! That's terrific!"

IMPEC! Exactly right! You said it!

IMPER, *m., abbr.* of **imperméable.** Raincoat. *Je préfère mon pébroc à mon imper.* "I'd rather take my umbrella instead of my raincoat."

IMPER À POPAUL/POPOL. Condom (lit. "Popaul's [dick's] raincoat"). *N'oublie pas las impers à Popaul.* "Don't forget the rubbers." Cf. K-WAY.

IN. Trendy (from Eng. "in"). *Chez les musulmans, Mahomet reste toujours un prénom très in.* "Among Muslims, Mohammed is always a fashionable first name."

INCENDIAIRE, *f.* Car-based prostitute who specializes in fellatio (lit. "arsonist"). *Il cherchait une incendiaire ardente pour lui faire un pompier.* "He was looking for an ardent head-job specialist to put out his phallic fire."

INCENDIER. To reprimand (lit. "to set fire to"). *Le prof a incendié l'élève inco.* "The teacher read the riot act to the incorrigible pupil."

INCO, *abbr.* of **incorrigible.** *Le cureton m'a dit que je n'étais pas inco.* "The padre said I wasn't past praying for."

INCOLLABLE. Unbeatable (lit. "nonstick"). *Aux jeux de la télé il est incollable sur les questions de musique.* "He can't be caught on music questions in TV game shows."

INCON, *adj.* and *m., f. n., abbr.* of **inconditionnel.** Staunch supporter. *C'est un inconditionnel de France Culture.* "He's hooked on France Culture (radio station)."

INCONNU AU BATALLION. S.o. the speaker has never heard of. *C'est un inconnu au batallion qui a renseigné la police.* "A total stranger informed the police."

INCONOBRÉ/INCONNOBLÉ, *adj.* and *n.* Unknown. *Ses parents refusaient qu'elle sorte avec cet inconobré.* "Her parents wouldn't let her go out with that stranger."

L'INCRUSTE. See TAPER L'INCRUSTE.

(S') INCRUSTER. To wear out one's welcome (lit. "to become imbedded"). *Je ne m'incruste jamais car, comme dit Franklin, "les poissons et les invités puent au bout de trois jours".* "I never overstay my welcome, because 'fish and guests begin to stink after three days,' as Franklin said."

INCRUSTEUR, -EUSE, *m., f.* Gate-crasher. *C'est un incrusteur de première.* "He's an accomplished gate-crasher."

INDÉCROTTABLE. Incorrigible (lit. "s.o/s.t. you can't get the crud off"). *(Ne) perds plus de temps avec lui; il est indécrottable.* "Don't waste any more time on him; he's hopeless."

INDIC, *m., abbr.* of **indicateur.** Police informer. *C'est connu de tous qu'il est un indic.* "Everybody knows he's a fink."

INFECT, -E. Revolting. *Ton copain est infect.* "Your buddy's a scuzzball."

INFECTADOS, *m.* Cheap cigar. *On ne voit jamais ce vieux schnoque sans son infectados.* "That old fogey's never without his stogie."

INFECTION, *f.* S.t. revolting. *Quand les égouts refoulent, c'est une infection.* "It's disgusting when the sewers overflow."

INFICHU, -E. Incompetent. *Elle est infichue de s'occuper du ménage.* "She can't keep up with running the house."

INFO, *f., abbr.* of **information.** Tip. *Le turfiste m'a filé une info pourrie.* "The racetrack tout gave me a bum steer."

INFOS, *f., pl.* News. *J'écoute les infos sur plusieurs canaux.* "I listen to the news on several stations."

INFOUTU = INFICHU.

INO, *abbr.* of **inoccupé.** Not busy or occupied. *Tu peux y aller; les chiottes sont inos.* "You can go now; the john's not occupied."

INSTALLER/EN INSTALLER. To show off. *Cesse d'installer; tu nous fatigues.* "Quit hamming it up; you bore us."

INSTIT, *m., f., abbr.* of **instituteur,-trice.** Elementary school teacher. *Mon fils aime bien sa nouvelle instit.* "My son likes his new elementary school teacher."

INSTRUMENT, *m.* Penis. *La plupart des mecs ne savent pas bien jouer de leur instrument.* "Most guys don't know how to use their equipment right."

INTELLO, from **intellectuel.** High-brow. *La pièce était trop intello pour nous.* "The play was too cerebral for us."

INTELLO, *m., f.* Intellectual. *Mao et Fidel exigeaient que les intellos soient aussi des manuels.* "Mao and Fidel required eggheads to be manual laborers too."

INTERDIT, -E DE SÉJOUR. Banned from. *Ce soulard est interdit de séjour dans cette boîte.* "This place is off-limits to that drunk."

INTERJO, *m.* Interest. *Tu as interjo à m'écouter.* "It's in your interest to listen to me."

INTERPELLER. To stir (lit. "call out to"). **Ça m'interpelle!** "That really gets to me." **Ça m'interpelle quelque part!,** ironic. *Ta kyrielle de plaintes, ça m'interpelle qq. part.* "Your endless litany of complaints has touched my heart!"

INTOX(E), *f.,* from **intoxication.** Disinformation. *L'intox sévit dans les médias.* "The media are loaded with propaganda."

INTOXIQUO = TOXICO.

INVITATION À LA VALSE. Invitation to pay the bill. *Quand on sort en groupe je redoute toujours l'invitation à la valse.* "When the bunch of us go out, I dread it when it's time to pay the piper."

INVITE, *f.* Invitation. *Procure-moi une invite.* Get me an invite.

IROQUOIS, *m., f.* Individual (punk, for instance) with a Mohawk haircut. *Une bande d'iroquois avait terrifié ma grand-tante.* "My great-aunt was terrified by a gang of Mohawk-headed punks."

IROQUOISE, *f.* Mohawk haircut. *Pépé veut se coiffer à l'iroquoise.* "Grandpa wants to get a Mohawk."

ISOLOIR, *f.* Urinal (lit. "voting booth"). *L'isoloir était une infection.* "The urinal was filthy."

ITALBOCHE/ITALGO/ITALO, *m., pej.,* dated. Italian. *Allons à ce nouveau resto italo.* "Let's go to that new guinea/dago restaurant."

ITOU. Also. **Et moi itou!** And me too!

IVOIRE, *m.* Ivory. **Écraser/taquiner l'ivoire.** To play the piano. *Si tu taquinais un peu l'ivoire, on pourrait danser.* "If you tickled the ivories a bit, we could dance."

IVRE-DÉZINGUÉ, -E. Dead drunk. *Ils étaient tous ivre-dézingués.* "They were all smashed out of their minds."

JACOT = JACQUOT.

JACQUES. Fool. **Battre/faire le Jacques,** *idiom.* To act the clown. *Paul se plaît à faire le Jacques.* "Paul enjoys playing the fool."

JACQUOT/JACQUES, *m.* **1.** Jimmy (orig. staff carried by pilgrims to St. James of Compostella). **2.** Safe-deposit box. *Le jacquot du casseur a forcé tous les jacquots de la banque.* "The burglar's crowbar jimmied every safe-deposit box in the bank." **3.** Penis; dildo. *Mon garagiste est bien monté, mais je préfère mon jacquot.* "My car mechanic's well hung, but I prefer my vibrator." **4.** Parrot. *As-tu déjeuné Jacquot?* "Polly want a cracker?"

JACTANCE, *f.* Smooth fast talk (lit. "haughtiness"). **Avoir de la jactance,** *idiom.* To have the gift of gab. *Il bégayait mais maintenant il a de la jactance.* "He used to stutter but now he's got the gift of gab."

JACTER. To talk. See ARGOMUCHE. **Jacter sur.** To badmouth. *Pour jacter, tu te poses là, mais évite de jacter sur les autres.* "You're a master gabber, but try not to badmouth others."

JAFFE, *f.* Food. **À la jaffe!** "Soup's on! Come and get it!"

JAFFER. To eat. *Tu ne penses qu'à jaffer.* "All you think about is eating."

JAFFLE = JAFFE.

JAJA, *m.* Wine. *Il ne peut jaffer sans jaja.* "He can't eat without wine."

JALIANCE = JALMINCE/JALMINCERIE.

JALMINCE. Jealous. *Tu ne serais pas jalmince, par hasard?* "Is it possible you're jealous?"

JALMINCE/JALMINCERIE, *f.* Jealousy. *La jalmincerie de mon mari est insupportable.* "My husband's jealousy is unbearable."

JAMBE, *f.* Leg. **Faire une belle jambe,** *idiom.* To be useless. *Ça nous fera une belle jambe!* "Fat lot of good that'll do us!" **Faire qch. par-dessous la jambe.** To do sloppy work. *Ce bricolo ne fait son boulot que par-dessous la jambe.* "That cowboy always does a bum job." See also LEVER LA JAMBE; PARTIE DE JAMBES; ROND DE JAMBE; TENIR LA JAMBE; TIRER…JAMBES; TRAITER…LA JAMBE.

JAMBE DU CHINOIS, *m.* Pastis (Pernod/Ricard, served in a narrow, yellow glass (lit. "Chinaman's leg"). *Dans un bistrot tout près de l'arsenal de Brest, on a apprécié le jambe du Chinois.* "In a bistro near the Brest dockyards we enjoyed a glass of pastis."

JAMBE DU MILIEU, *f.* Penis. *Il marche avec une canne, mais sa jambe du milieu est toujours vaillante.* "He walks with a cane but his middle leg's still sturdy."

JAQUETTE, *f.* Male homosexual (lit. "woman's jacket"). **Être/filer/refiler de la jaquette (flottante).** To be one of them. *Elle sait que son fils est de la jaquette.* "She knows her son's gay."

JAR, *m.,* from **jargon.** Criminals' slang. *Les gangsters avaient un jar à eux.* "The gangsters had their own brand of slang." See DÉBALLER LE JAR.

JARDIN DES ALLONGÉS, *m.* Cemetery. *La plupart de mes vieux amis sont déjà au jardin des allongés.* "Most of my old friends are already in the boneyard."

JARNAC. See COUP DE JARNAC.

JARRETELLE, *f.,* police. Tapped telephone conversation (lit. "garter"). *Le tribunal a refusé d'écouter les jar-*

retelles. "The court refused to listen to the bugged phone conversations."

JARS = JAR.

JASER. To gab; gossip. *Ça va faire jaser.* "There'll be talk about that."

JASPIN/JASPINAGE, *m.* Gossip. *Tout cela n'est qu du jaspinage.* "All that's just idle chatter."

JASPINER. To talk. *Il jaspine un anglais-lavabo.* "He speaks broken English." See ARGOMUCHE.

JASPINEUR, *m.* Lawyer. *Son jaspineur l'a vendue.* "Her mouthpiece sold her out."

JAVA, *f.* Wild party. *On va faire une java de toutes les javas.* "We're going to have a blast to end all blasts." See PARTIR EN JAVA; FILER UNE…JAVA.

JAVANAIS, *m.* Slang words created by inserting **-av-, -va-,** and **-ag-.** Examples: **chagatte = chatte; javardavin = jardin; javeudavi = jeudi; pavute = pute.** Lit. **Javanese,** also influenced by **j'avais.** Note: The computer language Java is unrelated.

JAVARDAVIN, *m.,* javanais of **jardin**. *Cultive ton javardavin.* "Cultivate your garden!"

JAVELLISÉ, *m.* Squeaky clean homosexual (lit. "chlorine bleached"). *Il ne couche qu'avec son javellisé, qui n'oublie jamais le préso.* "He only sleeps with his Mr. Clean, who never forgets rubbers."

JAVEUDAVI, *m.* javanais of **jeudi**. *Le javeudavi, je suis d'humeur joviale, j'honore Jupiter en ne travaillant pas.* "Thursdays I'm jolly; I honor Jove and don't work."

JAZZ-TANGO. Bisexual. *Son jules est jazz-tango.* "Her boyfriend swings both ways."

JAZZEUX, *m.* Jazz musician. *Elle est dingue de son jazzeux.* "She's nuts about her jazz musician."

JEAN-FESSE, *m.* Useless person. *Espèce de Jean-Fesse, tu ne fous rien!* "You lazybones, you do nothing!"

JEAN-FOUTRE, *m.* Worthless individual. *Je l'ai traité de grand Jean-Foutre.* "I told him he was a no-good bum."

JEANFOUTRERIE, *f.* Lazing around. *Cette famille n'est capable que de jeanfoutrerie.* "All this family can do is lie around on their butts and do nothing."

JEAN-NU-TÊTE. Penis (lit. "baldy-bean Johnny"). *J'ai pris mon jean-nu-tête dans la fermeture éclair.* "My dick got caught in the zipper."

JE-M'EN-FICHISME = JE-M'EN-FOUTISME.

JE-M'EN-FICHISTE = JE-M'EN-FOUTISTE.

JE-M'EN-FOUTISME, *m.* Indifference. *Le client n'est plus roi; c'est le je-m'en-foutisme qui règne.* "The customer is no longer king; what do I care?/what's it to me? is the prevailing attitude."

JE-M'EN-FOUTISTE. Indifferent person. *Son comportement est celui d'un je-m'en-foutiste.* "He acts as if he couldn't care less."

JE-SAIS-TOUT, *n.* and *adj.* Smart aleck. *C'est un Monsieur/une Madame Je-sais-tout.* He's/she's a (Mr./Mrs.) know-it-all.

JÈSE, *m.* Jesuit. *Il a étudié chez les jèses.* "He studied with the Jesuits."

JÉSUS, *m.* **1.** Teen-age homosexual. *Il est mort à Venise en contemplant son Jésus.* "He died in Venice contemplating his teenage darling." **2.** Erect penis. *Elle s'agenouillait devant son Jésus adoré.* "She knelt in adoration before his erect cock."

JETÉ, -E. Crazy. *Je fais tout pour l'éviter; il est jeté un max.* "I go out of my way to avoid him; he's totally bananas."

JETER. To throw. **En jeter.** To be impressive. *Sa julie et sa moto, elles en jettent!* "His broad and his bike are really hot stuff!" See CRAVATE.

JETER DU JUS/JETER SON JUS. To make a big impression. *Les fringues du trav jettent toujours du jus.* "The drag queen's clothes are always a knockout."

JETER SON VENIN. See VENIN.

(S'EN) JETER UN/S'EN JETER UN DERRIÈRE LA CRAVATE. To belt down a drink. *Et si on s'en jetait un avant le boulot?* "How about a shot before getting to work?"

JETON, *m.* Hit; punch (lit. "token"). *En réparant la lampe j'ai pris un jeton.* "I got a shock when repairing the lamp." See FAUX JETON; FAUX COMME UN JETON.

JETONS, *m., pl.* Jitters. *J'ai eu les jetons quand je l'ai vue évanouie par terre.* "I got the willies when I saw her passed out on the floor." See FOUTRE LES JETONS.

JEU. Game. **Faire/jouer/sortir le grand jeu,** *idiom.* To go all out. *On a eu le contrat mais il fallait jouer le grand jeu.* "We got the contract but we had to give it everything we had."

JÈZE = JÈSE.

JINJIN, *m.* Brains. *Tu n'as rien dans le jinjin.* "You haven't got a brain in your head."

JINJIN = JAJA.

JOBARD, -E. 1. Gullible (from the biblical Job). *Je ne te croyais pas aussi jobard.* "I didn't think you were that naïve." **2.** Crazy. *Il est jobard de t'avoir embrinqué dans une histoire pareille.* "He's nuts, getting you mixed up in s.t. like that."

JOBARD,-E. *m., f.* **1.** Dupe. *Ce combinard sait trouver les jobards.* "That slick operator has no trouble finding suckers." **2.** Crazy person. *Quelle bande de jobards!* "What a bunch of loonies!"

JOICE. Happy. *Tu n'as pas l'air joice aujourd'hui.* "You don't look very cheerful today."

JOIE, *f.* Joy. *Ce n'est pas la joie!* "It's no picnic/pleasure!"

JOISSE = JOICE.

JOJO. Attractive; great. *Tu n'es pas jojo dans ta robe et tout*

ce que tu me racontes n'est pas très jojo non plus.
"You're not very attractive in that dress and everything
you're telling me isn't very appealing either."

JOJO, *m.,* from biblical Joseph who resisted Potiphar's
advances. **Faire son jojo,** *idiom.* To behave prudishly. *Il
est assez lubrique mais aime faire son jojo.* "He's quite
lecherous but enjoys playing the Puritan."

JO-LA-BRICOLE. Petty criminal. *Le parrain se riait de ce
Jo-la-bricole.* "The godfather laughed at the small-time
hood."

JOLI, *m.,* ironic. Rotten (lit. "nice; pretty"). **C'est du joli!**
"That's a nice mess! That's a fine thing to do!" (Also
ironic in Eng.) **Faire du joli,** *idiom. Ça va faire du joli!*
"That's going to foul things up."

JONC, *m.* **1.** Gold (lit. "rush; rattan"). *Le jonc est en baisse.*
"(The price of) gold is going down." **2.** Money. **Avoir du
jonc,** *idiom.* To be rich. *Il a du jonc et pourrait être moins
près de ses sous.* "He's got plenty of money and could be
less tightfisted."

JONCAILLE, *f.* Gold jewelry. *Elle ne portait pas du toc,
mais de la joncaille.* "She wore gold jewelry, not junk."

JOSEPH. Se faire appeler Joseph. See ARTHUR.

JOUAL, *m.* Strongly accented, provincial Fr. with large
admixtures of Eng., spoken by some, but by no means all,
Fr. Canadians. From the pronunciation of **cheval.**
Beaucoup de Français ont du mal à piger le joual. "Many
French people have trouble understanding 'joual'."

JOUASSE = JOICE.

JOUE, *f.* Cheek. See (SE) CALER.

JOUER (À) LA FILLE DE L'AIR. To beat it; run away.
*Incapable de supporter l'internat, il a joué la fille de
l'air.* "He couldn't take boarding school and cleared
out."

JOUER À TOUCHE-PIPI. 1. To play doctor. *Les gosses
jouaient à touche-pipi.* "The kids played doctor." **2.** To

engage in heavy petting. *Ils jouaient à touche-pipi dans la bagnole.* "They fooled around in the car."

JOUER AU CON. To act like a jerk. *Il jouait au con et on en avait marre.* "He kept jerking around and we'd had enough."

JOUER DE LA FLÛTE. To fellate (lit. "to play the flute"). *Elle aimait jouer de la flûte en écoutant* La flûte enchantée *et en pensant à Pan, Krichna, et Kokopelli.* "She liked to play the skin flute while listening to *The Magic Flute* and thinking of Pan, Krishna, and Kokopelli." Cf. TURLUTER.

JOUER DE LA GRATTE. To play the guitar. *Des étudiants jouaient de la gratte dans le métro.* "Students were playing the guitar in the subway."

JOUER DES COMPAS/FOURCHETTES/FUSEAUX/ GUIBOLLES. To run off; to scram. *Dès qu'il a vu les flics il a joué des fuseaux.* "As soon as he saw the cops he ran off."

JOUER DES FLÛTES/UN AIR DE FLÛTE. To beat it. *Tu ne penses qu'à jouer un air de flûte, mais écoute-moi d'abord.* "All you want to do is hit the road, but listen to me first."

JOUER LA VEUVE DE PROVINCE/D'ALENÇON/DE CARPENTRAS/VIERZON, and so on, *finance.* To get scared and sell securities at a loss. *Pris de panique, il a joué la veuve de Vierzon.* "He got panicky and took a loss."

JOUER LE FILS DE LA REPASSEUSE. To hesitate before engaging a prostitute (lit. "to act the ironer's son." **Repasser** means "to walk past or back and forth; to iron clothes"). *Tu vas cesser de jouer le fils de la repasseuse, oui ou merde?* "You gonna quit jerkin' my strings? Are we gonna get it on or not?"

JOUER LES UTILITÉS. See UTILITÉ.

JOUER RIP. See RIP.

JOUER UN AIR DE CLARINETTE BAVEUSE. To fellate (lit. "to play a tune on the drooling clarinet"). *Après avoir joué un air de clarinette baveuse, elle a senti jouer tout un orchestre en soi.* "After going down on him, she heard a whole orchestra playing in her." Cf. JOUER DE LA FLÛTE.

JOUIR. 1. To have great pleasure/an orgasm. *"Il est jeune et beau et me fait jouir,"* a dit Arletty au tribunal. " 'He's young and handsome and makes me come,' said Arletty to the court." **2.** To experience pain, *ironic. Mon mal de dent me fait jouir.* "I've got a toothache that's driving me up the wall."

JOUISSIF, -IVE. Intensely pleasurable. *Jouissives nos amours au bord de l'eau, mais moins juissif la visite chez le toubib.* "Our lovemaking on the beach was ecstasy, but the visit to the doctor was less of a thrill."

JOURDÉ, *m.* Day. *Mes jourdés ne sont plus tristes à cause de toi.* "My days are no longer sad, because of you."

JOURNAILLE, *f.* = JOURDÉ.

JOURNALEUX, -EUSE, *m., f., pej.* Hack writer. *La critique de ce journaleux est déplorable.* "That hack's review is disgraceful."

JOURNANCHE, *f.* = JOURDÉ.

JOURNE, *m., f.* = JOURDÉ.

JOYEUSES, *f., pl.* Testicles. *Mes joyeuses souffrent sur la selle de bicyclette.* "My nuts ache on the bicycle seat."

JULES. Jules/Julius. **Se faire appeler Jules,** see ARTHUR.

JULES, *m.* **1.** Male. *Vous ne pouvez entrer dans cette boîte qu'accompagnée par un jules.* "You can't get into this place unless you're with a guy." **2.** Steady boyfriend; husband. *À ma connaissance, elle vit sans jules, ni amant ni mari.* "So far as I know, she doesn't have a lover or a husband." **3.** Pimp. *Ces filles travaillent pour le même jules.* "Those girls work for the same pimp."

JULIE, *f.* **1.** Female. *Il n'a pas encore trouvé la julie de ses rêves.* "He hasn't yet found the girl of his dreams." **2.**

Steady girlfriend/mistress; wife. *Il n'a été fidèle à aucune de ses julies, maîtresses ou épouse.* "He wasn't faithful to any of the women in his life, the mistresses or the Mrs."

JULIE DU BRÉSIL, *f.* Cocaine. *C'est la Julie du Brésil qui a ruiné sa carrière.* "Nose candy ruined her career."

JULOT = JULES 1, 2.

JUMELLES, *f., pl.* Buttocks (lit. "twin sisters"). *Ne pose pas tes jumelles sur ce banc fraîchement peint.* "Don't park your fanny on this freshly painted bench."

JUPÉ, -E. Drunk. *Son mari n'est supportable que jupé.* "Her husband is unbearable except when he's drunk."

JUPETTE, *f.* Drunkenness (lit. "short skirt"). *Elle a pris une jupette au champagne.* "She got drunk on champagne."

JUPON, *m.* Skirt. See COUREUR DE JUPONS.

JUPONNÉ = JUPÉ.

JUS, *m.* **1.** Water; liquid (lit. "juice"). See TIRE-JUS. **2.** Sperm. See LÂCHER LE JUS. **3.** Electricity. **Avoir du jus,** *idiom.* To be strikingly elegant. *Quoiqu'elle porte, elle a du jus.* "Whatever she wears, she's a classy lady." **Couper/mettre le jus,** *idiom.* To switch off or on. *L'orage a coupé le jus.* "The storm cut the electric current."

JUS DE CHAPEAU/CHAUSSETTE/CHIQUE, *m.* Weak coffee (lit. "hat/sock/tobacco juice"). *Ce jus de chaussette ne m'ennervera pas.* "This dishwater isn't going to make me jumpy."

JUTANT, *m.* Pimple. *Ça lui était jouissif de presser ses jutants.* "He really got off on squeezing his zits."

JUTE, *m.* Sperm. *La bouffeuse de bite se demandait si le jute était calorifique.* "The cocksucker wondered whether cum was calorific."

JUTER. 1. To ejaculate. *J'aime quand il met du temps avant de juter.* "I like it when he takes his time before coming." **2.** To be impressive = JETER; JETER...JUS. **3.** To be lucrative. *Leur commerce jute bien.* "Their business is making fat profits."

JUTEUX, -EUSE. Very profitable (lit. "juicy"). *Sa maison close est juteuse.* "Her brothel's a real money-maker."

KANGOUROU, *m.* Potential prostitute's client who doesn't hire her right away (lit. "kangaroo," when the potential client "hops" around before deciding). *Ce kangourou m'a fait perdre beaucoup de temps.* "That john made me lose a lot of time."

KANGOUROUS, *m., pl.* Menstruation. **Avoir ses kangourous,** *idiom.* To have one's period. *J'ai des kangourous très réguliers.* "My periods come on regularly."

KARNA, *f.,* backslang of **arnaque.**

KASBA(H), *f.* House; place. *On a été danser dans une de ces kasbahs!* "That was some joint we danced in!"

KAWA, *m.* (Cup of) coffee. *Je prépare le kawa.* "I'll prepare the java."

KEBLA, *adj.* and *n.,* backslang of "black." Black. *Des keblas vendaient leurs marchandises devant la basilique de Montmartre.* "Blacks were selling their wares in front of the Basilica of Montmartre."

KÉBOUR, *m.* Policeman. *Le kébour m'a donné seulement un avertissement.* "The cop gave me only a warning."

KÉBRA, backslang of **braquer.** To stick up. *Ils ont été kébra dans leur voiture.* "They were robbed in their car."

KEN, backslang of **niquer.**

KÉPA, *m.,* backslang of **paquet.** Dose of cocaine. *File-moi un képa.* "Pass me a coke fix."

KÉP'S = KÉBOUR.

(DU) KÈS = (DU) QUÈS.

KEUB = KEBLA.

KEUBA, *m.,* backslang of **bac.**

KEUBLA = KEBLA.

KEUD! = QUEUDE!

KEUF, *m.,* backslang of **flic.** Policeman. *Les keufs les ont toutes interrogées.* "The cops questioned them all."

KEUM, *m.,* backslang of **mec.** Guy. *Comment ça va, le keum?* "How you doin', fellah?"

KEUPON, *m.,* backslang of **punk.** Punk; punk rocker. *Je ne danse pas avec ces keupons.* "I'm not dancing with those punks."

KEUT, backslang of **ticket.** Ticket. *Prends un keut pour moi.* "Buy a ticket for me."

KEZACO? = QU'ES-ACO?

KIF, *m.* **1.** Hashish; mixture of tobacco and hashish. *Ce kif est dégueu.* "This junk is revolting." **2.** *m. C'est du kif!* "That's six of one, half dozen of the other."

KIF(F)ER. To get high or off on. *Ta gonze, je la kiffe.* "Your girl turns me on."

KIFKIF/KIF-KIF/KIF. The same. *Que j'aille en bus ou en métro, c'est kif-kif.* "It makes no difference whether I go by bus or subway."

KIF-KIF BOURRICOT/KIF-KIF LE MÊME SAC. Intensifiers of **KIFKIF/KIF-KIF/KIF.**

KIKI, *m.* **1.** Neck; Adam's apple. See SERRER LE KIKI. **2.** Child's penis. *Elle prenait bien soin de retracter le prépuce du kiki de son fils.* "She took care to retract her son's prepuce." **3.** Short-haired, casually dressed homosexual. *Des kikis arrivaient en moto.* "Clean-cut-looking gays arrived on motorbikes."

KISDÉ, *m.,* backslang of **déguisé.** (Plainclothes) policeman. *Fais gaffe, c'est un kisdé.* "Watch out, he's a cop."

KLEB/KLEBS/KLÉBARD = CLEB/CLEBS/CLÉBARD.

KOKÉ, *Fr. Caribbean.* To have sex. *Allons koké sous les palmiers.* "Let's get it on under the palm trees."

KOP, *m.* Football fanatic. *Des bandes de kops se bagarraient.* "Gangs of football fanatics brawled."

KRO, *f., abbr.* of **Kronenbourg®,** a brand of beer. Can of beer. *Il balançait les kros vides par la vitre de sa bagnole.* "He threw the empty beer bottles out of the car window."

(À) KROUM(E) = À CROUM(E).

KROUMIR, *m.* Old fogey. *C'est un club plein de vieux kroumirs.* "The club members are all old fossils."

KROUTCHOU, *f.* Hard drugs. *Sa kroutchou lui revient cher.* "His drug habit is costly."

KROUTCHOU, *m.,* backslang of **choucroute** (*sauerkraut*). Theft. *Il est accro et fait kroutchou souvent.* "He's a junkie and often steals."

K-WAY®, *m.* Condom (lit. "windbreaker"). *Le K-way a crevé, si puissant était son zob.* "His penis was so strong, the bag broke."

KYRIELLE, *f.* A string or series of s.t. *Elle est toujours entourée d'une kyrielle de gosses.* "She's always surrounded by a gang of kids."

LÀ. There; here. **Avoir qn. là,** *idiom.* To have had it with s.o. *Je l'ai là.* "I'm fed up with him."

(OH) LÀ! LÀ! (LA! LA!) My oh my (oh my)!; Isn't that s.t.! Just look at that!

LA BARBE! "Damn it, that's enough!"

LABATEM, louchébem* of **tabac.**

LAC, *m.* **1.** Lake. See TOMBER…LAC. **2.** Female genitalia (lit. "lake"). *Mon lac mouille toujours pour lui.* "My snatch always gets wet for him." See DESCENTE…LAC.

LÂCHAGE, *m.* Abandoning. *Ses deux récents lâchages l'ont déprimée.* "Two guys ditched her recently and she's depressed."

LÂCHER. To release. **Les lâcher.** To fork over money. *Mémé ne veut pas les lâcher.* "Granny won't come up with the dough."

LÂCHER DU FIGNE. See FIGNE.

LÂCHER L'AFFAIRE/LE COUDE/LES BASKETS À QN. To leave s.o. in peace (lit. "to release s.o.'s case/elbow/sneakers"). *Lâche-moi les baskets!* "Get off my case/back, will you!"

LÂCHER LA GRAPPE À QN. To leave s.o. in peace (stronger version of previous entry (lit. "to get off s.o.

---

* See explanation of **louchébem,** page 210.

genitals [male]"). *Veux-tu me lâcher la grappe.* "Will ya quit bustin' my balls!"

LÂCHER LE JUS/LA CRÈME/UNE GICLÉE. To ejaculate (lit. "to release the juice/cream/a spurt"). *Il aime limer avant de lâcher la crème.* "He likes to take his time before dropping his load."

LÂCHER LE MORCEAU/PAQUET. To confess. (Lit. "to drop the piece/package.") *Il a mis du temps avant de lâcher le morceau.* "It took some time before he spilled the beans; dropped the cookies."

LÂCHER LES COUILLES À QN. = LÂCHER LA GRAPPE.

LÂCHER SON VENIN. See VENIN.

LÂCHER UN COLIS/UNE CAISSE/LOUF(F)E/LOUISE/PERLE. To fart. *Qui vient de lâcher une louise ici?* "Who's been farting here?"

LÂCHER UN FIL/L'ÉCLUSE. To urinate (lit. "to release a thread; sluice gate"). *Il s'est précipité pour lâcher l'écluse.* "He ran out to take a leak."

LÂCHEUR, -EUSE, *m., f.* Unreliable person. *Quelle bande de lâcheurs; ils nous ont laissé tout le boulot.* "What a bunch of deadbeats; they left us all the work."

LACRYMO, *f.* short for **(bombe/grenade) lacrymogène.** Tear gas (bomb). *Dans la manif, fais gaffe aux lacrymos.* "Be on the lookout for tear gas during the demonstration."

LADÉ. Here; there. *Mets-toi ladé pour la photo.* "Stand over there for the photo."

LAFÉQUÉ/LAFÉQUÈS, *m.,* largonji of **café.** Coffee. *C'est l'heure du laféqué.* "It's time for a cup of coffee."

LA FERME! See FERME-LA!

LAGA/LAGO/LAGUCHE = LADÉ.

LAISS'BET'/LAISSE BÉTON, backslang of **laisse tomber!** Let it drop/ride!

LAISSE COURIR/PISSER/TOMBER! Let it go/drop! Forget it!

LAISSE PISSER LE MÉRINOS! Lit. "let the sheep piss." "Wait for the right moment! Bide your time! Let things take their course!"

LAISSER TOMBER COMME UNE VIEILLE CHAUS-SETE. To cast s.o. off like an old rag. *Il en pinçait pour une actrice qui l'a laissé tomber comme une vieille chaussette.* "He was infatuated with an actress who cast him off like an old rag."

LAIT, *m.* Milk. **Boire du petit lait,** *idiom.* To savor praise of o.s. *Je bois du petit lait quand il admire mes fringues.* "I just love it when he admires my clothes." See SOUPE AU LAIT.

LAIT DE CHAMEAU/PANTHÈRE/TIGRE, *m.* Pastis (lit. "camel/panther/tiger milk". *On a bu de l'ouzo, espèce de lait de tigre grec.* "We drank ouzo, a kind of Greek pastis."

LAÏUS, *m.* Speech (often long-winded). *Tout ça, ce n'est que du laïus!* "That's all a lot of hot air!"

LAÏUSSER. To speechify. *On s'endort quand il laïusse.* "We fall asleep when he drones on."

LAMEDÉ/LAMDÉ, *f.,* largonji of **dame.** Woman; wife. *Il a plaqué sa lamdé.* "He got rid of his wife."

LAMFÉ, *f.,* largonji of **femme.** Woman. *Sa lamfé a le popotin opulent.* "His broad's got a really fat ass."

LAMPE, *f.* Stomach. See (SE) METTRE QCH., ...LAMPE.

LANCE-FLAMMES, *m.* Cigarette lighter (lit. "flame launcher"). *J'ai paumé mon lance-flammes.* "I've lost my cigarette lighter."

LANCELOT, *m.* Fireman (play on **lancer l'eau** and **Lancelot** [Jack of clubs, as well as the figure from Arthurian legend]). *Les lancelots ont éteint l'incendie avec l'eau du lac.* "The firefighters put out the fire with water from the lake."

LANCE-PARFUM, *m.* Machine gun (lit. "perfume launcher"). *Les gangsters sortaient leurs lances-parfum.* "The gangsters took out their tommy guns."

LANCE-PIERRES, *m.* Catapult. See MANGER AU LANCE-PIERRES.

LANCEQUINE, *f.* **1.** Water; rain. *La lancequine a enfin cessé.* "It's finally stopped raining." **2.** Urine. *Il y a de la lancequine partout dans les chiottes.* "The toilet's covered with piss."

LANCEQUINER. To weep; rain; urinate. *L'argotnaute a traduit Verlaine par: "Il lancequine dans mon palpitant comme il lancequine sur le bled."* "The slang scholar translated Verlaine as: 'It's blubbering in my old pump, just as it's pissing rain on the city.'"

LANGOUSE = LANGUE.

LANGOUSTE/LANGOUSTINE, *f.* **1.** Prostitute (lit. "spiny lobster"). *Il cherchait une langoustine pour calmer son chagrin.* "He looked for a working girl to soothe his sorrow." **2.** Mistress. *Il y a eu plusieurs langoustes dans sa vie.* "He had several mistresses in his life."

LANGUE, *f.* Tongue. **Donner sa langue au chat,** *idiom.* To stop trying to guess (lit. "to give one's tongue to the cat." Cf. Eng. "cat got your tongue?"). *Aucune idée! Je donne ma langue au chat.* "No idea. I give up." **Avoir la langue bien pendue; ne pas avoir la/sa langue dans sa poche,** *idioms.* To be a fast or clever talker (lit. "to have a well-hung tongue; not to have one's tongue in one's pocket"). *Les représantants n'ont jamais la langue dans leur poche.* "Salesmen are never at a loss for words." **Avoir la langue qui fourche,** *idiom.* To make a slip of the tongue. *La fourche m'a langué.* "I made a tip of the slung." See SOUPE DE LANGUES; TIRER LA LANGUE.

LANGUE DE BOIS, *f.* Wooly/waffly talk (lit. "wooden tongue"). *Je ne pige rien à sa langue de bois.* "I make nothing out of his gibberish."

LANGUE DE VIPÈRE, *f.* Gossip-monger (lit. "viper's tongue"). *Méfie-toi de cette langue de vipère.* "Be careful of that scandal spreader."

LANGUE FOURRÉE, *f.* Wet kiss. *Il m'a fait une langue*

fourrée, inoubliable! "He French kissed me; it was unforgettable!"

LANGUETOUSE = LANGUE.

LANGUE VERTE, *f.* Slang. *Pépé, toujours très vert, se plaît à parler la langue verte.* "Grandpa, still spry, enjoys talking slang."

LANTERNE, *f.* **1.** Lantern. **Éclairer sa lanterne,** *idiom.* To elucidate one's ideas. *Éclaire un peu ta lanterne.* "Try to shed some light on what you're getting at." See VESSIE. **2.** Stomach. See (SE) METTRE QCH.; (SE) TAPER SUR LA LANTERNE.

LANTERNE ROUGE, *f.* Participant who brings up the rear. *Tâche de ne pas faire la lanterne rouge à la course.* "Try not to come in last in the race."

LANTERNES, *f., pl.* Eyes. *Allume tes lanternes!* "Open your eyes!"

LAPEUSE, *f.* Lap dancer, nude stripper who wiggles lasciviously and bumps and grinds on a client's lap (from Eng. "lap"). *Pas même la lapeuse n'arrivait à le faire bander.* "Not even the lap dancer could get him up."

LAPIN, *m.* Guy (lit. "rabbit"). **Un sacré lapin.** A swell fellow. *C'est un sacré lapin, ton pote.* "He's one hell of a guy, your buddy." See CHAUD LAPIN; COUP DU LAPIN.

LAPINE, *f.* Woman who gives birth to many children. *Marie-Thérèse et d'autres Habsbourgeoises étaient de vraies lapines.* "Maria Theresa and other Hapsburg ladies were real baby manufacturers."

LAPINER. To breed like rabbits. *Elle voulait bien se marier mais ne pas lapiner.* "She did want to get married but she didn't want to produce brat after brat."

LARBIN, -E, *m., f.* Waiter or waitress; servile person. *Il était larbin de métier et le larbin de sa langoustine.* "He worked as a waiter and was his mistress' doormat."

LARBINOS = LARBIN.

LARD, *m.* Pork fat. **Ne pas savoir; se demander si c'est du**

lard ou du cochon, *idiom.* Not to know what to make of s.t. *Sa proposition, je ne savais pas si c'était du lard ou du cochon.* "I couldn't make head or tail of his proposal." **Faire son lard; (se) faire du lard,** *idioms.* To put on the pounds. *Je me suis fait du lard pendant les vacances.* "I gained weight during my vacation." See RENTRER...LARD; TÊTE DE LARD.

LARDON, *m.* Small child. **(Avoir) un lardon dans le tiroir,** *idiom.* To be pregnant. *Je suis revenue de vacances avec un lardon dans le tiroir.* "I came back pregnant from my vacation."

LARGE, *m.* Open sea. **Être au large,** *idiom.* To be rich. *On est au large; on peut se payer des vacs.* "We're rolling in it; we can afford to go on vacation."

LARGEAU/LARGEO(T)LARGEOS. By far. *J'ai gagné, largeau!* "I won by a wide margin."

LARGONJI, from **jargon.** Slang system, possibly from former Fr. Indochina, in which "l" replaces the first letter; the original first letter is shifted to the final syllable that can end in **-é, -ès, em, ic, iche, oque, -uche.** Example: **café** becomes **laféké** or **laféquès.**

LARGUER. To dump; ditch (lit. "to release"). *Son jules l'a larguée.* "Her boyfriend dumped her."

LARGUER LES AMARRES. To go away (lit. "to cast off"). *On était content de larguer les amarres de ce bled maudit.* "We were glad to get the hell out of that damned town."

LARIGOT. See (À) TIRE-LARIGOT.

LARME/LARMICHETTE, *f.* Small quantity of liquid (lit. "tear"). *Je voudrais une larmichette de cognac.* "I'd like just a wee drop of cognac."

LASCAR, *m.* **1.** Shrewd dude; great guy. *Quel sacré lascar, ton pote.* "Your buddy's one hell of a guy." **2.** No-good bum. *Ce drôle de lascar ne m'inspire pas confiance.* "I don't trust that good-for-nothing."

LATTES, *f., pl.* Walking shoes. *Ma grand-tante ne porte* *que des lattes.* "My great-aunt wears only walking shoes."

LAUCHEM, largonji of **chaud.**

LAVABO, *m.* Confirmed alcoholic (lit. "washbasin." Lots of liquid goes down both the alcoholic and the sink). *Ce lavabo a bu toute la bouteille.* "That lush drank the whole bottle."

LAVASSE, *f.* Watery, poor tasting coffee, soup, and the like. *Ton potage c'est de la lavasse.* "Your soup's dishwater."

LAVETTE, *f.* **1.** Wimp (lit. "dishrag"). *Quelle vraie lavette tu fais!* "You come across as a real wimp!" **2.** Tongue. *Je me suis brûlé la lavette.* "I burned my tongue."

LÈCHE, *f.* Apple-polishing. **Faire de la lèche,** *idiom.* To bootlick. *Il fait de la lèche au prof.* "He brown-noses the teacher."

LÉCHÉ, -E. Well done (lit. "licked." Cf. Eng. "spit and polish"). *Son topo était bien léché.* "Her presentation was first-rate."

LÈCHE-BOTTES, *m., f.* Servile flatterer (lit. "bootlicker"). *C'est un lèche-bottes du PDG.* "He's one of the managing director's ass-kissers."

LÈCHE-COUILLES/LÈCHE-CUL, *m., f.* Ass-kisser (lit. "balls- or ass-licker"). *Cherche qn. d'autre pour faire le lèche-cul.* "Find somebody else to be your ass-kisser."

LÈCHE-POMPES = LÈCHE-BOTTES.

LÉCHER. To lick. See BABINES.

LECTURE, *f.* Reading. **Être en lecture,** *idiom,* prostitutes. To be with a client. *Il a dû attendre Mimi qui était en lecture.* "He had to wait for Mimi who was busy with a client."

LÉGER. Easy. **Faire du léger; dans le léger,** *idioms.* To take the line of least resistance. *Aux autres les risques; moi je ne fais que dans le léger.* "I let others take risks; I just go for a sure thing."

LÉGITIME, *f.* Wife. *Sa légitime était jalouse de sa langoustine.* "His wife was jealous of his mistress."

LÉGUME, *f.* See GROSSE LÉGUME.

LÉGUMISER. To lounge or bum around (from **légume** [vegetable]). *J'ai légumisé tout le week-end.* "I loafed all weekend."

LERCHE, largonji of **cher.** Expensive. *Rien n'est jamais trop lerche pour toi.* "Nothing's ever too pricey for you."

LESSIVÉ, -E. 1. Washed out. *J'étais lessivé par le déménagement.* "Moving left me limp with exhaustion." **2.** Washed up financially. *Il a été lessivé en jouant aux courses.* "The races wiped him out."

LEULEUR/LEUR, from **contrôleur.** Subway conductor. *J'ai voyagé à l'œil aujourd'hui; les leurs sont en grève.* "I rode free today; the conductors are on strike."

LEUR(S) ZIGUE(S). Them/themselves. *Méfie-toi de leurs zigues.* "Watch out for them."

LEVER LA JAMBE. To be a promiscuous woman (lit. "to lift the leg"). *On raconte qu'elle lève facilement la jambe.* "They say she's an easy lay."

LEVER LE COUDE. To drink heavily (lit. "to raise [bend] one's elbow"). *Depuis son divorce il lève le coude.* "He's been hitting the bottle since his divorce."

LÉVO, backslang of **voler.** To steal. *On s'est fait lévo notre radiocassette.* "Somebody swiped our radio tape recorder."

LEVRETTE, *f.* Greyhound bitch. **En levrette.** Doggy style. *Il aime tirer son coup en levrette.* "He likes to mount her from behind." See PRENDRE…LEVRETTE.

LEZ, *m.* Problem. *L'enregistrement s'est fait sans lez.* "The recording session came off without a hitch."

LÉZARD, *m.* Problem (lit. "lizard"). *(Il n') y a pas de lézard!* No problem!

LÉZARDER. To laze around (often in the sun). *J'aime lézarder sur le sable.* "I like to bask in the sun."

LÉZOUILLE = LEZ.

LICAILLE = LIQUETTE.

LICHAILLER = LICHER.

LICHER. To tipple. *Assez liché! Au boulot!* "Enough boozing! Get to work!"

LICHETTE, *f.* Tiny bit. *J'en veux bien une lichette.* "I'd like a nibble."

LIEUTE, *m.,* from **lieutenant.** Lieutenant. *Il est beau gosse, ton lieute.* "Your lieutenant's good-looking."

LIEUVE, *m., f.,* largonji* of **vieux.** Old person. *"Faites l'amour avec une lieuve; elle te sera si reconaissante,"* conseillait Franklin.* " 'Make love to an old woman; she'll be so grateful to you,' advised Ben Franklin."

LIME/LIMÉ, *m.* White wine with lemon soda. *Pas de lime aujourd'hui. Sers-moi un muscadet pur.* "No wine cooler today. Give me a muscadet straight."

LIMER. To copulate with slow concentration ("to file"). *J'aurais aimé la limer, mais il fallait faire vite.* "I would have liked a long, lengthy screw, but we had to hurry."

(SE) LIMER. To masturbate. *Les taulards se limaient dans leurs cellules.* "The jailbirds jerked off in their cells."

LIMITE. Barely. *On est arrivé avant le lever du rideau, mais c'était limite.* "We arrived before curtain time, but just barely."

(À LA) LIMITE. If need be. *À la limite, je veux bien te prêter de l'argent.* "If it's really necessary, I'll lend you money."

LIMITE DE L'ÉPURE, *f.* Edge of a drawing. **Dépasser/franchir/sortir des limites de l'épure,** *idiom.* To go beyond the pale or limits of a subject or situation. *Ses blagues grivoises sortaient des limites de l'épure.* "He went too far with his spicy stories."

LIMOGER. To dismiss high officials. *Après le scandale, le président a limogé des généraux et des ministres.* "After the scandal, the president sent generals and ministers to Coventry (put them out to pasture)."

LIMOGES, *m., f.* Provincial person (not necessarily from

---

* See explanation of **largonji,** page 205.

Limoges, famous for porcelain). *À la disco ce soir, que des Limoges.* "Nothing but squares from the sticks in the disco tonight."

(SE) LINGER. To get dressed up; to buy clothes. *Elle se linge chez les grands couturiers.* "She gets her duds from the great dress designers."

LION, *m.* Lion. **Avoir bouffé/mangé du lion,** *idiom.* To be raring to go. *À son dernier match il avait bouffé du lion.* "He was full of beans at his last match."

LIQUEMOUZE = LIQUETTE.

LIQUETTE, *f.* Shirt. *Je lui ai payé une nouvelle liquette Lacoste.* "I bought him a new Lacoste shirt."

LISBROQUE, *f.* Need to urinate. *Il a été pris soudain d'une lisbroque.* "He suddenly felt a strong urge to pee."

LISBROQUER/LISSEBROQUER, largonji of **pisser.** To urinate. *Il lisbroquait toutes les dix minutes.* "He took a leak every ten minutes."

LISBROQUEUSE, *f.* Men's room. *Cette tapette passe tout son temps à draguer dans les lisbroqueuses.* "That fag spends all his time cruising in men's rooms."

LISPOQUER = LISBROQUER.

LISSÉPEM = LISSEBROQUER.

LITRON, *m.* One-liter bottle of cheap wine. *Il buvait son litron à bicyclette.* "He used to drink his liter bottle of wine when riding his bike."

LOFFE = LOUFOQUE.

(À) LOILPÉ/À LOILPUCHE, largonji of **à poil.**

LOLITA, *f.* Underage prostitute; older prostitute trying to pass h.s. off as a teeny-bopper (influenced by the Nabokov novel). *Il n'aime que les lolitas, les mineures ou les plus âgées.* "All he likes is nymphets, or those pretending to be jailbait."

LOLO, *m.,* children. Milk. *Ça c'est du lolo!* "That's nice stuff!"

LOLOCHES/LOLOS, *m., pl.* Breasts. *Ses lolos dansaient quand elle courait.* "Her tits shimmied and shook when she ran." See SOUTIEN-LOLOCHES.

LONBEM, louchébem of **bon.** *Lonbem, ton frichti!* "Your grub's great!"

LONGUET. Rather long. *Ce film est un peu longuet sur les bords.* "This movie is a bit on the long side."

LOPAILLE/LOPAIL-LEKEM = LOPE.

LOPE, *f., pej.* **1.** Homosexual. *On ne savait pas qu'il était lope.* "We didn't know he was queer." **2.** Coward; informer. *Ce salaud de lope a dénoncé ses copains.* "That rotten coward informed on his buddies."

LOPER. To sodomize. *On t'a lopé en taule?* "Did you get corn-holed in the slammer?"

LOPESSE/LOPETTE = LOPE.

(SE) LOQUER. To dress. *Elle n'est pas belle, mais sait se loquer.* "She's not beautiful but knows how to dress."

LOQUES, *f., pl.* Clothing (lit. "rags"). *Elle crée et vend des loques.* "She's in the rag trade."

LOQUEUR, *m.* Tailor. *Les loqueurs de Saville Row à Londres sont réputés.* "London's Savile Row tailors are well known."

LOUB(S)/LOUBARD, *m.* Young thug. *Une bande de loubards terrorise la cité.* "A gang of hoodlums is terrorizing the housing development."

LOUBARDE = LOUPIOTE.

LOUCHE, *f.* **1.** Ladle. **À la louche.** Approximately. *C'est un bouquin de 300 pages, à la louche.* "The book comprises roughly 300 pages." **2.** Hand. *J'ai refusé de lui serrer la louche.* "I refused to shake his hand." **3.** Head. See (SE) PRENDRE LA LOUCHE.

LOUCHÉBEM/LOUCHERBEM, *m.* Variation of LARGONJI, created by Lyon and Paris butchers. The most common suffix is **-em,** often preceded by **b,** although other consonants are also found. Examples: **labatem = tabac; lonbem = bon; lounèmes = nous; louivème = oui; luctrème = truc.**

LOUCHERBEM, *m.* louchébem of **boucher.** Butcher. *Notre loucherbem est devenu végétarien!* "Our butcher has become a vegetarian!"

LOUF/LOUFTINGUE, largonji* of **fou.** Crazy. *Tu es louftingue de te mêler de ça.* "You're nuts to get mixed up in that."

LOUFERIE, *f.* Madness. *J'en ai marre de tes louferies.* "I'm fed up with your nuttiness."

LOUF(F)E, *f.* See LÂCHER UN COLIS…LOUF(F)E.

LOUF(F)ER. To fart. *Sa femme avait loufé, mais par galanterie il s'est déclaré coupable.* "His wife cut the cheese, but he gallantly took the blame."

LOUFOQUE = **LOUF/LOUFTINGUE.**

LOUFOQUERIE = **LOUFERIE.**

LOUISE. See LÂCHER UN COLIS….

LOUIVÈME, louchébem of **oui.** Yes. *Quand est-ce que tu me diras "Louivème!"?* "When will you say 'Yes!' to me?"

LOULOU, *m.* **1.** Hood. See LOUBARD. **2.** Darling. *Embrasse-moi, mon loulou.* "Kiss me, my sweet."

LOULOUTE, *f.* **1.** Flighty young girl. *C'est une drôle de louloute.* "She's a hard-to-figure, snippety thing." **2.** Darling. *On y va, les louloutes!* "Let's be on our way, my chickadees."

LOUNÈMES, louchébem of **nous.** We; us. *On y va, lounèmes aussi!* "Let's go, us too."

LOUP, *m.* Wolf. **Avoir connu/vu le loup,** *idiom.* To have had sex for the first time with a man (lit. "to have known or seen the wolf." Said of a young girl). *Ça fait longtemps que j'ai connu et apprivoisé le loup.* "It's been some time since I met and mastered the sexual animal, man."

LOUPER. To miss; fail. *Ça n'a pas loupé!* "That's just what I expected!"

LOUPER LE COCHE. To miss an opportunity (lit. "the coach"). *J'ai loupé le coche en tardant à me décider.* "I missed the boat by making up my mind too late."

---

* See explanation of **largonji,** page 205

(SE) LOUPER. To botch a suicide attempt. *Elle s'est loupée la première fois, mais pas la seconde.* "She bungled it the first time, but not on her second try."

LOUPIOT, -IOTTE, *m., f.* Child; kid. *Mon loupiot, tâche d'être sage.* "Try to behave y.s., my child."

LOUPIOTE, *f.* Small lamp. *Je te laisse une loupiote allumée.* "I'll leave a small light on for you."

LOURD, -E. 1. Heavy. **La faire lourde,** *idiom.* To drone on. *Tu la fais lourde et tu m'emmerdes.* "You're going on and on and bugging me." **2.** Rich. *Ton tonton est lourd de sous.* "Your uncle's loaded."

LOURDE, *f.* **1.** Door. *Elle est partie en claquant la lourde.* "She slammed the door when she left." **2.** Hard drug. *C'est une lourde dangereuse.* "That's a dangerous hard drug."

LOURDER. 1. To close up. *Les magazes sont déjà lourdés.* "The stores are already closed." **2.** To kick out; get rid of s.o./s.t. *Je me suis fais lourdé de tous les bars du bled.* "I've been thrown out of all the bars in town."

LOURDINGUE. Ham-handed; lame-brained. *Je ne te croyais pas aussi lourdingue.* "I didn't think you were that thick."

LOUSTIC, *m.* Joker (from Ger. **lustig** [jolly]). *C'est un drôle de loustic!* "He's an oddball." **Faire le loustic,** *idiom.* To play the fool. *Quand finiras-tu de faire le loustic?* "When are you going to stop acting like a jerk?"

LOUTE, *f.* **1.** Woman; girl. *Ma nouvelle loute est de Bordeaux.* "My new girlfriend is from Bordeaux." **2.** Darling. *Ma loute, je t'adore!* "My little honey, I adore you!"

LOVÉ, *m.* Money. *Va te lover avec ton lové, tu l'aimes tant.* "Go cuddle up with your money, you love it so much." Note: This **lové** is from Romany for "coin" and is not related to **se lover** (to coil).

LSD, *f.,* letters standing for *"elle suce debout"* (she sucks standing up). Tiny woman. *Il est un géant mais sa nana est une LSD.* "He's a giant but she's practically a dwarf."

LUC, *m.,* inversion of **cul.** *Assez de tes histoires de luc.* "Enough of your smutty stories."

LUCARNE, *f.* **1.** Dormer window; skylight. **Voir de sa lucarne,** *idiom.* To see s.t. from one's own point of view. *Vous voyez ça de votre lucarne.* "You see that from your own perspective." **2.** Posterior. *Ta lucarne va aimer ce lubrifiant à base de fleurs de lotus.* "Your ass is going to like this lotus-blossom lubricant."

LUCIOLE, *f.* Flamboyant homosexual (lit. "firefly"). *Luc, pédoque rentré, cache ses talents et fuit les lucioles.* "Closet queen Luke hides his light under a bushel and flees flaming faggots."

LUCTRÈME, *m.,* louchébem of **truc.**

LUISANT/LUISARD, *m.* Sun. *Oui, vénérez le luisant, mais soyez prudents.* "Yes, worship the sun, but be prudent."

LUNDI. See SAINT-LUNDI.

LUNE, *f.* Buttocks (lit. "moon"). *L'étudiant s'amusait à montrer sa lune.* "The student got off on mooning (displaying buttocks)." See CON...LUNE; TAPER...LUNE.

LUNÉ, -E. Être bien/mal luné. To be in a good/bad mood. *À cette heure-ci je ne suis jamais bien lunée.* "At this time of day I'm never in a good mood."

LUNES, *f., pl.* Menstruation. **Avoir ses lunes,** *idiom.* To have one's period. *Je l'évite quand elle a ses lunes.* "I stay away from her during her period."

LUSTUCRU? from **l'eusses-tu cru?** (would you have believed that?). "Well what do you know! Isn't that the living end!"

LUSTUCRU, *m.* Chump. *Ce combinard me prenait pour un lustucru.* "That slick operator thought I was a dope."

LUZERNE, *f.* Hashish (lit. "alfalfa"). *Des nuages de luzerne tourbillonaient dans la boîte.* "Clouds of hash swirled in the night club."

MABOUL. Crazy. *Tu es maboul si tu te jettes dans cette eau glacée.* "You're nuts if you dive into that cold water."

MAC = MAQUEREAU.

MACAB = MACCHABÉE.

MACACHE!/MACACHE BONO!/MACACHE BON-BON!/MACACHE ET MIDI SONNÉ. "Nothing doing! No way! No go!"

MACARONI, *m.* **1.** Italian, *pej. Elle ne sort qu'avec des macaronis.* "She only goes out with spaghetti-benders." **2.** Penis. *Le macaroni de mon marin est plein de sauce.* "My sailor's dick has plenty of spunk." See (SE) GRIFFER.

MACC(H)ABÉE/MACC(H)AB, *m.* Corpse. *La marée ammenait sur le sable les maccabées du naufrage.* "The tide deposited the corpses from the shipwreck on the sand."

MACDO, *m., abbr.* of McDonald's. **Se faire un macdo,** *idiom.* To go for a burger. *Le Ritz ce soir ou on se fait un macdo?* "The Ritz tonight, or shall we go for a burger?"

MACHIN, *m.* Whatsit. *Ça sert à quoi, ce machin?* "What's this gizmo good for?"

MACHIN(CHOSE)/MACHINCHOUETTE/MACHIN-TRUC = TARTEMPION.

MAGASE/MAGAZE, *m.,* from **magasin.** Store; shop. *C'est pas la première fois qu'on casse le magase.* "It's not the first time the store's been broken into."

MAGNE-TOI!/MAGNEZ-VOUS! "Get moving!"

(SE) MAGNER LE CUL/FION/POPOTIN/TRAIN/LA RONDELLE/LES FESSES. To move one's butt; hurry it up. See TRAIN.

MAGNES, *f., pl.* Affectation. See FAIRE DES MAGNES.

MAGO = MAGASE.

MAGOUILLARD = MAGOUILLEUR.

MAGOUILLE, *f.* Wheeling and dealing. *J'ai horreur des magouilles des politicards.* "I'm turned off by the politicians' horse trading."

MAGOUILLEUR, -EUSE. *m., f.* Sharp operator. *Ta copine est une sacrée magouilleuse.* "Your friend's a real wheeler and dealer."

MAHOMET, *m.* Sun (lit. Mohammed. Cf. MOULANA). *Je rêve de mahomet et de vacances.* "I'm dreaming of sunshine and vacation time."

MAHOUSSE = MAOUSSE.

MAIN, *f.* Hand. **Avoir un poil dans la main,** *idiom.* To be very lazy. *Qu'est-ce qu'on va faire avec ce gosse? Il a un poil dans la main.* "What are we going to do with that kid? He's chronically lazy." See BALADEUR; CLAQUER...MAINS.

MAISON. Excellent; immense. *On m'a promis une récompense maison.* "They promised me a huge reward."

MAISON J'T'ARQUEPINCE = MAISON POULA-GA...

MAISON CLOSE/MAISON DE PASSE, *f.* Brothel. *Les hôtels complets, je n'avais le choix qu'entre une maison de passe ou dormir à la belle étoile.* "The hotels were full and my only choice was between a whorehouse and sleeping outside."

MAISON POULAGA/POULMAN/PARAPLUIE, *f.* Police. *La maison poulaga est arrivée tard sur la scène du crime.* "The fuzz arrived late at the scene of the crime."

MAL. Bad. **Ça va faire mal!** *idiom.* To have a strong effect. *Si ses parents apprennent son larcin, ça va faire mal!* "If his parents find out about his thieving, things are going to get hairy." **Ça la fout mal!** *idiom.* "That makes a bad impression." **Ça me ferait mal!** *idiom.* "Don't give me that! Tell me another!"

MALABAR, *m.* Well-built man. *Son gosse est devenu un sacré malabar.* "Her kid's become quite a muscle man."

MAL-BAISÉ, -E, *m., f.* Sexually uptight person; difficult individual (lit. "ill-fucked"). *Ça se voit, c'est une mal-baisée.* "It's obvious she's all screwed up (because she's not getting laid)."

MALBAR, *m.* Bouncer. *Aussi malabar qu'il était, le malbar avait la trouille de se mêler à la bagarre.* "As brawny as he was, the bouncer was afraid of getting mixed up in the brawl."

MAL DE CHIEN, *m.* Great difficulty. *J'ai eu un mal de chien à obtenir ces places de théâtre.* "I had a hell of a time getting these theater tickets." See (SE) DONNER....

(IL Y A) MALDONNE. There's a mistake. *(Il) y a mal-donne avec ce rencart.* "There's a mix-up concerning the appointment."

(DE) MALHEUR. Damned. *Débranche ce bigo de malheur!* "Disconnect that (god)damned telephone."

MALLE, *f.* Trunk. **Se faire la malle** (lit. "to pack one's trunk"), *idiom.* To pick up and go. *Ralbol de notre appart; on se fait la malle!* "We've had it up to here with our apartment; we're getting out."

MALPT!, *abbr.* of **Merde à la puissance treize!** (Shit to the thirteenth power). "All the luck in the world!" See MERDE **2.**

MAMOURS, *m., pl.* Hugs and kisses. **Faire des mamours,** *idiom.* To spoon. *Après l'école on se faisait des mamours dans la bagnole.* "After school we used to neck in the jalopy."

MANCHE, *f.* Sleeve. **Faire/taper la manche,** *idiom.* To beg. *C'est triste de voir toute cette jeunesse faire la manche dans le métro.* "It's sad to see all those young people begging in the subway."

MANCHE, *m.* Handle (broom, and so on). **Avoir le manche,** *idiom.* To have an erection. *Coincé contre une nana dans le métro, il avait le manche.* "Pressed against a girl in the subway, he had a boner."

MANCHE À BALAI, *m.* **1.** Skinny person (lit. "broomstick"). *Ce mannequin n'est qu'un manche à balai.* "That model's just skin and bones." **2.** Penis. *On finit de balayer et ensuite je te montrerai comment je me sers de mon manche à balai à moi.* "We'll finish sweeping up and then I'll show you how I use my rod."

MANCHE À COUILLES, (lit. "handle with balls") = **MANCHE À BALAI 2.**

MANDOLINE, *f.* Mandolin. **Jouer de la mandoline,** *idiom.* To masturbate (female). *Elle était aux anges en jouant de la mandoline.* "She was in ecstasy playing with herself."

MANETTE, *f.* Lever. **À fond les manettes!** "At full speed/throttle!"

MANGER À TOUS LES RÂTELIERS. To play the field to one's advantage (lit. "to eat at every trough"). *Il se démerde pour manger à tous les râteliers.* "He sees to it that he gets his gravy no matter where it comes from."

MANGER AU LANCE-PIERRES. To grab a quick bite to eat. *J'en ai marre de manger au lance-pierres; fais-moi un bon gueuleton.* "I'm sick of eating on the run; make me a big meal."

(SE) MANGER/SE MANGER LES DENTS/LA FACE/FIGURE. To fall; fall flat. *Il s'est mangé la face en VTT.* "He took a fall on his mountain bike."

MANGEUSE D'HOMMES/DE MECS, *f.* Strongly sexed woman. *C'est une mangeuse d'hommes, laide, mais populaire.* "She's an unattractive but popular nymphomaniac."

(SE) MANIER = SE MAGNER.

MANIF, *f., abbr.* of **manifestation.** Demonstration. *Elle participe à toutes les manifs de gauche, et aussi, parfois de droite.* "She takes part in all the left- and some right-wing demonstrations too."

MANITOU, *m.* Big wheel; boss. *J'ai essayé de voir le grand manitou, sans succès.* "I tried, unsuccessfully, to see the big cheese."

MANOUCHE, *m.* Gypsy; gypsy language. *Beaucoup de mots d'argot proviennent du manouche.* "Many slang words come from gypsy talk."

MANQUE DE BOL!/MANQUE DE POT! Tough luck!

MANQUER UNE CASE. Not to have all one's marbles. *Il lui manque une case.* "He's not playing with a full deck."

(NE PAS) MANQUER D'AIR. To have some nerve. *Il ne manque pas d'air, le mec, de me faire du rentre-dedans.* "That guy's got some nerve, making advances to me."

MAOUS, -SE. Humongous. *Il s'est payé une maousse de voiture.* "He bought a huge car."

MAQ = MAQUEREAU.

MAQUAGE, *m.* Cohabitation. *Ils vivent en maquage.* "They're shacking up together." Note: The legal term for cohabitation is **concubinage.**

(SE) MAQUER. To cohabit. *Ils ont décidé enfin de se maquer.* "They finally decided to live together."

MAQUEREAU, *m.* Pimp. *Ce réalisateur emploie deux maquereaux.* "That movie director has two pimps working for him."

MAQUERELLE, *f.* Procuress; brothel madam. *Lola a l'allure d'une maquerelle.* "Lola looks like a madam."

MARAVE, *f.* From Romany for "to beat." Fisticuffs. **Chercher marave,** *idiom.* To be out for a fight. *Fais gaffe, c'est un type à chercher marave pour un rien.* "Watch out, that guy is quick to let go with his fists."

MARAVER. 1. To beat up. *Ce soulard voulait tous nous*

maraver. "That drunk wanted to beat us all up." **2.** To be excessive. *Ça marave dur dans resto.* "They really hit you hard in this restaurant (the bill is steep)."

MARCHAND DE BARBAQUE/BIDOCHE/FLEURS, *m.* Pimp; white slaver (lit. "meat or flower seller"). *Il est repoussant, ce marchand de barbaque.* "That flesh peddler is revolting."

MARCHAND DE MORT SUBITE, *m.* Bad doctor (lit. "dealer in sudden death"). *N'appelle surtout pas ce marchand de mort subite.* "By no means call that quack sawbones."

MARCHANDE D'AIL, *f.* Lesbian. *C'est un couple de marchandes d'ail.* "They're a lesbian couple."

MARCHANDE D'AMOUR, *f.* Prostitute. *C'est une marchande d'amour qui ne vend pas cher son amour!* "She's a hooker who doesn't charge much for her favors."

MARCHANDE DE CHAIR HUMAINE, *f.* Brothel keeper; madam. *La marchande de chair humaine régnait en abbesse sur une collection de belles filles.* "The madam reigned like an abbess over a group of beautiful girls."

MARCHE À L'OMBRE! "You'd better lay low (lit. "walk in the shade")."

MARCHE OU CRÈVE! "Keep on going or croak!" "Do or die!"

MARCHER. 1. To participate (lit. "to walk"). *Je comprends ce que vous voulez, mais je ne marche pas.* "I know what you want, but count me out." **2.** To fall for s.t. *Tu essaies de me faire marcher?* "Are you putting me on?"

MARCHER À CÔTÉ DE SES POMPES. See POMPE.

MARCHER À L'ALCOOL/À LA DYNAMITE/AU CAFÉ/AUX DROGUES. To function by means of alcohol, cocaine, coffee, or drugs. *Il marche au beaujolpif; sa femme marche au café.* "He's never without his Beaujolais; his wife can't live without coffee."

MARCHER À L'OUBLI. To pretend not to know; function

by means of repressing. *Il nie ses crimes et marche à l'oubli.* "He denies his crimes and goes about his business in seeming ignorance of them."

MARCHER AU RADAR. See RADAR.

MARGOULETTE, *f.* Face. *Il voulait lui casser la margoulette.* "He wanted to smash his face in." **Se casser la margoulette,** *idiom.* To fall flat on one's face. *Il voulait montrer son astuce, mais il s'est casse la margoulette.* "He wanted to show how smart he was but he fell flat on his face."

MARGOULIN, *m.* Sharp business operator. *Tu n'auras pas d'aubaine chez ces margoulins.* "You won't get any bargains from those sharks."

MARGUERITE, *f.* Condom (lit. "daisy"). *Ça l'émoustillait d'exposer ses marguerites de toutes couleurs et tous parfums.* "It turned him on to display all his rubbers in many colors and scents."

MARI, *m.* Pimp with several girls working for him (lit. "husband"). *Ce mari ne prend pas bien soin de ses femmes.* "That pimp doesn't take good care of his women."

MARIE-COUCHE-TOI-LÀ, *f.* Floozie (lit. "Marie, lie down here"). *Elle a une gueule de Marie-couche-toi-là.* "She looks like an easy piece."

MARIDA. To marry. *Ma fille est à marida.* "My daughter is of marrigeable age."

(SE) MARIDA. To get married. *Elle voulait tout de suite qu'on se marida.* "She wanted us to get married right away."

MARIÉE, *f.* Glass or mug of beer with a big head (lit. "bride" [dressed in white]). *Il buvait mariée sur mariée.* "He drank one foaming mug after another."

MARIE-JEANNE, *f.* Marijuana. *Elle a mis de la marie-jeanne dans l'omelette.* "She put grass into the omlette."

MARIE-LOUISE = LOUISE.

MARIE-PISSE-TROIS-GOUTTES. *f.* Very young girl (lit. "Marie-piss-three-drops"). *Il veut une bandeuse, pas une Marie-pisse-trois-gouttes.* "He wants a sexpot, not a dry little slip of a girl."

MARIE-POPO(T)TE, *f.* Woman who spends all her time cooking. *Il cherche une Marie-popote comme épouse.* "He's looking for a homebody/good cook to be his wife."

MARIE-SALOPE, *f.* **1.** Slovenly woman. **2.** Bloody Mary (vodka and tomato juice). *Cette Marie-salope se soûle à la Marie-salope.* "That sloppy cow gets drunk on Bloody Marys."

MARIOLE, -OLLE, *m., f.* Clown. *Cesse de faire le mariole!* "Quit fooling around."

MAROLEPE!, backslang of **ma parole!** "You don't say!"

MARQUER LE COUP. To note; celebrate an occasion. *Le père a marqué le coup pour la réussite de son fils.* "The father celebrated his son's success."

MARRANT, -E. Very funny. *Zape; le film n'est pas marrant.* "Change channels; the movie isn't very funny."

MARRE. Enough. **En avoir marre,** *idiom.* To be fed up with. *J'en ai marre de toutes vos disputes.* "I'm sick and tired of your quarrels." *(Il) y en a marre!* "That's enough, damn it!"

MARRER. To laugh. *Tu me fais marrer!* "You crack me up!"

(SE) MARRER. To enjoy o.s. *Qu'est-ce qu'on s'est marré à la teuf!* "What a blast we had at the party!"

MARTEAU. Crazy. *Tu es marteau de sortir ton bateau par cette tempête.* "You're nuts to take your boat out in this storm."

MASO, *abbr.* of **masochiste,** *adj.* and *n.* *Il faut être maso pour t'aimer.* "Loving you means having to be a masochist."

MASTOC. Huge; oversized. *Je n'aime pas cette architecture mastoc.* "I don't like that megalomaniac architecture."

(SE) MASTURBER LES MÉNINGES, stronger variant of **se creuser… méninges.** See MÉNINGES.

MAT'/MATE, *m., abbr.* of **matin.** *Il part au boulot à trois heures du mat'.* "He leaves for work at three in the morning."

MATHEUX, -EUSE, *m., f.* Mathematician; eager math student. *Aucun n'est matheux dans la famille.* "Nobody in the family's any good at math."

MATHS, *m., pl.* Mathematics. *Ma frangine a la bosse des maths.* "My sister has a flair for math."

MAX, *abbr.* of **maximum. Un max.** The greatest; mostest. **Assurer un max,** *idiom.* To be stunning. *Dans sa robe fendue elle assure un max.* "She's a knockout in her dress, open at the side."

MEC, *m.* Guy; dude; boyfriend. *Il y avaient de beaux mecs sur la plage, mais elle n'avait d'yeux que pour son mec.* "There were handsome guys on the beach, but she had eyes only for her boyfriend."

MECA, backslang of **came.**

MÉCA, backslang of **camé.**

MEC À MEC/MEC POUR LES MECS, *m.* A man among men but not among women. *Elle a failli épouser un mec pour les mecs.* "She almost married a guy who goes for guys."

MEC À PASSIONS, *m.* Male in search of prostitutes for kinky sex. *Les filles redoutaient le Marquis de Sade, un sacré mec à passions.* "Whores feared the Marquis de Sade who was out for kinky sex."

MÉCANIQUES, *f., pl.* Shoulders. See ROULER LES MÉCANIQUES.

MÉCHANT, -E. Powerful (lit. "mean"). *Mary a un méchant service au tennis.* "Mary has a wicked tennis serve."

MÈCHE, *f.* Wick. **Être de mèche,** *idiom.* To be in cahoots/partnership with. *Pour mon anniversaire-surprise ma femme et ma fille étaient de mèche.* "For my surprise birthday party my wife and daughter teamed up."

MEFFE = MEUF.

MEG, *variant* of **meg,** *abbr.* of **méga** (huge). **Le Meg des Megs/le grand Meg/Mec.** God. *C'est une mangeuse de mecs qui croit très fort au Meg des Megs!* "She's a nympho who believes strongly in the Big Guy in the Sky."

MÉGALO, *m., f., adj.* and *n., abbr.* of **mégalomane.** Megalomaniac. *Ce sont tous les deux des mégalos de première.* "Both of them are total ego trippers."

MÉGOTER. To skimp. *Il n'a pas mégoté pour marier sa fille.* "He spared no expense for his daughter's wedding."

(LA) MEILLEURE. The best one yet. **Ça, c'est la meilleure!** "That takes the cake! That's unbelievable!"

MEK À MEK = MEC À MEC.

MÉLASSE, *f.* Molasses. **Être dans la mélasse,** *idiom.* To be in the soup. *Depuis qu'il chôme il est dans la mélasse.* "He's been in a pickle ever since he lost his job."

(SE) MÊLER. To interfere. **De quoi je me mêle?** *idiom.* "What business is that of yours?"

MÊLÉ-CASS, *m.* Cassis with brandy (or vermouth). **Voix de mêlé-cass.** Raspy voice (orig. due to alcohol abuse). *Cesse de chanter; ta voix de mêlé-cass me casse les oreilles.* "Stop singing; your screechy voice is busting my ears."

MÉLO, *m., abbr.* of **mélodrame.** Tearjerker. *Tes amours sont de véritables mélos!* "Your love affairs are real soap operas."

MELON, *m.* **1.** Head. *Pour couvrir son melon déplumé il porte un chapeau melon.* "He wears a derby to cover his bald head." **2.** Arab, *pej. Il est raciste et pour lui ils ne sont que des "bougnoules" ou des "melons".* "He's a racist and for him they're just 'gooks' or 'Ay-rabs.'"

MEMBRÉ. Limbed. **Bien/mal membré.** With a large/small penis (lit. "strong- or weak-limbed"). *Mon nouveau mec est foutrement bien membré.* "My new boyfriend is wonderfully well hung."

MÉMÉ, *f.* Granny; Grandma. *Mémé et pépé fêtent leurs noces d'or.* "Grandma and Grandpa are celebrating their golden wedding anniversary."

MÉMÈRE, *f., adj* and *n.* Granny; old lady. *Ce chapeau fait mémère.* "That hat makes you look dowdy."

MÉNAGÈRE, *f.* Prostitute posing as a housewife (lit. "housewife"). *La ménagère racolait au marché.* "The whore, posing as a housewife, solicited at the market."

MENDIGOT, -E. Beggar; vagrant. *Ma grand-tante donne des bonbons aux mendigots.* "My great-aunt gives candies to beggars."

MENER LE PETIT/POPAUL AU CIRQUE. To get one's end in; have sex (lit. "to take the little lad to the circus"). *Ce soir j'espère mener le petit au cirque.* "I'm hoping to get laid tonight."

MENER UNE VIE DE BÂTON DE CHAISE. To live riotously. *Après avoir mené une vie de bâton de chaise, elle est partie en quête d'un gourou dans l'Himalaya.* "After a wild life, she left to look for a guru in the Himalayas."

MÉNINGES, *f., pl.* Brains (lit. "meninges"). **Se creuser/ fatiguer/fouler/remuer les méninges,** *idioms.* To rack one's brains. *Je vais me creuser les méninges pour préparer ce topo.* "I'm going to put my thinking cap on to prepare that report." **Faire marcher ses méninges,** *idiom.* To use one's head. *Si tu faisais marcher tes méninges, tu trouverais la réponse.* "With a little mental effort, you'd find the answer." See also stronger MAS-TURBER....

MER, *f.* Sea. **Ce n'est pas la mer à boire,** *idiom.* "That's not asking too much!" See PISSER...MER.

MERDAILLON, *m.* Nasty kid or individual. *Fout le camp, espèce de petit merdaillon.* "Beat it, you little shit."

MERDE, *f.* Excrement; trash; shit. **C'est de la merde! C'est une merde!** "That's junk/crap!" **C'est la merde! C'est une de ces merdes!** "That's a real/damned mess!"

Être dans la merde, *idiom.* To be up shit's creek. *Depuis qu'il chôme ils sont dans la merde.* "Since he's been unemployed they've been in a bad way." **Foutre/semer la merde,** *idiom.* To create disorder. *Tu adores semer la merde là où tu passes.* "You love to screw things up wherever you go." **Ne pas se prendre pour de la/pour une (petite) merde,** *idiom.* To have an inflated opinion of o.s. *Le sénateur ne se prend pas pour une petite merde.* "The senator thinks his shit doesn't stink/thinks he's hot shit." See FOUILLE-MERDE.

MERDE!/MERDE ALORS! Goddamnit! Holy shit!

MERDE! Good luck! *Avant d'entrer en scène tous lui ont dit "merde!"* "Before she went out on stage everybody said " 'break a leg!' " Cf. MALPT!

(OUI OU) MERDE? Yes or no? *"Je serai ton vice président? Oui ou merde?," a dit Nixon à Eisenhower.* " 'Am I going to be your vice president? Shit or get off the pot!' said Nixon to Eisenhower."

MERDER. To fail to function; fuck up. *Juste au moment de partir la voiture a merdé.* "The car conked out just as I was going to leave."

MERDEUX, -EUSE, *m., f.* Pretentious kid; nasty individual. *Cette merdeuse se gare toujours devant ma porte de garage.* "That fucking bitch always parks in front of my garage door."

MERDIER, *m.* Terrible mess. *Dans quel merdier je me suis mis?* "What kind of a damned mess have I gotten myself into?" **Foutre le merdier = foutre la merde,** see MERDE.

MERDIQUE. Rotten. *Cet hôtel est vraiment merdique.* "This hotel's a real dump."

MERDOUILLE, *f.* Crap; bad scene. *"Quelle merdouille! Cette machine est toujours en panne.* "What a crock of shit! That machine is always going on the blink."

MERDOUILLER/MERDOYER. To get screwed up. *À mon exam j'ai merdouillé.* "I screwed up on my exam."

MERLAN, *m.* **1.** Whiting (fish). See REGARDER...MERLAN. **2.** Pimp. *J'aimerais changer de merlan.* "I'd like a new main man."

MES COUILLES! "You're full of it!" "Nuts to you!"

METTRE. To beat (lit. "to put"). *Qu'est-ce que les flics lui ont mis!* "The cops really worked him over!"

METTRE AU RANCART. See RANCART.

METTRE DU BEURRE DANS LES ÉPINARDS. To improve one's lot (lit. "to put butter in the spinach"). *Elle chante dans les églises pour mettre du beurre dans les épinards.* "She sings in churches to pick up a nice bit of extra money."

METTRE EN PERCE. To tap a barrel. **Mettre une fille en perce,** *idiom.* To take a girl's virginity. *Ça n'a pas été, facile mais je l'ai enfin mise en perce.* "It wasn't easy, but I finally popped her cherry."

METTRE LA GOMME. To accelerate; go all out. *Pour en finir j'ai mis toute la gomme.* "To get it done, I gave it the gun."

METTRE LE GRAPPIN SUR. To get one's hooks into. *Sa grand-dabe voulait qu'elle mette le grappin sur le comte.* "Her grandmother wanted her to get her hooks into the count."

METTRE LE JUS. See JUS **2.**

METTRE LE PAQUET/LA SAUCE. See PAQUET; SAUCE **1.**

METTRE LE POISSON DANS LE BOCAL. To copulate (lit. "to put the fish into the bowl"). *Mon mec n'a que ça dans la tête, mettre le poisson dans le bocal.* "All my boyfriend thinks about is screwing."

METTRE LES ADJAS. See ADJA.

METTRE LES BOUCHÉES DOUBLES. See BOUCHÉE.

METTRE LES PIEDS DANS LE PLAT. To put one's foot in it. *Pour mettre les pieds dans le plat, tu t'y connais.* "When it comes to making goofs, you're in your element."

(SE) METTRE EN ROGNE. See ROGNE.

226

(SE) METTRE QCH./S'EN METTRE JUSQUE-LÀ/S'EN METTRE PLEIN LA GUEULE/LAMPE/LANTERNE/PANSE. To indulge in gluttony (lit. "to put it away; put it in to the limit; stuff one's face or belly"). *Les vins et les desserts étaient à volonté et on s'en est mis plein la lampe.* "Wines and desserts were unlimited with the meal so we really stuffed our faces."

MEUF, backslang of **femme,** used also for *"girl."* *Elle est sympa cette meuf!* "She's a nice chick!"

MEUMEU. Outstanding. *Ce qu'il est meumeu, ton blouson.* "What a neat jacket!"

MÉZIG(UE)/MÉZIGO, *pron.* Me; myself; yours truly. *Quant à mézig, je dis non.* "As for me, I say no." Cf. TÉZIG(UE); SÉZIG(UE); NO(S)ZIGUE(S); VOZIGUE; LEUR(S) ZIGUE(S).

MÉZIG(UE), *m.,* police slang. Self-important person. *Le lieute Colombo triomphe toujours des mézigues criminels qui le toisent.* "Lt. Colombo always gets the better of the smart-ass criminals who look down on him."

MICHÉ, *m.* Prostitute's client. *Pour restreindre la prostitution, les flics agrafent aussi les michés.* "To discourage prostitution, the cops are arresting johns too."

MICHES, *f., pl.* **1.** Buttocks (lit. "loaves; buns"). **Avoir les miches (à zéro/à glagla)/avoir les miches qui font bravo,** *idioms.* To be very afraid. *À la vue des extraterrestres, on avait les miches à glagla.* "When we sighted the aliens from outer space, we were scared shitless." See (SE) CAILLER LES MICHES. **2.** Breasts. *On reluquait ses petites miches dans son corsage et ses grosses miches dans sa jupe.* "We ogled her titties in her blouse and her ass in her skirt."

MICHET = MICHÉ.

MIEL! *euph.* for **merde!** Shoot! Sugar!

MILLEFEUILLE, *m.* **1.** Layered, creamy pastry. *C'est du millefeuille!* "That's a piece of cake." **2.** Female genitalia. *Quel délice, son millefeuille!* "How delicious, her box!"

MIMI. Cutesy. *C'est pas mimi, ça?* "Isn't that precious?"

MIMINE, *f.* Darling. *Viens avec moi, mimine!* "Come with me, sweetheart!"

MIMINES, *f. pl.* Hands. *Mimi avait les mimines froides.* "Mimi's hands were cold."

MINA-MINA, *m.* Successful compromise. *Ce mina-mina sera avantageux pour nous deux.* "That trade-off will be good for both of us."

MINARET, *m.* Penis (lit. "minaret"). See DÉFROMAGER LE MINARET.

MINCE (ALORS)! *euph.* for **merde (alors)!** "Gosh darn!" "Holy cow!"

MINE, *f.* Look. **Avoir bonne mine,** ironic. To look foolish (lit. "to be looking good"). *Si tu loupes cette occasion tu auras bonne mine.* "You'll look like an idiot if you let that opportunity pass you by."

MINE DE RIEN! Unprepossessing; casually; just like that. *Mine de rien, tu as réussi à obtenir ce que tu voulais.* "No one would have thought it, but you succeeded in getting what you want."

MINET, *m.* **1.** Female genitalia (lit. "pussycat"). *Ton minet me fait de l'œil sous ton bikini.* "Your pussy is winking at me from your bikini." **2.** Effeminate fop. *Il est minet mais pas travelo.* "He's a dandy but not a transvestite."

MINETTE, *f.* **1.** Young girl (lit. "pussycat"). *Chaque samedi soir on draguait les minettes.* "Every Saturday night we tried to pick up broads." **2.** Pussy ("cat" and "female genitalia"). **Faire minette,** *idiom.* To perform cunnilingus. *D'abord je lui ai fait minette, ensuite je l'ai prise en levrette.* "First I ate pussy, then I took her doggy style."

MINOU = MINET 1.

MINUS, *m.* Insignificant person. *Tu t'intéresses à ce minus?* "You're interested in that nobody?"

MINUTE, PAPILLON! Hold on a minute there! Hold your horses!

MIOCHE, *m., f.* Little kid. *Les mioches ont bousillé le jardin avec leurs ballons.* "The kids have messed up the garden with their balloons."

MIRAUD = MIRO.

MIRETTES, *f., pl.* Eyes. *Il rêvait souvent des mirettes d'Arletty.* "He often dreamed of Arletty's eyes."

MIRO. With poor vision. *T'as rien trouvé? T'es miro?* "You didn't find anything? Do you need glasses?"

MISER. To fuck; sodomize (lit. "to place a bet"). *Le croupier m'a souvent misée, mais je n'ai jamais gagné à la roulette.* "The croupier often screwed me, but I never won at roulette."

MISO, *m. abbr.* of **misogyne.** Misogynist. *Après son quatrième divorce il est devenu miso.* "After his fourth divorce he became a woman hater."

MISTIGRI, *m.* = **MINET 1; MINETTE 2.**

MITA-MITA = MINA-MINA.

MOB, *f., abbr.* of **mobylette** *(nom déposé).* Mobylette®. *J'ai eu ma mob d'occase.* "I bought a used pedal bike."

MOELLE, *f.* Marrow. See OS À MOELLE; TIRE-MOELLE.

MŒURS, *f.* Morals. **Les Mœurs,** short for **la brigade de la police des mœurs.** The Vice Squad. *La "Ligue Pour La Suppression des Vices" voulait que les Mœurs soient plus vigilants.* "The 'League for the Suppression of Vice' wanted the Vice Squad to be more watchful."

(C'ÉTAIT) MOINS UNE! That was a close shave/call!

MOIS, *m.* Month. See TOUS…MOIS.

MOLASSE/MOLASSON, -ONNE. *Adj.* Slow as molasses. *Merde, que tu es molasse!* "Damn it, you're some slowpoke!"

MOLASSON, -ONNE, *m., f.* Lazy or flabby person. *Quelle bande de molassons!* "What a bunch of spineless louts!"

MOLLO(-MOLLO). Easily. **Y aller mollo(-mollo),** *idiom.* To take it easy. *Allons-y mollo!* "We'd better take it easy."

MÔME, *f.* Young girl. *"Jolie Môme" est une belle chanson de Léo Ferré.* " 'Pretty Girl' is a nice song by Leo Ferré."

MÔME, *m., f.* Kid. **Pisser un môme.** To give birth. *Chaque année elle pissait un môme.* "She shit out a brat every year." (Note that Fr. slang is more on the mark, anatomically, than the equivalent Eng. expression.) See TIRE-MÔME.

MONACOS, *m., pl.* Money. *J'étais sans monacos à Monte Carlo.* "I had no bread in Monte Carlo."

MON CUL! "My ass!" "You're full of it!"

MON (PETIT) CHAT/CHOU/LAPIN. My (little) honey/sweetie/dearie/darling.

(LA) MONDAINE = LES MŒURS.

MONDE, *m.* World. **Il y a du monde!** That packs a punch. That's really s.t. (in standard Fr. "it's crowded"). *Ta nouvelle moto, il y a du monde!* "That's one mountain of power, your new bike!" See FAIRE UN MONDE.

(IL Y A DU) MONDE AU BALCON. See BALCON.

MONNAIE, *f.* Coin; currency. **Monnaie courante.** Widespread. *Beaucoup de mots d'argot sont devenus monnaie courante.* "Many slang words are in common use." See COMMENCER…MONNAIE.

MONNAIE DE SINGE. See PAYER EN MONNAIE DE SINGE.

MONORGUE = MÉZIGUE.

(BIEN/MAL) MONTÉ. See MEMBRÉ.

MONTÉ COMME UN ÂNE/BOURRICOT/CHEVAL/TAUREAU. To be hung like a mule/horse/bull. *Il se croit monté comme un taureau; quel con!* "He thinks he's hung like a bull; what a fool!"

MONTÉ COMME UN SERIN. To be hung like a canary; have minimal sexual equipment. *Il était complexé d'être monté comme un serin.* "He was self-conscious about his tiny pecker."

MONTER EN AMAZONE. See AMAZONE **1.**

MONTGOLFIÈRE, *f.* Prostitute more interested in sex

than money; nymphomaniac (lit. "hot air balloon"). *La montgolfière le transporte toujours au septième ciel.* "The nympho always takes him to seventh heaven."

MONTGOLFIÈRES, *f., pl.* **1.** Testicles. *Ses montgolfières sortaient de son slip étroit.* "His balls popped out of his tight briefs." **2.** Breasts. *Ses montgolfières prenaient l'air au dessus de son soutien gorge.* "Her lovely bunch of coconuts were out in the air above her bra."

MONTPARNO, from **Montparnasse** (lit. "Mt. Parnassus"), a district in Paris. *Avant de prendre le train pour la Bretagne, on a visité le cimetière de Montparno.* "Before taking the train for Brittany, we visited Montparnasse Cemetery."

MONTRER SA BOUTIQUE. See BOUTIQUE.

MORCEAU, *m.* Piece. **Bouffer/cracher/lâcher le morceau,** *idiom.* To confess. *Il a enfin craché le morceau à la mondaine.* "He finally sang to the Vice Squad."

MORDRE. To understand (lit. "to bite"). *Tu mords?* "(Do) you get it?"

MORDU, -E. Taken with s.o./by s.t. *Son mec, elle en est mordue, mais lui il est plus mordu des courses de chevaux.* "She's nuts about her guy but he's more hung up on the ponies/horse racing."

MORFAL(E), *m.* Glutton. *Cessez de manger comme des morfales!* "Stop eating like pigs."

MORFALER/SE MORFALER. To eat gluttonously. *En taule je rêvais de me morfaler.* "I dreamed of pigging out when I was in stir."

MORFALOU = MORFALE.

MORGANE/MORGANÉ, -E. Smitten; gone on. *Elle aimait fredonner la chanson* Morgane de toi. "She liked to hum the song *Hooked on You.*"

MORLINGUE, *m.* Wallet. **Constipé du morlingue,** *idiom.* Stingy. *Pas drôle de sortir avec ce constipé du morlingue!* "No fun going out with that tightwad!"

MORPION, *m.* Pubic louse. *Elle ne savait pas qui lui avait* *collé ses morpions.* "She didn't know who'd given her crabs."

(À) MORT. Totally; all out (lit. "to death"). *N'oublie pas de chauffer à mort la salle de bains.* "Don't forget to put the heat up high in the bathroom."

MORT. See RAIDE DEF; RAIDE MORT.

MORT AUX VACHES! "Down with the cops/fuzz/pigs! (lit. "death to the cows")."

MORTEL!, youth. Fantastic! (lit. "deadly"). *Mortel le week-end!* "The weekend was awesome!"

MORTIBUS. Dead as a doornail. *Plus d'espoir; il est mortibus.* "No hope; he's stone-cold dead."

MORUE, *f.* **1.** Slut (lit. "cod [fish]"). *Une bande de morues arpentait les couloirs de l'hôtel.* "A bunch of hookers made the rounds of the hotel corridors." **2.** Nasty woman. *Vieille morue!* "Old bag/hag/bitch!"

MORVE, *m.* Nasal mucus; snot. See TIRE-MORVE.

MORVEUX, -EUSE, *m., f.* Jerk (lit. "snotty-nosed brat/individual"). *Espèce de petit morveux!* "You dumb little nerd!"

MOT DE CAMBRONNE, *m.* The "S" word (*euph.* for **merde,** esp. in the sense "Good luck!") *Avant mon concours ma grand-tante m'a chuchoté, "le mot de Cambronne!"* "Before my exam my great-aunt whispered the S word to me." See CAMBRONNE.

MOT DE CINQ LETTRES = MOT DE CAMBRONNE.

MOTTE, *f.* Vagina; mons veneris (lit. "mound"). *La motte de beurre sur la table, et ta motte à côté de moi au plumard—quelle vie heureuse!* "A block of butter on the table and your box next to me in bed—life is wonderful!"

MOTUS (ET BOUCHE COUSUE)! "Mum's the word!" "Keep it quiet!" "Button your lip." (Note: **Motus** is pseudo Latin for **mot** [word]. **Bouche cousue** is "mouth stitched up.")

MOU, *m.* Stomach. See BOURRER...MOU; RENTRER...MOU.

MOU, MOLLE. Flabby. See BANDER MOU.

MOUCHACHA, *f.,* from Sp. **muchacha.** Girl. *Il est mordu de cette mouchacha.* "He's nuts about that chick."

MOUCHACHO, *m.,* from Sp. **muchacho.** Boy. *On a envoyé le mouchacho en colo.* "We sent the kid off to camp."

MOUCHARDER. To inform. *Quel salaud, il nous a tous mouchardés!* "That SOB, he finked on all of us!"

MOUCHE, *f.* Fly. See ENCULER LES MOUCHES.

MOUCHER. To reprimand (lit. "to blow" [nose]). **Les morveux veulent moucher les autres,** *proverb.* "That's like the pot calling the kettle black."

MOUFLET, -ETTE, *m., f.* Kid. *On ne la voit jamais sans ses mouflets.* "You never see her without her kids."

MOUFTER/MOUF(F)ETER. To protest; grumble. **Sans moufter; ne pas moufter,** *idioms.* Not to bat an eyelid. *Quand les flics lui ont demandé ses paps, il n'a pas moufté.* "When the cops asked for his ID, he didn't turn a hair."

MOUILLE, *f.* Mouth. *Donne-moi un baiser sur la mouille.* "Give me a wet one."

MOUILLER. To experience vaginal/clitoral orgasm (lit. "to wet"). *Elle mouille un max avec moi.* "The earth really moves for her when she's with me." **(En) mouiller pour qn.** To be sexually excited by s.o. (of either sex). *Il en mouille pour elle.* "He's got the hots for her."

MOUILLER LA BARBE/LAITUE. To urinate (said of women). Lit. "to wet the beard/lettuce." *La bière me donne envie de mouiller la barbe.* "Beer makes me want to pee."

MOUILLER LE GOUPILLON. To get one's end in (lit. "to moisten the holy water sprinkler"). *Il avait toujours rêvé de mouiller le goupillon avec une bonne sœur.* "He'd always dreamed of dipping his wick into a nun."

MOUILLER SA CHEMISE/LIQUETTE. To work very hard (lit. "to wet one's shirt", as in "to sweat"). *Il n'a pas*

233

peur de mouiller sa chemise pour aider sa famille. "He's not afraid of knuckling down and doing work to help his family."

MOUILLER/MOUILLER SA CULOTTE ET SON FROC. To be afraid (lit. "to wet one's underpants and pants"). *Il mouille pour un rien.* "He pisses in his pants over the slightest little thing."

MOUILLER UNE ARDOISE. To urinate (lit. "to wet a slate"). *Verse-moi encore une chope; je vais mouiller une ardoise.* "Pour me another mug (of beer); I'm going to take a leak."

MOUILLES, *f., pl.* Buttocks. *Elle est molle aux mouilles.* "She's got a tender ass."

MOUILLES = MICHES 1.

(SE) MOUILLER. To take a risk. *Il n'a pas voulu se mouiller par peur des représailles.* "He didn't want to stick his neck out because of possible reprisals."

MOUISE, *f.* Poverty; hard luck. **Être dans la mouise,** *idiom.* To be hard up financially. *Elle a été dans la mouise un an avant de retrouver un boulot.* "She had a year of rough going before she found a job again."

MOUKÈRE, *f., pej.* North African woman; woman; prostitute (from Sp. **mujer**). *Ce maq bat ses moukères.* "That pimp beats his women."

MOULANA, *m.* Scorching sun (from Ar. for "Our Master," a title of Allah [God]. Cf. MAHOMET). *On a visité les temples des dieux solaires sous un moulana brûlant.* "We visited the temples of the solar deities under a blazing sun."

MOULE, *f.* **1.** Female genitalia (lit. "mussel"). *Sa moule bien musclée s'accrochait à ma colonne.* "Her well-muscled snatch clutched my column (cock)." Note: Mussels cling to **bouchons** (posts) placed in coastal waters. **2.** Luck. **Avoir de la moule.** To be very lucky. *Elle a eu de la moule à la loterie.* "She hit it big in the lottery." **3.** Fool. *Quelle moule!* "What a dumb jerk!"

MOULE À GAUFRE(S), *m.* Real idiot (lit. "waffle iron"). *Cesse de me prendre pour un moule à gaufres.* "Stop treating me like a lamebrain."

MOULE-BOULES/MOULE-BURNES, *m.* Tight-fitting jeans (lit. "balls' molder"). *Je l'avais trouvé sexy dans son moule-boules, mais quel minus au lit!* "I thought him sexy in his tight jeans but what a loser in bed!"

MOULÉ. Molded. **Bien moulée.** Very shapely. *Sacrément bien moulée, la strip-teaseuse!* "The stripper's got curves in all the right places."

MOULER UN BRONZE. To defecate (lit. "to cast a bronze statue"). See BRONZE.

MOUMOUTE, *f.* Wig; toupee. *Ça se voit que le présentateur de télé porte une moumoute.* "It's obvious the TV announcer is wearing a rug."

MOUQUÈRE = MOUKÈRE.

MOURON, *m.* Pimpernel (herb of the primrose family whose flowers close at the approach of bad weather). **Se faire du mouron,** *idiom.* To worry o.s. sick. *Ne vous faites pas de mouron; les prisonniers seront libérés.* "Don't be upset; the prisoners will be rescued."

MOUSCAILLE, *m.* Excrement; trouble. *Ils sont dans une mouscaille pas possible.* "They're really in deep doo-doo."

MOUSMÉ, *f.* Girl; woman. *Il a épousé une mousmé japonaise.* "He married a Japanese girl."

MOUSSE, *f.* **1.** Froth. **Se faire de la mousse,** *idiom.* To get all worked up. *Tu te fais de la mousse pour rien.* "You're getting in a lather for nothing." **2.** Beer. *On se tape une bonne mousse?* "Shall we go for a nice beer?"

MOUSSER. To foam. **Se faire mousser,** *idiom.* To praise o.s. *Il ne loupe jamais une occasion de se faire mousser.* "He never misses an opportunity to blow his own horn." **Se faire mousser le créateur.** To jerk off; cream one's jeans (lit. "to get the creator all frothy/lathered up"). *Il ne pouvait plus prier et s'est fait moussé le créateur.* "He couldn't pray anymore and jerked off."

MOUSTACHE, *f.* Mustache. See (SE) CALER.

MOUSTACHUE, *f.* Butch homosexual. *Cette tantouze ne veut coucher qu'avec des moustachues.* "That old queen just wants to get it on with he-man gays."

MOUSTAGACHE, *f.* javanais of moustache. *Le kaiser et Clemenceau avait des moustagaches impressionantes.* "The kaiser and Clemenceau had impressive mustaches."

MOUTARD, *m.* Young boy; apprentice. *C'est un moutard sympa.* "He's a nice lad."

MOUTON, *m.* Sheep. **Se conduire en moutons de Panurge.** To show no initiative. *On n'embauche pas ceux qui se conduisent en moutons de Panurge.* "We're not hiring yes-people."

MOUTON À CINQ PATTES, *m.* **1.** Rarity (lit. "sheep with five feet"). *Les manuscrits de Descartes, Racine, sont des moutons à cinq pattes, réclamés par mes clients.* "Manuscripts by Descartes and Racine are great rarities sought after by my customers." **2.** Strange bird or duck. *Il se méfie de Dolly, qu'il trouve un mouton à cinq pattes.* "He doesn't trust Dolly, whom he takes to be a real weirdo."

MOUTRAVE. To urinate (from Romany). *Moutrave au jardin, ça fait pousser les orties.* "Pissing in the garden makes the nettles grow."

-MUCHE. Slang suffix. Examples: **argotmuche = argot; fatmuche = fatma; trucmuche = truc.**

MULE, *f.* Mule. See TÊTE DE MULE.

MULE AVEUGLE, *m.* Unwitting drug carrier (lit. "blind mule"). *Les stups de l'aéroport ont agrafé la mule aveugle.* "The airport narcs nabbed the unsuspecting mule."

MULTIPRISE, *m.* Female/passive male homosexual, open to all comers (lit. "electrical adaptor"). *Es-tu prêt à t'envoyer la multiprise assise au bar?* "Are you ready to get it on with that slut at the bar?"

MÛR, -E. Drunk (lit. "ripe"). *Après tous ces cocktails elle était bien mûre.* "After all those cocktails she was well pickled."

MURGE, *f.,* Drunkenness. *Ils avaient tous une sacrée murge.* "They were all dead drunk."

(SE) MURGER. To get drunk. *On s'est foutrement murgé hier soir au Quartier Latin.* "We really tied one on last night in the Latin Quarter."

MUSEAU, *m.* Face (lit. "muzzle"). See (SE) SUCER LE MU-SEAU.

MUSICO/MUSICOS, *m.* Musician. *Le musicos se démer-dait pour créer de l'ambiance.* "The musician did his best to liven things up."

MUSIQUER. To complain. *Tu vas encore longtemps musi-quer?* "Will you be playing your violin much longer?"

MUTCHELL! Silence!

MYTHO, *m., abbr.* of **mythomane. 1.** Pathological liar. *Je n'en crois rien; c'est un mytho de première.* "I don't believe any of it; he's an out-and-out liar." **2.** Lie. *Ton laïus est pétri de mythos.* "Your long-winded speech is full of lies."

MYTHO, *adj.* Lying. *Il est incroyablement mytho.* "You wouldn't believe how full of crap he is."

NANA, *f.* Girl. *Les nanas sont de sortie ce soir.* "The girls are out tonight."

NANAR(D), *m.* Low budget '30s and '40s movies. *Je ne regarde que les nanars.* "All I watch are trashy '30s and '40s movies."

NARPI, backslang of **pinard.**

NARVALO, *m.* from Romany. Zany good-for-nothing. *C'est un narvalo mais rigolo!* "He's a no-good nut, but he's amusing."

NARZO, backslang of **zonard.**

NATCHAV!, from Romany. "Let's blow this hole!" Cf. TCHAVE.

NATÜRLICH, HEINRICH/ULRICH! from Ger. "naturally" + first names. "You bet, Fred! Sure thing, Bing!"

NAVET, *m.* **1.** Turnip. See SANG DE NAVET. **2.** Trashy book or movie. *Et le livre et le film sont des navets.* "Both the book and the movie are trash."

NÉGIFRAN, *f.,* backslang of **frangine.** Sister; sis. *J'suis pas jalouse de ma négifran.* "I'm not jealous of my sister."

N'EN AVOIR RIEN A FOUTRE, *idiom.* To be totally indifferent to s.t. *Tes emmerdes, je n'en ai rien à foutre!* "Your problems are no skin off my nose!"

NÉNÉS, *m., pl.* Breasts. *Elle n'a que douze ans mais trou-*

ve ses nénés trop petits. "She's only twelve but thinks her titties are too small."

NÉNETTE, *f.* **1.** Girl. *Quelle sacrée nénette!* "She's one hell of a chick!" **2.** Head. See (SE) CASSER LA NÉNETTE.

NÉNUPHAR, *m.* Female genitalia (lit. "waterlily"). *Courbet, Monet, et tous les grands auraient adoré peindre son nénuphar.* "Courbet, Monet, and all the great ones would have loved to paint her bush."

NET, *abbr.* of Internet. *Est-ce que l'on peut te trouver sur le net?* "Can I find you on the Web?"

NETTE = SAVONETTE.

NEUILLE = NOILLE.

NEUNEU. Foolish. *Ce qu'elle peut être neuneu, ta frangine!* "Your sister is sometimes really birdbrained!"

NEUNŒIL = NŒIL.

NEZ, *m.* Nose. **Avoir qn. dans le nez,** *idiom.* To be hostile to s.o. *Après cette vacherie, je l'aurai à vie dans le nez.* "After that dirty trick I'll hate him forever." See (SE) BOUFFER LE NEZ; (SE) CASSER LE NEZ; COUP...NEZ; DOIGTS...NEZ; PIQUER DU NEZ; SENTIR...NEZ; VERRE.

NIAFFE = GNAF.

NIAULE = GNÔLE.

NIBARDS/NIBS = NICHONS.

NI CHAUD NI FROID. Indifferent. *Tes sarcasmes me font ni chaud ni froid.* "I couldn't care less about your sarcastic remarks."

NICHE, *f.* **1.** Doghouse (lit. "niche"). **À la niche!** "To your doghouse" (to a dog). "Beat it"; "hit the road!" (to a human). **2.** Practical joke; dirty trick. **Faire une niche à qn.,** *idiom. Il passe son temps à me faire des niches.* "He spends his time playing jokes on me."

NICHONS, *m., pl.* Breasts. *Très jeune, elle avait déjà d'énormes nichons.* "She already had big knockers when she was very young."

NIÔLE = GNÔLE.

NIOUZES, *f., pl.,* phonetic Fr. rendering of "news". News (TV and Internet). *Mémé ne loupe jamais l'heure des niouzes.* "Granny never misses the news on TV."

(SE) NIPPER. To dress. *Elle n'a jamais su se nipper.* "She never knew how to dress."

NIQUER. To copulate. **Va te faire niquer!** "Fuck off!" **Nique ta mère/père/sœur,** and so on! "Go fuck your mother, and so on!"

NITOUCHE, from **n'y touche (pas).** See SAINTE NITOUCHE.

NŒIL, *m.* Eye. *Le froid me fait pleurer les nœils.* "The cold makes my eyes tear."

NŒUD, Knot. **Un sac ou paquet de nœuds,** *idiom.* A tangle of problems. *Laissons tomber ce sac de nœuds.* "Let's not get into that can of worms." See POMPER...NŒUD; TÊTE DE NŒUD.

NOILLE/NOÏE, *f.* Night. *Le comte ne sort que la noille.* "The count only goes out at night."

(AU) NOIR. See AU BLACK/NOIR/SCHWARZ.

NOISETTE, *f.* Testicle (lit. "hazelnut") See CASSE-NOISETTES.

NOIX, *f.* Jerk (lit. "walnut"). *Quelle vielle noix!* "What an old fool!"

(À LA) NOIX/À LA NOIX DE COCO. Crummy (lit. "coconut"). *C'est un roman à la noix.* "That's a trashy novel."

NOM DE DIEU DE BORDEL DE MERDE! "Goddamn' fuckin' shit almighty!"

NOM DE NOM! For God's sake!

NOM D'UN CHIEN/NOM D'UNE PIPE! "For heaven's sake!" "Ye Gods!"

NO(S)ZIGUE(S). Us. *C'est pas pour noszigues, ça.* "That's not for us."

NOUBA, *f.* Party. **Faire la nouba,** *idiom.* To party. *Ils ont fait la nouba trois jours durant.* "They partied for three days straight."

NOUILLE, *f.* Idiot (lit. "noodle"). **Quelle nouille!** "What a jackass!"

NOUILLE DE MER, *f.* Condom floating on water (lit. "sea noodle"). *La marée descendante déposait les nouilles de mer sur le sable mouillé.* "The ebbing tide left the aquatic rubbers on the wet sand."

NOUNE, *f.* Female genitalia. *Dès le matin de mon adolescence ma noune s'ouvrait à la lumière de l'amour.* "In early adolescence my pussy opened to the light of love."

NOYE = NOILLE.

NUL À CHIER/NULACHE. Really rotten. *Ces rappeurs sont nulaches!* "Those rappers are shitty!"

NUMERNAUTE, *m.* TV channel surfer. *Je ne lâche plus ma piaule car ma vie de numernaute est sensass!* "I don't leave my pad anymore because my TV traveling is great!"

NUMÉROTER. To number. See ABATTIS.

NUNU/NUNUCHE. Gullible; goofy (from **ingénu**). *J'annule l'abonnement de cette revue trop nunuche.* "That review is too idiotic and I'm canceling my subscription."

NUTS = backslang of thunes.

-O. Frequently found slang suffix, as in **alcoolo = alcoolique; apéro = apéritif; intello = intellectuel; préso = préservatif; proxo = proxénète; réglo = réglementaire.**

OBÉIR AU DOIGT ET À L'ŒIL. To be absolutely obedient. *J'insupporte qu'on ne m'obéisse pas au doigt et à l'œil.* "I won't put up with not being obeyed to the letter."

OBLIGADO/OBLIGEMAN. Required. **Faire qch. obligado.** To be pressured into doing s.t. *J'ai sorti la poubelle obligado.* "I was strong-armed into taking out the garbage."

OCCASE, *f.* Occasional prostitute. *Ça change d'aller au radada avec une occase.* "Getting it on with an occasional hooker makes for a change."

(D')OCCASE, from **d'occasion.** Secondhand. *Je l'ai eu d'occase.* "I got it secondhand."

OCCUPE-TOI DE TES FESSES!/T'OCCUPE! "Mind your own damned business! Keep your own nose clean."

-OCHE. Suffix that can make a word humorous, casual, or pej. Examples: **cinoche = cinéma; fastoche = facile; téloche = télévision.**

OD, *f., pron.* as in Fr. **(odé),** from Eng. "to OD." **Faire une OD.** To die of a drug overdose. *Vas-y mollo, sinon tu feras une OD!* "Go easy or you'll OD!"

ŒIL, *m.* Eye. **Avoir qch. à l'œil,** *idiom.* To get s.t. free. *On* *a eu nos places à l'œil.* "Our tickets were complimentary." **Avoir qn. à l'œil.** To keep an eye on s.o. *L'État omniprésent vous a à l'œil.* "Big Brother is watching you." See (SE) FOURRER; OBÉIR; (SE) RINCER; TAPE-À-L'ŒIL; TAPER DANS L'ŒIL.

ŒIL AU BEURRE NOIR, *m.* Black eye. *À part un œil au beurre noir, il s'en est bien sorti.* "Apart from a black eye, he came through pretty well."

ŒUF, *m.* Egg. **Aller se faire cuire un œuf,** *idiom.* To go fly a kite. *Si tu crois que je marche dans ta combine, va te faire cuire un œuf!* "If you think I'm part of your scam, you can go jump in the lake!" See CASSER SON ŒUF; FACE.

ŒUFS SUR LE PLAT. Tiny titties (lit. "(two) fried (sunnyside up) eggs"). *Avec ses œufs sur le plat elle n'a aucune chance de devenir la Reine des Vendanges.* "Flat-chested as she is, she has no chance of becoming Harvest Queen."

OIGNON, *m.* **1.** Luck. **Avoir de l'oignon; avoir l'oignon qui décalotte,** *idioms.* *À la roulette de Monte Carlo nous avons eu de l'oignon!* "We were lucky at roulette in Monte Carlo." **2.** Anus. **Défoncer l'oignon or foutre/taper dans l'oignon.** To sodomize. *Il le lui a foutu dans l'oignon.* "He gave it to him up the ass." **Passer/taper sous l'oignon.** To penetrate vaginally from behind. *Elle préfère que je lui passe sous l'oignon pour une meilleure pénétration.* "She likes me to go in from behind for better penetration."

OIGNONS, *m., pl.* Onions. **Mes/tes/ses/nos/vos/leurs oignons.** My (and so on) own business. *Laisse tomber; ce sont ses oignons et pas les tiens!* "Let it drop; it's her business, not yours."

(À) OILP/OILPÉ, backslang of **à poil.** See POIL.

OINJ, backslang of **joint.**

OLKIF = OLPICHE/OLPIF.

OLPÈTE/OLPETTE = OLPICHE/OLPIF.

OLPICHE/OLPIF. Excellent. *Tout à la teuf était olpiche.* "Everything was peachy at the party."

OLRÈT/OLRETTE!, horse racing. OK; all right. *Olrette pour ce jockey qui a minci!* "OK for that jockey who's lost weight."

OR, *m.* Gold. **C'est de l'or en barre.** "That's rock solid; as good as gold!" See ROULER SUR L'OR.

(EN) OR, *m.* **En or.** Wonderful. *J'ai un dab en or!* "My father's just wonderful."

ORDURE, *f.* Rotten person (lit. "filth"). **Quelle (sale) ordure!** "What a sleazebag!"

OREILLE, *f.* Ear. See SORTIR PAR...OREILLE.

OREILLES EN FEUILLES DE CHOU. See FEUILLES... CHOU.

ORPHELINES, *f., pl.* Testicles (lit. "orphans"). *Les eunuques de la cité interdite ont récuperé leurs orphelines.* "The eunuchs of the forbidden city got their balls back."

ORTEILS = DOIGTS DE PIEDS.

OS, *m.* Bone. **Jusqu'à l'os.** Thoroughly; utterly. *Son maq l'a possédée jusqu'à l'os.* "Her pimp owned her totally." See TOMBER...OS.

-OS. Suffix much used by youth from the 1960s to the 1980s. Examples: **braquos = braquemard; cassetos = cassette; musicos = musicien; rapidos = rapide; zygos = zygomatique.**

OS À MOELLE, *m.* **1.** Nose (lit. "marrow bone"). *Quelle renommée, l'os à moelle de Jimmy Durante et celui de Cyrano.* "How famous were Jimmy Durante's and Cyrano's schnozzes!" **2.** Penis. *Son os à moelle a taché ma jupe.* "His cock stained my skirt."

OSEILLE, *m.* Money (lit. "sorrel"). *As-tu vu* Prends l'oseille et tire-toi *de Woody Allen?* "Have you seen Woody Allen's *Take the Money and Run?*"

OUAH! "Wow! Ooh!"

OUAIS. "Yup; yeah."

OUALLOU! "No way! Nothing doing!"

OUA-OUA, *m., pl.,* children. Toilet. *Jusqu'à dix ans elle refusait d'aller aux oua-oua toute seule.* "Till she was ten, she wouldn't go to the toilet alone."

OUATÈRES = WATERS.

OUBLI, *m.* Forgetting; omission. See MARCHER À L'OUBLI.

OUILLE! "Ouch!"

-OUILLE. Ending on slang words, often *pej.* Examples: **magouille; merdouille; papouille; petzouille.**

OUIOUINE, *f.* Sanitary napkin. *Je n'utilise plus les ouiouines.* "I don't use sanitary napkins anymore."

OUI OU MERDE? See (OUI OU) MERDE?

OÙ JE PENSE! The place I'm thinking of; where the sun don't shine. *Votre critique, vous pouvez vous la foutre, où je pense!* "You can stuff your review you know where!"

OURS, *m., pl.* Bears. **Avoir ses ours,** *idiom.* To have one's menstrual period. *J'avais mes ours et une méchante migraine.* "I was having my period and a nasty headache."

OURSIN, *m.* Sea urchin. **Avoir des oursins dans la fouille/poche/le morlingue,** *idioms.* To be stingy (lit. "to have spiny sea urchins in one's pocket/wallet"). *Mes vioques ont des oursins dans la fouille.* "My parents are really tightfisted."

-OUSE/OUZE. Slang suffix, sometimes *pej.* Examples: **partouse = party; picouse/piquouse = piqûre; pinouze = pinard; planquouse = planque; sidouze = SIDA; tantouze = tante.**

OUST(E)!/ALLEZ OUST(E)! "Get going! Get a move on!"

OUTIL, *m.* Tool. See REMBALLER SES OUTILS.

OUTILLÉ. Equipped with tools. **Être bien outillé,** *idiom.* To have a large tool (penis). *Ce bas-duc est bien outillé.* "That runt's well hung."

OUVRIR LES GRANDES EAUX DE VERSAILLES. To start crying. *Je cède dès qu'elle ouvre les grandes eaux* *de Versailles.* "Once she turns on the tears, I give in." Note: The palace of Versailles was famous for its waterworks and fireworks.

(L') OUVRIR/OUVRIR SA GRANDE GUEULE. To open one's big fat mouth. *Ne te crois pas obligé de l'ouvrir.* "Don't feel you have to open your big mouth."

OVERDOSE = OD.

(LA) P..., *euph.* for **prostituée; putain; pute.** *Ma tante refusait de lire* La P...*respectueuse de Sartre.* "My aunt refused to read Sartre's *The Respectful Prostitute.*"

PACSIF/PACSON. Package. **Gagner/toucher le pacson.** To make a bundle. *Mémé a touché le pacson.* "Granny struck it rich."

PAF. Drunk. *Le cocktail m'a rendue complètement paf.* "The cocktail totally plastered me."

PAF, *m.* Penis. *Il était trop paf pour trouver son paf pour pisser.* "He was too pissed to find his dick and take a piss." See BEAU...PAF; SAUTE-AU-PAF.

PAGE. See TOURNER LA PAGE.

PAGETOURNER. To end a relationship and move on. *J'aimerais avoir le courage de le pagetourner.* "I wish I were strong enough to get rid of him."

PAIN. 1. Bread. **Avoir du pain sur la planche** (lit. "to have bread on the board"), *idiom.* To have a lot of work. *Avec le déménagement, j'ai du pain sur la planche.* "What with moving, I've got a lot on my plate." **2.** Whack. *Sa joue a gonflé après le pain qu'elle lui a fiché.* "His check swelled up after the smack she gave him." **3.** Wrong note. *Malgré tous les pains, ses accros étaient ravis.* "Despite all the wrong notes, her fans were delighted."

PAIX, *f.* Peace. **La paix!** "Shut up, that's enough now!"

Ficher/foutre la paix à qn. To leave s.o. in peace. *Fiche-moi la paix!* "Quit bugging me!"

PALPER. To make a bundle (lit. "to feel"). *L'avocat a dû palper au passage.* "The lawyer probably lined his pockets along the way (in the course of a transaction)."

PALPITANT, *m.* Heart. *Son palpitant a lâché.* "His ticker gave out."

PALUCHE, *f.* Hand. *Liszt avait des paluches impressionantes.* "Liszt had impressive hands."

(SE) PALUCHER. To masturbate. *Après avoir joué du Rachmaninoff, il s'est paluché.* "After playing Rachmaninoff, he saw Dr. Jerkoff."

PANADE, *m.* Bread soup. **Être dans la panade,** *idiom.* To be in the soup. *Il est dans la panade depuis son licenciement.* "He's been down on his luck ever since he lost his job."

PANAIS, *m.* Penis (lit. "parsnip"). **Dégraisser/dérouiller/planter/tremper son panais.** To have sexually; dip one's wick. *Il ne laisse jamais passer l'occasion de tremper son panais.* "He never misses an opportunity to get his."

PANAM(E), dated. Paris. *Elle était venue à Paname pour gagner des ronds.* "She had come to Paris to make money."

PANARD, *m.* Foot. *Elle lui écrasait toujours les panards en dansant.* "She always stepped on his feet when dancing." See PRENDRE SON PANARD.

PANET = PANAIS.

PANIER, *m.* Basket. **Mettre dans le même panier,** *idiom.* To lump together. *Elle est lui sont à mettre dans le même panier.* "The two of them are of the same ilk." **Mettre la main au panier,** *idiom.* To pinch or grope s.o.'s behind. *S'il essaie de me mettre la main au panier il aura un pain.* "If he tries to goose me, I'll slap him." See CON…PANIER.

PANIER À SALADE, *m.* Police van (lit. "salad shaker"). *La flicaille les a tous embarqués dans le panier à salade.* "The fuzz took them all away in the paddy wagon."

PANIER D'AMOUR, *m.* Vagina. *Catherine la Grande les aimait bien montés pour bien remplir son panier d'amour impérial.* "Catherine the Great liked men who were well endowed to fill up her imperial love box."

PANIER DE CRABES, *m.* Place full of tension and hostility (lit. "crab cage"). *Je suis heureuse d'être sortie de ce panier de crabes.* "I'm glad to be out of that vipers' nest."

PANSE, *f.* Belly. See (SE) METTRE QCH. DANS…PANSE.

PANTOUFLARD, -E, *m., f.* Stay-at-home (from **pantoufle,** "slipper"). *Mes vioques sont des pantouflards.* "My parents are old sticks-in-the-mud."

PANTRUCHE = PANAM.

PAPA GÂTEAU, *m.* **1.** Overindulgent father. *Elle a eu de la chance d'avoir eu un papa gâteau.* "She was lucky to have had a generous dad." **2.** Sugar daddy. *Je n'ai jamais eu de boulot, grâce à mon papa gâteau.* "I've never had a job, thanks to my sugar daddy." See BAISER À LA PAPA.

PAPE, *m.* Pope. **Sérieux comme un pape.** Solemn-faced; serious. *La gosse triste était sérieuse comme un pape.* "The sad little girl was solemn-faced." See TÉLÉPHONER AU PAPE.

PAPELARDS, *m., pl.* Identity papers. *Les flics m'ont demandé mes papelards.* "The cops asked for my ID."

PAPIER, *m.* Paper. **Être dans les petits papiers de qn.,** *idiom.* To be in s.o.'s good books. *Il fait tout pour être dans les petits papiers de la patronne.* "He's trying hard to be on the good side of the boss."

PAPIER-CUL/PAPIER Q, *m.* Toilet paper. *Elle achète du papier Q parfumé.* "She buys scented toilet paper."

PAPILLON, *m.* Parking ticket (lit. "butterfly"). *J'ai une collection de papillons non payés.* "I have a collection of unpaid parking tickets."

PAPILLON D'AMOUR, *m.* Pubic louse (lit. "love butterfly"). *T'inquiète; il ne t'a refilé que des papillons d'amour!* "Take it easy; all he gave you was crabs!"

PAPILLON DU SÉNÉGAL, *m.* Penis. *Elle s'était essayée*

à toute une collection de papillons du Sénégal. "She tried out a whole gamut of cocks."

PAPOUILLE, *f.* Tickle. **Faire des papouilles,** *idiom.* To feel up. *Il m'a fait des papouilles en dansant.* "He pawed me when we were dancing."

PAP'S = PAPELARDS.

PÂQUERETTE, *f.,* **1.** Daisy. **Au ras des pâquerettes,** *idiom.* At base level. *Je ne suis pas pimbêche, plutôt au ras des pâquerettes.* "I'm not stuck up, rather, down to earth." **2.** Vagina. *Il aime baiser en levrette sa paquerette.* "He likes to hump her doggie-style."

PAQUET, *m.* Package. *Mettre le paquet.* To go all out; shoot the wad. *Pour en finir ce soir, j'ai mis le paquet.* "I went whole hog to finish tonight."

PARANO, *adj., abbr.* of **paranoïaque.** Paranoid. *Qu'est-ce qu'il est parano!* "God, is he uptight!"

PARANO, *m., f., abbr.* of **paranoïaque.** Paranoiac. *Même les paranos ont des ennemis.* "Even paranoiacs have enemies."

PARANO, *f., abbr.* of **paranoïa.** Paranoia. *Te voilà repartie en complète parano!* "There you go off the deep end again."

PARAPLUIE, *m.* Umbrella. **Avoir avalé un parapluie,** *idiom.* To be a stuffed shirt. *Il semble toujours avoir avalé un parapluie.* "He seems uptight all the time."

PARE-BRISE, *m.* Eyeglasses (lit. "windshield"). *Il a paumé son pare-brise.* "He lost his glasses."

PARE-CHOCS, *m., pl.* Breasts (lit. "bumpers"). *Ces pare-chocs étaient irrésistibles.* "Her front bumpers were overpowering."

PAREIL. Similar. **C'est du pareil au même.** "It's six of one, half a dozen of the other."

PARIGOT, -E, *adj.* Parisian. *Elle a perdu son accent parigot.* "She lost her Parisian accent."

PARIGOT, -E, *m., f. Cette provinciale est devenue on ne peut plus Parigote.* "That girl from the provinces has become ultra-Parisian."

PARLOT(T)E, *f.* Idle talk. *C'est de la parlote pour ne rien dire.* "That's just hot air."

PAR TERRE. On the ground. See (SE) ROULER PAR TERRE.

PARTI, -E. Slightly drunk; stoned. *À la Saint Sylvestre ses vioques étaient bien partis, mais lui, il était complètement parti.* "On New Year's Eve his parents were tipsy but he was spaced out."

PARTIE CARRÉE, *f.* Orgy with two couples. *Elle n'aime que les parties carrées.* "All she goes for are foursomes."

PARTIE DE BALAYETTE INFERNALE. See BALAYETTE.

PARTIE DE JAMBES EN L'AIR, *m.* Lovemaking. *Le pique-nique s'est terminé par une partie de jambes en l'air.* "The picnic ended up with a roll in the hay."

PARTIES/PARTIES HONTEUSES, *f. pl.* Genitals. *Ce moraliste a honte de ses parties honteuses.* "That moralist is ashamed of his private parts."

(C'EST) PARTI MON KIKI! Off you go! Away we go!

PARTIR EN COUILLE(S). To go down the drain, *idiom. Mon exam loupé; c'est une année de travail partie en couille.* "I failed my exam; there's a year's work in the garbage."

PARTIR EN JAVA. To have a ball. *On est parti en java sur la plage.* "We had a blast on the beach."

PARTIR SUR LES CHAPEAUX DE ROUES. See CHAPEAU DE ROUE.

PARTOUSARD, -E, *m., f.* Participator in group sex. *Ce bled est un nid de partousards.* "This town is a nest of wife-swappers."

PARTOUSE, *f.* Group sex. *Leurs réunions ne sont que des partouses.* "Their get-togethers are just orgies."

PARTOUSER. To participate in group sex. *Je ne voulais*

plus partouser et mon mari m'a quittée. "I didn't want any more group sex and my husband left me."

PARTOUZARD = PARTOUSARD.

PARTOUZE = PARTOUSE.

PAS DÉGUEULASSE! Not half-bad (lit. "not disgusting"). *Pas dégueulasse ton petit vin de derrière les fagots.* "Not bad at all, your special reserve wine."

PAS FOLICHON! Not very agreeable. *Nos repas de famille ne sont pas très folichons.* "Our family dinners aren't much fun."

PAS FOLLE LA GUÊPE! Not as dumb as s.o. looks; not as foolish as s.t. seems (lit. "the wasp's not crazy"). *Elle a fait sa valise sans oublier le fric—pas folle la guêpe!* "She packed her bags without forgetting the money— she's no fool!"

PASSADE, *f.* Brief affair. *Je lui ai pardonné ses passades, mais je n'accepte pas sa nouvelle liaison.* "I've pardoned his little flings but I can't accept his new relationship."

PASSE, *f.* Pass. **En passe de,** *idiom.* On the point of. *Elle est en passe de devenir une grande star.* "She's about to become a big star." **Faire une passe,** *idiom.* To turn a trick. *Pour plaire à son maq elle fait le plus possible de passes.* "To please her pimp she turns as many tricks as possible."

PASSE BOURGEOISE, *f.* Paid sex with a married woman. *Son mari savait qu'elle faisait des passes bourgeoises pour arrondir leurs fins de mois.* "Her husband knew she did a little screwing on the side to help with the monthly bills."

PASSEPORT, *m.* Condom. *Je n'entre jamais sans passeport.* "I never go in without a rubber."

PASSE RAIDE, *f.* Basic price for a session with a prostitute. *Ma passe raide est très raisonnable.* "My price for a quickie is very reasonable."

PASSER À L'AS. See AS.

PASSER À TABAC. To beat up. See TABAC.

PASSER L'ARME À GAUCHE/Y PASSER, *idioms.* To die. *Il a failli y passer.* "He almost lost his life."

PASSER QCH. À L'AS. See AS.

PASSER UN SAVON. See SAVON.

PASSE SÈCHE/SIMPLE = PASSE RAIDE.

(QUEL) PATAQUÈS! What a fuss/scandal!

PATATE. Head (lit. "potato"). **En avoir gros sur la patate,** *idiom.* To have a lot on one's mind; be distressed. *Elle en avait gros sur la patate quand il l'a laissée tomber.* "She was distraught when he dropped her." See RAS…PATATE.

(ET) PATATI ET PATATA. And so on and on.

PATAUGER DANS LA SEMOULE = PÉDALER.

PATIN, *m.* Tongue kiss (lit. "skate"). **Filer/rouler un patin.** *Il m'a filé un des ces patins.* "He gave me a real wet one."

PATINER LE CHINOIS. To fellate; have oral sex. *Ils cherchent toujours à patiner le chinois.* "They're always looking for oral sex."

PATRAQUE. Slightly sick. *Aujourd'hui je me sens patraque.* "I'm feeling a bit under the weather today."

PATTE, *f.* Leg. (lit. "animal leg; paw"). **Aller à pattes,** *idiom.* To go on foot. **En avoir plein les pattes,** *idiom.* To be fed up. *J'en avais plein les pattes de toujours aller à pattes au boulot.* "I was sick and tired of always hoofing it to work." See CLAQUER…PATTES; TIRER…PATTES.

PAUMÉ, -E, *adj.* Bewildered. *On était tous les deux paumés.* "We were both all mixed up."

PAUMÉ, -E, *m., f.* Misfit. *C'est un enfant de paumés.* "The child's parents are dropouts."

PAUMER. To lose. *Je paume sans cesse mes clefs.* "I keep losing my keys."

(SE) PAUMER. To be all mixed up. *Je me paume sur la carte routière à toutes les sorties d'autoroute.* "I'm completely lost with the road map every time I get off the highway."

PAUVRE. Poor. *Pauv' type!* "What a jerk/washout/loser!" See PIANO DU PAUVRE; PRENDRE...PAUVRE. PAUVRE CON/TARÉ/TYPE!

PAVUTE, javanais of **pute.**

PAXON = PACSON.

PAYE, *f.* Long time (lit. "pay"; "payroll"). *Ça fait une paye qu'on ne s'est pas pris de vacs!* "It's been ages since we've had a vacation."

(ÇA) PAYE! What a scream/howl/gas!

PAYER. To treat (lit. "to pay"). *Tu me paies un pot?* "Will you buy me a drink?"

PAYER EN MONNAIE DE SINGE. (lit. "to pay in monkey money"). To fob off; welch. *Cet escroc de promoteur a payé ses ouvriers en monnaie de singe.* "That crooked real estate developer let his workers whistle for their money."

(SE) PAYER. To have to endure (ironic use of the lit. meaning "to treat o.s. to"). *Le même mois je me suis payé un accident de voiture et une jambe cassée au ski.* "The same month I had the luck to smash up my car and break my leg skiing."

(SE) PAYER LA FIOLE/GUEULE/POIRE/TÊTE DE QN. To make fun of s.o. *Tu te paies ma tête?* "Are you putting me on?"

(SE) PAYER UN JETON (DE MATE) = PRENDRE UN JETON (DE MATE).

(S'EN) PAYER/S'EN PAYER UNE TRANCHE. To have a good time. *Ce dernier weekend on s'en est payé.* "Last weekend we had a blast."

PD = PÉDÉ.

PEAU, *f.* Skin. **Avoir qn. dans la peau,** *idiom.* To be madly in love with. *Son gangster de jules, elle l'a vraiment dans la peau.* "She's really gone on her gangster boyfriend." **Avoir la peau de qn./faire la peau à qn.,** *idioms.* To kill s.o. *Les truands ont fait la peau de deux otages.* "The gangsters knocked off two hostages." **Bien/mal dans sa peau.** To feel comfortable/uncomfortable. *Entourée d'aristos au resto rup je me sentais mal dans ma peau.* "I felt ill at ease in the ritzy restaurant surrounded by aristocrats." See RAS...PEAU.

PEAU DE BALLE = PEAU DE BITE/ZÉBI/ZOB.

PEAU DE BANANE, *f.* Snare (lit. "banana peel"). *Méfie-toi de cette association—c'est une peau de banane!* "Don't trust that association—it's a trap!"

PEAU DE BITE/ZÉBI/ZOB, *f.* Nothing (lit. "dick skin"). *Ce boulot te rapportera peau de balle.* "You'll get zilch from that job."

PEAU DE CHIEN, *f.* Old whore (lit. "dog skin"). *Comme dit la chanson: "À la Bastille on aimait bien Nini peau de chien."* "As the song says: in the Bastille district, everyone loved Nini, the dear old whore."

PEAU DE SAUSS/SAUCISSON, *f.* Shoddy merchandise (lit. "sausage skin"). *Ça ne vaut rien; c'est de la peau de saucisson!* "That's worth nothing; it's junk!"

PEAU DES FESSES, *f.* Very expensive (lit. "skin of the buttocks"). *Ça m'a coûté la peau des fesses.* "That cost me an arm and a leg."

(À LA) PEAU DE TOUTOU, *f.* Bungled. *C'est un travail à la peau de toutou.* "That's a sloppy job."

PEAU DE VACHE, *f.* Bitch; SOB. *Son prof est une vraie peau de vache.* "Her teacher's a real bastard."

PÉBROC/PÉBROQUE, *m.* Umbrella. *Ma grand-tante se servait de son pébroc pour se défendre.* "My great-aunt used her umbrella to defend h.s."

PÊCHE, *f.* **1.**. Peach. **Poser sa pêche.** To defecate. *Le chien a posé sa pêche devant ma porte.* "The dog pooped in front of my door." **2.** Head. **Avoir la pêche,** *idiom.* To look great; be in great shape. *En ce moment j'ai la pêche.* "Right now, I'm feeling great." See (SE) FENDRE...PÊCHE. **3.** Blow. *Il a pris une pêche en pleine gueule.* "He got whacked right in the kisser." See FILER UNE PÊCHE.

PÉCHO, backslang of **choper.**

PECLO, backslang of **clope.**

PÉCORE = PEDZOUILLE.

PÉCU = PAPIER-CUL.

PÉDALE, *f.* Male homosexual. **Être de la pédale,** *idiom.* To be a homosexual. *J'ignorais qu'il était de la pédale.* "I didn't know he was gay."

PÉDALER DANS LA CHOUCROUTE/SEMOULE/LE YAOURT. To be getting nowhere fast (lit. "to be pedaling in sauerkraut/semolina/yogurt"). *Les négociations pédalent dans la semoule.* "The negotiations are bogged down."

PÉDÉ, *abbr.* of **pédéraste.** *m.* Homosexual. **Pédé comme un phoque.** Really queer. *Marc est fier d'être pédé comme un phoque.* "Mark is proud of being a flaming faggot."

PÉDOQUE = PÉDÉ.

PEDZOUILLE, *m.* Yokel. *Des pédés parigots draguaient les pedzouilles.* "Parisian queens were cruising country bumpkins."

PÈGRE, *f.* The underworld. *Le maire a été acheté par la pègre.* "The mayor was in the mob's pocket."

PEIGNE-CUL/PEIGNE-DERCHE, *m.* Lazy good-for nothing (lit. "ass comb"). *Moi, je turbine pendant que ce peigne-cul se la coule douce.* "I slave away while that lazy bum takes it easy."

PEIGNÉE, *f.* Beating. *Tu vas voir la peignée que je vais te flanquer.* "Just wait until you get the beating I'm going to give you."

PEIGNER LA GIRAFE. To waste time in idle pursuits (lit. "to comb the giraffe"). *Dans ma vie j'ai peigné des troupeaux de girafes.* "I've spent my life in no end of useless projects."

PEIGNE-ZIZI = PEIGNE-CUL.

PEINARD, -E. Cushy. *Notre vie est peinarde.* "We've got an easy life."

PEINARD, *adv.* With no problems. *Je fais mon jogging chaque jour peinard.* "I do my daily jogging in peace and quiet."

PEINARDEMENT = PEINARD. *(adv.)*

PEINTURE, *f.* Painting. **Ne pas pouvoir voir qn. en peinture,** *idiom.* To find s.o. unbearable. *Son mari, je ne peux pas le voir en peinture.* "I hate the sight of her husband."

PELÉ, *m.* Bald man (lit. "peeled"). See TROIS...TONDU.

PELLE, *f.* **1.** Shovel. **À la pelle.** In quantity. *Les couples désunis, il y en a à la pelle.* "The world is full of people who've fallen out of love." **2.** Fall; flop. See PRENDRE...PELLE; RAMASSER...PELLE. **3.** Tongue kiss. See ROULER UNE PELLE.

PELOTAGE, *m.* Petting. *Papa ne permet pas le pelotage à table.* "Dad doesn't permit smooching at the table."

PELOTE, *f.* Fortune (lit. "ball of yarn"). **Faire sa pelote,** *idiom.* To make a mint. *Ils se sont fait une petite pelote en travaillant au noir.* "They made a small fortune moonlighting."

PELOTER. To feel up. *Il ne peut pas m'approcher sans me peloter.* "He can't come near me without pawing me."

PELOTES, *f., pl.* Testicles. *Dédé ne pouvait plus rentrer ses pelotes dans son jean rétréci.* "Andy could no longer get his balls into his tight (shrunk) jeans."

PELOTEUR, *m.* Groper. *Les peloteurs du métro attendent les rames bondées.* "Subway mashers wait for crowded trains."

PELOTEUR DE GRAND-MÈRE, *m.* Street or subway musician slang. Double bass player. *Notre peloteur de grand-mère s'accompagnait en chantant.* "Our double bass player accompanied h.s. in a song."

PENDRE AU CUL/NEZ. To be hanging over one's head (lit. one's "ass or nose"). *La grève, ça nous pend au nez.* "We're faced with the strike that's looming."

PENDU, *m.* Hanged man. **Avoir une veine de pendu,** *idiom.* To be very lucky. *Il a une veine de pendu; son* *roman sera édité.* "He's a lucky devil; his novel's going to be published."

PENDULE, *f.* Clock. **Remettre les pendules à l'heure,** *idiom.* To make s.t. clear. *Son patron était trop entreprenant et Lili a dû remettre les pendules à l'heure.* "Her boss was too forward and Lili had to set things straight for him."

PENSEUSE, *f.* Head. See COURT-JUS...PENSEUSE.

PENTE, *f.* Slope. **Avoir la dalle en pente,** *idiom.* To drink a lot (lit. "to have a slating slope," as in one for liquor to slide down easily). *Mon dab a la dalle en pente.* "My dad's a lush."

PÉPÉ, *m.* Grandpa. *Pépé voulait se remarier à 95 ans.* "Gramps wanted to get married again at 95."

PÉPÉE, *f.* = **NANA.**

PÉPÈRE, *m.* and *adj.* Comfy; easy. *Casse-cou à vingt ans, mais à quarante il mène une vie pépère.* "At twenty he was a daredevil but at forty he's living a soft life."

PÉPIN = PÉBROC.

PÉPIN, *m.* Problem (lit. "pip"). *Il a eu un gros pépin avec sa voiture.* "He had a major problem with his car."

PÉQUENOT = PEDZOUILLE.

PERDRE LA BOUSSOLE. See BOUSSOLE.

PERDRE LES PÉDALES, *idiom.* To lose one's head. *Je m'inquiète de perdre les pédales pour un rien.* "It upsets me when I go nuts over trifles."

PERDRE SA FLEUR (D'ORANGER). To lose one's virginity. *Il n'a pas su que j'avais perdu ma fleur d'oranger sur la plage.* "He didn't find out that I had lost my cherry on the beach."

PÉRIF/PÉRIPH, *m., abbr.* of **périphérique.** Beltway. *Prenons la départementale; le périf bouchonne.* "Let's take the secondary road; the main road is bumper to bumper."

PERLE, *f.* Fart. See LÂCHER UN COLIS...PERLE.

PERME, *f. abbr.* of **permission.** Leave of absence. *Le marin a eu une perme de huit jours.* "The sailor got an eight-day leave."

PERPÈTE/PERPETTE, *f., abbr.* of **perpétuité.** Life sentence. *Il avait pensé éviter la perpette mais on l'a condamné à perpette.* "He thought he wouldn't get life, but he did."

(À) PERPETTE (LES ALOUETTES/BAINS/OIES). In the back of the beyond. *Ils ont quitté Paris pour s'installer à Perpette-les-Bains!* "They left Paris to live in the boonies."

PERROQUET, *m.* Absinthe; pastis with menthe (lit. "parrot"). See ÉTOUFFER...PERROQUET.

PERVENCHE, *f.* Female traffic cop (lit. "periwinkle"). *J'ai évité le papillon en faisant du charme à la pervenche.* "I didn't get a ticket because I turned on the charm to the meter maid."

PET, *m.* Fart. **Ne pas valoir un pet (de lapin),** *idiom.* To be worthless. *Tes pets-de-nonne ne valent pas un pet de lapin.* "Your fritters (lit. "nun's farts") aren't worth a rabbit's fart."

PÉTARD, *m.* **1.** Noise (from firecrackers, backfiring, and the like). **Faire du pétard,** *idiom.* To create an uproar/scandal. *Quand ils apprendront la nouvelle ça fera du pétard.* "When they find out about that, it's going to make waves." **2.** Revolver. *Il a tout de suite sorti son pétard.* "He took out his revolver right away." **3.** Posterior. *Lili a un pétard aguichant.* "Lily has an attractive ass." See RAS...PÉTARD. **4.** Cannabis cigarette. *Il fume un pétard aux WC; son pétard le fait planer.* "He's smoking a joint in the john; he gets high on his own petard."

PÉTASSE, *f.* Slut. *Vise cette pétasse à vélo!* "Look at that broad on the bike!" **Avoir la pétasse** = **avoir la pétoche.** See PÉTOCHE.

PÈTE = PÉTARD 3, 4.

PÉTÉ, -E. Drunk; stoned. *Il est rigolo quand il est un peu* *pété, mais moins drôle quand il l'est à donf.* "He's a riot when he's a little high, but less funny when he's completely pissed."

PÈTE-DANS-LE-SABLE, *m., f.* Short person (lit. "ass in the sand"). *C'est ce pète-dans-le-sable qui veut jouer au basket?* "Is that the little runt who wants to play basketball?"

PÉTER DANS LA SOIE. See SOIE.

PÉTER LA FAIM/DALLE = CREVER LA FAIM/ DALLE.

PÉTER LA FORME/SANTÉ. To be in top shape. *Au retour de vacances je pète toujours la santé.* "I'm always bursting with health when I get back from vacation."

PÉTER LE FEU. To be full of energy. *Le travail avance car il pète le feu.* "The work's making progress because he's full of zip."

PÉTER LES BOUTONS DE BRAGUETTE. To turn on (lit. "to bust the buttons of one's fly"). *Elle et sa sœur me font péter les boutons de braguette.* "She and her sister really get me horny."

PÉTER LES PLOMBS. To blow a fuse. *Quand je les vois ensemble, je pète les plombs.* "When I see them together I blow a gasket."

PÉTER PLUS HAUT QUE SON CUL/DERRIÈRE. To be pretentious (lit. "to fart higher than one's ass"). *Depuis qu'elle a épousé le duc elle pète plus haut que son cul.* "Since marrying the duke she's swell-headed."

(SE) PÉTER LA GUEULE. To get smashed. *Après s'être pété la gueule au whisky et au shit il s'est pété la gueule en voiture.* "After getting smashed on whisky and hash he smashed up his car."

(SE) PÉTER LA PANSE/SOUVENTRIÈRE. To overeat. *Au gueuleton on s'est bien pété la panse.* "We really stuffed our bellies at the feast."

(SE) PÉTER LA RUCHE. See RUCHE.

PÈTE-SEC, *m.* Authoritarian, sharp-tongued person (lit.

"dry-ass"). *Pas drôle de jacter avec ce pète-sec.* "No fun talking to that martinet."

PÉTEUX, *m.* = **PÉTARD.**

PÉTEUX, -EUSE, *m., f.* Pretentious person. *Toutes des péteuses, ces nanas du 16ème (arrondissement)!* "Those girls from the 16th **(arrondissement)** are all stuck-up!"

PETIT CADEAU, *m.* Prostitute's fee. *Quand un miché oublie mon petit cadeau, mon maq le lui rappelle.* "When a john forgets my little consideration, my pimp reminds him."

PETIT CHAPEAU, *m.* Condom (lit. "little hat"). *Il se balade avec plein de petits chapeaux dans la poche.* "He walks around with plenty of rubbers in his pocket."

PETIT CHAUVE À COL ROULÉ, *m.* Penis (lit. "little baldie in a turtleneck"). *Son petit chauve à col roulé était immense.* "His pecker was huge."

PETIT COIN, *m.* Toilet. *Le bigo sonnait pendant que j'étais au petit coin.* "The phone rang while I was in the can."

PETIT CREVÉ, *m.* Cheap little punk/mobster. *Ce petit crevé s'est fait tout de suite agrafer.* "That little punk got nabbed right away."

PETIT DÈJ, *abbr.* of **petit déjeuner.** *Je n'aime pas sauter mon petit déj.* "I don't like skipping breakfast."

PETIT FRÈRE, *m.* Penis (lit. "little brother"). *Son petit frère ne supporte pas l'eau glacée.* "His dick doesn't like very cold water."

PETIT FRIPÉ, *m.* Anus (lit. "the little wrinkled one"). *Le roman de Burroughs met en valeur un petit fripé qui parle.* "Burrough's novel features a talking anus."

PETIT GUICHET, *m.* Anus (lit. "the little ticket window"). **Être du petit guichet = être de la pédale.**

(LE) PETIT JÉSUS EN CULOTTE DE VELOURS, *m.* Succulent food or drink (lit. "the baby Jesus in velvet britches"). *Le banquet était une succession de petits Jésus en culottes de velours.* "The banquet was a succession of exquisite dishes and drinks."

PETIT NOIR, *m.* An espresso coffee. *Il y avait plus de sucre que de café dans son petit noir.* "There was more sugar than coffee in his espresso."

(AUX) PETITS OIGNONS. Excellent. *Votre soirée était aux petits oignons.* "Your party went off perfectly."

PÉTOCHE, *f.* Fear. **Avoir la pétoche,** *idiom.* To be afraid. *J'ai la pétoche quand il roule trop vite.* "It scares me when he drives too fast."

PÉTOUILLE = PÉTOCHE.

PETSEQUE = PÈTE-SEC.

PETZOUILLE = PEDZOUILLE.

PEUCLO = PECLO.

PÈZE, *m.* Money. *As-tu du pèze à me prêter?* "Got any bread to lend me?"

PHALLO, from **phallocrate.** Male chauvinist pig. *Il ne bande plus, mais il est toujours aussi phallo.* "He doesn't get it up anymore, but he's still as sexist as ever."

PHOQUE, *m.* **1.** Seal. **Les avoir à la phoque.** Work-shy individual (lit. "with turned-in flippers" or "hands"). *On ne peut compter sur lui; il les a à la phoque.* "There's no counting on him; he's a goldbrick." **2.** Homosexual; limp wrist (again, the connection is with "inversion" or "turning in"). *Notre fils se plaît au milieu des phoques.* "Our son likes to hang out with fags." See EN ÊTRE.

PHOSPHORER. To think long and hard. *Elle a phosphoré toute la nuit avant de prendre sa décision.* "She cogitated all night before making her decision."

PIANO, *m.* Restaurant oven. *Le maître cuisinier tenait à l'œil son piano.* "The great chef kept an eye on his oven."

PIANO DU PAUVRE/PIANO À BRETELLES, *m.* Accordion. *Ce rameux est un virtuose du piano du pauvre.* "That strolling subway musician is an accordion virtuoso."

PIAULE, *f.* Room. *C'est toujours le bordel dans sa piaule.* "His pad's always a mess."

PIAULER. To sleep; live. *Je ne piaule pas chez mes vioques.* "I don't live with my parents."

PICAILLON, *m.* Small change; cash. **Avoir des picaillons,** *idiom.* To be rich. *Je crois qu'elle a des picaillons.* "I think she's got big bucks."

PICHOUN = PITCHOUNET.

PICOLER. To tipple. *Ils picolent tous dur dans cette famille.* "They all hit the bottle in that family."

PICOUSE = PIQUOUSE.

PICOUSER = PIQUOUSER.

PICRATE, *m.* Cheap wine. *Le prof les a bernés en versant un picrate dans une bouteille de Mouton-Rothschild.* "The prof fooled them by serving cheap wine in a Mouton-Rothschild bottle."

PIED, *m.* Foot. **Faire du pied à qn.,** *idiom.* To play footsy/kneesies. *Son mari me faisait du pied sous la table.* "Her husband played footsy with me under the table." **Mettre le pied quelque part à qn.,** *idiom.* To kick s.o. in the backside. *Tu vas avoir mon pied quelque part si tu continues à m'emmerder.* "I'll give you a kick in the ass if you keep bugging me." See COMME UN PIED; COUP DE PIED EN VACHE; COUPS DE PIED AU CUL...; COUP DE PIED DE VÉNUS; PRENDRE SON PIED.

(C'EST) LE PIED! (That's) sensational; orgasmic; mind-blowing!

PIED-DE-BICHE, *m.* Beggar; vagrant; door-to-door salesman (lit. "doe's foot"; "crowbar." May derive from a door knocker shaped liked a deer's foot.). *L'ancien PDG est devenu pied-de-biche.* "The former CEO's become a beggar." See TIRER...BICHE.

PIED DE GRUE, *m.* Crane's foot. **Faire le pied de grue,** *idiom.* To be kept waiting. *Tâche d'etre à l'heure; j'ai horreur de faire le pied de grue.* "Try to be on time; I hate to hang around for nothing."

PIED DE NEZ, *m.* Thumbing one's nose at s.o. *Quel imper-*

tinent, ce mouflet; il m'a fait un pied de nez. "What an impudent brat; he thumbed his nose at me!"

PIED-NOIR, *m., f.* Algerian-born Fr. person. *La famille de pieds-noirs regrettait sa terre natale.* "The Algerian-Fr. family missed their native land."

PIEDS, *m., pl.* **Faire des pieds et des mains,** *idiom.* To go all out. *J'ai fait des pieds et des mains pour obtenir ce boulot.* "I moved heaven and earth to get that job." **Faire les pieds à qn.,** *idiom.* To teach s.o. a lesson. *Il n'a rien foutu de l'année—s'il loupe son exam, ça lui fera les pieds!* "He goofed off all year—if he fails his exam it'll serve him right." See BÊTE…PIEDS; CASSE-PIEDS; CASSER LES PIEDS; CON COMME SES PIEDS; (S')EMMÊLER LES PIEDS.

PIEU, *m.* Bed (lit. "stake"). *Je rêvais d'un pieu au bord de la mer.* "I dreamed of a bed by the sea."

(SE) PIEUTER. To hit the sack. *J'adore me pieuter à la belle étoile.* "I love to sleep under the stars."

PIF. Nose; schnozz. **Au pif.** By a rough estimate. *Au pif, il a 100 mètres d'ici au garage.* "I'd say it was about 100 meters from here to the garage."

PIF(F)ER. To smell. **Ne pas pouvoir piffer qn.** To find s.o. unbearable. *Ce prof n'a jamais pu me piffer.* "That teacher could never stand me."

(AU) PIF(F)OMÈTRE = AU PIF.

PIFFRER = PIF(F)ER.

PIGE, *f.* Year. *Je me sens toujours jeune avec mes 80 piges.* "I still feel young at 80."

PIGER. To understand. *Je te planque. Tu piges?* "I'm ditching you. Have you got that?"

(N'Y) PIGER QUE COUIC/DALLE/POUIC. To understand nothing at all. *Dans son argomuche je n'y ai pigé que couic.* "I couldn't make head or tail of his slang talk."

PIGNOLE, *f.* Masturbation. *Une petite pignole, ça te dit?* "Do you feel like a hand job?"

(SE) PIGNOLER. To masturbate. **Se pignoler à quatre**

mains, *idiom.* To delude o.s. *Si tu crois que ça va marcher tu te pignoles à quatre mains!* "If you think that's going to work, you're kidding y.s. (lit. "jerking off with four hands")."

PIGNOUF, *m.* Boor. *Quelle bande de pignoufs!* "What a pack of louts."

PILPOIL. Perfectly. *Ça me convient pilpoil.* "That suits me to a T."

PILULE, *f.* Pill. See AVALER LA PILULE; DORER LA PILULE.

PINAILLER. To nitpick. *Cesse de pinailler tout le temps.* "Stop splitting hairs all the time."

PINARD, *m.* Wine. *Il n'y a pas de bon pique-nique sans pinard.* "A picnic's not a picnic without wine."

PINCE, *f.* Hand. See SERRER…PINCE.

PINCEAUX = PIED.

PINCE-CUL/PINCE-FESSES, *m.* Party; dance (lit. "pinch ass"). *Ils vont chaque samedi au pince-fesses.* "They go to the dance every Saturday."

PINCER. To arrest. *On l'a pincé sur le fait.* "They nabbed him red-handed."

(EN) PINCER POUR QN., *idiom.* To be infatuated with s.o. *Il en pince pour moi.* "He's taken a shine to me."

PINCES = PINCETTES 1.

(À) PINCES/PINCEAUX/PINGOTS. On foot. *Par ce froid je n'ai pas envie de rentrer à pinces.* "I don't feel like walking back in this cold."

PINCETTES, *f., pl.* **1.** Pair of tweezers; fire tongs. **Qn. pas à prendre avec des pincettes.** S.o. dirty or angry and thus not fit to go near. *Sa nana l'a quitté et il n'est pas à prendre avec des pincettes.* "His girl left him and there's no going near him (with a ten-foot pole)." **2.** Legs. **Remuer les pincettes,** *idiom.* To dance. *Pépé sait toujours bien remuer les pincettes.* "Gramps is still a good dancer."

PINE, *f.* Penis. *Molly Bloom se plaignait que les mecs ne se* *lavaient jamais la pine.* "Molly Bloom complained that guys never washed their dicks." See RENTRER...BRAS.

PINER. To have sexually. *Il ne pense qu'à piner.* "All he thinks about is getting laid."

PINGLOT/PINGOT = PIED.

PINOUZE = PINARD.

PINTER. To guzzle alcohol (from **pinte,** "pint," a measure no longer used in Fr.). *Tu ferais bien de pinter moins.* "It'd be a good idea for you to booze it up less."

PIOCRE, *m.* Louse. *Tous les gosses au bahut avaient des piocres.* "All the kids in school had lice."

PIOGER. To live. *Je n'y pioge plus.* "I don't live there anymore.

PIÔLE = PIAULE.

PION, -NNE, *m., f. adj.* and *n.* Drunk. *Ils étaient tous pions, sauf moi.* "They were all soused, except me."

PION(N)ARD, *m.* Drunk. *Je ne veux plus le voir, ce pionard.* "I don't want to see that drunk anymore."

PIONCER. To sleep. *Je pionce toujours au cours le lundi matin.* "I always get forty winks in school Monday morning."

(SE) PIONER/SE PIONARDER. To get drunk. *Je me suis pioné mais ça n'a pas aidé.* "I got drunk but it didn't help."

PIPE, *f.* **1.** Fellatio (lit. "pipe"). **Faire/tailler une pipe** (lit. "to do/trim a pipe"). To perform fellatio. *Je ne fais pas de pipe à des pines malpropres.* "I don't go down on dirty dicks." **2.** Head. See CASSE-PIPE; CASSER SA PIPE; (SE) FENDRE LA PIPE; NOM D'UNE PIPE; TÊTE DE PIPE.

PIPELETTE, *m.* Talkative person. **Quelle pipelette!** "What a chatterbox."

PIPI DE CHAT = PISSE D'ÂNE.

PIQUE-ASSIETTE, *m., f.* Sponger. *C'est un pique-assiette de première.* "He's a first-class freeloader."

PIQUE-FESSES, *f.* Nurse. *J'oublie le stress des piquouzes* *avec cette aguichante pique-fesses.* "That sexy nurse makes me forget the stress of the injections."

(PAS) PIQUÉ DES VERS/HANNETONS. Not half-bad at all. *Son soufflé n'était pas piqué des vers.* "Her soufflé was really excellent."

PIQUER. To take; swipe. *Shakespeare et Homer ont piqué leurs sujets à plusieurs sources.* "Shakespeare and Homer took their subjects from many sources."

PIQUER DU NEZ. To snooze. *Je piquais du nez au boulot, tellement j'étais crevée.* "I was so pooped I nodded off at work."

PIQUER DU ZEN = PIQUER DU NEZ. See ZEN 1.

PIQUER UNE BÂCHE/UN ROUPILLON. See BÂCHE; ROUPILLON.

PIQUER UNE COLÈRE/CRISE. To fly off the handle. *Elle pique une colère chaque fois que sa frangine lui pique ses fringues.* "She hits the ceiling every time her sister pinches her clothes."

PIQUER UNE TÊTE. To dive. *Chaque jour il aimait piquer une tête dans la piscine.* "He liked to dive into the pool every day."

PIQUER UN FARD/SOLEIL. To blush. *Elle pique un fard pour un rien.* "She blushes for the slightest little thing."

(SE) PIQUER LA RUCHE. See RUCHE.

PIQUETTE, *f.* **1.** Inferior wine. *Ils n'ont servi que de la piquette.* "All they served was cheap wine." **2.** Defeat. **Prendre/ramasser une piquette,** *idiom.* To get a real licking. *Il a pris une de ces piquettes au tennis.* "He was soundly beaten at tennis."

PIQUOUSE/PIQUOUZE, *f.* Injection; drug fix. *Il a la trouille des piquouses.* "He's afraid of injections."

PIQUOUSER/PIQUOUZER. To inject; shoot drugs. *Les flics ont vu qu'il se piquouzait.* "The cops saw that he was a mainliner."

PISSE, *f.* Urine. *Dans les WC il y a de la pisse partout.* "There's piss all over that john."

PISSE-COPIE, *m.* Bad journalist. *Incroyable; ce pisse-copie a eu le prix Pulitzer!* "I don't believe it; that hack got the Pulitzer Prize."

PISSE D'ÂNE, *f.* Unsavory drink (lit. "donkey piss"). *Son café, c'est toujours de la pisse d'âne.* "Her coffee always tastes like dishwater."

PISSE-FROID, *m.* Cold fish. *Quel pisse-froid!* "What a wet blanket!"

PISSENLIT, *m.* Dandelion. **Bouffer/sucer les pissenlits par la racine,** *idiom.* To be dead and buried (lit. "to eat/suck the dandelions by the root"). *Il fumait trop! Maintenant il suce les pissenlits par la racine!* "He smoked too much. Now he's pushing up daisies!"

PISSE-MENU, *m.* Nonentity. *Ce pisse-menu se prend pour quelqu'un!* "That piddling jerk thinks he's somebody."

PISSER. To urinate. **Ne plus se sentir pisser,** *idiom.* To be conceited (lit. "not to feel or notice o.s. pissing anymore"). *Il ne se sent plus pisser depuis qu'il habite un château.* "He thinks his shit doesn't stink anymore since moving into the castle." See LAISSE PISSER; LAISSER PISSER...; PLEUVOIR...PISSE.

PISSER AU CUL DE QN. To despise s.o (lit. "to piss on s.o.'s ass"). *Je te pisse au cul!* "Go fuck y.s.!"

PISSER DANS UN VIOLON/LA MER. To do s.t. useless (lit. "to piss into a violin/the sea"). *Essayer de le raisonner c'est comme pisser dans un violon.* "Trying to reason with him is like farting against the wind."

PISSER DES LAMES DE RASOIR. To have painful gonorrhea (lit. "to piss razor blades"). *Malgré la pénicilline, il pissait des lames de rasoir.* "Despite the penicillin, the clap hurt him like hell."

PISSER EN L'AIR = CRACHER EN L'AIR.

PISSER UN MÔME. See MÔME.

PISSETTE, *f.* **1.** A (small) pee. **Faire pissette,** *idiom.* To urinate. *Il faut que je fasse pissette.* "I've got to take a leak." **2.** Windshield wiper. *Fais marcher la pissette.* "Turn the windshield wiper on." **3.** Firehose nozzle. *L'eau ne sortait plus de la pissette.* "The water stopped running from the nozzle."

PISSEUX, -EUSE. Dingy (lit. "pissy"). *Je n'aime pas ce café pisseux.* "I don't like that dingy café."

PISSOIR, *m.* Men's room; urinal. *Plutôt pisser dans l'herbe que dans ce pissoir dégueu.* "I'd rather piss on the grass than use that filthy john."

PISSOIRE, *f.* = **PISSOIR.**

PISSOTIÈRE, *f.* Men's room; "tearoom" (homosexual). *La flicaille surveille toutes les pissotières du parc.* "The cops are watching all the tearooms in the park."

PISSOTTE, *f.* Vagina. *Elle avait la pissotte peu accueillante.* "Her pussy wasn't very hospitable."

PISTON, *m.* String pulling (lit. "piston"). *Il a eu son poste par piston.* "He got his job through pull."

PISTONNER. To pull strings. *Il s'est fait pistonner pour entre à la banque.* "He got his bank job through connections."

PITCHOUNET, -TE. Tiny. *Son fils est beau mais pitchounet.* "Her son's handsome but tiny."

PLANCHE, *f.* Board. **Planche à repasser; à pain** (lit. "ironing board; bread board"). Flat-chested woman. *Les mannequins sont souvent des planches à pain.* "Models are often flat-chested."

PLANCHER, *m.* Floor. **Débarasser le plancher,** *idiom.* To clear out. *Débarassez le plancher illico!* "Get out of here now!"

PLANCHER. 1. To work on s.t. for school. *J'ai planché deux heures sur un problème de maths.* "I sweated two hours over a math problem." **2.** To make a verbal presentation (from student slang for being "called to the blackboard"). *Au motel il va plancher sur l'immobilier.* "He's going to talk about real estate at the motel."

PLANER. To be high; stoned (lit. "to soar"). *Impossible de lui parler; il plane complet.* "Impossible to talk to him; he's totally spaced out."

PLAN-PLAN = PLON-PLON.

PLANQUARÈS. Hidden. *Le gangster est toujours planquarès.* "The gangster's still hiding out." See PLANQUER 1.

PLANQUE, *f.* **1.** Easy job. *Son nouvel intérim c'est la planque!* "Her new temp job is really cushy." **2.** Hideout. *Les flics ont découvert leur planque.* "The cops discovered their hiding place."

PLANQUÉ, -E, *m., f.* S.o. with an easy job. *Ces planqués de fonctionnaires parlent de faire la grève.* "Those gold-bricking civil servants are talking about going on strike."

PLANQUER. 1. To hide. *Elle a planqué la came dans sa pissotte.* "She hid her stash in her twat." **2.** To keep under surveillance. *Les paparazzi ne cessaient de planquer la princesse.* "The paparazzi constantly kept tabs on the princess."

(SE) PLANQUER. To go into hiding. *Ils se sont planqués avec le butin.* "They went into hiding with the loot."

PLANQUOUSE = PLANQUE.

PLANTER SON PANAIS. See PANAIS.

(SE) PLANTER. 1. To have an accident. *Le skieur s'est planté en plein slalom.* "The skier crashed in full slalom." **2.** To make a mistake. *Tu vas te planter à nouveau.* "You're going to get it wrong again."

PLANTE VERTE. 1. Green plant. **Faire la plante verte,** *idiom.* To be decorative but useless. *Je n'a pas envie de faire la plante verte ici.* "I don't feel like just being a fixture/part of the furniture here." **2.** Guard stationed in one place. *Les plantes vertes gardent les ambassades.* "Guards are stationed in front of the embassies."

PLAQUER. To abandon. *Non seulement il a plaqué son job mais sa famille aussi.* "He not only quit his job, he walked out on his family too."

PLAT, *m.* Dish. **Faire du plat à qn.,** *idiom.* To make advances to s.o. *Il me fait du plat mais je m'en fiche.* "He comes on to me but I'm not interested." **Faire (tout) un plat de qch.,** *idiom.* To make a fuss about s.t. *Il ne faut pas en faire un plat.* "You don't have to make such a song and dance about it."

PLATES-BANDES, *f., pl.* Flower beds. **Marcher sur/ piétiner les plates-bandes de qn.,** *idiom.* To encroach on s.o.'s territory. *J'insupporte qu'il marche sur mes plates-bandes!* "I won't have him trespassing on my turf."

PLEIN AUX AS. See AS.

(À) PLEIN NEZ. See SENTIR.

(À) PLEINS TUBES. At maximum power. *Ils faisaient marcher leur télé à pleins tubes.* "They had their TV on full blast."

PLEURER. To weep. **Faire pleurer son aveugle/la fau- vette/le colosse,** *idiom.* To urinate. *Le jogging me fait souvent pleurer le colosse.* "Jogging makes me take a leak often."

PLEUVOIR COMME VACHE QUI PISSE. To rain cats and dogs. *Impossible de jouer au foot; il pleuvait comme vache qui pisse.* "Impossible to play football; it was rain- ing buckets."

PLI, *m.* Fold. *Ça ne fait pas un pli!* **1.** That's just perfect! **2.** That's sure as shootin'. **3.** That's as good as done!

PLOMB DANS L'AILE. See AILE.

PLOMBE, *m.* **1.** Hour. *Il m'a raconté sa vie pendant des plombes.* "He spent hours telling me his life story."

PLOMBÉ, -E. Infected with VD. *Les filles de ce maq sont plombées.* "That pimp's whores are all clapped/syphed up."

PLOMBER. 1. To riddle with bullets. *Mon dab a été plombé lors de la St Valentin à Chicago.* "My father got a belly full of lead during the St. Valentine's Day massacre in Chicago." **2.** To infect with VD. *Ce salaud m'a plombée et plaquée.* "That bastard gave me a dose and ditched me."

PLONGE, *f.* Dishwashing. *Étudiante, je faisais la plonge pour payer ma piaule.* "When I was a student I washed dishes to pay for my room."

PLONGEUR, -EUSE. *m., f.* Dishwasher (lit. "diver"). *Ce resto embauche des plongeurs.* "This restaurant is hiring dishwashers."

PLON-PLON. Easygoing. *Le prince est plon-plon, et assez populaire, mais la monarchie ne sera jamais restaurée.* "The prince is laid back, and popular enough, but the monarchy will never be restored."

PLOUC. Unsophisticated. *Le marquis a l'air plouc.* "The marquess has a rough manner."

PLOUC/PLOUQUE, *m.* Country bumpkin. *Ce sont deux ploucs.* "They're a couple of yokels."

PLUMARD, *m.* Bed. *Mon plumard n'est pas trop petit pour nous deux.* "My bed isn't too small for the two of us."

PLUME, *f.* Feather. **Voler dans les plumes de qn.,** *idiom.* To go after s.o. verbally and physically (lit. "to fly into s.o.'s feathers." Cf. Eng. "the fur will fly"). *Dès que je vois sa poufiasse j'ai envie de lui voler dans les plumes.* "Just the sight of his slut makes me want to pull her hair out/lay into her."

PLUMER. To steal (lit. "to pluck"). *Ils l'ont plumé, lui et son appart.* "They robbed him, and cleaned out his apartment."

POÊLANT = POILANT.

(SE) POÊLER = SE POILER.

POGNE, *f.* Hand. **Être à la pogne de qn.,** *idiom.* To be under s.o.'s thumb. *Il est à la pogne de sa regulière.* "He's under his wife's thumb." **Se faire une pogne,** *idiom.* To masturbate. *Je me sers des deux mains pour me faire une pogne.* "I use both hands to jerk off."

POGNER. To masturbate. *Il se pognait tous les soirs devant les vidéos pornos.* "He whacked off every night looking at porn videos."

POGNON, *f.* Money. *On m'a piqué mon pognon dans le*

métro. "They stole my dough in the subway." See (SE) FAIRE DU POGNON.

POIGNER = POGNER.

POIGNET, *m.* Wrist. See VEUVE.

POIL, *m.* Hair. **À poil.** Naked. *J'aime me baigner à poil.* "I like to skinny-dip." **Au (petit) poil; au quart de poil,** *idiom.* Perfect. *Ce resto est au poil.* "This restaurant is tops." **Au poil (du cul) près; à un poil (de grenouille) près,** *idiom.* Excellent to the last detail. *Ça me va au poil près.* "That suits me to a T." **D'un poil.** Barely. *Elle a loupé son vol d'un poil.* "She just missed her flight." **De bon/mauvais poil.** Good/bad mood. *Elle est toujours de mauvais poil le matin.* "She's always in a bad mood in the morning."

POILANT, -E. Hilarious. *Tout le film est poilant.* "The whole movie is a scream."

(SE) POILER. To laugh uproariously. *On s'est poilé avec ces comiques.* "We never stopped laughing with those comics."

POILU, -E. Courageous (lit. "hairy"). *Ces petits branleurs se veulent poilus.* "Those little jerks think they're spunky."

POILU, *m.,* homosexual slang. Hairy-chested hunk. *Cette tapette n'aime que les poilus.* "That queen only goes for hairy hunks."

POINT D'EAU, *m.* Bar. *Il y a un chouette point d'eau dans cette rue.* "There's a nice watering hole on this street."

POINTURE, *f.* Outstanding person (lit. "size"). *En saut à ski, c'est la grande pointure.* "She's a superstar in ski jumping."

POIRE, *f.* 1. Face (lit. "pear"). *Il a une bonne poire.* "He has a friendly face." 2. Individual. See RAMMENER SA POIRE. 3. Naïve person; sucker. *Je suis trop bonne poire—c'est ça mon problème.* "I'm too much of a good egg—that's my problem."

POIREAU. 1. Penis (lit. "leek [vegetable]"). **Souffler dans**

le poireau, *idiom.* To fellate. *Pourquoi tu ne me souffles pas un peu dans le poireau?* "Why won't you blow me a little?" **2.** Lone individual at a restaurant table. *C'est mort ce soir! Que quelques poireaux.* "It's dead tonight. Just a few loners."

(FAIRE LE) POIREAU, *m.* To wait around. *Elle m'a fait faire le poireau devant son appart.* "She kept me waiting in front of her apartment."

POIREAUTER. To let s.o. cool his or her heels. *J'ai poireauté deux heures en l'attendant.* "I was left to twiddle my thumbs for two hours while waiting for him."

(SE) POIRER = SE POILER.

POIROTTER = POIREAUTER.

POISCAILLE/POISSECAILLE, *m.* **1.** Fish. *Au port ça sent le poiscaille.* "The port smells of fish." **2.** Pimp. See POISSON 2.

POISSON, *m.* **1.** Fish. **Engueuler comme du poisson pourri.** To yell and scream at s.o. *Je l'ai engueulé comme du poisson pourri quand il est rentré bourré.* "I really ripped into him when he came home drunk." **2.** Pimp. *Ce poisson l'a pourrie.* "That pimp corrupted her."

POIVROT, -E, *m., f.* Alcoholic. *La poivrote s'est fait désintoxiquer.* "The lush went to a drying-out tank."

POLAR, *m.* Detective story or movie. *Maman ne lit que des polars.* "Mom just reads whodunits."

POLAR, from **polarisé** (centered on). Eager beaver; workaholic. *Il est complètement polar.* "He just lives for his work."

POLICHINELLE, *m.* Punch(inello) [puppetry; theater]. **Avoir un polichinelle dans le tiroir,** *idiom.* To be pregnant. *À quatorze ans elle avait déjà un polichinelle dans le tiroir.* "Already at fourteen she had a bun in the oven." **C'est le secret de Polichinelle,** *idiom.* "It's an open secret."

POLIR L'ASPHALTE/LE BITUME. See ASPHALTE; BITUME.

(SE) POLIR LE CHINOIS. To masturbate (lit. "to polish the Chinaman"). *Nous nous polissons le chinois de concert.* "We beat the meat together."

POLITESSE, *f.* Politeness. **Faire une politesse,** *idiom.* To perform fellatio. *La femme de l'ambassadeur ne l'aimait pas, mais elle faisait souvent une politesse à son mari.* "The ambassador's wife didn't like it, but she often obliged her husband by going down on him."

POLTRON, *m.* Fart (lit. "coward"). *Qn. de la classe avait lâché un poltron.* "S.o. in the class let go a furtive fart."

POMMADE, *f.* Ointment. **Passer de la pommade à qn.,** *idiom.* To flatter. *Elle sait lui passer de la pommade quand elle veut qch.* "She knows how to butter him up when she wants s.t."

POMMADER. To flatter. *Il sait très bien pommader son supérieur.* "He's good at sucking up to his boss."

POMME, *f.* **1.** Apple. **Tomber dans les pommes,** *idiom.* *À la vue du sang je suis tombé dans les pommes.* "I fainted at the sight of blood." **2. Ma/ta/sa pomme/nos pommes.** Individual (me/you, and so on). *D'abord ma pomme, ensuite vos pommes.* "I look out for number one, then you guys." **3.** Face. *Voici ma foto. J'espère que ma pomme te plaît.* "Here's my photo. I hope you like the kisser." See also (SE) SUCER....

POMPE, *f.* **1.** Shoe. **Être/marcher à côté de ses pompes,** *idiom.* Not to be with it (because one is daydreaming or mentally distraught). *Depuis son divorce il marche à côté des ses pompes.* "He's been beside h.s. since his divorce." See CIRER...POMPES; LÈCHE-POMPES. **2.** Pump. **Le/un coup de pompe,** *idiom.* Drained feeling. *Je crains les coups de pompe.* "I'm afraid of being overcome by attacks of fatigue."

POMPÉ -E. Exhausted. *Après le concours j'étais pompée.* "I was bushed after the competitive exam."

POMPER. 1. To pump. **Pomper l'air; les pomper,** *idiom.* To get on s.o.'s nerves. *Il me pompe l'air en se plaignant sans cesse.* "He bugs me with his constant complaining."

2. To copy; plagiarize. *Pendant l'exam il a pompé sur son voison.* "He copied from his neighbor during the exam."

POMPER LE DARD/GLAND/NŒUD À QN. To fellate. *Je t'offrirai la lune si tu me pompes le gland.* "I'll give you anything you want if you'll suck me off."

POMPETTE. Slightly drunk. *Une coupe de champagne et la voilà pompette.* "She gets tipsy after just one glass of champagne."

POMPIER/POMPLARD, *m.* Fellatio (lit. "fireman"). **Faire/tailler un pompier,** *idiom.* To fellate. *Son maq exige qu'elle lui fasse des pompiers souvent.* "Her pimp insists that she give him head frequently."

PONTIFE, *m.* **1.** Big shot; pundit (lit. "pontiff [the Pope])." *Il se prend pour un pontife.* "He thinks he's a big shot." **2.** Penis. **Se faire tutoyer le pontife,** *idiom.* To get s.o. to give one a blow job (lit. "to have the Pope/penis addressed in the **tu** (intimate) form"). *Il se fait tutoyer le pontife chaque soir.* "He gets s.o. to blow him every evening."

PONTONNIÈRE, *f.* Prostitute who works on, under, or near bridges. *La vieille pontonnière est toujours fidèle au poste sur le Pont Neuf.* "The old hooker is always at her post on the Pont Neuf."

POPAUL, *m.* Penis. See EMMENER POPAUL…; MENER POPAUL…

POPOF(F)/POPOV, *adj.* and *n.* Russian (from a common Russian family name). *Les Popofs dansaient et jouaient de la balalaïka.* "The Rooskies danced and played the balalaika."

POPOL = POPAUL.

POPOTE, *f.* Cooking. *J'en ai marre de faire la popote.* "I'm sick and tired of doing the cooking." See MARIE-POPOTE.

POPOTIN, *m.* Posterior. **Tortiller du popotin; se trémousser le popotin.** To wiggle one's hips when walking. *Elle les émoustille en tortillant du popotin.* "She turns them on when she wiggles her fanny." See (SE) MAGNER LE POPOTIN.

POPULO, *m.* Crowd; riffraff. *Il y avait un des ces populos dans la rue.* "There was quite a mob in the street."

PORTE-COUILLES, *m.* **1.** Husband (lit. "balls carrier"). *Je déteste son porte-couilles.* "I don't like her husband." **2.** Proficient lover. *Elle est dingue de son nouveau porte-couilles.* "She's mad about her latest stud."

PORTÉ SUR LA BAGATELLE/CHOSE. See BAGATELLE; CHOSE.

PORTER LE CHAPEAU. To take the blame. *Les autres se sont sauvés et lui, il a porté le chapeau.* "The others took off and he was left holding the bag."

PORTILLON, *m.* Gate. **Se bousculer au portillon. 1.** To crowd in. *Lors des soldes ça bouscule au portillon.* "During the sales they knock t.s. out getting in." 2. To fall over one's words. *J'étais très stressée et ça se bousculait au portillon.* "I was very tense and could hardly get my words out."

PORTO/PORTOCHE/PORTOS(S), *adj.* and *n.* Portuguese. *Les portoches foulent toujours les raisins du porto avec les pieds.* "The Portuguese still press the grapes for port wine with their feet."

PORTUGAISE, *f.* Ear (from the shape of oysters called **portugaises**). **Avoir les portugaises ensablées,** *idiom.* To be hard of hearing. *Après le match de boxe il avait les portugaises ensablées.* "After the boxing match he was half deaf."

POSER UN LAPIN À QN. To stand s.o. up. *Il m'a posé un lapin; je ne veux plus le revoir.* "He didn't show up; I don't want to see him again."

(SE) POSER LÀ. To be a prime example of. *Comme tombeur, il se pose là!* "He's one hell of a Don Juan."

POSTÈRE/POSTÉRIEUR, *m.* Posterior. *Son postère m'a fait de l'œil!* "Her derriere caught my eye."

POT, *m.* **1.** Cooking pot. See TOURNER...POT. **2.** Drink. *Viens prendre un pot de beaujolpif!* "Come for a spot of Beaujolais!" **3.** Luck. **Avoir du pot,** *idiom.* To be lucky.

Elle n'a jamais eu de pot dans sa vie. "She never had any luck in life." **4.** Posterior. **Avoir le pot près des talons.** (lit. "to have one's rump close to one's heels"). To be short. *Elle est une perche mais sa sœur a le pot près des talons.* "She's a giant but her sister's ass is very close to the ground." See DÉFONCER LE POT.

POTASSER. To study hard. *Il a potassé toute la nuit son exam.* "He crammed all night for his exam."

POT D'ÉCHAPPEMENT, (lit. "exhaust pipe; muffler") = **POT 4.**

POT-DE-VIN, *m.* Bribe. *Sans pots-de-vin, rien ne se fait.* "You get nowhere if you don't grease some palms."

POTE/POTEAU, *m., f.* Chum. *"Touche pas à mon pote!", disait le slogan.* " 'Keep your hands off my buddy,' said the slogan."

POU, *m.* Louse. **Chercher des poux (dans la tête) à qn.,** *idiom.* To pick a quarrel. *C'est son genre de chercher des poux aux autres.* "It's his nature to go looking for a fight with others."

POUFFE = POUF(F)IASSE.

POUF(F)IASSE, *f.* Bitch; slut. *Sa femme n'est qu'une pouffiasse.* "His wife's just a floozy."

POUIC = COUIC.

POULAGA/POULARD/POULARDIN/POULMANN = POULET.

POULE, *f.* **1.** Young girl; chick (lit. "hen"). *Comment vas-tu, ma poule?* "How're you doin', my little chickadee?" **2.** Prostitute. *À la Madeleine tu trouveras des poules de luxe.* "In the Madeleine district you'll find high-class whores."

POULE MOUILLÉE, *f.* Cowardly person (lit. "wet chicken"). *Ne fais pas la poule mouillée.* "Don't be chicken; a scared rabbit."

POULET, *m.* Policeman (lit. "chicken"). *Les poulets ont fait une descente dans le métro.* "The fuzz raided the subway station."

POULETTE = POULE 1.

POULICHE = POUFFIASSE.

POUPÉE = POULE 1.

POURLÉCHER. To lick one's lips. See BABINES.

POUSSE-CROTTE, *m.,* homosexual. **1.** Active homosexual; sodomizer (lit. "shit pusher"). *La tapette rêvait d'un pousse-crotte en sirotant son pousse-café.* "The old queen dreamed of a stud while sipping his after-dinner drink." **2.** Sodomy. *Je te ferai une pipe mais je n'aime pas le pousse-crotte.* "I'll blow you but I don't like browning."

POUSSE-MOULIN = CHÂTEAU-LAPOMPE.

POUSSER. To exaggerate. **Faut pas pousser mémé dans les orties!,** *idiom,* lit. "not necessary to shove granny into the nettles." "You don't have to go overboard." See (À LA) VA-COMME…POUSSE.

POUSSER LE BOUCHON (UN PEU/TROP LOIN). See BOUCHON **1.**

POUSSER UN COUP DE GUEULE/UNE GUEULANTE. To yell. *Il va pousser un coup de gueule quand il verra le gnion de sa voiture.* "He's gonna let out a holler when he sees the dent in his car."

POUVOIR (TOUJOURS) S'ALIGNER. See (S')ALIGNER **3.**

POUSSIÈRE, *f.* Dust. See ET DES POUSSIÈRES.

PQ = PAPIER-CUL.

PRALINE, *f.* **1.** Bullet; slug (lit. "sugar-coated almond"; "chocolate"). *Il aurait tué davantage mais il n'avait plus de pralines.* "He would have done more killing but he ran out of bullets." **2.** Clitoris. **Avoir la praline en délire,** *idiom.* To be very stimulated sexually. *Un seul baiser et j'avais la praline en délire.* "Just one kiss and I was hit by clitoral electricity."

PRÉCIEUSES, *f., pl.* Testicles. *Son zob est à peine visible et ses prècieuses sont ridicules.* "His dick's practically invisible and his family jewels are a joke."

(DE) PREMIÈRE. First-rate. *C'est un artiste de première.* "She's a top-notch artist."

(EN) PRENDRE DE LA GRAINE. To serve as an example. *Ton dab turbine; il faudrait que tu en prennes de la graine.* "Your dad's a hard worker; you should take a leaf from his book."

(EN) PRENDRE PLEIN LA GUEULE. To be taken with. *En l'écoutant chanter, j'en ai pris plein la gueule.* "I got carried away listening to her sing."

PRENDRE DE LA BOUTEILLE/DU BOUCHON/ CARAT. See BOUTEILLE.

PRENDRE DE L'AIR = CHANGER D'AIR.

PRENDRE DU CHOUETTE, *homosexual.* To sodomize. *Il prend souvent du chouette et se balade avec lubrifiant et présos.* "He has sex with lots of guys and walks around with a lubricant and rubbers."

PRENDRE DU GALON. To move up in the world (lit. "to get a military promotion"). *Depuis qu'elle a pris du galon elle ne se prend pas pour une petite merde.* "Ever since she's moved up in the world she thinks she's hot shit."

PRENDRE LA TÊTE (EN RAPPEL) À QN. To exasperate. *Et le prof et ses cours me prennent la tête.* "That teacher and his courses drive me nuts."

PRENDRE LE CAFÉ DU PAUVRE. To have sex (lit. "to have the poor man's coffee." Real coffee was scarce during wartime; sex was not). *On se console de toutes les tuiles en prenant le café du pauvre.* "We make up for all our hard luck by creating our own entertainment."

PRENDRE LE LARGE. To beat it (lit. "to head for the open sea"). *Trop de fumée ici; prenons le large!* "Too smoky here; let's blow this hole!"

PRENDRE LE THÉ. To be a sodomite; have anal sex (lit. "to have tea"). *Pendant la partouze à la bague on a tous pris le thé.* "During the daisy chain orgy we all buggered each other."

PRENDRE QCH. EN PLEINE GUEULE/SUR LE COIN DE LA GUEULE. To get hit in the face with s.t. *J'ai pris son parapluie en pleine gueule.* "His umbrella hit me right in the kisser."

PRENDRE QN. EN FILOCHE. See FILOCHE.

PRENDRE SA PAUME. To sell securities at a loss. *Je savais que tu allais prendre ta paume avec ces titres.* "I knew you were going to take a beating on those stocks."

PRENDRE SON PANARD/PIED. 1. To experience orgasm. *Avec mon dernier jules je prenais mon pied à chaque fois.* "Every time I got it on with my last boyfriend, the earth moved." **2.** To experience pleasure. *Bill prend son pied en jouant du saxo.* "Bill gets off on saxophone playing."

PRENDRE UN BOL D'AIR. See BOL.

PRENDRE UN BOUILLON. See BOUILLON.

PRENDRE UN COUP DE VIEUX. To age noticeably. *Il a pris un sacré coup de vieux, mais joue toujours les jeunes premiers.* "He's showing his age but still playing romantic leads."

PRENDRE UNE ARDOISE À L'EAU = MOUILLER UNE ARDOISE.

PRENDRE UNE BITURE. See BITURE.

PRENDRE UNE CAISSE/CUITE. To get drunk. *Il s'est pris une bonne cuite ce week-end.* "He got thoroughly soused this weekend."

PRENDRE UNE CLAQUE. To suffer severe damages/losses. *Il a pris une claque magistrale aux elections.* "He was soundly beaten in the elections."

PRENDRE UNE PIQUETTE. See PIQUETTE 2.

PRENDRE UNE RUE EN LEVRETTE. To use a one-way street illegally (lit. "to go in from the back"). *Si je prends une rue en levrette, j'aurai une contredanse salée.* "If I go the wrong way on a one-way street I'll get a stiff fine." See (EN) LEVRETTE.

PRENDRE UN GADIN/UNE BÛCHE/GAMELLE/ GAUFRE/PELLE. See RAMASSER…PELLE.

PRENDRE UN JETON (DE MATE). To see a sex show. *On a pris un jeton de mate de première.* "We saw a terrific sex show."

PRENDRE UN POT/VERRE. See POT 2; VERRE.

(SE) PRENDRE LA LOUCHE. To be self-important. *Depuis qu'il a gagné cette médaille, il se prend la louche.* "Ever since winning that medal, he's been swell-headed."

(SE) PRENDRE UNE BARRE. To split one's sides laughing. *On s'est pris une barre quand il a mimé le patron.* "We died laughing when he imitated the boss."

(SE) PRENDRE UNE (PEAU DE) BANANE. See BANANE 1.

PRÈS DE SES SOUS. Tight-fisted (lit. "close to one's money"). *Mon tonton est très près de ses sous.* "My uncle's a tightwad."

PRÉSO, *m.* from **préservatif.** Condom. *Elle lui achète des présos de haute qualité.* "She buys high-quality rubbers for him."

PRIMO. Firstly. *Primo ça ne me plaît pas; deuxio je n'ai pas le temps.* "First of all I don't like it; second of all, I haven't the time."

PRINCESSE, *f.* Princess. **Aux frais de la princesse,** *idiom.* At s.o. else's expense. *Sa voiture est aux frais de la princesse.* "His car is paid for by the company." *Le restaurateur déclarait que le gâteau d'anniversaire était aux frais de la princesse.* "The restaurant owner announced that the birthday cake was on the house."

PRISE, *f.* race track. High, last-minute bet. *La prise était une grosse perte et il s'est consolé avec une prise de cocaïne.* "The bet was no good and he consoled himself with a snort of coke."

PRISE DE BEC, *f.* Run-in. *On a eu une prise de bec avec le proprio.* "We had a row with the landlord."

PRISEUR DE CAME, *f.* Cocaine addict. *Aux priseurs de came il leur faut leur dose journalière.* "Cocaine users need their daily dose."

PRIX D'ATTAQUE, *m.* Lowest price. See ATTAQUE **2.**

PROBLOC/PROBLOQUE = PROPRIO.

PROPRIO, *m., f., abbr.* of **propriétaire.** Proprietor; landlord; landlady. *La proprio nous a fait des facilités de paiement.* "The landlady arranged payment terms for us."

PROUT, *m.* Fart. *Ces flageolets me donnent des prouts.* "Those beans give me gas."

PROUT-PROUT!/PROUT-PROUT, MA CHÈRE!, homosexual. "Get you, Mary!" "My, you're such a lady!"

PROXÉMAC = PROXÉNÈTE/PROXO.

PROXO, *abbr.* of **proxénète.** Procurer. *Ce proxo fait travailler trois putes.* "That pimp has three hustlers working for him."

PRUNES, *f., pl.* Plums. **Des prunes!** "Not on your life!" "No way!" **Pour des prunes.** For nothing; practically nothing. *Je ne travaille pas pour des prunes.* "I don't work for peanuts."

PSY, *m., f. abbr.* of **psychonalyste.** Psychoanalyst. *Ça coûte cher, les psys.* "Psychiatrists are expensive."

PSY, *abbr.* of **psychiatrique.** Crazy. *Sa mère est un peu psy sur les bords.* "Her mother's a bit whacko."

PUCE, *f.* Flea; computer chip. See SAC À PUCES.

PUCIER = SAC À PUCES 1.

PUISSANT. Marvelous. *Puissant, ton blouson!* "Your jacket's stunning!"

PURÉE! "For heaven's sake!"

PUTAIN, *adj.* Sycophantic. *Il est assez putain pour accepter ta proposition.* "He's enough of an ass-kisser to accept your proposition."

PUTAIN, *f.* Prostitute. *Cette rue grouille de putains.* "This street is swarming with hustlers."

PUTAIN! Damn it!

PUTAIN DE...! Filthy rotten! *Ralbol cette putain de pluie!* "I'm fed up with this goddamned rain!"

PUTAIN (DE BONDIEU) DE BORDEL (DE MERDE)! Holy fucking shit! *Putain de bordel—arrêtez vos conneries et foutez-moi le camp!* "Damn you all to hell—cut the crap and get the fuck out of here!"

PUTAIN DE MERDE! "God damn it!"

PUTASSE, *f.* Cheap whore. *Il m'a traité de putasse.* "He called me a low whore."

PUTASSIER = PUTAIN. *(adj.)*

PUTE = PUTAIN. *(adj.*and *n.)*

PV, *abbr.* of **procès-verbal.** Traffic ticket; fine. *Non seulement ils m'ont filé un PV, mais ils m'ont retiré mon permis.* "They didn't just give me a ticket; they took away my driver's license too."

(AU) QUART DE TOUR, *m.* At a quarter turn. **Comprendre/piger/biter au quart to tour,** *idiom.* To be quick on the uptake. *Elle a compris au quart de tour que c'était de la blague.* "She caught on right away that it was a joke." **Démarrer/partir au quart de tour.** To start right away. *La voiture a démarré au quart de tour.* "The car started right away."

QUARTIER CHAUD, *m.* Red-light district. *Il est chaud lapin et fréquente le quartier chaud.* "He's a horny guy and hangs out in the red-light district."

QUAT', *abbr.* of **quatre. Un de ces quat'.** One of these days. *J'irai chez le toubib un de ces quat'.* "I'll go to the doctor one of these days."

QUATRE PELÉS ET UN TONDU = TROIS…TONDU.

QUATRE-VINGT-HUIT, *m.* Kiss (lit. "88"). *Et pour moi un petit 88, vite fait, avant de prendre la route!* "And a nice little kiss for me before I get under way!"

QUE COUIC = QUE DALLE.

QUE DAL(L)E. Nothing at all. *Ce problème de maths, je n'y pige que dalle.* "I understand zilch about that problem in math."

QUELLE CHIASSE! What a filthy mess!

QUELLE CHIERIE! What a bummer!

QUELQUE CHOSE DE BIEN, ironic. A real job of s.t. *Il*

a bousillé sa voiture quelque chose de bien. "He car was totaled, completely."

QUELQUE PART. Somewhere. **Aller quelque part,** *euph.* To go to the toilet. *Il faut que j'aile quelque part.* "I've got to wash my hands." **Se foutre/mettre qch. quelque part,** *idiom.* To stick s.t. you know where. *Ton cadeau, tu peux te le foutre quelque part.* "You can take your present and shove it."

QUENOTTES, *f., pl.* Teeth. *Elle a de belles quenottes.* "She has beautiful teeth."

QUÉQUETTE. Penis. *Les gosses s'amusaient à se montrer leurs quéquettes.* "The kids fooled around showing their peckers to each other."

QU'ES-ACO/QUÈS ACO? What on earth is that? *Tu me lâches pour ce p'tit con—qu'es-aco?* "You're leaving me for that jerk—what the hell's going on?"

QUÈS, *f.,* from question. *Limitons-nous à ce cas en quès!* "Let's stick with the case in question."

QUÈS, *m.* Same. *C'est du quès.* "It's six of one, half a dozen of the other."

QUEUDE = QUE DALLE.

QUEUE, *f.* Penis (lit. "tail"). *"Con de Manon! Queue de des Grieux!," c'est un de ses jurons préférés.* "'Manon's cunt! Des Grieux's dick!'" That's one of his favorite cuss words." (Ref. to characters in the Abbé Prévost's novel *Manon Lescaut.*) See COUP DE QUEUE.

QUEUNER = QUEUTER.

QUEUTARD, -E, *m., f.* Person always out for sex. *C'est un queutard de première.* "He's a real sex fiend."

QUEUTER. 1. To fail. *Elle a queuté à son exam de conduite.* "She flunked her driving test." **2.** To copulate. *Les soldats nous ont queutées nuit et jour.* "The soldiers ravished us night and day."

QUINCAILLE, *m.* Parisian outdoor bookseller who also offers cheap souvenirs. *Le quincaille du pont vend des* *tours Eiffel dorées.* "The bookseller by the bridge also sells gilded Eiffel Towers."

QUINCAILLERIE, *f.* **1.** Computer hardware (lit. "hardware store"). *La quinquaillerie sur catalogue coûte moins cher.* "Hardware is cheaper by catalog." **2.** Military decorations; cheap jewelry. *Au repas de famille les grand-dabes avaient sorti toute leur quincaillerie.* "At the family dinner, Grandpa and Grandma got out their military decorations and junk jewelry."

QUINQUETS, *m., pl.* Eyes (lit. "oil lamps") *Garde-les bien ouverts, tes quinquets!* "Keep your peepers peeled!"

QUIQUE/QUIQUETTE = QUÉQUETTE.

QUIQUI = KIKI 2.

R.A.B. See BRANLER **1.**

RAB, *m.* Second helping. *Oliver Twist réclamait du rab.* "Oliver Twist asked for more." **Faire du rab,** *idiom.* To work overtime. *Le patron nous a fait faire du rab.* "The boss made us work overtime."

(SE) RABIBOCHER. To reconcile. *Après six mois de séparation, ils se sont rabibochés.* "After a six-months separation, they kissed and made up."

RABIOT = RAB.

RABIOTER. To scrounge; wangle. *Il cherche toujours à rabioter qch.* "He's always trying to get s.t. extra on the side."

RACCROCHER LES WAGONS. See WAGON.

RACLÉE, *f.* Beating. *Le parti a pris une de ses raclées.* "The party was soundly defeated." See FILER UNE RACLÉE; FLANQUER UNE RACLÉE; FOUTRE UNE RACLÉE.

RACLURE, *f.* Despicable person (lit. "scraping," as in s.t. you'd scrape up). *Pas la peine de me parler de cette raclure.* "No point talking to me about that sleazebag/ scuzzball."

RADADA, *m.* Posterior. **Aller au radada.** To have sex; a piece of ass. *Lili voulait aller au radada, mais Lulu venait de me pomper.* "Lily wanted us to make it, but I'd already given my all to Lulu." See RONDIBÉ.

RADAR, *m.* Radar. **Marcher au radar,** *idiom.* To function mechanically. *J'ai la gueule de bois et marche au radar.* "I've got a hangover and I'm walking around in a fog."

RADIN, -E. Miserly. *On ne peut être plus radin que lui.* "He's as stingy as they come."

RADINER/SE RADINER. To show up fast. *Radine-toi, sinon je pars seul.* "Get over here fast or I'll leave without you."

RADIS, *m.* Cent (lit. "radish"). *Je suis partie sans un radis sur moi.* "I left without a cent in my pocket."

RAFFUT, *m.* Noise. **Faire du raffut,** *idiom.* To cause a commotion. *Ses révélations ont fait un de ces raffuts!* "Her revelations really made waves!"

RAGNAGNAS, *m., pl.* Menstrual period. *Elle a ses ragnagnas.* "She's got the rag on."

RAIDE. 1. Erect (lit. "stiff"). *Dès qu'elle s'approche de lui, il l'a raide.* "He gets a hard-on the minute she comes near him." 2. Penniless. *Elle est toujours raide en fin de mois.* "She's always broke at the end of the month." 3. Incredible. *Ses histoires sont un peu raides.* "His stories are a bit hard to swallow." 4. Drunk. See RAIDE/RAIDE DEF/MORT.

RAIDE AMOUREUX/DINGUE. Madly in love. *Elles étaient toutes raides amoureuses de Valentino.* "They were all crazy about Valentino."

RAIDE MORT. Stone-cold dead. *On les a trouvées raides mortes.* "They found them dead as a doornail."

RAIDE/RAIDE DEF/MORT. Dead drunk; drugged. *Ils était raides après le troisième sérieux.* "They were dead drunk after the third mug of beer."

RAISIN, *m.* Blood (lit. "grape"). See (SE) CAILLER LE RAISIN.

RALBOL, *m.* Exasperation. *Quel ralbol, cette grève des transports!* "What a crock of shit, this transportation (train/bus/air) strike!"

RAMASSER LES BALAIS. To come in last in a race; fail. *J'ai ramassé les balais à cause d'une crampe.* "I came in last because of a cramp."

RAMASSER UNE PIQUETTE. See PIQUETTE 2.

RAMASSER UN GADIN/UNE BÛCHE/GAMELLE/ GAUFRE/PELLE. To fall down/fall flat on one's face. *Le même jour, j'ai ramassé un gadin dans le métro et une pelle au boulot.* "On the same day, I had a fall in the subway and got egg on my face at work."

(SE) RAMASSER. To fall down (lit. "to pick o.s. up"). *Le premier de la classe s'est ramassé au concours.* "The star student fell flat on his face at the competitive exam."

RAMBOUR = RENCARD.

RAMDAM = RAFFUT.

RAME/RAMÉE, *f.* Oar. **Ne pas en ficher/foutre une rame.** Not to do a damned thing. *Dès que j'ai le dos tourné, ils n'en foutent pas une rame.* "As soon as my back is turned, they all goof off."

RAMENER SA FRAISE/POIRE. 1. To show up. See (SE) RAMENER. **2.** To put an oar in. *Il faut toujours qu'il ramène sa fraise.* "He always has to put in his two cents worth."

(SE) RAMENER. To show up. *On ne sait quand elle se ramènera.* "We don't know when she'll put in an appearance."

RAMER. To work hard (lit. "to row"). *Ça fait longtemps que nous ramons.* "We've been working away for months."

RAMEUX, -EUSE, *m., f.* Subway musician. *J'ai toujours de la monnaie pour les rameux.* "I always have a few coins for the music makers in the subway."

RAMONER (LA CHEMINÉE D') UNE FEMME. To have a woman sexually (lit. "to sweep a woman's fireplace/chimney"). *Son mari ferait bien de la ramoner plus souvent.* "Her husband ought to screw her more often."

RANCARD = RENCARD.

RANCART, *m.* Scrap. **Mettre au rancart,** *idiom.* To junk. *Il pense que nous sommes bons à mettre au rancart.* "He thinks we're ready for the glue factory."

RAOUSSE! "Get going!" "Get out!" (from Ger. **raus,** "out!").

RÂPÉ. Shredded. *C'est râpé!* "It's curtains!" "It's all over!"

RAPIDO/RAPIDOS. Very fast. *Il s'est taillé rapidos.* "He cleared out in a hurry."

RAPLAPLA(T). Exhausted. *Après le jogging elle était raplaplat.* "She was bushed after jogging."

RAPPER. To perform or dance to rap music. *Ils rappent mieux qu'ils ne chantent.* "They rap better than they sing."

RAPPEUR, -EUSE, *m., f.* Rap musician. *C'est devenu une mode pour les rappeurs d'employer le passé simple.* "It's become an in-thing for rappers to use the past definite tense."

RAPTER. To monopolize s.o. *À l'entrée de l'immeuble je me suis fait rapter par la concierge.* "The concierge got hold of me at the entrance and wouldn't let me go."

RAQUER. To pay up. *Pour ne pas raquer, il est sorti avant qu'on présente la note.* "So as to not have to shell out (his share), he left before the check arrived."

RAS. Close-cropped; short. **En avoir ras le bol/cul/pot/la cale/caisse/patate/les couilles.** See BOL 3.

RASE-BITE/RASE-BITUME, *m., f.* Short person (lit. "scrape pavement"). *Il est maigrichon et rase-bitume.* "He's a skinny half-pint."

RASER. To bore (lit. "to shave"). *Le cours de ce prof m'a rasée.* "That professor's course bored me stiff."

(SE) RASER (À CENT SOUS DE L'HEURE). To be bored to death. *Quand je vais chez eux je me rase à cent sous de l'heure.* "When I visit them I'm bored to death."

RASIBUS. Very short. *On s'est sauvé rasibus!* "We escaped just in the nick of time."

RAS-LE-BOL = RALBOL.

RAS LE BONBON/CRESSON/PÉTARD/PÈTE/LA TOUFFE. At pubic/pelvic level. *Les arpenteuses se* *fringuent ras le bonbon.* "Streetwalkers wear the miniest of skirts."

RASOIR. Boring. *Le film ce soir est rasoir au possible.* "Tonight's movie is excruciatingly boring."

RAT, *m.* Rat. **S'emmerder/s'ennuyer comme un rat mort,** *idiom.* To be bored out of one's mind. *Aux réunions je m'emmerde comme un rat mort.* "At the meetings I'm bored beyond endurance." See FACE.

RATE, *f.* Spleen. **Ne pas se fouler la rate,** *idiom.* To not strain o.s. *Tu ne t'es pas foulé la rate pour faire cette bouffe.* "You didn't knock y.s. out making this dinner."

RATÉ, -E, *m., f.* Failure. *Tu ne penses pas épouser ce raté?* "You're not thinking of marrying that deadbeat are you?"

RÂTELIER, *m.* **1.** Hayrack; trough. See MANGER…RÂTELIERS. **2.** False teeth. *Son râtelier a coûté bonbon mais il ne s'en sert pas.* "His dentures were expensive, but he doesn't use them."

RATER. To fail. **Ne pas en rater une.** To never fail to make a mistake. *Ce mec n'en rate pas une.* "That guy always puts his foot in it."

RATIBOISER. To clean out. *Il a été ratiboisé aux cartes.* "He was wiped out at cards." **Se faire ratiboiser (la colline),** *idiom.* To get scalped. *Il s'est fait ratiboiser.* "He got a baldie haircut."

RATTE, *f.,* youth. Worthless slut. *Ce lascar largue ratte sur ratte.* "That no-good lout dumps one worthless broad after another."

RAYER LE CASQUE. To bite while fellating (lit. "to scratch the helmet"). *Elle te fera un pompier sans rayer le casque.* "She'll blow you without biting."

RAZIF, *m.* Razor; knife. *Fais gaffe, il a sorti son razif.* "Watch it, he's got his knife out."

REBELOTE! Here we go again! *Et rebelote—j'ai encore oublié mes clefs!* "Just like me—I've forgotten my keys again!"

REBEU = BEUR.

RECHARGER LES ACCUS. To recharge one's batteries. See ACCUS.

RÉCHAUFFÉ. Reheated. **C'est du réchauffé.** "That's old news."

RECTIFIER. To kill (lit. "to correct"). *Il s'est fait rectifier par la pègre.* "He got sanctioned/bumped off by the mob."

RDV, from **rendez-vous.** Date; appointment. *Je rêve d'un RDV avec elle.* "I dream about a date with her."

REFAITE, *f.* Porn star much enhanced by plastic surgery (lit. "redone"). *Cette refaite ne me fait plus bander.* "That remade porn queen doesn't get me up anymore."

REFILER DE LA BAGOUSE. See BAGOUSE **2.**

REFILER DE LA JAQUETTE. See JAQUETTE.

REFILER LE BÉBÉ À QN. To pass the buck (lit. "the baby"). *Il a foutu le camp en refilant le bébé à son pote.* "He beat it and left his buddy holding the bag."

REFILER UNE AVOINE. See AVOINE.

REGARDER LA FEUILLE À L'ENVERS. See FEUILLE.

REGARDER QN. AVEC DES YEUX DE MERLAN FRIT/DE CRAPAUD MORT D'AMOUR. To look at s.o. with lovesick eyes (lit. "with the eyes of a fried whiting [fish]/a toad that died of love"). *Ça me fait rire quand tu me regardes avec des yeux de merlan frit.* "I laugh when you look at me like a lovesick dog."

RÉGLO. Honest. *Confie-lui ce boulot; c'est un type réglo.* "Let him do the job; he's a regular guy."

RÉGULIER/RÉGULE = RÉGLO.

RÉGULIÈRE, *f.* Wife; steady girlfriend. *Aujourd'hui, il s'affiche avec sa régulière.* "Today he's out in public with his missus/mistress."

RELUQUER. To observe. *As-tu fini de reluquer mes nichons?* "Have you finished staring at my breasts?"

REMBALLER SES OUTILS. To put one's pants on again (lit. "to rewrap one's tools"). *Vite fait, bien fait, il a rem-*

ballé ses outils. "In practically no time he hitched up his trousers again."

REMPILER. To start; do over (lit. "to reenlist"). *Il a dû rempiler un an au bahut.* "He had to repeat a school year."

(SE) REMPLUMER. To recover health or finances. *Elle s'est remplumée en touchant l'héritage.* "Her finances improved when she came into the inheritance."

REMUER LES PINCETTES. See PINCETTES **2.**

RENAUDER. To complain. *Cesse de renauder!* "Quit grousing!"

RENCARD, *m.* Date. *J'ai un rencard avec cette nana.* "I've got a date with that gal."

RENCARDER. To make a date. *Il m'a rencardée pour vingt heures au resto.* "He made a date with me for eight o'clock in the restaurant."

(SE) RENCARDER. To get information. *Tu peux me rencarder sur ce type?* "Can you give me the lowdown on that guy?"

RENCART = RANCART.

RENDÈVE, *m.,* from **rendez-vous.** *J'ai un rendève chez le dentiste.* "I've got a dental appointment."

RENDRE LA MONNAIE. To make change. See COMMENCER À RENDRE LA MONNAIE.

RENIFLE. *f.* Cocaine; the police (from **renifler,** "to sniff"). *La renifle, surtout les stups, est en quête de renifle.* "The police, especially narcs, look for coke."

RENIFLETTE = RENIFLE.

RENOI, *m., f.,* backslang of **noir.** Black person. *Peu de renois assistaient à la conférence sur la négritude.* "Few blacks were present at the lecture on negritude."

RENTRE-DEDANS, *m.* Heated confrontation (lit. "hand-to-hand combat"). *Hier au Sénat il y a eu du rentre-dedans.* "They went at it hot and heavy in the Senate yesterday." **Faire du rentre-dedans,** *idiom.* To make amorous advances. *Il m'a fait du rentre-dedans, mais je* *l'ai envoyé balader.* "He tried to get it on with me but I sent him packing."

RENTRER À DEUX. To come home drunk. *Depuis que sa femme l'a quitté, il rentre à deux chaque soir.* "Ever since his wife left him, he comes home drunk every night."

RENTRER (AVEC) LA BITE/PINE SOUS LE BRAS. To not score with s.o. (lit. "to come back with one's dick under one's arm"). *Je me suis décarcassé pour coucher avec elle, mais je suis rentré la pine sous le bras.* "I knocked m.s. out trying to make her, but I didn't score."

RENTRER DEDANS. To beat to a pulp. *Je n'avais qu'une envie, c'était de lui rentrer dedans.* "All I wanted to do was knock his block off."

RENTRER DANS LE CHOU/LARD/MOU = RENTRER DEDANS.

RENVOYER L'ASCENSEUR. See ASCENSEUR.

REPASSEUR. See JOUER LE FILS DE LA REPASSEUSE.

RESTAU = RESTO.

RESTER. To remain. **Y rester.** To die. *C'est un turbin à y rester.* "That job's enough to kill anybody."

(EN) RESTER BABA. See BABA, *adj.*

(EN) RESTER COMME DEUX RONDS DE FLAN. To be left speechless. *Pour une fois il était à l'heure; j'en suis resté comme deux ronds de flan.* "He was on time for once; I was dumbfounded."

(EN) RESTER SUR LE CUL. To be extremely astonished. *Quand j'ai appris qu'il avait violé sa fille, j'en suis restée sur le cul.* "When I learned he'd raped his daughter, it floored me."

RESTER EN CARAFE. To be left to wait. *Je suis resté en carafe à son rendève.* "I had a date with him but he stood me up."

RESTER LE BEC DANS L'EAU. To be left in the lurch. *Il m'a joué rip et je suis restée le bec dans l'eau.* "He ran off and I was left high and dry."

RESTIF = RESTO.

RESTO, *m.* Restaurant. *C'est une rue pleine de restos sympas.* "It's a street with many appealing restaurants."

RÉTAMER. To smash up. *Lui et sa voiture étaient rétamés après l'accident.* "He and his car were smashed up after the accident."

(SE) RÉTAMER. To get drunk. *Il se rétame à chaque fête.* "He gets smashed at every party."

RETAPE, *f.* Soliciting. **Faire de la retape.** To be a prostitute. *La veuve s'est mise à faire de la retape.* "The widow started hustling." **Faire de la retape pour.** To beat the drums for. *Il fait de la retape pour vendre sa camelote.* "To sell his junk he has to give it the hard sell."

RETOURNER QN. COMME UNE CRÊPE/UNE VIEILLE CHAUSSETTE. To wind s.o. around one's little finger. *Sa nana sait le retourner comme une vieille chaussette.* "His woman can get him to do whatever she wants."

(SE) RETROUVER LE BEC DANS L'EAU = RESTER LE BEC DANS L'EAU.

(SE) RETROUVER (TOUT SEUL) COMME UN CON. To find o.s. alone in an unpleasant situation. *Elle n'est pas venue à notre rendève et je me suis retrouvé comme un con.* "She didn't show up for our date and I was left to stand there like an idiot."

RICAIN, -E, *pej.* American. *Elle a surtout une clientèle de ricains.* "Most of her clients are Americans."

RIC-RAC/RIC ET RAC/RIC À RAC. 1. Precisely. *Sa facture est toujours ric-rac.* "His bill is always calculated down to the last detail/penny." **2.** Barely. *Elle a réussi à son exam, mais c'était ric-rac.* "She barely squeezed through on her exam."

RIFLARD, *m.* Umbrella. *Ce riflard est riquiqui pour nous deux.* "This umbrella's too small for the two of us."

RIGOLADE, *f.* Fun. **C'est de la rigolade! 1.** That's as easy as pie! **2.** That's a lot of hogwash! See BOYAU.

RIGOLBOCHE = RIGOLO.

RIGOLER. 1. To laugh. *Ça me fait rigoler.* "That makes me laugh." **2.** To kid (around). *Mais tu rigoles!* "You must be joking!"

RIGOLO, -TE, *m., f.* **1.** Amusing person. *Elle est rigolote en travesti.* "She's a scream dressed like a man." **2.** Unreliable individual. *On ne peut pas se fier à ce rigolo.* "There's no trusting that jokester."

RIKIKI. Ridiculously small; measly. *Ta chemise fait rikiki.* "Your shirt looks undersized."

(SE) RINCER LA DALLE/LES AMYGDALES. To wet one's whistle. *J'ai une de ces envies de me rincer la dalle!* "Boy do I need a drink!"

(SE) RINCER L'ŒIL. To take a long/good look. *Il se rinçait l'œil quand elle se déshabillait.* "He got an eyeful when she undressed."

RINGARD, -E. Dated; corny. *Costumes et mise en scène étaient totalement ringards.* "The costumes and staging were definitely behind the times."

RINGARD, -E, *m., f.* **1.** Second-rate actor; has-been. *On me traite de ringard, mais j'ai toujours de l'espoir.* "They call me a has-been, but I still have hopes." **2.** Nonentity; fuddy-duddy. *Ce banquet était une réunion de ringards.* "That banquet was a convention of squares."

RIPA, backslang of **Paris.** *Quand irons-nous à Ripa?* "When are we going to Paris?"

RIPATON, *m.* Foot. *J'ai mal aux ripatons.* "My feet hurt."

RIPER. To scram. *Ils ont tous ripé à l'arrivée des flics.* "They all beat it when the cops arrived."

RIPOU, *m.,* backslang of **pourri** (rotten). Crooked. *Ce promoteur n'est qu'un ripou.* "That real estate developer's no more than a crook."

RIQUIQUI = RIKIKI.

RIRE. To laugh. See (SE) TORDRE…RIRE.

RITAL, -E, *m., f., pej.* Italian. *Ces ritals ne s'arrêtent pas de chanter.* "Those wops never stop singing."

ROBERTS, *m., pl.* Breasts (from the name of a manufacturer of baby bottles). *L'artiste aime peindre et sculpter les roberts de ses modèles.* "The artist likes to paint and sculpt his models' breasts."

ROGNE, *f.* Anger. **Se foutre/mettre en rogne,** *idiom.* To hit the ceiling. *Il se met en rogne dès que je lui parle de fric.* "He blows his top every time I talk about money."

ROGNER LES AILES DE QN. To clip s.o.'s wings. *Il est temps de rogner les ailes de ce phallo.* "It's time to take that male chauvinist pig down a peg or two."

ROMBIÈRE, *f.* Old lady. *Cette une drôle de (vieille) rombière!* "She's a strange old bag."

ROND, RONDE. 1. Round. See TOURNER EN ROND; TOURNER ROND. **2.** Drunk. See ROND COMME UNE BARRIQUE.

ROND, *m.* **1.** Cent. **Avoir des ronds,** *idiom.* To be very rich. *Mes vioques ont des ronds; moi je n'ai pas un sou.* "My parents are loaded but I haven't got a red cent." **2.** Anus. *Il a le rond irrité.* "His ass is sore."

ROND COMME UNE BARRIQUE. To be rolling drunk (lit. "drunk as a barrel"). *Quand il sort du chai il est rond comme une barrique.* "When he leaves the wine storehouse he's high as a kite."

ROND COMME UNE BOULE/BILLE/QUEUE DE BILLARD = ROND COMME UNE BARRIQUE.

ROND DE FLAN. See (EN) RESTER…FLAN.

ROND DE JAMBE, *m.* Circular leg movement in ballet. **Faire des ronds de jambe,** *idiom.* To be excessively polite. *L'épicier du coin me fait des ronds de jambe pour que j'achète chez lui.* "The local grocer's sugar-sweet to me to get me to buy from him."

RONDELLE, *f.* Anus. See CASSER/DÉFONCER…RONDELLE; (SE) MAGNER LA RONDELLE.

RONDIBÉ (DU RADADA). Anus. **Espèce de rondibé du radada!** "You dumb asshole!"

RONDS DE CHAPEAU. See (EN) BAVER DES RONDS DE CHAPEAU.

ROPLOPLOS, *m., pl.* Breasts. *Avec de tels roploplos elle fera carrière.* "With jugs like that, her career is assured."

ROSE, *f.* Rose. **Ça sent la rose!,** ironic. "What a stench!" **Envoyer qn. sur les roses,** *idiom.* To tell s.o. where to get off. *Je l'ai envoyé sur les roses quand il m'a demandé des ronds.* "I told him where to go when he asked me for money."

ROSE DES VENTS, *f.,* homosexual. Anus (lit. "wind rose"). *Ta rose des vents doit être épuisée après tant de mecs.* "Your rosebud must be exhausted after so many guys."

ROSETTE, *f.* **1.** Rosette. **Avoir la rosette (de la Légion d'honneur).** To be an officer of the Legion of Honor. *Mon mari aura bientôt la rosette.* "My husband will soon be named an officer of the Legion of Honor." **2.** Anus. **Amateur de rosette; chevalier de la rosette.** Active homosexual (sodomizer). *La tapette rêvait de trouver un chevalier de la rosette.* "The fag dreamed of finding a knight to ride his rosebud."

ROSETTE DE LYON, *f.* Salami sausage. *La rosette de Lyon, quel délice!* "Lyon salami, how delicious!"

ROTEUSE, *f.* Bottle of champagne (lit. "belcher"). *Voici un bouchon spécial pour cette roteuse.* "Here's a special cork for the bottle of bubbly."

ROTEUX, *m.* Champagne (lit. "belcher"). *Je préfère un roteux brut.* "I prefer brut champagne."

ROTOPLOS/ROTOTOS = ROPLOPLOS.

ROTULES, *f., pl.* Kneecaps. **Sur les rotules,** *idiom.* Exhausted. *La course de V.T.T. m'a mis sur les rotules.* "The mountain bike race really knocked me out."

ROUBIGNOLLES, *m., pl.* Testicles. *Ses roubignolles exècrent l'eau froide.* "His balls loathe cold water."

ROUGE. Red wine. *Buvons un coup de ce gros rouge qui tache.* "Let's light into this rough-and-ready red wine."

ROULÉ, -E, *m., f.* Well-built person. *J'aime les filles bien roulées.* "I like girls who are really stacked."

ROULER. To roll. See (SE) FAIRE ROULER.

ROULER LA CAISSE/LES BISCOTOS/ MÉCANIQUES. To swagger. *Il aime les rouler, les mécaniques, devant les belles.* "He likes to strut his stuff in front of pretty girls."

ROULER SA BOSSE. See BOSSE.

ROULER SUR L'OR. To be very rich. *Ils ne roulent pas sur l'or mais ils ne manquent de rien.* "They haven't got money to burn, but they don't have to do without."

ROULER UN PATIN/UNE ESCALOPE/GALOCHE/ PELLE. To tongue kiss (lit. "to roll a skate/cutlet/clog/ shovel). *Il m'a roulé une pelle en me tripotant.* "He French kissed me as he felt me up."

(SE) ROULER PAR TERRE. To laugh uproariously. *Ses histoires sont à se rouler par terre.* "Her stories are side-splittingly funny."

ROULURE, *f.* Slut. *Tu peux la sauter facilement; c'est une roulure.* "You can screw her easily; she's a tramp."

ROUPETTES = ROUBIGNOLLES.

ROUPILLER. To snooze. *Il roupille devant la télé.* "He nods off in front of the TV."

ROUPILLON, *m.* Nap. *Je piquerais bien un petit roupillon.* "I'd like to get a little shut-eye."

ROUSCAILLE = ROUSPÉTANCE.

ROUSCAILLER = ROUSPÉTER.

ROUSPÉTANCE, *f.* Complaining. *Retournez au boulot; pas de rouspétance!* "Get back to work; no bellyaching!"

ROUSPÉTER. To complain. *Dans ce resto il faut toujours rouspéter pour être bien servi.* "You always have to bitch to get good service in that restaurant."

ROUSTE/ROUSTÉE, *f.* Beating. *Tu l'auras, la roustée, si tu me casses ma bagnole.* "I'll knock your block off if you mess up my car."

ROUSTONS, *m., pl.* Testicles. *Il a reçu le ballon dans les roustons.* "The football hit him in the balls."

RUCHE, *f.* Nose (lit. "beehive"). **Se péter/se piquer la ruche.** To tipple. *On aime bien se piquer la ruche au vin.* "We like tying one on with wine."

RUP. High-class. *Cherchons un hôtel moins rup.* "Let's look for a less posh hotel."

RUPIN, -E = RUP.

RUPIN, *m., pej.* Very rich person; moneybags. *C'est un resto pour rupins.* "That's a ritzy restaurant."

RUSSCOF/RUSSKOFF/RUSSKI, *adj.* and *n.* Russian. *Si l'on allait bouffer ce soir chez les Russkoffs?* "How about eating in a Russian restaurant tonight?"

SABIR, *m.* Mumbo-jumbo; pidgin (a mixture of Fr., Sp., Ital. and Ar. From Sp. **saber,** "to know"). *Qui peut piger son sabir?* "Who can understand his gibberish?"

SABOT, *m.* Wooden shoe. See VENIR.

SABRE, *m.* Penis. **Filer un coup de sabre** (lit. "to make a saber thrust"). To copulate. *L'officier a eu juste le temps de lui filer un coup de sabre.* "The officer had just enough time to plug her."

SABRER. To fuck (lit. "to cut down with a sword"). *Le lieute était troup paf pour me sabrer.* "The lieutenant was too stewed to screw me."

SABRER LE CHAMPAGNE. To crack open a bottle of champagne (orig. by using a sword or knife). *Elle est toujours prête à sabrer le champagne.* "She's always ready to crack open a bottle of champagne."

SAC, *m.* Bag. **Vider son sac,** *idiom.* To confess; own up to (lit. "to empty one's bag"). *Vide enfin ton sac.* "Come on, spit it out now." See FAIRE UN SAC.

SAC À BITES, *m.* Prostitute (lit. "bag for dicks"). *Tu veux épouser ce sac à bites?* "You want to marry that super slut?"

SAC À PUCES, *m.* **1.** Bed, *dated* (lit. "fleabag"). *Il faut balancer ce sac à puces.* "We've got to throw out this bed." **2.** Computer (lit. "microchip bag"). *Il met une fortune dans ses sacs à puces.* "He spends a fortune on his computers."

SAC À SPERME, *m.* Easy lay. *Toute la bande est passée sur ce sac à sperme.* "The whole gang's had her."

SAINTE-BARBE. See BARBE 2.

SAINTE-NITOUCHE, *f.* Prudish woman. *Elle est baiseuse mais aime faire la Sainte-nitouche.* "She's a sexpot but likes to play the Puritan."

SAINTE TOUCHE, *f.* Payday (from **toucher,** "to get money"). *Ils célèbrent la Sainte-Touche au bistrot.* "They celebrate payday at the bistro."

SAINT-FRIC. Money. *Dans leur réligion on bénit Hermès, Mercure, Lakchmi, et le Saint-Fric.* "In their religion they bless Hermes, Mercury, Lakshmi, and Almighty Money."

SAINT-FRUSQUIN, *m.* **1.** The whole works. *Elle a vidé tout le saint-frusquin du grenier.* "She cleared everything out of the attic." **2.** Male genitalia. *Il est fier de son saint-frusquin.* "He's proud of his equipment."

SAINT-GLINGLIN. Indefinite date. **(Jusqu')à la Saint-Glinglin.** Never in a month of Sundays. *Tu peux attendre jusqu'à la Saint-Glinglin.* "You can wait till hell freezes over."

SAINT-JEAN, *f.* Midsummer. **En Saint-Jean.** Naked. *À Carnac, pour les feux de la Saint-Jean, les néo-druides dansaient en Saint-Jean.* "In Karnak, on Midsummer Eve, the neo-Druids danced in the all-together around the bonfires."

SAINT-LUNDI, *f.* **Faire/fêter la Saint-Lundi,** *idiom.* To take Monday off. *Fêtons la Saint-Lundi et partons à la campagne.* "Let's declare Monday a holiday and go to the country."

SAINT-TROU-DU-CUL, vulgar equivalent of SAINT-GLINGLIN.

SALADE, *f.* **1.** Stupid/untrue story; mess (lit. "salad"). *Ne nous emmerde pas avec toutes tes salades.* "Quit bugging us with all that bullshit." **2.** Fuss. **En faire toute une salade,** *idiom.* To make a fuss. *Il va en faire toute une* *salade.* "He's going to make a big to-do about that." See ARRÊTER.

SALADIER, *m.* **1.** Mouth (lit. "salad bowl"). See TAPER DU SALADIER. **2.** Fast talker. *Ce saladier devient de plus en plus chiant.* "That glib babbler bugs me more and more."

SALAMALECS, *m. pl.,* from Ar. for "peace be with you." Unctiousness. *Reçois-les sans faire de salamalecs.* "Greet them without fawning."

SALAUD, *m.* SOB. *Espèce de salaud!* "You bastard!"

SALE GUEULE, *f.* Repulsive face. *Quelle sale gueule!* "What a nasty mug!" **Faire une sale gueule,** *idiom.* To give a dirty look/cold shoulder. *Elle m'a fait une sale gueule pour ne pas être rentré de la nuit.* "She gave me the cold shoulder for not having come home at night."

SALÉ, -E. Excessive (lit. "salty"). *Dans ce resto la carte des vins est salée.* "In this restaurant the wine list is steep."

SALER LA SOUPE, sports. To take drugs (lit. "to salt the soup"). *Il avait salé la soupe et a perdu sa médaille.* "He'd taken drugs and lost his medal."

SALIGAUD = SALAUD.

SALOP/SALOPARD = SALAUD.

SALOPE, *f.* **1.** Bitch. *C'est la vraie salope!* "She's a real bitch!" See MARIE-SALOPE **1.** **2.** SOB. *Son mari est une sacrée salope!* "Her husband is a damned bastard!"

SALOPER. To botch. *Il ne sait rien faire sans saloper.* "He can't do anything without bungling it."

SALOPERIE, *f.* **1.** Bitchy comment. *Espèce de mal elevé, ravale tes saloperies.* "You boor, take back those nasty cracks!" **2.** Dirty trick. *Elle lui a fait une saloperie en couchant avec son frère.* "She played a dirty trick on him by sleeping with his brother." **3.** Trash. *Elle a acheté une saloperie comme souvenir.* "She bought a piece of junk as a souvenir."

SALPÊTRE, *m.* Saltpeter. See VACCINÉ AU SALPÊTRE.

SANDEC = SANS DEC'.

SANG, *m.* Blood. **Avoir du sang de navet,** *idiom.* To be gutless/a wimp (lit. "to have turnip's blood"). *Alors, tu y vas ou tu n'y vas pas? Tu as du sang de navet?* "Well are you going to or not? Are you chicken?" See (SE) CAILLER...SANG.

SANISETTE, *f.,* registered trademark in the sense of "toilet." Prostitute who works in toilets, alleys, hallways, and so on (lit. "public coin toilet"). *Impossible de pisser—les sanisettes sont au turbin.* "Impossible to take a piss—the working girls are at it."

SANS BLAGUE! No kidding!

SANS DÉBANDER. Nonstop (lit. "without losing an erection"). *On est parti faire la java trois jours sans débander.* "We partied three days nonstop."

SANS DEC', *abbr.* of **sans déconner.** No fooling. No kidding. *Tu l'as sautée, ta cousine? Sans dec'?* "You banged your cousin? No shit?"

SAPE, *f.* The garment industry. *Elle bosse pour la sape au Sentier.* "She works for the rag trade in the garment district."

SAPÉ, -E. Dressed. *Elle est toujours bien sapée.* "She's always well dressed."

SAPER. To sentence (lit. "to undermine"). *On l'a sapé à dix piges.* "He got sent away for ten years."

SAPES, *f., pl.* Clothes. *Tes sapes sont trempées.* "Your clothes are wet through."

(SE) SAPER. To dress; buy clothes. *Je me sape aux Puces de Clignancourt.* "I get my clothes at the Clignancourt flea market."

SAQUER. 1. To give low marks. *Ils l'ont saqué à l'exam.* "They flunked him on the exam." **2.** To endure. *Sa gonzesse, je ne peux pas la saquer.* "I can't stand that broad of his."

SARDINE, *f.* Sardine. See ÉGOUTTER LA/SA SARDINE.

SATANÉ, -E! Damned. **Satanée pluie!** Damned rain!

SATURER. To be fed up (lit. "to saturate"). *Je sature sur les voisins.* "I've had it up to here with the neighbors."

SATYRE. Lecher; flasher. *Ce vieux satyre a son coin dans le bois de Boulogne.* "That old lecher's turf is in the Bois de Boulogne park."

SAUCE, *f.* **1.** Sauce. **Envoyer/mettre la sauce,** *idiom.* To go all out. *Ils ont mis toute la sauce pour gagner.* "They went all out to win." **2.** Sperm. *Après son rêve mouillé les draps étaient pleins de sauce.* "After his wet dream the sheets were full of sperm."

SAUCÉE, *f.* Downpour. *Mes sapes ont reçu la saucée.* "My clothes got drenched."

SAUCER. 1. To copulate (lit. "to dunk in sauce"). *Messalina aimait se faire saucer.* "Messalina loved getting laid." **2.** To scold. *Je te l'ai saucé le gamin, après sa bêtise!* "I gave that kid a good dressing down after his mischief."

SAUCIFLARD, *m.* Sausage. *On n'a que du sauciflard à bouffer.* "Sausage is all there is to eat."

SAUCISSON, *m.* **1.** Sausage. See PEAU DE SAUSS. **2.** Golden oldie, music. *Il aime réécouter les mêmes saucissons.* "He likes to listen to the same old stuff."

SAUCISSONNÉ, -E. Bulging out of one's clothes. *Vise un peu comme elle est saucissonnée!* "Just look at how she's stuffed into her clothes!"

SAUTE-AU-CRAC, *m.* Satyr (lit. "jumps to crack [vagina]"). *Ton pote, c'est un vrai saute-au-crac.* "Your buddy's a real gash hound."

SAUTE-AU-PAF, *f.* Nymphomaniac (lit. "jumps to penis"). *Trouver une saute-au-paf, c'était son rêve d'ado.* "Finding a nympho was the dream of his adolescence."

SAUTER. 1. To jump. **Et que ça saute!** "Jump to it!" "Step on it!" **2.** To copulate. *Au turbin, il l'a sautée aux WC.* "At work, he screwed her in the john."

SAUTERELLE, *f.* **1.** Tall person (lit. "grasshopper"). *Vise* *un peu les gambettes de cette sauterelle norvégienne!* "Take a look at that Norwegian gal's legs!" **2.** Female, sometimes *pej. J'ai vu ta sauterelle arpenter la rue Saint Denis.* "I think I saw your girlfriend working St. Denis Street."

SAUVAGE. Marvelous! (lit. "wild"). *Sauvage le concert rock!* "The rock concert was terrific!"

SAV = SAVONNETTE.

SAVOIR Y FAIRE. To be competent. *Tu ne sais pas y faire.* "You don't know how to go about it."

SAVON, *m.* Soap. **Passer un savon à qqn.,** *idiom.* To tell s.o. off. *Elle lui a passé un de ces savons.* "She chewed him out good."

SAVONNER. To stammer (lit. "to soap up"). *Tu savonnes— explique-toi mieux.* "You're spluttering—explain yourself better."

SAVONNETTE, *f.* Cannabis (lit. "small bar of soap"). *Je n'ai plus qu'une savonnette.* "All I've left is a little stash of grass/hash."

SCAILLES = CHAILLES.

SCALPER. To arrest (lit. "to scalp"). *Les flics l'ont scalpé.* "The cops nabbed him."

SCAPHANDRE, *m.* Diving suit; space suit. **Scaphandre de poche.** Condom. *Elle lui a mis un scaphandre de poche.* "She put a rubber on him."

SCATO, *abbr.* of **scatologique.** Scatological. *Le prof de philo aime l'humour scato.* "The professor of philosophy loves bathroom humor."

SCHBEB, *m.* Homosexual (esp. in prison/the military [from Ar. for "pretty"]), *pej. Il était déjà schbeb à l'internat avant de faire de la tôle.* "He was already gay in boarding school before he did time."

SCHLAFFE/SCHLOF, *m.* Sleep (from Ger. **schlafen**). **Aller à/au schlof** or **faire schlof.** To go to bed. *C'est l'heure de faire schlof.* "It's time to hit the sack."

SCHMITT, *m.* Policeman. *Il y a du schmitt!* "The cops are here!"

SCHNOC/SCHNOQUE, *m.* Idiot, "shnook." *C'est un vieux shnoque, ton tonton!* "Your uncle's an old fool."

SCHNOUF(FE), *f.* Heroin. (from Ger. for "snuff" and "sniff"). *Elle marche à la schnouffe.* "She's on big doses of the big H."

(SE) SCHNOUFFER. To shoot heroin. *Il ne se schnouffe plus.* "He no longer mainlines heroin."

SCHPROUM, *m.* Ruckus (from Ger. **sprung** [to jump]). **Aller au schproum.** To make a scene. *Pourqoui toujours aller au schproum?* "Why do you always make a scene?"

SCHTIB(E), *m.* Prison (either a variant of **Schtilibem** or from Ger. **Stübchen,** "little room"). *Il a appris à méditer au schtib.* "He learned how to meditate in the clink."

SCHTILIBEM, *m.* Prison (Gypsy parlance, with possible influence of Ger. **Stilleben** [still life]). *Le gitan chantait au schtilibem.* "The gypsy sang in the slammer."

SCHTOUILLE = CHTOUILLE.

SCHTUC, *m.* Little bit (from Ger. **Stück** [piece]). *Donne-m'en juste un schtuc.* "Give me just a smidgeon."

SCOTCHÉ. Stuck (from "Scotch tape®"). *Il a les yeux scotchés sur la télé.* "His eyes are glued to the TV."

SCOUZE! = SCUZMI.

SCRIBOUILLARD(E), *m., f., pej.* Journalist; pen pusher. *Ce scribouillard rêve d'écrire un grand roman.* "That journalist dreams of writing a great novel."

SCROGNEUGNEU, *m.* Old grouch; Col. Blimp. *Ce scrogneugneu fait la guerre à tous.* "That old grouch is hostile to everybody."

SCROGNEUGNEU! Hell and damnation! Damn it!

SCROUM = SCHPROUM.

SCUZMI! Excuse me (from Eng. or It.) *Scuzmi, je suis à la bourre!* "Excuse me, I'm in a hurry!"

SEC, *adv.* Dryly. **Boire sec**. To drink a lot. *Elle boit sec, ta belle-doche!* "Your mother-in-law really puts it away!" See AUSSI SEC; CUL SEC!

SÉCATEUR, *m.* Pruning shears. **Baptiser au sécateur,** *pej.* To circumcise. *Avant de se convertir à l'Islam, il s'est fait baptiser au sécateur.* "Before converting to Islam, he was circumcised." **Baptisé au sécateur,** *pej.* Jewish. *On ne savait pas qu'il était baptisé au sécateur.* "We didn't know he was Jewish."

SECOUER LA BABASSE. See BABASSE.

SECRET DE POLICHINELLE, *m.* See POLICHINELLE.

SÉCU, *f. abbr.* of **la Sécurité sociale,** Fr. health/pension system. *Son accident est pris en charge par la Sécu.* "Her accident is covered by medical insurance."

SEFFE, *f.,* backslang of **fesse**.

SEIGNEUR-TERRASSE, *m.* Person who spends much time but little money in a café (lit. "terrace lord"). *Plusieurs seigneurs-terrasse sirotaient leur café.* "Several table hogs sipped their coffee."

SÉMAPHORE, *m.* **1.** Traffic cop (lit. "semaphore"). *Ce sémaphore doit avoir les poumons noirs.* "That traffic cop's lungs must be black." **2.** Orchestra director. *On dit que les sémaphores vivent longtemps.* "They say conductors are long-lived."

SEMER QN. To shake s.o. off (lit. "to sow; scatter"). *Je ne sais pas pourquoi il m'a semée.* "I don't know why he ditched me." See ZIZANIE.

SEMOULE, *f.* Semolina. **Être dans la semoule,** *idiom.* To be confused. *Je suis toujours dans la semoule pour remplir des formulaires.* "I'm always muddled when I have to fill out forms." See PÉDALER. **Balancer/envoyer la semoule.** To ejaculate. *Il avait du mal à balancer la semoule.* "He had a hard time coming."

SENSASS, from **sensationnel**. Wonderful. *Le film était sensass.* "The film was terrific."

SENTIR L'AIL. See AIL.

SENTIR À PLEIN NEZ. To be obvious. *Ça sent à plein nez les accros.* "It's as plain as the nose on your face they're junkies."

(LE/LA) SENTIR PASSER. To experience s.t. unpleasant. *L'addition du Ritz, il l'a sentie passer.* "He won't forget the bill at the Ritz."

(SE) SENTIR PISSER. See PISSER.

SÉRIEUX, *m.* Liter glass of beer. *Il ne se prend pas au sérieux, peut-être parce qu'il aime la convivialité et s'envoie un sérieux chaque soir.* "He doesn't take h.s. very seriously, perhaps because he likes conviviality and belts down a big glass of beer every evening."

SERIN, *m.* Ninny (lit. "canary"). *Espèce de petit serin, change de disque!* "You nitwit, put on another record."

SERINETTE, *f.* Homosexual. *Je ne sais pas s'il en est, mais tous ses amis sont des serinettes.* "I don't know if he's 'one of them,' but all his friends are gay."

SERINGUER. To riddle with bullets (**seringue** = "syringe"). *Son mec l'a seringuée joliment.* "Her guy plugged her full of lead."

SERRER LA CUILER/LOUCHE/PINCE. To shake hands (lit. "the spoon/ladle/claw"). *En Europe on se serre la pince pour un oui, pour un non.* "In Europe people shake hands all the time."

SERRER LE KIKI. To strangle. *Si tu lui donnes encore du gin, je te serre le kiki.* "If you give him any more gin, I'll wring your neck."

SERRER LES FESSES. 1. To grit one's teeth (lit. "to squeeze one's buttocks together"). *Le toubib m'a dit de serrer les fesses avant de me charcuter.* "The doctor told me to grit my teeth before cutting me." **2.** To be afraid. *Je serre les fesses quand il roule trop vite.* "I get all tensed up when he drives too fast."

(SE) SERRER LA CEINTURE. See CEINTURE.

SERVICE, *m.* Service. **Service trois pièces.** Male genitalia (lit. "three-piece dish set"). *Son service trois pièces—*

quelle sacrée trinité! "His family jewels—what a trinity!"

SÉZIG(UE). Him; her. *C'est un cadeau de sézigue.* "It's a present from him."

SHIT, *m.* Hashish (from Eng.). *Passe-moi une boulette de shit.* "Pass me a hash pellet."

(SE) SHOOTER/SHOUTER. To inject o.s. with drugs. *Ils aiment se shouter ensemble.* "They enjoy shooting up together."

SHOOTEUSE/SHOUTEUSE, *f.* Drug needle. *Elle a toujours sa shooteuse avec elle.* "She's always got her syringe with her."

SIDATEUX, -EUSE/SIDATIQUE, *m., f., pej.* Person with AIDS. *Il y a des centres pour aider les sidatiques.* "There are centers for helping people with AIDS."

SIDOUZE, *m.* AIDS. *Fais gaffe au sidouze!* "Be careful of AIDS."

SIFELLE = CIFELLE.

SIFFLER. To whistle. **Siffler un verre,** *idiom.* To belt down a drink. *Entre, juste le temps de siffler un verre.* "Come in for a quick drink."

SIFFLET, *m.* Throat (lit. "whistle"). See COUPER LE SIFFLET.

SINGE, *m.* **1.** Monkey. See PAYER EN MONNAIE DE SINGE. **2.** Corned beef. *À l'armée il bouffait du singe.* "In the army he ate corned beef." **3.** Boss. *Le singe nous a mis en chômage technique.* "The boss laid us off temporarily."

SINOC/SINOQUE/SINOQUET. Crazy. *Il est devenu complètement sinoc.* "He's gone completely around the bend."

SIPHONNÉ, -E. Crazy. *Ce type est siphonné; il m'a bousillé la voiture.* "That guy's bonkers; he screwed up my car."

SIX-À-NEUF = SOIXANTE-NEUF.

SMALA, *f.* Large family; entourage. *Il va venir avec toute sa smala.* "He'll come with his whole tribe."

SNIF, *m.* Cocaine. *Il trouve du snif pas cher.* "He gets inexpensive nose candy."

SNIFFER. To inhale cocaine and other things. *Il lui fallait sniffer de plus en plus.* "He grew more and more addicted to snow."

SNUFF = SNIF.

SŒUR, *f.* Sister. See ET TA SŒUR!

SŒURS, *f., pl.* Prostitutes who work for the same pimp, whom they call "husband." *Notre mari tient la bride haute à mes sœurs et à moi.* "Our husband keeps a tight rein on my sisters and me."

SOIE, *f.* Silk. **Péter dans la soie,** *idiom.* To live the life of Riley (lit. "to fart in silk [undies, etc.]"). *Après avoir pété dans la soie, il est tombé dans la misère.* "After having lived high on the hog, he fell on hard times."

SOIF, *f.* Thirst. **Il fait soif!,** *idiom.* "I need a drink in this weather!" See COUPE-LA-SOIF.

SOIF, *m.* Tip (from **poursoif,** variant of **pourboire**). *Il n'est payé qu'aux soifs.* "His only wages are in tips."

SOIGNÉ, -E. Intense (lit. well-groomed). *J'avais un rhume soigné.* "I had a dirty rotten cold."

SOIGNER. To treat. **Il faut te faire soigner!** "You need to see a shrink!"

SOISSONAIS (ROSE), *m.* Clitoris (lit. "bean"). *Il m'a frotté le soissonais et j'ai senti un petit frisson.* "I felt a little thrill when he rubbed my clit."

SOIXANTE-NEUF, *m.* Simultaneous oral sex. *Elle est individualiste mais elle adore le soixante-neuf.* "She's an individualist but she loves 69."

SOLEIL, *m.* Sun. See PIQUER UN SOLEIL.

SONNÉ, -E. 1. Knocked out; groggy. *Après sa chute à ski elle était sonnée.* "She was dazed after her fall when skiing. **2.** Crazy. *Il est un peu sonné sur les bords.* "He's slightly cracked."

SONNER. To ring. *Elle a ses quarante ans bien sonnés.* "She's forty if she's a day."

SONNER LES CLOCHES À QN. To reprimand severely.

On lui a sonné les cloches pour avoir sécher l'école. "They read him the riot act for having played hooky from school."

SONORGUE = **SÉZIG(UE).**

SORTIE, *f.* Exit. **Être de sortie,** *idiom.* To be out/away/missing. *La boniche est de sortie aujourd'hui.* "Today's the maid's day off."

SORTIR PAR LES YEUX (ET LES OREILLES)/PAR LES TROUS DE NEZ. To leave (lit. "to be coming out of one's eyes (ears), nostrils"). To have a snoot/belly full of s.t. *Je l'évite car il me sort par les yeux.* "I avoid him because I've had as much of him as I can take."

SOUDÉ. Jammed (said of traffic; lit. "welded"). *Le périf est archisoudé à 17 heures.* "The beltway is completely bottlenecked at 5:00 P.M."

SOUK, *m.* Disorder (from Ar. for "market"). *Sa chambre est devenue un souk invivable.* "His room's become a pigsty."

SOÛLARD, -E. *m., f.* Drunkard. *C'est un couple de soûlards.* "He and she are both lushes."

SOÛLAUD/SOÛLOT = **SOÛLARD.**

SOUPE À LA GRIMACE, *f.* A hostile reception. *Quand il rentre bourré, il a soupe à la grimace.* "He gets the cold shoulder when he comes home drunk."

SOUPE AU LAIT, *f.* Person quick to fly off the handle (milk added to boiling soup rises rapidly). *Il n'a aucune patience. Quelle soupe au lait!* "He has no patience. What a hothead!"

SOUPE DE LANGUES, *f.,* youth. Long Fr. kiss (lit. "tongue soup"). *Les ados sont friands de soupes de langues.* "Adolescents are fond of long wet kisses."

SOUPER. To have supper. **En avoir soupé,** *idiom.* To be fed up with s.t. *J'en ai soupé de faire le ménage après le boulot.* "I'm sick and tired of doing the housework after coming home from work."

SOURDINGUE. Deaf. *Parle moins fort; je ne suis pas sourdingue.* "Don't talk so loud; I'm not deaf."

SOURIS, *f.* Young girl (lit. "mouse"). *Il ne pense qu'aux souris.* "All he thinks about is chicks."

SOURIS DE SACRISTIE, *f.* Sanctimonious church lady. *Ma grand-tante est une souris de sacristie.* "My great-aunt is a Holy Joe."

SOUS-FIFRE/SOUS-FIFRESSE, *m., f.* Underling. *Le chirurgien fait sa ronde avec ses sous-fifres et sous-fifresses.* "The surgeon makes his rounds with his junior associates."

SOUS-PRÉFET, *m.* Subprefect. See AGACER…PRÉFET.

SOUTIEN-LOLOCHES = SOUTIF.

SOUTIF, *m.* Brassiere. *Elle ne porte jamais de soutif.* "She never wears a bra."

SPEEDÉ, -E. Hyper. *Ils étaient speedés lors du viol collectif.* "They were wired during the gang rape."

SPEEDER. To accelerate. *Je speede dès le matin.* "I've been going nonstop since morning."

SPROUM = SCHPROUM.

SQUATTER. To occupy illegally. *La gare désaffectée est squattée.* "Squatters are occupying the former railroad station."

STUP, *m., abbr.* of **stupéfiant.** Narcotic. *Il a fait de la taule pour un trafic de stup.* "He was in stir for drug dealing."

STUPS, *m., pl.,* from **Brigade des stups.** Narcotics squad. *Des stups américains et français devaient collaborer.* "American and French narcs were supposed to work together."

SUBITO(S)/SUBITO PRESTO. Suddenly; on the double. *Il nous a quitté subitos.* "He left us all of a sudden."

SUÇADE, *f.* Fellatio. *La suçade lui plaisait mieux avec la capote.* "She found frenching more pleasing with a rubber."

SUÇAGE, *m.* = **SUÇADE.**

SUCER LA POMME/LE MUSEAU. To kiss (lit. "to suck the face/muzzle"). *Le baisemain, c'est bien, mais* *j'aimerais mieux que tu me suces la pomme.* "A kiss on the hand is nice, but I'd rather you gave me a real kiss."

SUCRE, *m.* Sugar. **Casser du sucre sur le dos de qn.,** *idiom.* To speak ill of s.o. *Méfie-toi de cette garce qui ne cesse de casser du sucre sur ton dos!* "Be careful of that bitch who's always running you down."

SUCRER LES FRAISES. To have one foot in the grave (lit. "to sugar the strawberries"). *Heureusement nos parents ne sucrent pas encore les fraises.* "Fortunately our parents aren't on their last legs yet."

(SE) SUCRER. To feather one's nest. *L'agent immobilier s'est sucré en vendant ma boutique.* "The real estate agent lined his pockets in selling my boutique."

SUER. To sweat. **Faire suer qn.,** *idiom.* To bore/annoy s.o. extremely. *Tu me fais suer!* "You really piss me off." **Se faire suer,** *idiom.* To be extremely bored. *Sortons d'ici! On se fait suer.* "Let's get out of here. This is a real drag."

SUP, *abbr.* of **supplémentaire.** *Il n'a pas payé mes heures sup.* "He hasn't paid me for my overtime."

SUPERBLIME. Marvelous (from **super** and **sublime**). *Le concert était superblime.* "The concert was fantabulous."

SURBOUM, *f.* Wild party. *On s'est bien pété la gueule à la dernière surboum.* "We all got smashed at the last big bash."

SURGÉ, *m.,* school, *abbr.* of **surveillant général.** Vice principal. *Le surgé est une peau de vache.* "The vice principal's a real SOB."

SUR LES BORDS. See BORDS.

SUR LE VIF. On the spot; live. *L'enregistrement a été fait sur le vif.* "It's a live recording."

SURPATTE = SURBOUM.

SUSHI, *m.* Jap. fish dish. **Rouler/faire un sushi.** See ROULER UNE PELLE.

SYMPA. Pleasant. *Il nous a dégoté un coin sympa pour pique-niquer.* "He found a nice spot for our picnic."

SYNOQUE = SINOQUE.

SYPH/SYPHLOTTE, *f.,* from **syphilis.** *Fais gaffe, qu'il ne te colle pas la syphlotte aussi.* "See to it that he doesn't syph you up too."

SYSTÈME, *m.* System. **Courir/taper sur le système à qn.,** *idiom.* To get on s.o.'s nerves (lit. "to run/hit on s.o.'s [nervous] system"). *L'entendre chanter faux me tape sur le système.* "Listening to his off-key singing grates on me."

SYSTÈME D (for **DÉBROUILLE/DÉMERDE),** *m.* Resourcefulness. *"Comment as-tu réussi à faire ça?"* *"Système D."* "How'd you manage that?" "Smarts!"

TAB, *f.,* drugs, *abbr.* of **tablette.** Amphetamine tablet. *Il avale tab sur tab.* "He pops speed constantly."

TABAC, *m.* **1.** Tobacco. **Passer à tabac,** *idiom.* To beat up. *La police l'a passé à tabac.* "The police worked him over." **2.** Success. **Faire un tabac,** *idiom.* To be very successful. *Cette diva a fait un tabac.* "That diva had a resounding success."

TABASSER. To beat up. *Ils l'ont tabassé à la sortie du match.* "They beat him up after the game."

TAC. Taxi. *Il vase et les tacs sont rares.* "It's pouring and cabs are scarce."

TACHE, *f.* **1.** Stain. **Faire tache,** *idiom.* To stick out like a sore thumb. *Dans sa robe rouge Jézabel faisait tache.* "Jezebel stuck out like a sore thumb in her red dress." **2.** Nonentity. *Pour moi, ce n'est qu'une tache.* "For me he's just a dud."

TACO(T) = TAC.

TAFANARD, *m.* Posterior. *En taule, il avait souvent le tafanard irrité.* "His ass often hurt in jail."

TAFFE = TOUFFE 2.

TAG, *m.* Graffiti maker's signature; graffito. *Le bus était couvert de tags.* "The bus was covered with graffiti."

TAGGER = TAGUEUR.

TAGUER. To spray graffiti. *Ce petit morveux a tagué la* *maison.* "That little jerk has spray-painted the house."

TAGUEUR, -EUSE, *m., f.* Graffiti sprayer. *Le tagueur se balade avec sa bombe de peinture.* "The graffiti sprayer walks around with his can of spray paint."

TAILLER UNE BAVETTE. See BAVETTE.

TAILLER UNE PIPE. See PIPE.

TAILLER UNE PLUME. To fellate. *Il aime mieux tailler une plume, plutôt que de se faire turluter.* "He'd rather blow than be blown."

(SE) TAILLER. To beat it. *Dès que je le vois, je me taille.* "I split as soon as I see him."

TAL, *m.* Money. *J'ai besoin de tal.* "I need money."

TALA, *m., f.* Militant Roman Catholic (from the liaison in **vont à la [messe]**). *C'est un tala, de ceux qui vont à la messe!* "He's a Holy Joe, a mass goer."

TALOCHE, *f.* Slap. See ALLONGER...TALOCHE.

TAMBOUILLE, *f.* Food. *Le resto du coin fait de la bonne tambouille.* "The local restaurant serves good food."

TAM-TAM ARABE = TÉLÉPHONE ARABE.

TANGEANTE, *f.* Tangent. **Prendre la tangeante.** To make o.s. scarce; to shirk s.t. *Ne pense pas à prendre la tangeante.* "Don't think of slipping off."

TANTE, *f.* Homosexual (lit. "aunt"). *C'est une belle brochette de tantes!* "What a bunch of fairies!"

TANTOUSE/TANTOUZE = TANTE.

TAPÉ, -E. Crazy (lit. "hit [in the head]"). *Il est bien tapé depuis qu'elle l'a quitté.* "He's been really bananas since she left him."

TAPE-À-L'ŒIL, *m.* Flashy stuff. *Chez eux le décor est très tape-à-l'œil.* "Their place is gaudily decorated."

TAPE-CUL, *m.* Rattletrap vehicle (lit. "ass hitter"). *Son bahut est un vrai tape-cul.* "His car's a real bone-shaker."

TAPÉE, *f.* A large amount. *Je ne supporte pas leur tapée de marmots.* "I can't stand their pack of brats."

TAPER. 1. To hit on; mooch (lit. "to hit; tap"). *Je peux te taper d'une clope?* "Can I bum a cigarette off you?" **2.** To stink. *Il adore les fromages qui tapent.* "He loves smelly cheeses."

TAPER DANS LA LUNE. To sodomize. *Il aime lui taper dans la lune.* "He likes to stick it up her ass."

TAPER DANS L'ŒIL. To impress. *Son diamant m'a tapé dans l'œil.* "Her diamond blew me away."

TAPER DES ARPIONS. To have smelly feet. *Mon mari tape toujours des arpions.* "My husband's feet are always smelly."

TAPER DU BEC/SALADIER. To have bad breath. *Elle le repousse parce qu'il tape du saladier.* "She keeps him distant because he's got bad breath."

TAPER L'AIL. To be a lesbian. See AIL.

TAPER L'INCRUSTE. To invite o.s.; be a gate-crasher. *Personne ne le soupçonnait d'avoir tapé l'incruste.* "Nobody knew he was a gate-crasher."

TAPER SUR LE SYSTÈME. See SYSTÈME.

(SE) TAPER. 1. To treat o.s. to s.t. *On s'est tapé un resto trois étoiles.* "We treated ourselves to a three-star restaurant." **2.** To have sex. *Elle se tape un nouveau mec chaque soir.* "She bangs a different guy every night." **3.** To tackle s.t. difficult. *C'est moi qui me tape toujours la vaisselle.* "I'm the one who always gets stuck with the dishes."

(SE) TAPER LA CLOCHE. To eat a lot. *On s'est bien tapé la cloche chez mémé.* "We had a big feed at Grandma's."

(SE) TAPER LE CUL PAR TERRE. See ASTAP(E) 1.

(SE) TAPER SUR LA LANTERNE. To be hungry. *Ça fait un moment que je me tape sur la lanterne.* "I've been hungry for some time now."

TAPETTE, *f.*, *pej.* Flaming faggot (lit. "flyswatter"). *Ce bar est un nid à tapettes.* "This bar is a home for flaming faggots."

TAPIN, *m.* Prostitution. **Faire le tapin = Tapiner.**

TAPINER. To work as a prostitute. *Elle ne veut plus tapiner.* "She doesn't want to be a hooker anymore."

TARBOUIF, *m.* Nose. *Pour se sauver elle l'a cogné dans le tarbouif.* "To get away she hit him in the schnozz."

TARÉ, -E, *m., f.* Idiot. *C'est une famille de tarés.* "They're retards, that family."

TARIN = **TARBOUIF.**

TARPÉ, backslang of **pétard 4.**

TARTE, *adj.* Stupid. *Tu as l'air tarte avec ce chapeau.* "You look idiotic in that hat."

TARTE, *f.* **1.** Tart. **C'est pas de la tarte!** That's no picnic/piece of cake! **2.** Whack. See ALLONGER…TARTE.

TARTE AUX POILS, *f.* Female genitalia (lit. "fur pie"). *Elle peignait tous les matins sa tarte aux poils.* "She combed her hairy snatch every morning."

TARTEMPION, *m.* What's-his/her-name. *Monsieur et Madame Tartempion ont acheté l'appart d'en face.* "What's-their-name bought the facing apartment."

TARTIGNOLE = **TARTE.** (*adj.*)

TAS DE FERRAILLE, *m.* Old heap of a car (lit. "pile of scrap metal"). *Tu n'as acheté qu'un tas de ferraille qu'on devrait retirer de la circulation.* "All you bought was a pile of junk that should be taken off the road."

TASSE/TASSE À THÉ = **THÉIÈRE 2.**

(SE) TASSER LA CLOCHE = **(SE) TAPER LA CLOCHE.**

TATA = **TANTE.**

TATANE, *f.* Shoe; foot. **Filer un coup de tatane.** To kick. *Elle lui a filé un coup de tatane dans les roubignolles.* "She gave him a kick in the balls."

TAULARD, -E, *m., f.* Convict. *Elle fera une taularde si elle continue.* "She'll wind up a jailbird if she keeps on."

TAULE, *f.* **1.** Home; room. *Tu veux monter à ma taule?* "You want to come to my place?" **2.** Jail. *Il a fait deux ans de taule pour vol.* "He was in stir for two years for larceny."

TBM. 1. Very well hung (*abbr.* of **très bien monté**). *Elle m'a dans la peau car je suis TBM.* "She's nuts about me because I'm hung like a mule." **2.** Very good-looking guy (*abbr.* of **très beau mec**). *Elle n'a d'yeux que pour les TBM.* "She has eyes only for handsome guys."

TC, *f., abbr.* of **télécommande.** TV remote control. *Où est la TC?* "Where's the remote?"

TCHAO, phonetic rendering of Ital. **ciao.** "So long/see you."

TCHATCHER. 1. To gab; yak. *On tchatchait au café.* "We were shooting the breeze in the café." **2.** To smooth-talk; sweet-talk. *Ne me tchatche pas.* "Don't hand me a line."

TCHATCHEUR, -EUSE, *m., f.* Glib talker. *C'est un sacré tchatcheur.* "He's a real smooth talker."

TCHAVE, *m.* from Romany. Departure. **Se faire la tchave,** *idiom.* To shove off. *Faisons la tchave!* "Let's blow this hole!" Cf. NATCHAV!

TCHI/T'CHI, from Romany. Nothing. *Ton argot, je n'y pige que tchi!* "I don't understand a word of your slang."

TCHIN-TCHIN! A toast. "Cheers! Bottoms up!"

TCHOUCH, *m.,* street vendor slang. Free gift. *J'ai eu ce lapin en peluche en tchouch.* "I got this stuffed bunny as a freebie."

TDP, *m., abbr.* of **tour de poitrine.** Bust size. *Elle a donné son TDP dans son CV.* "She gave her bust size in her curriculum vitae."

TEBI/TÉBI = TEUBE.

TÉCÉ = TC.

TÉCI, *f.* City (backslang of **cité**). Low-rent housing development. *La drogue circule dans cette téci.* "Drugs are plentiful in this project."

TÉDÉPÉ = TDP.

TÉLÉ, *f., abbr.* of **télévision; téléviseur.** Television set; TV set. *Chez eux il y a une télé dans chaque pièce.* "They've got a TV in every room."

TÉLÉMUCHE, *m.* Telephone. *Elle passe son temps au télémuche.* "She spends her time on the telephone."

TÉLÉPHONE ARABE, *m.* Grapevine. *Par le téléphone arabe j'arrive à tout savoir.* "I get to know everything through the grapevine."

TÉLÉPHONER AU PAPE. To go to the can; to defecate. *Au Vatican, je devais téléphoner au pape mais impossible de trouver les chiottes!* "At the Vatican I had to shit but it was impossible to find the can."

TÉLÉPHONER DANS LE VENTRE. To fellate. *Après lui avoir téléphoné dans le ventre, elle avait de l'amour dans la boudine.* "After giving him head, she had love in her belly."

TÉLOCHE = TÉLÉ.

TENIR. To hold. **En tenir une couche; en tenir.** To really stupid. *Il en tient une couche; pas possible de discuter.* "He's as thick as a board; discussion is impossible."

TENIR LA JAMBE DE QN. To hold s.o. up by talking (lit. "to hold s.o.'s leg"). *Elle m'a tenu la jambe une heure.* "She buttonholed me for an hour."

TENIR LE BON BOUT. See BOUT.

TENIR LE COUP. To withstand. *Je craignais de ne pas pouvoir tenir le coup.* "I was afraid I wouldn't be able to stick it out."

(SE) TENIR À CARREAU. To watch one's step (from the Tarot cards). *Depuis sa dernière engueulade il se tient à carreau.* "Since his last chewing out he watches his step."

TÊTE, *f.* Head. **Être une tête,** *idiom.* To be brainy. *C'est une tête!* He's a brain! **Avoir la grosse tête,** *idiom.* To be swell-headed. *Depuis qu'il a hérité, il a la grosse tête.* "Since coming into money he's been on an ego trip." **Ça (ne) va pas la tête?** "Are you nuts?" **À la tête du client.** Depending on appearance. *Il fait son prix à la tête du client.* "He charges what the traffic will bear." See CASSE-TÊTE; CASSER/(SE) CASSER LA TÊTE; COUP DE TÊTE; (SE) CREUSER LA TÊTE.

TÊTE À CLAQUE, *m.,* police slang. Nighttime brothel customer. *Les keufs tenait ce tête à claque à l'œil.* "The cops kept an eye on the night owl brothel goer."

TÊTE À CLAQUES/À GIFLES, *f.* Repulsive face. *Ce mec a une tête à claques.* "That guy's got a mug that cries out for a whack in the mouth."

TÊTE DE COCHON/LARD/MULE, *f.* Stubborn person. *C'est une sacrée tête de lard; on ne peut pas raisonner avec lui.* "He's really pigheaded; there's no reasoning with him."

TÊTE DE NŒUD, *f.* Jackass. *Va te faire niquer, tête de nœud!* "Fuck off, asshole!"

(PAR) TÊTE DE PIPE, *f.* Per capita. *Le repas nous a coûté 300 FF par tête de pipe.* "The meal cost each one of us 300 francs."

TÉTER. To booze it up (lit. "to suck at"). *Il téte sans arrêt.* "He drinks like a fish, nonstop." **Va te faire téter!** Fuck/piss off!

TÊTU COMME UNE BOURRIQUE. See BOURRIQUE.

TEUBE/TEUBI, *m.,* backslang of **bite.** Penis. *Son petit teube le complexe.* "He's self-conscious about his little dick."

TEUCH, *m.,* drugs, backslang of **shit.** Hashish. *Ils ont toujours du teuch sur eux.* "They've always got hashish on them."

TEUCHE, *f.,* backslang of **chatte.** Female genitalia. *Sa teuche est toujours prête.* "Her beaver is always eager."

TEUF, *f.,* backslang of **fête.** Party. *Ils aiment faire la teuf.* "They like to party."

TEUF-TEUF, *m.* **1.** Choo-choo train (children's language). *On va prendre le teuf-teuf.* "We're going to take the choo-choo." **2.** Rattling old car. *Il sortait tout courbaturé de son teuf-teuf.* "He was stiff all over when he got out of his old heap."

TÉZIG(UE). You. *J'aimerais danser avec tézigue.* "I'd like to dance with you."

TGV, *abbr.* of **train grande vitesse** (high speed train). **1.** Prostitute who turns tricks quickly. *Ce soir Marc a du temps, pas de TGV pour lui.* "Mark's got time tonight, and doesn't want a quickie." **2.** Really fast horse. *Il a misé sur un TGV.* "He bet on a fast horse." **3.** Amphetamine; cocaine. *Il se bourre de TGV.* "He loads up on speed."

THÉ, *m.* Intoxicating drink (lit. "tea"). *Il marche au thé.* "He's an alcoholic." See PRENDRE LE THÉ.

THÉIÈRE, *f.* **1.** Head (lit. "teapot"). *Il n'a pas grand-chose dans la théière.* "He hasn't got much between the ears." **2.** Public urinal frequented by homosexuals (lit. "teapot"). *La tata trouvait la théière dégueu, mais y allait souvent quand même.* "The queen found the tearoom repulsive, but went there often anyway."

THUNE, *f.* Money (orig. a five-franc coin, then any coin, then money in general). *Je n'ai plus de thune.* "I don't have any more money."

THUNER. To beg. *Ça thune dans le métro!* "Lots of begging (goes on) in the subway!"

THURNE, *f.* Room; messy house. *Elle loue des thurnes à des étudiants.* "She rents rooms to students."

TICHE, *m.,* youth. T-shirt (from Eng.). *Elle vend des tiches dans la rue.* "She sells T-shirts on the street."

TICKET, *m.* Ticket. **Avoir un ticket avec qn.,** *idiom.* To make a hit with s.o. *Je crois avoir un ticket avec elle.* "I think she finds me attractive."

TICKSON/TICSON, *m.* Ticket. *Sans tickson, pas d'entrée.* "No tickee, no entry."

TIFS, *m., pl.* Hair. *Ses tifs ont à nouveau changé de couleur.* "Her hair's a different color again." See COUPE-TIFS.

TIFTIRE, *m.* Hairdresser. *Elle s'est fait tirer les tifs chez le tiftire.* "She had her hair done at the hairdresser's."

TIGE, *f.* **1.** Cigarette (lit. "stalk"). See GRILLER...TIGE. **2.** Penis. See BROUTER LA TIGE.

TILLEUL, *m.* Mix of red and white wine (lit. "linden"; often used in herb teas). *Merci, pas de tilleul, je les* *préfères sépararément.* "No thanks, I prefer red and white wine separately."

TIMBRÉ, -E. Crazy. *Il est timbré de rouler aussi vite.* "He's bonkers, driving that fast."

TINTIN! Nothing at all! No way!

(FAIRE) TINTIN. To have to do without. *Je voulais partir en vacances mais j'ai dû faire tintin.* "I wanted to leave on vacation but I had to give it up."

T'INQUIÈTE! from **ne t'inquiète pas.** "Don't sweat it!"

TIR, *m., abbr.* of **Transports Internationaux Routiers** (International Highway Shipments). Teamster who makes international trips. *Les tirs pensent faire la grève.* "The truckers are planning to strike."

TIRAGE, *m.* Friction. *Il y a du tirage dans leur couple.* "Things are strained in their relationship."

TIRE-AU-CUL/TIRE-AU-FLANC, *m.* S.o. who avoids work. *Ne compte pas sur lui; c'est un tire-au-flanc.* "Don't count on him; he's a lazy good-for-nothing."

TIRE-FESSES, *m.* Ski lift; ski tow. *Fais gaffe en prenant le tire-fesses.* "Be careful when you take the ski lift."

TIRE-GOSSE = TIRE-MÔME.

TIRE-JUS. Handkerchief; snot rag. *Il s'est branlé dans son tire-jus.* "He jerked off into his handkerchief."

(À) TIRE-LARIGOT. In quantity. *Il fume des clopes à tire-larigot.* "He smokes cigarettes like a chimney."

TIRE-MOELLE = TIRE JUS.

TIRE-MÔME, *m., f.* Obstetrician; midwife. *C'est une tire-môme contre les faiseuses d'anges.* "She's a midwife hostile to back alley abortionists."

TIRE-MORVE = TIRE JUS.

TIRER. 1. To endure (lit. "to pull; shoot"). *Il y a encore deux moix à tirer devant les vacances.* "Still two months to get through before vacation." **2.** To steal. *On m'a tiré ma bécane.* "Somebody swiped my bike."

TIRER AU FLANC. To shirk. *Ne tirez pas au flanc avant*

la fin du boulot. "No goldbricking before the job's done."

TIRER DANS LES JAMBES/PATTES DE QN. To make things difficult for s.o. *Cesse de me tirer dans les pattes.* "Quit giving me a hard time."

TIRER LA LANGUE. To be in need (such as financially) [lit. "to be panting"]. *Je tire la langue quand arrive le mois des impôts.* "I'm really strapped for money when it's tax-paying time."

TIRER LE PIED-DE-BICHE. To beg from house to house; sell from door to door. *C'est pas drôle, tirer le pied-de-biche quand il neige.* "It's no picnic, selling from door to door when it's snowing."

TIRER LES FICELLES. 1. To pull strings. *Il sait tirer les ficelles pour obtenir ce qu'il veut.* "He knows how to pull strings to get what he wants." **2.** To run the show. *C'est lui qui tire les ficelles.* "He's the power behind the scenes."

TIRER LES VERS DU NEZ. See VER.

TIRER SA CRAMPE/CRAMPETTE = TIRER SON COUP.

TIRER SA FLEMME. To be idle. *J'aime tirer ma flemme le week-end.* "I like lazing about on weekends."

TIRER SON PETIT COUP. To have a quickie. *Moi, je cherche la tendresse, mais la plupart des mecs ne pensent qu'à tirer leur petit coup.* "I want tenderness, but with most guys it's just 'wham, bam, thank you ma'am'."

TIRER SUR LA FICELLE. To stretch too far (lit. "to pull on the thread"). *S'il te plaît, ne tire pas sur la ficelle.* "Come on now, don't push it."

TIRER UN/SON COUP. To have sexually; shoot a load. *Il aime tirer son coup avant de dormir.* "He likes to get his rocks off before going to sleep."

(SE) TIRER. To clear out. *J'ai hâte de me tirer d'ici.* "I'm in a hurry to get out of here."

(SE) TIRER DES ADJAS. See ADJA.

(SE) TIRER LA BOURRE/DES BOURRES. To compete

fiercely. *Les lutteurs se tiraient la bourre.* "The wrestlers really battled it out."

TIREUR, *m.* Pickpocket (lit. "marksman"). *C'est un habile tireur.* "He's a skillful pickpocket."

TISANE, *f.* Fuel (lit. "herb tea"). *Ma meule bouffe beaucoup de tisane.* "My motorbike's a gas eater."

TITI, *m.* Brash or resourceful kid. *Le titi parisien ne se plaisait pas à la cambrousse.* "The Paris urchin didn't like it in the country."

TITILLER LE ZYGOMATIQUE. See ZYGOMATIQUE.

TOC, *m.* Trashy, fake material. *C'est du toc.* "It's junk."

TOCANTE, *f.* Watch. *Ta tocante retarde.* "Your watch is slow."

TOCARD, -E. Cheap; tinselly; shoddy. *Il a des goûts tocards.* "He has trashy taste."

TOCCIN = TOQUANT.

T'OCCUPE! See OCCUPE.

TÔLARD = TAULARD.

TÔLE = TAULE.

TOMATES, *f., pl.* Tomatoes. **Avoir ses tomates,** *idiom.* To have one's period. *J'avais mes tomates, mes j'ai quand même bien nagé.* "I was having my period but I swam well anyway."

TOMBEAU, *m.* Tomb. **À tombeau ouvert.** At breakneck speed. *Elle skie à tombeau ouvert.* "She skies at breakneck speed."

TOMBER. To fall. **Laisse tomber!** "Forget it!"

TOMBER À L'EAU/DANS LE LAC. To go down the drain. *Nos beaux projets sont tombés dans le lac.* "Our splendid plans went down the drain."

TOMBER DANS LES POMMES. See POMME **1.**

TOMBER EN BOTTE(S)/COUILLE(S) = PARTIR EN COUILLE(S).

TOMBER EN CARAFE. To break down. *Je suis tombé en*

carafe en pleine nuit. "My car broke down in the middle of the night."

TOMBER FAIBLE = TOMBER DANS LES POMMES.

TOMBER SUR UN BEC/OS. To hit a snag. *Je suis tombée sur un bec et j'ai pris du retard.* "I ran into a hitch and was delayed."

TOMBEUR, *m.* Seducer. *C'est un tombeur—méfie-toi!* "He's a Don Juan—be careful!"

TONDU, *m.* S.o. with close-cropped hair. See TROIS... TONDU.

TONORGUE = TÉZIG(UE).

TONTON, *m.* Police informer (lit. "uncle"). *Le tonton les a dénoncés.* "The informer snitched on them."

TOPO, *m.* Report; short talk. *Elle a bien travaillé son topo.* "She worked up a nice report." **C'est toujours le même topo.** "It's always the same old story/spiel."

TOQUANT, *m.* Heart. *Mon toquant fait tic-tac pour toi.* "My ticker ticks for you."

TOQUANTE = TOCANTE.

TOQUARD = TOCARD.

TOQUÉ, -E. 1. Slightly crazy. *Ton pépé est toqué.* "Your grandpa's a bit cracked." **2.** Smitten. *Il est vraiment toqué d'elle.* "He's really infatuated with her."

TORCHE = TORCHÉE.

TORCHE-CUL, *m.* **1.** Toilet paper (lit. "ass wiper"). *Prends-moi du torche-cul triple épaisseur.* "Get me triple-ply toilet paper." **2.** Low-end newspaper. *Tu lis ce torche-cul?* "You read that rag?"

TORCHÉE, *f.* Beating. *Il a reçu une sacrée torchée.* "He was thoroughly beaten up."

TORCHER. To dash off (lit. "to wipe"). *Bravo, tu as bien torché ta lettre!* "Congrats, you knocked off your letter quickly and well."

(SE) TORCHER. To wipe o.s. **Se torcher (le cul) de qch.,**

idiom. To not give a damn. *Tous tes projets, je m'en torche!* "I don't give a shit about all your projects."

TORCHON, *m.* Theater curtain (lit. "cloth"). *Elle a eu beaucoup de levers de torchon aux rappels.* "She got many curtain calls after the performance."

TORCHONNER = TORCHER.

TORDANT, -E. Hilarious. *Elle est tordante dans ce sketch.* "She's a scream in that sketch."

TORD-BOYAUX, *m.* Rotgut alcohol. *Assez de ton tord-boyaux de fine!* "That's enough of your rotgut brandy."

(SE) TORDRE LES BOYAUX (DE RIRE)/SE TORDRE DE RIRE = (SE) BOYAUTER.

TOSCH = TEUCH.

TOSSER. To get high. *Il tossait dur.* "He was really high."

TOTOCHES = DOUDOUNES.

TOUBIB, *m.* Doctor (from Ar. **tbib**). *Son toubib va à domicile.* "Her doctor makes house calls."

TOUCHE, *m.* Key (on keyboard). **Faire une touche,** *idiom.* To make a hit with s.o. *Elle a fait une touche avec le facteur.* "She and the postman have hit it off." See SAINTE TOUCHE.

TOUCHE-PIPI. See JOUER À TOUCHE-PIPI.

(SE) TOUCHER. To masturbate. *Le curé demandait s'ils se touchaient.* "The priest kept asking them if they played with themselves."

TOUFFE, *f.* **1.** Female pubic hair (lit. "tuft"). *Elle se rase la touffe.* "She shaves her box." See RAS LA TOUFFE. **2.** Puff on a cigarette. *Passe-la moi pour tirer une touffe.* "Let me have a little drag on your cigarette."

TOUPET, *m.* Impudence. *Quel toupet!* "What nerve/gall/chutzpah."

TOURNER AUTOUR DU POT. To beat about the bush. *Cesse de tourner autour du pot et accouche!* "Quit beating about the bush and spit it out!"

TOURNER DE L'ŒIL. To faint. *Attendre longtemps*

debout la fait tourner de l'œil. "She passes out if she has to wait on her feet for a long time."

TOURNÉE DES GRANDS-DUCS, *f.* Night on the town. *On s'est payé la tournée des grands-ducs pour nos noces d'or.* "We treated ourselves to a night on the town for our golden wedding anniversary."

TOURNER EN ROND. To go around in circles. *Depuis longtemps l'affaire tourne en rond.* "There's been no progress on the deal for some time."

TOURNER LA PAGE. 1. To put an end to s.t. *Je ne veux plus le voir; j'ai tourné la page.* "I don't want to see him anymore; I've closed the book on him." **2.** To turn over for vaginal or anal penetration. *Elle avait ses règles et on a tourné la page.* "She had her period so I turned her over for sex."

TOURNER ROND. To run smoothly. *Enfin ça tourne rond au bureau.* "Finally, things are going right at the office." **Ne pas tourner rond.** To be a bit cracked. *Mes vioques ne tournent pas rond.* "My parents are a little nuts."

TOUS AZIMUTS. See AZIMUT.

TOUS LES TRENTE-SIX DU MOIS. Once in a month of Sundays. *Mon fils ne vient me voir que tous les trente-six du mois.* "My son practically never comes to see me."

(À) TOUT CASSER. See CASSER.

TOUT DE GO. Right away. *Elle a dit oui tout de go.* "She said yes right away."

(ET) TOUT LE BASTRINGUE/BATACLAN/FOUR-BI/SAINT-FRUSQUIN/TRALALA; TREMBLEMENT. See BATACLAN; FOURBI; SAINT-FRUSQUIN; TOUTIM **2**; TRALALA; TREMBLEMENT.

(À) TOUTE BARRE/BITURE. At full speed. *Le capitaine du* Titanic *a donné l'ordre d'avancer à toute barre.* "The captain of the *Titanic* gave the order to advance at full speed."

TOUTIM. 1. Short TV newscast on which an announcer is heard but not seen (from **toute-image**). *J'ai juste le* *temps de regarder les toutims.* "All I have time to watch are news briefs." **2. Tout le toutim.** The whole bunch. *Dans son camping-car il y a cousins, belles-doches, et tout le toutim.* "In his camper he's got his cousins, mothers-in-law, the whole kit and caboodle."

TOUTOU, *m.* **1.** Doggie. **Filer comme un toutou,** *idiom.* To be easily led. *Elle n'est pas du genre à filer comme un toutou.* "She's not the sort who can be dictated to." See (À LA) PEAU...TOUTOU. **2.** Prostitute (Fr. African). *Les toutous attendaient au bar.* "The prostitutes were waiting at the bar."

TOUZEPAR, *f.,* backslang of **partouze.** Orgy. *La touzepar l'a fatigué.* "The orgy tired him out."

TOXICO, *m., f., abbr.* of **toxicomane.** Drug addict. *Je ne savais pas qu'il était toxico.* "I didn't know he was a junkie."

TOXIPUTE, *m., f.* Drug-addicted prostitute. *La toxipute faisait du yoyo pour racler du fric.* "The junkie whore turned lots of tricks to get money."

TRADALLE = TRADUC.

TRADUC, *f., abbr. of* **traduction.** *Fais-moi la traduc de ton jargon.* "Translate your slang for me."

TRAFALGAR. See COUP DE TRAFALGAR.

TRAIN. Backside (lit. "train"). **Se magner/manier le train,** *idiom.* To get a move on. *Magne-toi le train, sinon tu loupes le bus.* "Move your butt or you'll miss the bus." See COLLER AU TRAIN.

TRAÎNER SES GROLLES. To go; frequent. *Où as tu encore traîné tes grolles pour être en retard?* "Where've you been hanging/gallivanting around so that you're late again?"

TRAITER QN. PAR-DESSOUS/PAR-DESSUS LA JAMBE. To treat s.o. in a shabby or offhanded manner. *Au boulot c'est stressant d'être traité par-dessus la jambe.* "It's stressful, being treated like a fifth wheel at work."

TRALALA, *m.* Frills; fuss. *Ils se sont mariés sans tralala.* "They had a simple wedding." **Et tout le tralala.** And all the rest. *Il me dit qu'il m'adore et tout le tralala.* "He tells me he adores me, and so on and so forth."

TRANCHE, *f.* Slice. **S'en payer une tranche,** *idiom.* To have a great time. *Eh dis, tu t'en es payé une tranche ce soir!* "Well, you're really having a ball tonight." See (S'EN) PAYER UNE TRANCHE.

TRANS, *m., f., abbr.* of **transsexuel, -elle** (transsexual). *C'est une boîte frequentée par des trans.* "Transsexuals hang out in that night club."

TRAV = TRAVELO.

TRAVAILLER DU CHAPEAU/CHOU. To be a bit cracked. *Tu dis que ton tonton travaille de sa tête —moi, je dis qu'il travaille du chapeau!* "You say your uncle works with his head—I say he's off his rocker."

TRAVAILLER EN ARTISTE. To do a sloppy job. *Mon mari travaille en artiste quand il essaie de réparer la plomberie.* "My husband makes a mess when he tries to repair the plumbing."

TRAVELO, *m.* Transvestite. *Vise la robe du travelo!* "Get a load of the drag queen's dress!"

(DE) TRAVIOLE. Lopsided. *Il marchait tout de traviole.* "He walked leaning to one side."

TRÈFLE/AS DE TRÈFLE. Posterior (lit. "clubs; ace of clubs"). *Il se grattait l'as de trèfle.* "He scratched his ass."

TREMBLEMENT, *m.* Trembling. **Et tout le tremblement.** The whole kit and caboodle. *Ils ont vidé le grenier, la cave et tout le tremblement.* "They emptied out the attic, cellar, the whole works."

TREMPE, *f.* Beating. *Il a reçu une bonne trempe.* "He got a real walloping." See FILER UNE TREMPE.

TREMPER SON BAIGNEUR/BISCUIT = TREMPER SON PANAIS.

TREMPER SON PANAIS. To have sexually (lit. "to dip one's parsnip"). See PANAIS.

TRENTE ET UN. Thirty one. **Se mettre sur son trente et un,** *idiom.* To get all dressed up. *Elle s'est mise sur son trente et un pour voir son jules.* "She dressed to kill to see her boyfriend."

TRENTE-SIXIÈME. Thirty sixth. **Être dans le trente-six-ième dessous,** *idiom.* To be depressed; be at rock bottom financially. *Elle était dans le trente-sixième dessous après l'accident.* "She was really down after the accident."

TRIFOUILLER. To rummage around. *J'ai horreur que tu trifouilles dans mes papiers.* "I can't stand your messing around in my papers."

(SE) TRIMBALLER. To cart or drag around. *Je me trimballais toute la marmaille chaque dimanche.* "I had that bunch of kids on my neck every Sunday."

TRINGLE, *f.* Curtain rod. **Avoir la tringle,** *idiom.* To have or get an erection. *Il avait la tringle en visant du porno.* "He got a hard-on when looking at porn."

TRINGLER. To copulate. *Il l'a tringlée vite fait.* "He gave her a fast fuck."

TRINGLETTE, *f.* Nice little screw. *Une petite tringlette de temps en temps, ça fait du bien.* "A nice little screw now and then does you good."

TRINQUER. To take the rap (lit. "to clink glasses"). *Avec les flics c'est toujours les beurs qui trinquent.* "It's always the young Arabs who get the worst of it from the cops."

TRIQUE, *f.* Cudgel. **Avoir la trique,** *idiom.* To have an erection. *Il avait la trique en regardant les stripteaseuses.* "He got hard when looking at the strippers."

TRIQUETTE, *f.* Semierection. *Les sex-shops lui donnaient la triquette.* "The sex shops gave him a semierection."

TROGNE, *f.* Face, often *pej.* *"Quand je vois rougir ma trogne, je suis fier d'être Bourguignon,"* chante Papa. "'When I see my mug turn red (from drinking wine), I'm proud to be from Burgundy,' sings Dad."

TROIS PELÉS ET UN TONDU. Small/sparse audience

(lit. "three peeled persons, and one shorn one"—the idea is sparse, as hair). *C'est dommage, il n'y avait que trois pelés et un tondu au concert.* "It's too bad there was only a handful at the concert."

TROIS PIÈCES. See SERVICE TROIS PIÈCES.

TROM'/TROMÉ, *m.,* youth. Subway (backslang of **métro**). *Le dernier trom' est à minuit.* "The last subway's at midnight."

TRONCHE, *f., pej.* Face. **Faire la tronche,** *idiom.* To sulk. *Ne fais pas cette tronche.* "Don't pull a sour puss like that." See (SE) GRIFFER.

TRONCHE À CHIER DESSUS = GUEULE À CHIER DESSUS.

TRÔNER, youth. To astonish (lit. "to sit enthroned"). *Il m'a trônée en me montrant ses tatouages.* "He knocked me for a loop when he showed me his tattoos."

TROTTOIR, *m.* Sidewalk. **Faire le trottoir,** *idiom.* To solicit for prostitution. *Elle préfère faire le trottoir même en hiver.* "She prefers streetwalking even in the winter."

TROU, *m.* Hole. **Boire comme un trou,** *idiom.* To drink like a fish. *Il a bu comme un trou à la noce.* "He drank like a fish at the wedding."

TROU DE BALLE (lit. "gunshot hole") = **TROU DU CUL.**

TROU DE BITE/PINE. See YEUX EN....

TROU DU CUL, *m.* Asshole (lit. and fig., by metonymy [part for the whole], in this case "asshole," for the whole person). *Lui et ses copains, ce sont tous des trous du cul!* "He and his friends are all assholes." See SAINT...CUL.

TROUF/TROUFIGNARD/TROUFIGNON = TROU DU CUL.

TROUFION, *m.* Fool (lit. "private soldier"). *Ce ne sont que des troufions.* "They're all a bunch of assholes."

TROUILLARD, -E. Cowardly. *Ses copains le jugeaient trouillard.* "His friends thought him chicken."

TROUILLE, *m.* Fear. **Avoir la trouille,** *idiom.* To be afraid. *Elle a la trouille d'être attaquée la nuit.* "She's afraid of being attacked at night." See FOUTRE À LA PORTE.

TROUILLOMÈTRE, *m.* Fear indicator (hum. coinage. Cf. CONOMÈTRE; PIFOMÈTRE). **Avoir le trouillomètre à zéro,** *idiom.* To be scared stiff. *Quand j'ai vu les casseurs, j'avais le trouillomètre à zéro.* "When I saw the burglars I was scared stiff."

TROUS DE NEZ. See SORTIR…TROUS.

TROUSSER. To have intercourse quickly (lit. "to truss"). *Il l'a troussée sur l'herbe.* "He got it off with her on the grass."

TRUAND, *m.* Mobster. *Ces ados sont déjà de petits truands.* "Those adolescents are already little gangsters."

TRUANDER. To swindle. *Ils se sont fait truander.* "They got swindled."

TRUC, *m.* **1.** Whatsit. *D'où sors-tu ce truc?* "Where'd you get that thing?" **2.** Thing. *La boxe, c'est pas mon truc.* "Boxing isn't my thing." See CHACUN.

TRUCMUCHE, *m.* Unidentified person or thing. *Tu as fourré ton trucmuche dans la sac de Trucmuche.* "You put that thingamajig in what's-his-name's bag."

TRUQUEUR, *m.* Phony prostitute who takes money but doesn't render services. *L'étranger a été truandé par un truqueur.* "The foreigner was tricked by a phony prostitute."

TTBM = **TBM** with an extra **très.**

TUBAR, *m.* Connection. *C'est un boursier qui a de bons tubars.* "He's a stock market trader with good connections."

TUBARD, -E, *m., f.* Consumptive. *Ici c'est pas un climat pour tubards.* "This is no climate for TB sufferers."

TUBE, *m.* Great success. *Cette chanson fera un tube.* "That song'll be a big hit." See (À) PLEINS TUBES.

TUER LE VER. To have a wake-up snorter (lit. "to kill the worm"). *Sa journée commence en tuant le ver.* "His day starts with a shot of alcohol."

TUILE, *f.* Unexpected hard luck (lit. "tile," or one that drops on your head). *Quelle tuile!* "What a bummer."

TUNE = THUNE.

TUNER = THUNER.

TURBIN, *m.* Daily grind. *C'est un vache de turbin!* "This is one rotten job!"

TURBINER. To slave at a job. *Je turbine toute la journée.* "I slave away all day."

TURLUPINER. To bother. *Les gosses me turlupinent sans cesse.* "The kids bug me constantly."

TURLUT(T)E, *f.* Fellatio (lit. "fishing rod," with probable influence of **turlurette** [small flute]). *Mon prix ne comprend pas la turlute.* "My price doesn't include a blow job."

TURLUTER. To fellate (lit. "to tootle the flute"). *Laisse toutes ces histoires et viens me turluter.* "Forget all those stories and come blow me."

TURNE = THURNE.

TUTU = TOUTOU 2.

TYPE, *m.* Guy. *Que penses-tu de ce type-là?* "What do you think of that guy?"

TYPESSE, *f., pej.* Female. *Je ne peux pas la blairer, cette typesse.* "I can't stand that broad."

-UCHE. Slang suffix that imparts a sense of familiarity; for example, **galuche** = **Gauloise** (cigarette)**; loilpuche = à poil; Pantruche = Paris; paluche = patte.**

UNE, *f.* Front page (newspaper). *Ce scandale a fait la une.* "That scandal was front page news."

UNIF, *m.,* from **uniforme.** *Oui, il est beau en unif, mais même plus beau à poil.* "Yes he's handsome in uniform, but even more handsome in the all-together."

UNITÉ, *f.* 10,000 francs. *Son ardoise était de deux unités.* "He owed 20,000 francs."

UPER, youth. To stink (backslang of **puer**). *Ça upe!* "That stinks."

USINER. 1. To work long and hard (from **usine,** "factory"). *Elle usine chaque jour au zinc.* "She slaves away at the bar every day." **2.** To engage in sex. *Ne les dérange pas— ils usinent toujours.* "Don't disturb them—they're still screwing."

UTILITÉ, *f.* Theater. Minor part; small part (lit. "usefulness"). **Jouer les utilités.** To play bit parts; play second fiddle. *Avant de devenir une star, je jouais les utilités et bien sûr, je les ai jouées à merveille.* "Before becoming a star, I played minor parts and of course I played them perfectly."

VACANCES, *f., pl.,* drugs. Withdrawal time (lit. "vacation"). *L'accro a pris deux semaines de vacances.* "The junkie was clean for two weeks."

VACANT. Flat broke (lit. "vacant"). *À Las Vegas on était vacant.* "We were flat broke in Las Vegas."

VACCINÉ, -E. Impervious (lit. "vaccinated"). *Cesse tes lamentations; je suis vaccinée.* "Quit your groaning; I've heard it before."

VACCINÉ AU SALPÊTRE. Habitual drinker (lit. "vaccinated with saltpeter"). Saltpeter, according to boys' boarding school legend, is allegedly administered to institutional food to discourage "horniness." The connection to alcohol may lie in the fact that alcohol is said to increase sexual desire but diminishes performance. *Vise un peu tous les vaccinés au salpêtre autour du zinc.* "Take a look at all the habitual drinkers around the bar."

VACCINÉ AU VINAIGRE (lit. "vaccinated with vinegar"). In a bad mood. *Il se lève toujours vacciné au vinaigre.* "He's always got a sour puss when he gets up."

VACHE, *adj.* Nasty. *Il a un côté vache, ce type là.* "That guy's got a mean streak."

VACHE, *f.* Cow. **Ah, la vache! 1.** That's incredible! (astonishment; admiration) *Ah, la vache! Notre équipe a gagné!* "Mind-blowing! Our team won!" **2.** Damn it! *(Ah) la vache, il a piqué ma bécane!* "Damn it, he's made off

with my bike." See COUP…VACHE; PEAU DE VACHE; PLEU-
VOIR…PISSE.

VACHEMENT. Extremely. *Non seulement elle baise vachement bien mais elle est vachement intelligente.* "She's not only a terrific lay, but she's also super intelligent."

VACHERIE, *f.* Nasty comment or deed. *Non seulement il me balance des vacheries, mais il m'en fait.* "Not only does he bad-mouth me, he also plays dirty tricks on me."

VACHETEMENT = VACHEMENT.

(À LA) VA-COMME-JE-TE-POUSSE. Any old way (lit. "like this is how I give you a little shove"). *Il a fait le boulot à la va-comme-je-te-pousse.* "He did a really sloppy job."

VACS, *f., pl.,* from **vacances.** Vacation. *Que de la flotte pendant les vacs.* "All it did was pour during our vacation."

VAGUE, *f.* Pocket (lit. "wave"). *Cherche de la monnaie dans tes vagues.* "Look for some change in your pockets."

VAGUER. 1. To go through s.o.'s pockets. *La police l'a vagué.* "The police frisked him." **2.** To wander; bum around. *Il vague dans la zone.* "He wanders around the shanty town."

(SE) VAGUER. To fumble in one's pockets. *Il se vaguait sans trouver sa carte d'identité.* "He fumbled in his pockets without finding his ID."

VALDINGUER. To fall down. **Envoyer valdinguer.** To throw out; send packing. *J'ai tout envoyé valdinguer, lui et tout son foutoir.* "I threw him and all his junk out."

VALEUR, *f.* Value. **Valeur à la casse.** Scrap value. *Ce paumé? C'est une valeur à la casse.* "That bum? He's ready for skid row."

VALOIR UN PET DE LAPIN. See PET.

VALSE-HÉSITATION, *f.* Shilly-shallying. *Tu ne sais danser que la valse-hésitation. Tu viens, oui ou merde?* "All you can do is dilly-dally. Are you coming, yes or no?"

VALSEUR, *m.* Ass (lit. "waltzer"). *Son valseur est bien moulé dans sa robe.* "Her fanny is shapely in that dress." **Filer; onduler du valseur.** To wiggle one's bottom; mince (homosexual). *Tâche de moins onduler du valseur!* "Try not to shake your ass so much."

VALSEUSES, *f., pl.* Testicles (lit. "waltzers"). *Elle lui a foutu un coup dans les valseuses.* "She hit him in the balls."

VANNE, *f.* Sluice gate. **Balancer; envoyer une vanne; des vannes à qn.** To take verbal swipes at s.o; lash out at. *Il ne sait que balancer des vannes.* "All he can do is dump on people." (The idea is to let s.o. have it, like the sudden rush of water when a sluice gate is opened.)

VANNÉ, -E. Tired out (lit. "winnowed"). *En fin de journée on était tous vannés.* "At the end of the day we were all bushed."

VANTERNE, *f.* Window. *Les vanternes sont de nouveau sales.* "The windows are dirty again."

VAPÉ, -E. Zonked; smashed. *Après l'accident, j'étais vapée.* "I was in a daze after the accident."

VAPES, *f., pl.,* from **vapeur** (vapor; steam). **Être dans les vapes,** *idiom.* To be dead to the world. *Avec tout cet alcool il sera demain dans les vapes.* "With all that alcohol, he'll be dead to the world tomorrow." Note: This expression, and the preceding one, are not arch or genteel, in the manner of vapid Victorian ladies who frequently had "the vapors," or "felt faint."

VAPEUR. See VOILE.

VASELINER. To flatter (lit. "to apply vaseline"). *Il sait vaseliner ses supérieurs quand il le faut.* "He knows how to butter up the bosses when necessary."

VASER. To rain. *Ça a vasé toute la journée.* "It's been pouring all day."

VASEUX, -EUSE. Woozy; hazy (lit. "muddy"). *Après cette bringue, nous étions tous vaseux.* "After that bash, we were all woozy."

VASOUILLARD, -E. Wishy-washy; unclear. *Ses explications sont vasouillardes.* "His explanations are as clear as mud."

VÉCÉS, *m., pl.* = **WC.**

VEILLE, *f.* The day before. **C'est pas demain la veille** (lit. "tomorrow isn't the day before [s.t. will happen]"). That won't happen for a long time. *C'est pas demain la veille qu'on lui fera à nouveau confiance.* "Don't hold your breath waiting for us to trust him again."

VEINARD, -E. *m., f.* Lucky person. *Quel veinard! Il a décroché le job.* "What a lucky devil! He got the job."

VEINE, *f.* Luck (lit. "vein"). **Avoir de la veine,** *idiom.* *Elle n'a pas de veine avec sa bagnole toujours en panne.* "She's had no luck with her car that keeps breaking down." See COUP DE BOL/VEINE. CF. DÉVEINE.

VENDRE DE L'AIL. To be a lesbian. See AIL.

VENIN, *m.* Venom. **Cracher; filer; jeter; lâcher son venin** (lit. "to spit; hurl; leave one's venom"). To ejaculate. *Il a craché son venin et m'a quitté.* "He got his rocks off and left me."

VENIR. To come. **Voir venir qn. (avec ses gros sabots)** (lit. "to see s.o. coming [in their clodhoppers]"). To see what s.o. is getting at. *Je te vois venir! Tu veux du fric.* "I know what you're driving at. You want money."

VENT, *m.* Wind. **Avoir du vent dans les voiles** (lit. "to have wind in one's sails"). To be drunk. *Les pompons rouges avaient du vent dans les voiles.* "The (Fr.) sailors were three sheets to the wind." **Être dans le vent,** *idiom.* To be fashionable (lit. "to be in the wind; air current, or **au courant**). *Elle est toujours dans le vent malgré son grand âge.* "She's always up-to-date despite her advanced years."

VENTRE, *m.* Abdomen. See TÉLÉPHONER…VENTRE.

VÉNUS. Venus. **Recevoir un coup de pied de Vénus.** To get VD (lit. "to get kicked by Venus"). *Malgré la capote, il a reçu un coup de pied de Vénus.* "Despite the rubber, he caught a dose of the clap."

VER, *m.* Worm. **Tirer les vers du nez à qn.,** *idiom.* To worm s.t. out of s.o. *Les flics lui ont tiré les vers du nez et il a enfin avoué.* "The cops finally wormed a confession out of him." See (PAS) PIQUÉ...; TUER LE VER.

VERDURE, *f.* **1.** Greenery. **Faire de la verdure,** *idiom.* To look for sex; offer sex for sale in a park. *En été j'aime faire de la verdure.* "In the summer I enjoy soliciting in parks." **2.** Freshness; vigor. *Grand-dab a 80 piges mais la joie et la verdeur le caractérisent toujours.* "Grandpa is 80 but he's still joyous and vigorous."

VERJO = VERNI.

VERLAN (backslang of **l'envers**), *m.* Backslang, created by reversing or rearranging letters or syllables. Letters can be dropped or added, as in **barjo(t)/bargeot** (crazy) for **jobard** (crazy; gullible), **narca** from **canard** (newspaper).

VERNI, -E. Lucky (lit. "varnished; glazed"). *Qu'il est verni! Il a pu vendre son tas de ferraille.* "What a lucky devil! He was able to sell his old wreck of a car."

VERRE, *m.* Drink (lit. "glass"). **Prendre un verre,** *idiom.* To have a drink. *Avant le train on a pris un verre, vite fait.* "Before the train we had a quick snort." **Avoir un verre dans le nez,** *idiom.* To be drunk. *On ne peut pas l'approcher quand il a un verre dans le nez.* "There's no going near him when he's plastered." See SIFFLER UN VERRE.

VERT, -E. Green. See LANGUE VERTE.

VERSAILLES. See OUVRIR...VERSAILLES.

VERSIGO = VERSAILLES.

VERT, -E. Slangy (lit. "green"). See LANGUE VERTE.

VESSE, *f.* Silent, foul-smelling fart. *Il accusait le chien d'avoir lâché une vesse.* "He alleged the dog cracked the sneaky, stinky fart."

VESSER. To fart. **Vesser du bec,** *idiom.* To have bad breath. *Va voir le dentiste; tu vesses du bec.* "Go see the dentist; your breath stinks."

VESSIE, *f.* Bladder. **Prendre des vessies pour des**

lanternes, *idiom.* To be very gullible and make blunders. *Ce n'est pas la première fois qu'il prend des vessies pour des lanternes.* "It's not the first time he's been sold the Brooklyn Bridge."

VÉTÉTEUX, *m.* Avid mountain biker. *Ils font partie d'une équipe de vététeux.* "They belong to a team of mountain biking fans."

VÉTO, *m.* Veterinary. *Le véto a vacciné le chien contre la rage.* "The vet vaccinated the dog against rabies."

VEUVE, *f.* Widow. **Aller chez la Veuve Poignet,** *idiom.* To visit Mme. Palm and her five daughters (lit. "to visit the Widow Wrist"). Masturbate. *Il est allé chez la Veuve Poignet car elle le repoussait.* "He jerked off because she rejected him."

VIANDE, *f.* Meat. **Viande à pneus.** Reckless pedestrian (lit. "meat for tires"). *Fais gaffe aux viandes à pneus—tu conduis trop vite.* "Watch out for reckless pedestrians—you're driving too fast."

VICELARD, -E. *m., f.* Depraved individual. *Je me méfie de lui—c'est un vicelard.* "I don't trust him—he's a dirty old man."

VICE-VERSAILLES, *joc.* variation on **vice versa.** Reciprocally. *On s'est branlé, vice-versailles.* "We engaged in mutual masturbation."

VIDÉ, -E. Exhausted (lit. "emptied"). *Après tant de nuits blanches, je suis vidée.* "After so many sleepless nights, I'm all played out."

VIDER. 1. To fire (lit. "to empty"). *Son patron l'a vidée.* "Her boss fired her." **2.** To throw out. *Il cherche la bagarre et se fait vider de tous les bars.* "He looks for trouble and gets thrown out of all the bars."

VIDER LES BURETTES. See BURETTES.

VIDER SON SAC. See SAC.

VIDEUR, *m.* Bouncer. *Parce qu'il est balèse on l'a pris comme videur.* "Because he's beefy they hired him as a bouncer."

VIEILLE CHAUSSETTE, *f.* Old sock. See LAISSER... CHAUSSETTE; RETOURNER...CHAUSSETTE.

VIEUX, *m., pl.* Parents (lit. "old people"). *Mes vieux ne me comprennent pas.* "My parents don't understand me."

VIF, *m.* The quick. **Couper; tailler; trancher dans le vif.** To take decisive action (lit. "to cut to the quick"). *Finies les valses-hésitations; il faut trancher dans le vif.* "That's enough shilly-shallying; we've got to come on strong now." See SUR LE VIF.

VIF-ARGENT, *m.* Quicksilver. *Ton pote, c'est du vif-argent.* "Your buddy's a real live wire."

VINAIGRE, *m.* Vinegar. **Faire vinaigre,** *idiom.* To hurry up. *Fais vinaigre ou tu seras en retard!* "Get a move on or you'll be late." See VACCINÉ AU VINAIGRE.

VINASSE, *f.* Poor wine. *Ton grand cru, c'est de la vinasse.* "Your fine vintage wine is lousy."

VINGT-DEUX. Twenty-two. **Vingt-deux, v'la les flics!** "Watch out, here come the cops!"

VIOC = VIOQUE.

VIOLETTE, *f.* Tip; little extra (lit. "violet"). *Le serveur s'attendait à une violette.* "The waiter expected a tip." See DOIGTS DE PIEDS.

VIOLON, *m.* **1.** Violin. **Violon d'Ingres.** Artistic hobby. *Son violon d'Ingres, c'est la peinture.* "He's a Sunday painter." See PISSER...VIOLON. **2.** Jail. *Pris dans la manif, il a passé la nuit au violon.* "He was arrested during the demonstration and spent the night in the slammer."

VIOQUE, *m., f.* Old person; mother; father. *Il est de dab breton et de vioque parisienne.* "His father's a Breton, his mother a Parisian."

VIOQUES, *m., pl.* Parents. *Elle prend grand soin de ses vioques.* "She takes good care of her parents."

VIPÈRE, *f.* Viper. **Vipère brousailleuse** (lit. "snake in the underbrush"). Penis. *Il lui courait après, la vipère brousailleuse à la main.* "He ran after her, holding his tool."

VIRÉE, *f.* **1.** Jaunt. *Elles font une petite virée au parc.* "They're on a little outing in the park." **2.** Barhop. *Les marins partaient en virée.* "The sailors went barhopping."

VIRER. To expel (lit. "to turn"). *Il s'est fait virer de tous les bahuts de la ville.* "He's been expelled from every school in town."

VISER. To look at (lit. "to aim at"). *Vise un peu la bath moto.* "Take a look at that cool (motor)bike."

VISU, *m.* Meeting; eyeballing. *Il faut qu'on fasse un visu.* "We've got to get a look at each other."

VITAMINE, *f.* Dope. **Vitamine A.** Acid; LSD. **Vitamine C.** Cocaine. **Vitamine E.** Ecstasy. *Il prenait des vitamines jusqu'à l'OD.* "He took lots of drugs until he OD'd."

VITE FAIT. In no time at all. *Avant le boulot elle prépare le déj vite fait.* "Before work she gets breakfast ready in a jiffy." **Tirer un coup vite fait,** *idiom.* To have a quickie (sexual). *Après avoir pris un pot vite fait, on a tiré un coup vite fait.* "After a quick snort, we had a quickie."

VITE FAIT, BIEN FAIT = preceding entry, but indicates that swift action was also smooth action.

VIVANT, *m.,* race track. Favorite (lit. "living being; live one"). *Il regrette d'avoir misé sur le vivant.* "He's sorry he bet on the favorite."

VIVRE À LA COLLE. To live together (**colle** = "glue; paste"). *Ils ont vécu à la colle dix ans avant de se marier.* "They shacked up together for ten years before getting married."

VOILE, *f.* Sail. **Être; aller; marcher à voile et à vapeur,** *idioms.* To be bisexual (the idea is to be both a "sailing ship" and a "steamship"). *Elle ne fréquente que les mecs qui marchent à voile et à vapeur.* "She dates only guys who swing both ways." See VENT.

VOIR LA FEUILLE À L'ENVERS. See FEUILLE.

VOIR LES ANGES. To have an orgasm (lit. "to see the angels"). *Pour plaire à mon mari, je fais souvent sem-*

blant de voir les anges. "To please my husband, I often pretend to have an orgasm."

VOITURE-BALAI, *f.* Last train; bus (lit. "broom vehicle," or one that "sweeps up" the latecomers). *Pour coucher avec moi tu as loupé exprès la voiture-balai.* "You missed the last bus deliberately so you could sleep with me."

VOIX IN, *f.,* movies. Voice and visual presence on screen. *Je préfère les toutims aux nouvelles voix in.* "I prefer to see the news without the news reporters."

VOIX OFF, *f.,* movies. Voice-over; off-screen voice. *Les grandes stars font souvent des spots publicitaires voix off.* "The big stars often make commercials in which they're heard, not seen."

VOL À L'ABORDAGE/À L'ARRACHÉ. Drive- or pass-by crime; mugging. *Il y a des vols à l'arraché sur les Bvds. de Paris.* "Purses get snatched on Paris boulevards."

VOLAILLE, *f.* 1. Girl, esp. bar girl (lit. "poultry"). *Les étrangers cherchent la volaille de Pigalle.* "Foreigners seek out the B-girls of Pigalle." 2. Police. *La volaille est à la sortie du métro Les Halles.* "The cops are at the Les Halles subway station exit."

VOLANT, *m.* Steering wheel (car). See AS DU VOLANT.

VOLÉE, *f.* Beating (lit. "flight"). *Rentré trop tard il a reçu une sacrée volée.* "Because he came back too late, he got a real thrashing."

VOLEUR, *m.,* race track. Horse likely to "steal" the race (lit. "thief"). *Les initiés parieront sur ce voleur.* "Insiders will bet on that dark horse."

VOLIÈRE, *f.* Whorehouse (lit. "aviary"). *Cette poulette finira à la volière.* "That chick's gonna wind up in the cathouse." Note the avian connection in "chick" and "bird" (Brit. slang for "girl," although some say "bird" in the sense "girl" derives from "burd," an obsolete word for "girl"). Cf. also VOLAILLE 1.

VOLO, *f., abbr.* of **volonté. À volo.** Unlimited. *Le prix du* *repas comprend le vin à volo.* "The price of the meal includes all the wine you want."

VOLUME, *m.* Volume. **Faire du volume,** *idiom.* To throw one's weight around (lit. "to be bulky"). *Il ne se prend pas pour de la petite bière et aime faire du volume.* "He's conceited and likes to throw his weight around."

VOUZAILLES = VOZIQUE.

VO(S)ZIG(UE)S/VOZIGUE. You. *J'ai pris ceci pour vozigue.* "I bought this for you."

VRAI, -E DE VRAI, -E, *m., f.* The real thing; the real McCoy. *C'est un breton, un vrai de vrai.* "He's a Breton, through and through."

VRILLE, *f.* Dominant lesbian (lit. "tendril"). *Je suis vrille, mais je n'ai pas du tout une allure virile.* "I'm a bull dyke but I don't look at all butch."

VTT, *m., abbr.* of **vélo tout terrain** (mountain bike). *Le vététeux prend soin de son VTT.* "The mountain biking enthusiast takes care of his bike."

(À) VUE DE NEZ = AU PIF.

VULGOS, from **vulgaire.** Vulgar. *Il y en a qui l'ont trouvé innovateur son film; d'autres qui l'ont jugé vulgos.* "Some found her movie innovative; others thought it coarse."

VURDON, *m.* Gypsy caravan of trailers. *Je rêve de partir en vurdon avec un violoneux gitan.* "I dream of going off in a trailer with the gypsies and a gypsy violinist."

WAGON, *m.* Wagon; railroad car. **Raccrocher les wagons.** To put things right again (lit. "to hook the rail cars together again"). *L'affaire s'est faite car j'ai pu raccrocher les wagons.* "The deal went through because I was able to smooth things over."

WAGONNIÈRE, *f.* Prostitute who solicits on trains. *Les wagonnières voyageaient à tarif réduit.* "The train trollops rode at reduced rates."

WATERLOO, *m.* Catastrophe; bad luck (from the famous battle). *Je n'ai connu qu'une kyrielle de waterloos.* "All I've had is a string of rotten luck." Cf. COUP DE TRAFALGAR.

WATERS, *m., pl.* Toilet. *S'il vous plaît, où sont les waters?* "Where's the john, please?"

WATRIN, *m.* Pair of pants. *Quel watrin sexy!* "What sexy pants!"

WC, *abbr.* of "Water Closet." *Les WC du bar sont dégueulasses.* "The bar's toilets are revolting."

X, *m.* X. **Avoir les jambes en x.** To be knock-kneed. *Elle les trouve belles, les jambes en x de son mari.* "She thinks her husband's knock-knees are attractive."

X, *f.,* pronounced either as in Fr. *(eeks)* or as in Eng. Ecstasy (the drug). *Il dépense tout son fric pour l'X.* "He spends all his money on ecstasy."

XÉROX®, *m., f.* Unoriginal or robotic individual. *Au bureau ils sont tous des xérox.* "They're all just ciphers at the office."

Y ALLER AU BÉGUIN. See BÉGUIN **2.**

(N')Y ALLER QUE D'UNE FESSE. To undertake s.t. half-heartedly. *Si tu n'y vas que d'une fesse, tu saloperas le boulot.* "If you go at it half-heartedly, you'll do a half-assed job."

Y ÊTRE. To understand. *Tu y es? Oui, j'y suis!* "You get it? "Yes, I see." See ÇA Y EST!

Y ÊTRE POUR QCH. To have s.t. to do with. *J'ai fait carrière dans la musique et mon mari y est pour qch.* "I made a career in music and it's partially my husband's doing." **Ne pas y être pour rien,** *idiom.* Not to be responsible for. *Mais je n'y suis pour rien; c'est ton talent qui a triomphé.* "But I had nothing to do with it; it's your talent that triumphed."

YAOURT, *m.* **1.** Yoghurt. See PÉDALER...YAOURT. **2.** Gobbledygook. *Il croyait chanter en anglais, mais c'était du yaourt!* "He thought he was singing in English, but it was gibberish."

YEUX, *m., pl.* **Ne pas avoir les yeux en face des trous,** *idiom.* To not see the obvious; not feel up to par. *Tu n'avais pas les yeux en face des trous pour faire une connerie pareille.* "You must have been asleep; sick; dreaming to do s.t. so stupid." See COÛTER LES YEUX DE LA TÊTE; SORTIR...YEUX.

YEUX DE CRAPAUD MORT D'AMOUR. See REGARDER.

YEUX DE MERLIN FRIT. See REGARDER.

YEUX EN TROU DE BITE/PINE, *m., pl.* Tiny, deep-set eyes (not "cockeyed" but lit. "eyes like the meatus [opening] of the penis"). *Il me regardait, médusé,avec ses yeux en trou de bite.* "He looked at me dumbfounded, with his beady little eyes."

YÉYÉ, *m.* **1.** Sixties rock (from Eng. "yeah, yeah"). *Ils écoutent toujours le yéyé.* "They still listen to sixties rock." **2.** Sixties' rock fan. *Mes vioques étaient des yéyés.* "My parents were sixties rockers."

YIÈCHE = IÈCHE.

YOUDE/YOUDI = YOUPIN.

YOUPIN, -E, *m., f., pej.* Jew. *Il bouffait du youpin avant d'apprendre qu'il etait juif lui-même.* "He used to be violently antisemitic before finding out that he was Jewish h.s."

YOUVOI, *m.,* backslang of **voyou.** Hooligan. *Il est devenu youvoi.* "He's become a thug."

YOYO, *m.* Yo-yo®. **Faire du yoyo,** *idiom.* To turn a succession of tricks. *Pour plaire à mon mac je fais du yoyo.* "To please my pimp I turn lots of tricks."

ZAPPER. 1. To change TV channels; zap. *Elle zappait avant de se coucher.* "She channel-surfed before going to bed." **Zapper qn.** To shut s.o. out (shut off like a TV channel). *Après toutes ses vacheries je l'ai zappé.* "I dumped him after all his dirty tricks." **2.** To go away. *On reste ou on zappe?* "Do we stay or blow this hole?"

ZAPPETTE, *f.* Remote control. *Je paume souvent la zappette.* "I often misplace the remote."

ZAPPEUR, -EUSE, *m., f.* Inveterate channel surfer. *Les zappeurs suivent plusieurs films à la fois.* "Zappers follow several movies at once."

ZAP-ZAP, *m.* = **ZAPPETTE.**

ZARB/ZARBI. Weird (backslang of **bizarre**). *C'qu'il est zarb, ce gus!* "That guy's a real weirdo!"

ZEB, *m.* = **ZOB.**

ZÉBER, backslang of **baiser.** To fuck. *Il ne pense qu'à zéber.* "All he thinks about is screwing."

ZÉBI = **ZOB.** See PEAU…ZÉBI.

ZÈBRE, *m.* Guy. *C'est un drôle de zèbre!* "He's an odd one."

ZARMAZONE, *f.* Feminist. *Les zarmazones du IXème arrondissement sont militantes et intellos.* "The feminists in the 9th district (Paris) are militant and intelligent."

ZEF, *m.,* from **zéphyr.** Wind; fart. *Que vous ayez toujours le* *zef dans le dos, et qu'il ne soit jamais le vôtre.* "May the wind always be at your back, and may it never be your own."

ZEN, *m.* **1.** Nose (backslang of **nez**). **Piquer du zen,** *idiom.* To nod off. *Papa piquait du zen devant la TV.* "Pop nodded off in front of the TV." **2.** Zen (Buddhism). **Rester zen.** To stay calm. *Elle restait zen en toute circonstance.* "She kept her cool in all circumstances."

ZEPPELIN, *m.* Huge cigarette of *cannabis.* *Le zeppelin était la star de la noce.* "The huge joint was the star of the wedding party."

ZÉRO, *m.* **1.** Zero. **C'est un zéro fini!** "He's a total zero." **Les avoir à zéro,** *idiom.* To be very afraid. *En conduisant en montagne je les avais à zéro.* "When driving in the mountains I was very afraid." **2.** High-grade hashish. *Il est accro au zéro.* "He's hooked on quality hash."

ZETOUPAR, *f.,* backslang of **partouze.** Orgy. *Puritaine que je suis, j'ai refusé de participer à leurs zetoupars.* "Puritan that I am, I refused to take part in their group sex parties."

ZGUEG, *m.* Penis. *Il ne se lave jamais le zgueg.* "He never washes his dick."

ZIB, *m.* Penis. *Il prétend que son zib a sa propre volonté.* "He claims his dick's got a will of its own."

ZIC/ZICMU, *f.* backslang of **musique.** Music. *Ta zic, c'était de la merde.* "Your music was lousy."

ZIEUTER = ZYEUTER.

-ZIG(UE). Suffix used to create slang forms of the peronal pronouns. See MÉZIG(UE)/ MÉZIGO.

ZIGOMAR/ZIGOTO/ZIGUE, *m.* Guy. *Que fout-il, ce zigomar?* "What's that guy doing?" **Faire le zigoto,** *idiom.* To act the fool. *Arrête de faire le zigoto!* "Quit horsing around."

ZIGOUIGUI, *m.* **1.** Female genitalia. *J'essaye d'approfondir les grands mystères de son zigouigui.* "I'm trying to get to the bottom of the great mysteries of her box."

2. Penis. *Il n'a pas de zigougui dont je peux me vanter.* "He hasn't got a cock I can brag about." **3.** Thingamajig. *À quoi ça sert, tous ces zigouiguis?* "What are all those thingamabobs for?"

ZIGOUILLER. To kill. *Le casseur a zigouillé le gardien.* "The burglar knocked off the security guard."

ZIG-ZIG, *m.* Sex. **Faire zig-zig.** To have sex. *Veux-tu faire zig-zig avec moi?* "You wanna get it on with me?"

ZINC, *m.* Counter in a bar; café. *Il est chaque soir au zinc.* "He's at the bar every night."

ZINZIN. Crazy. *C'est lui le plus zinzin.* "He's the zaniest of them."

ZINZIN, *m.* **1.** Whatsit. *Voilà un drôle de zinzin.* "That's an odd little object." **2.** Noise. *Arrête enfin ton zinzin!* "Quit that racket, will you."

ZINZINS, *m., pl.,* stock market. Institutional investors (from the liaisons in **les investisseurs institutionnels**). *Les zinzins boudent les nouvelles actions.* "The institutional investors aren't buying the new stocks."

ZIZANIE, *f.* **1.** Rye grass (a weed). **2.** Discord. **Mettre; semer la zizanie.** To create ill feeling. Zizanie de Fragonard *était son parfum préféré, mais elle n'a jamais semé la zizanie.* "Zizanie de Fragonard was her favorite perfume, but she never stirred up trouble."

ZIZI, *m.* Sex organs (male or female). *Les enfants se montraient leurs zizis.* "The children showed each other their privates."

ZIZIQUE, *f.* Music. *Coupe ta zizique—je veux dormir.* "Shut off your music—I want to sleep."

ZOB, *m.* Penis (from Ar.). **Mon zob!** My eye! My ass! See PEAU...ZOB.

ZOMBLOU, *m.,* backslang of **blouson.** Jacket. *Il s'est acheté un zomblou d'aviateur.* "He bought a bomber jacket."

ZONARD, *m.* **1.** Vagrant. *Elle a créé un foyer pour zonards.*

"She founded a shelter for the homeless." **2.** Punk; tough. *Il ne fréquente que des zonards.* "He just hangs out with hooligans."

ZONER. 1. To hang out. *Il a zoné tout l'été.* "He just loafed all summer." **2.** To size s.o. up. *Je l'ai zonée au premier coup d'œil.* "I sized her up at first sight."

ZOUAVE, *m.* Guy; clown (orig. a soldier in military units formed in Algeria in 1831). **Faire le zouave,** *idiom.* Act the fool; waste time. *Il s'amusait à faire le zouave.* "He enjoyed horsing around."

ZOZORES, *f., pl.* Ears. *Ouvre tes zozores et écoute-moi.* "Open your ears and listen to me."

ZUT!/ZUT ALORS! Darn it! Damn it! Hang it!

ZUT POUR VOUS! Go to the devil! Nuts to you!

ZYEUTER. To scrutinize. *Il ne cesse de me zyeuter.* "He keeps staring at me."

ZYGOMATIQUE, *m.* Zygomatic (facial muscle). **Titiller le zygomatique de qn.** To make s.o. laugh. *Le comique a titillé le zygomatique de tous.* "The comic tickled everyone's funny bone."

ZYGOS/ZYGOSSES, *m., pl.,* from **zygomatique.** *J'ai mal aux zygos d'avoir tant ri.* "My face aches from laughing so much."